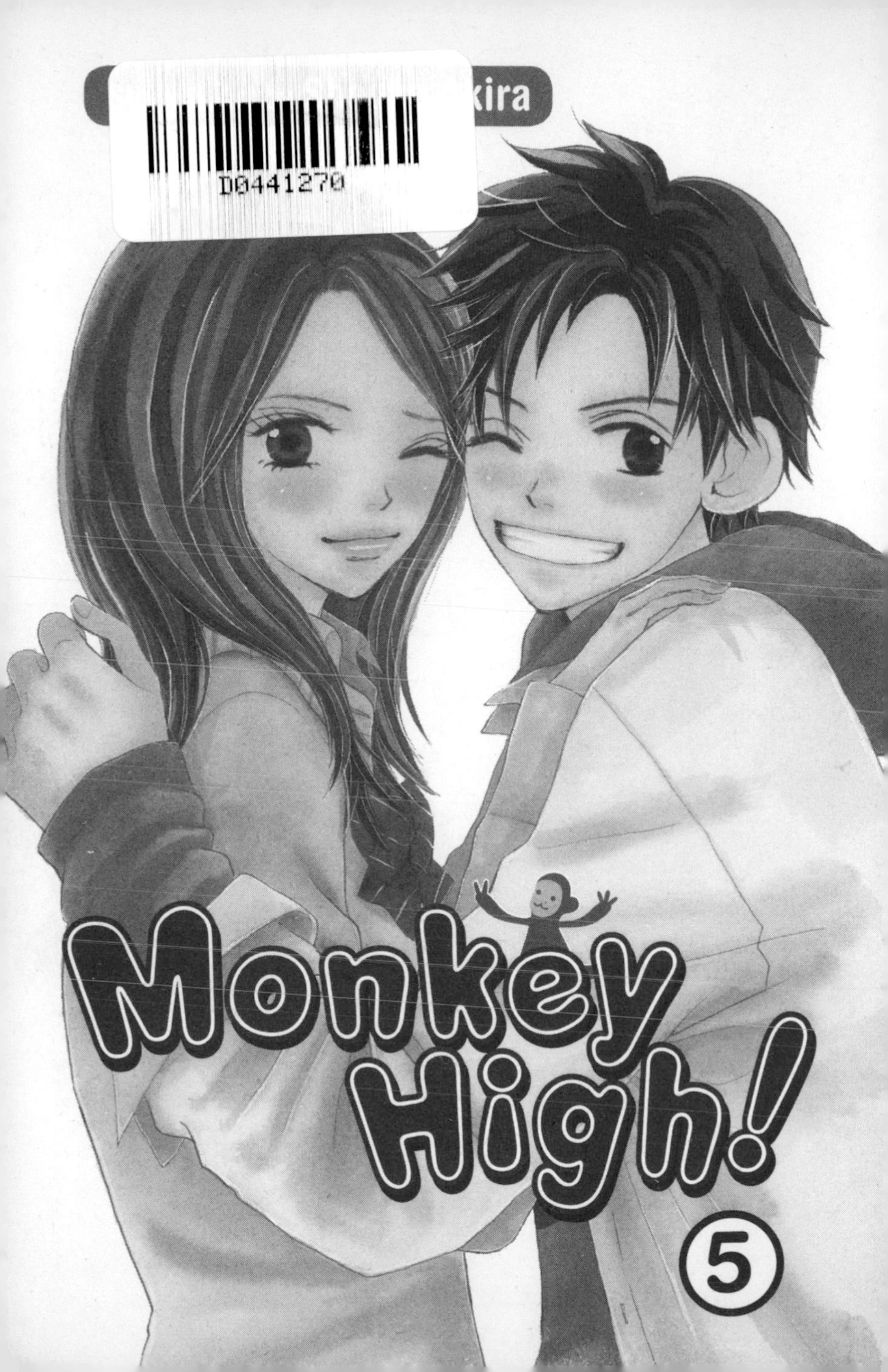
Monkey High!
5

Monkey High!

⑤

CONTENTS

Story Thus Far

Masaru Yamashita
(Nickname: Macharu)

Haruna starts going out with Macharu (often teased and called a baby monkey) at her new school. Every day is like a carnival with her rowdy classmates. So many events and happenings…
The annual school festival approaches, and Macharu and the whole class are beside themselves, but…?!

Haruna Aizawa

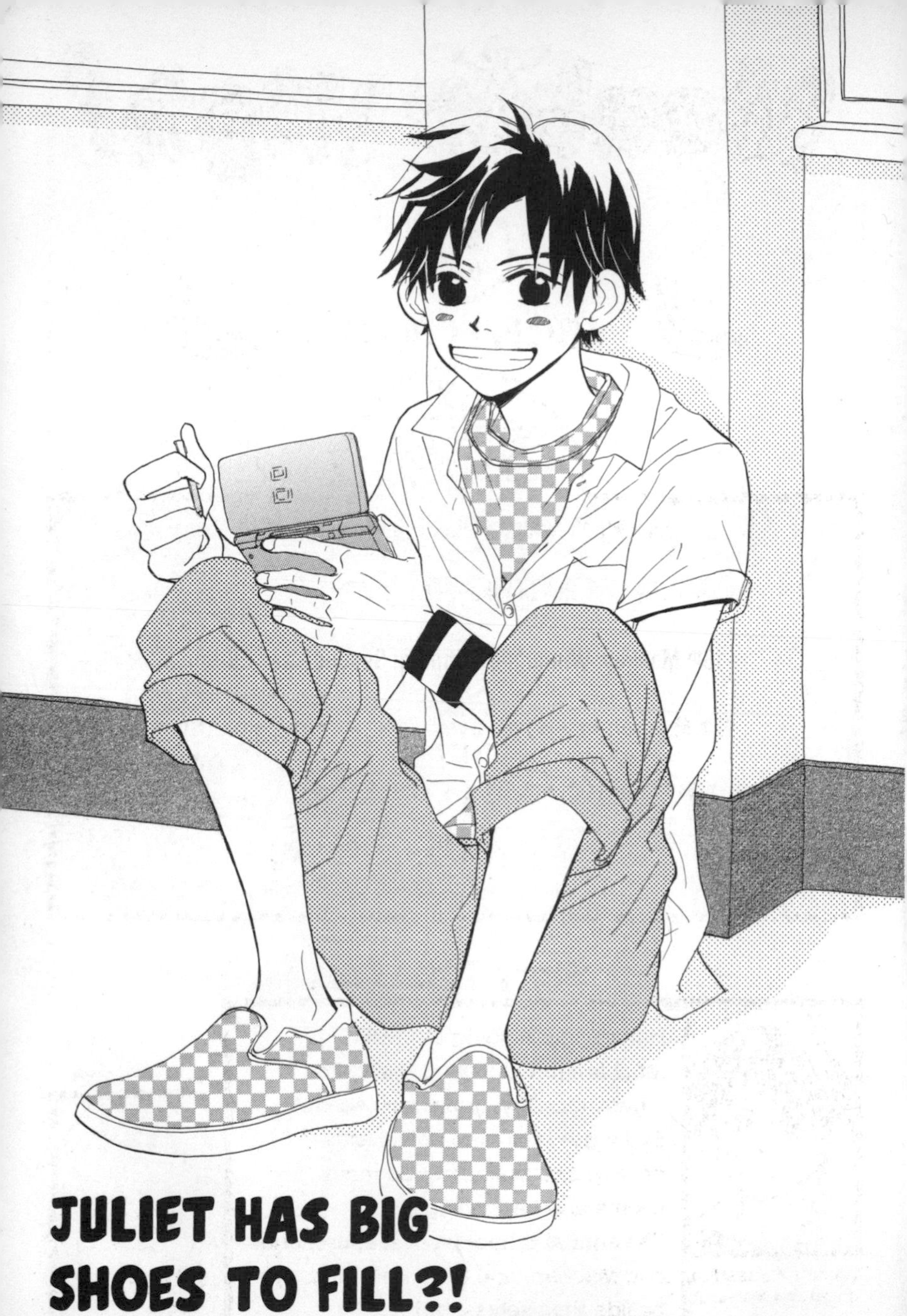

JULIET HAS BIG SHOES TO FILL?!

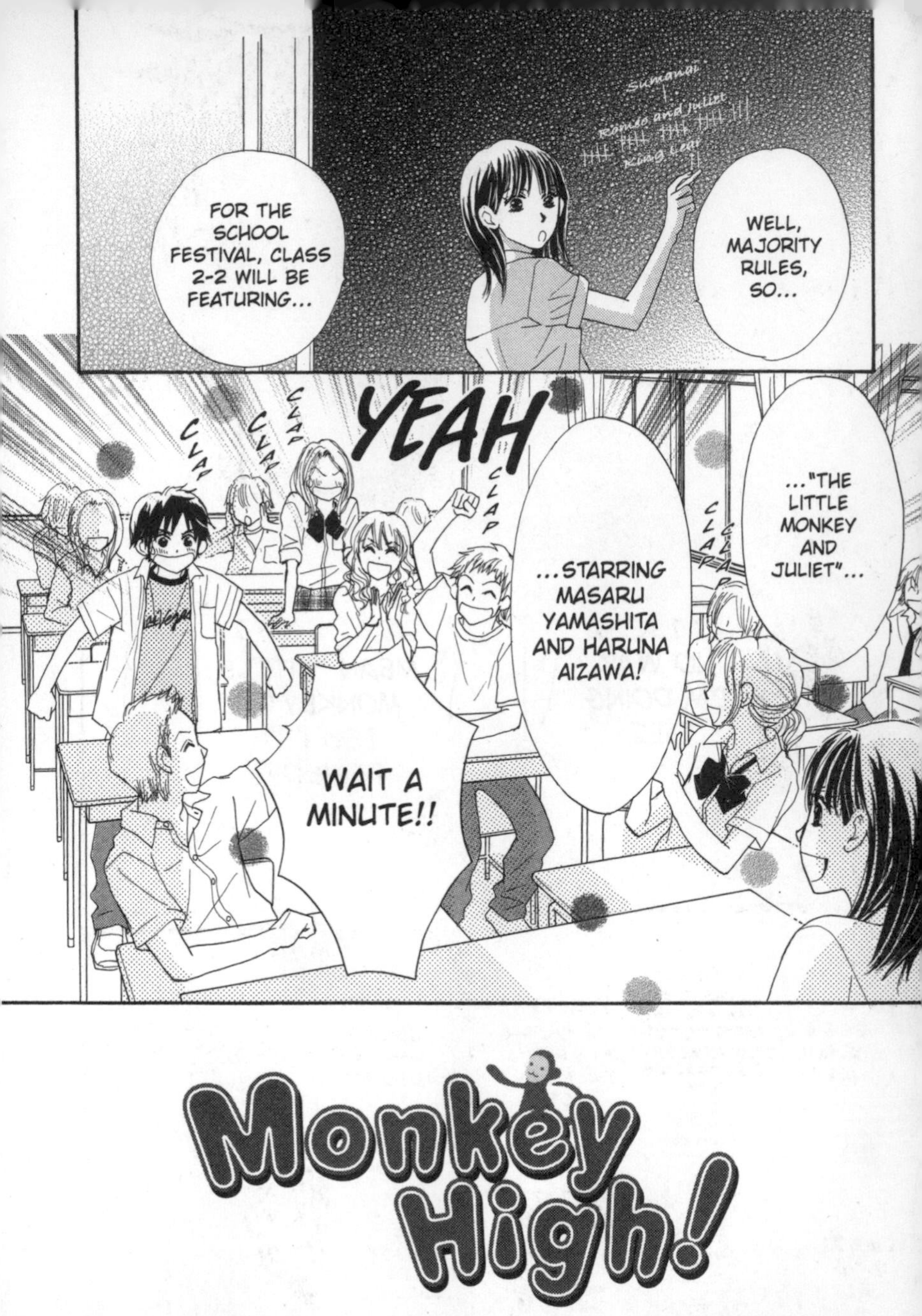
WELL, MAJORITY RULES, SO...
Romeo and Juliet
King Lear
FOR THE SCHOOL FESTIVAL, CLASS 2-2 WILL BE FEATURING...
..."THE LITTLE MONKEY AND JULIET"...
...STARRING MASARU YAMASHITA AND HARUNA AIZAWA!
CLAP CLAP
CLAP
YEAH
CLAP CLAP
CLAP
WAIT A MINUTE!!

Monkey High!

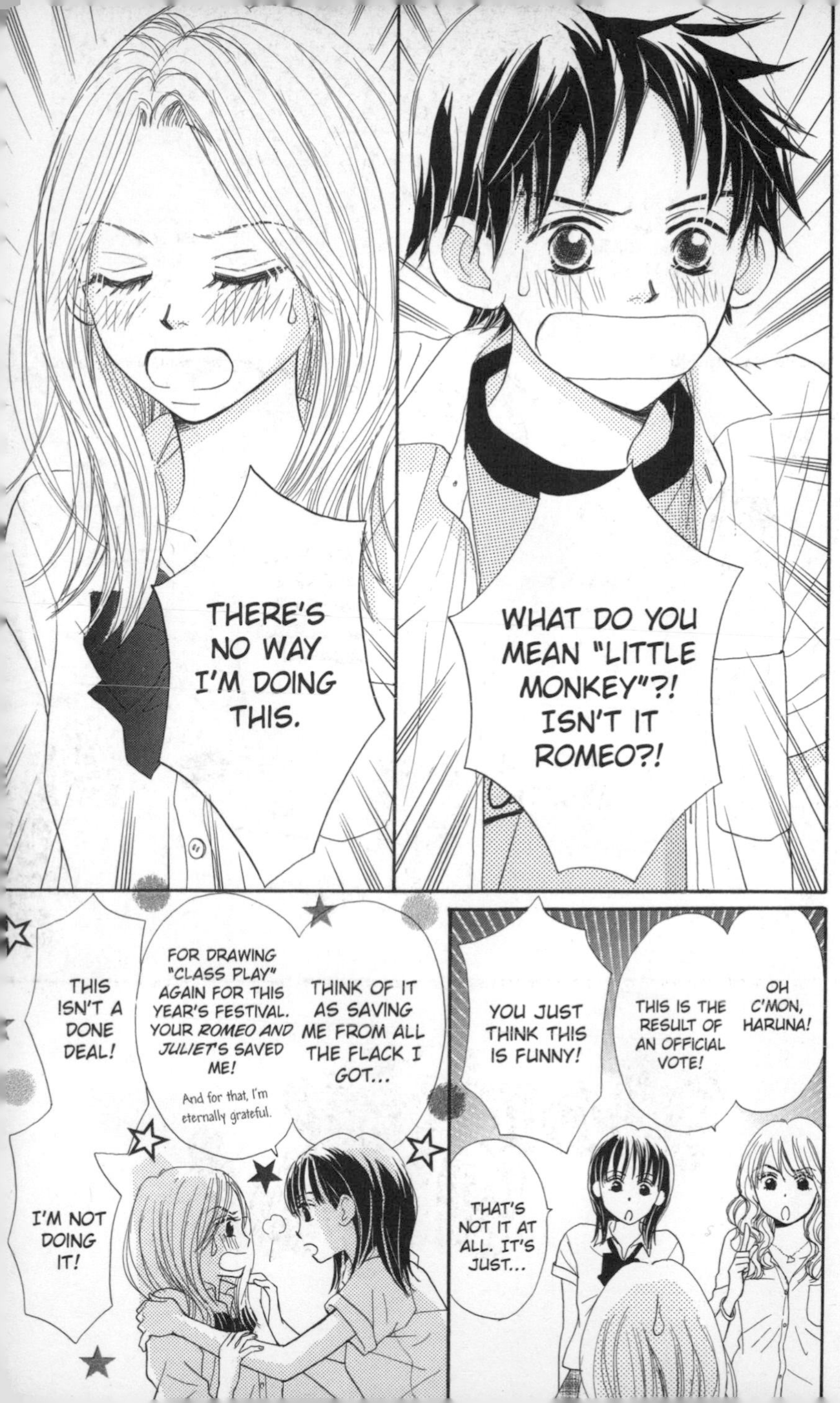
WHAT DO YOU MEAN "LITTLE MONKEY"?! ISN'T IT ROMEO?!
THERE'S NO WAY I'M DOING THIS.
OH C'MON, HARUNA!
THIS IS THE RESULT OF AN OFFICIAL VOTE!
YOU JUST THINK THIS IS FUNNY!
THAT'S NOT IT AT ALL. IT'S JUST...
THINK OF IT AS SAVING ME FROM ALL THE FLACK I GOT...
FOR DRAWING "CLASS PLAY" AGAIN FOR THIS YEAR'S FESTIVAL. YOUR *ROMEO AND JULIET*'S SAVED ME!
And for that, I'm eternally grateful.
THIS ISN'T A DONE DEAL!
I'M NOT DOING IT!

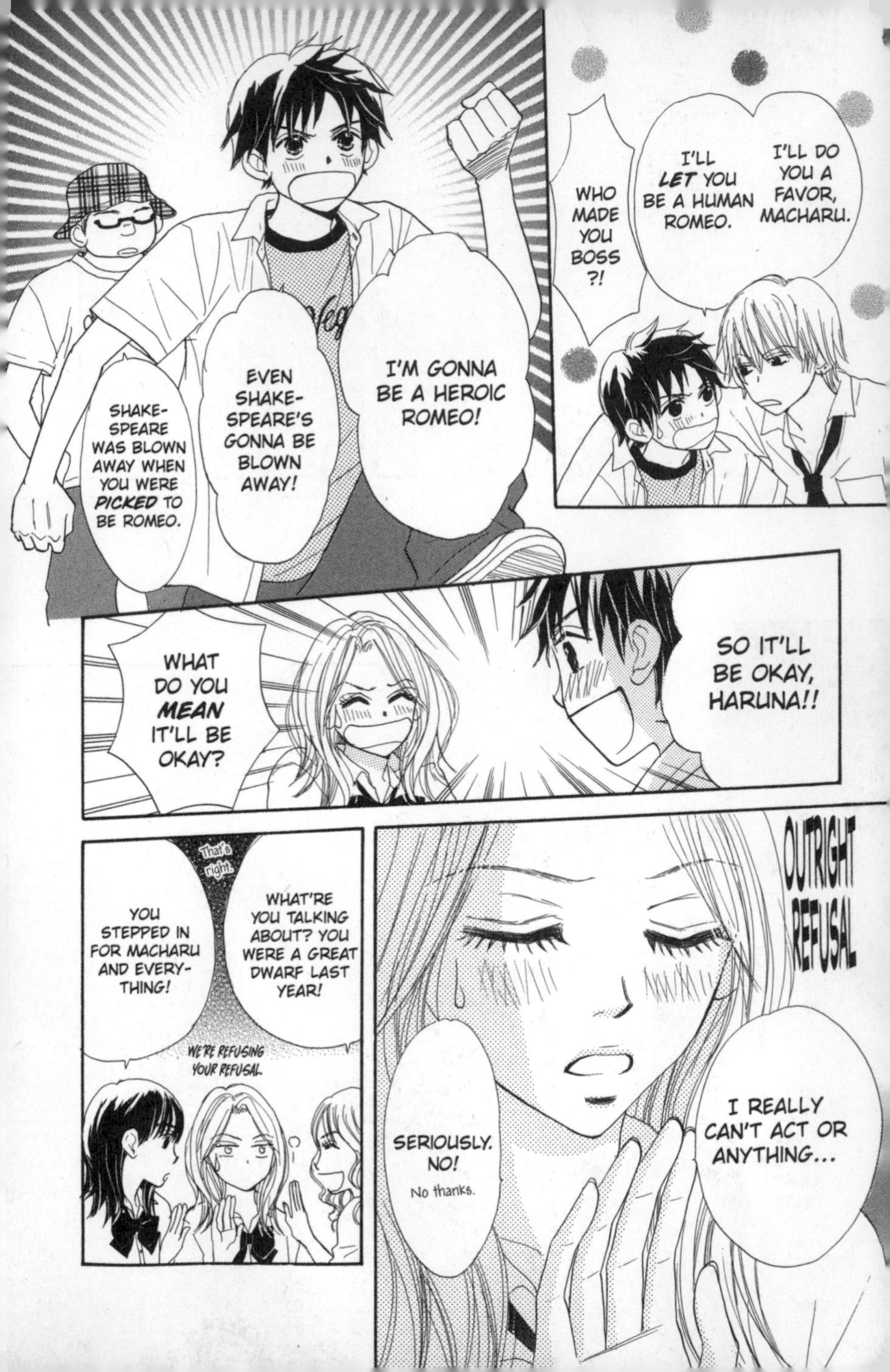
I'LL DO YOU A FAVOR, MACHARU.
I'LL *LET* YOU BE A HUMAN ROMEO.
WHO MADE YOU BOSS ?!
I'M GONNA BE A HEROIC ROMEO!
EVEN SHAKE-SPEARE'S GONNA BE BLOWN AWAY!
SHAKE-SPEARE WAS BLOWN AWAY WHEN YOU WERE *PICKED* TO BE ROMEO.
SO IT'LL BE OKAY, HARUNA!!
WHAT DO YOU *MEAN* IT'LL BE OKAY?
OUTRIGHT REFUSAL
I REALLY CAN'T ACT OR ANYTHING...
SERIOUSLY. NO!
No thanks.
WHAT'RE YOU TALKING ABOUT? YOU WERE A GREAT DWARF LAST YEAR!
That's right.
YOU STEPPED IN FOR MACHARU AND EVERY-THING!
WE'RE REFUSING YOUR REFUSAL.

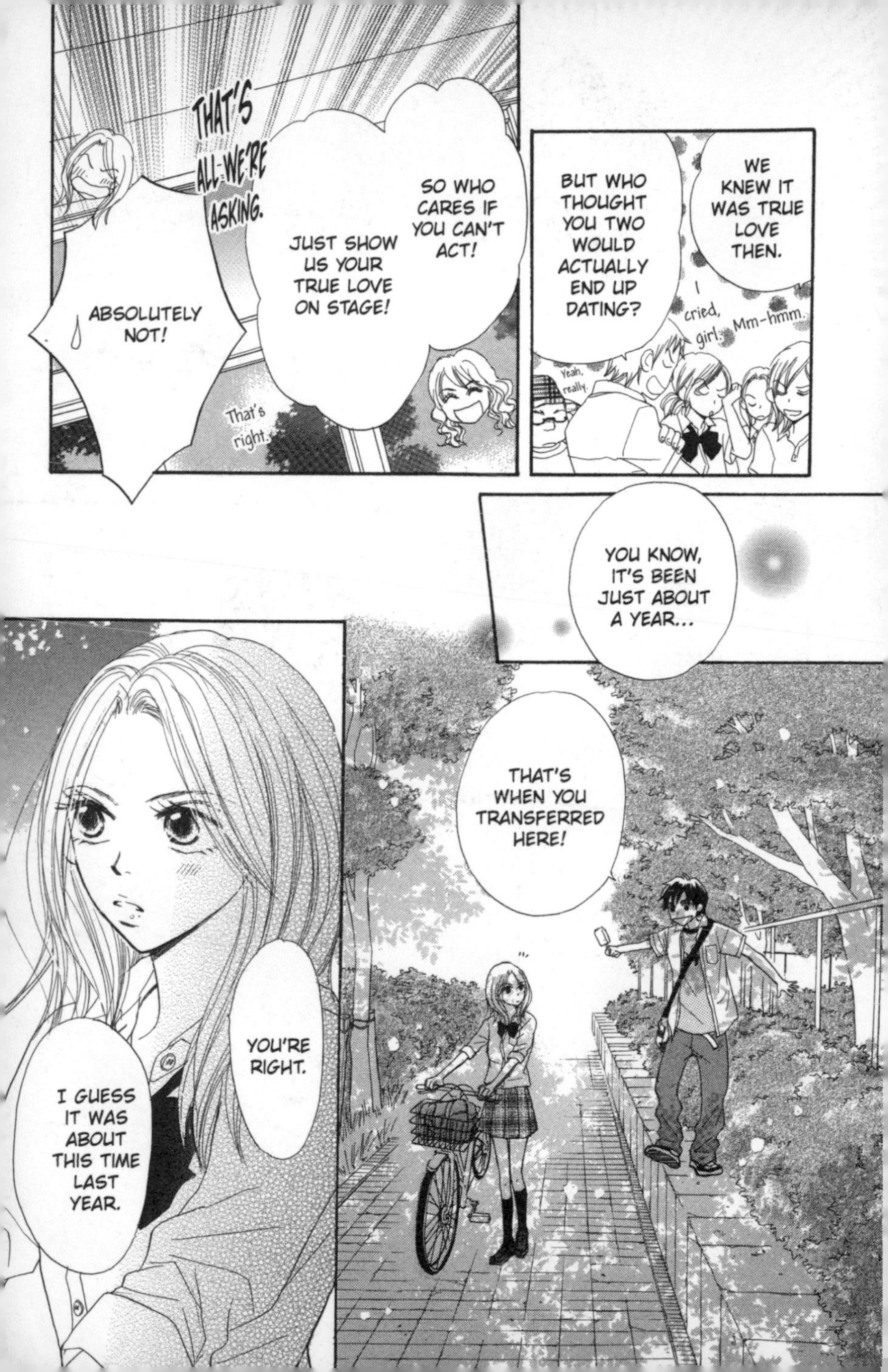
WE KNEW IT WAS TRUE LOVE THEN.
BUT WHO THOUGHT YOU TWO WOULD ACTUALLY END UP DATING?
Mm-hmm.
I cried, girl.
Yeah, really.
SO WHO CARES IF YOU CAN'T ACT!
JUST SHOW US YOUR TRUE LOVE ON STAGE!
THAT'S ALL WE'RE ASKING.
That's right.
ABSOLUTELY NOT!
YOU KNOW, IT'S BEEN JUST ABOUT A YEAR...
THAT'S WHEN YOU TRANSFERRED HERE!
YOU'RE RIGHT.
I GUESS IT WAS ABOUT THIS TIME LAST YEAR.

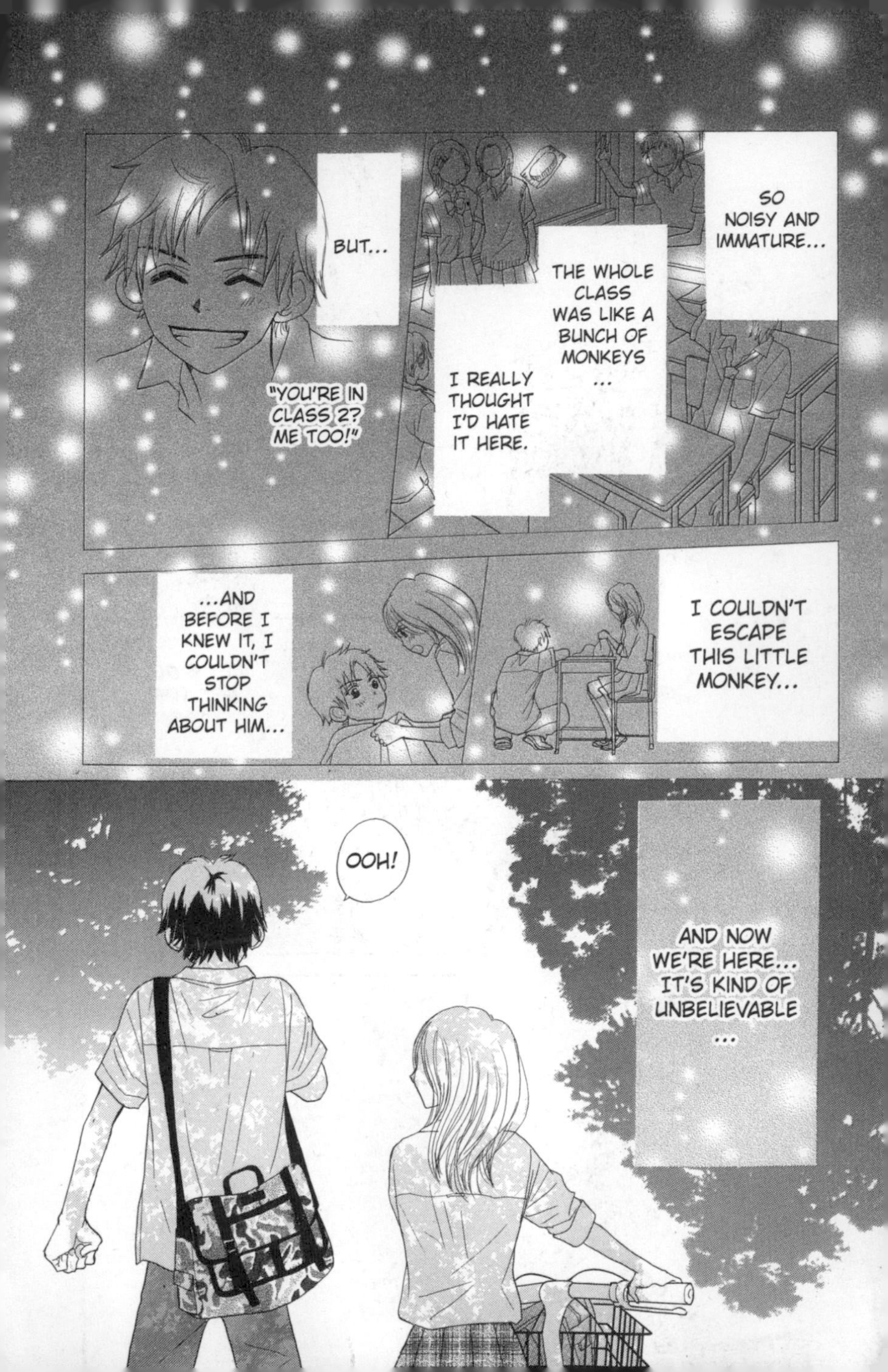
SO NOISY AND IMMATURE...
THE WHOLE CLASS WAS LIKE A BUNCH OF MONKEYS ...
I REALLY THOUGHT I'D HATE IT HERE.
BUT...
"YOU'RE IN CLASS 2? ME TOO!"
I COULDN'T ESCAPE THIS LITTLE MONKEY...
...AND BEFORE I KNEW IT, I COULDN'T STOP THINKING ABOUT HIM...
AND NOW WE'RE HERE... IT'S KIND OF UNBELIEVABLE ...
OOH!

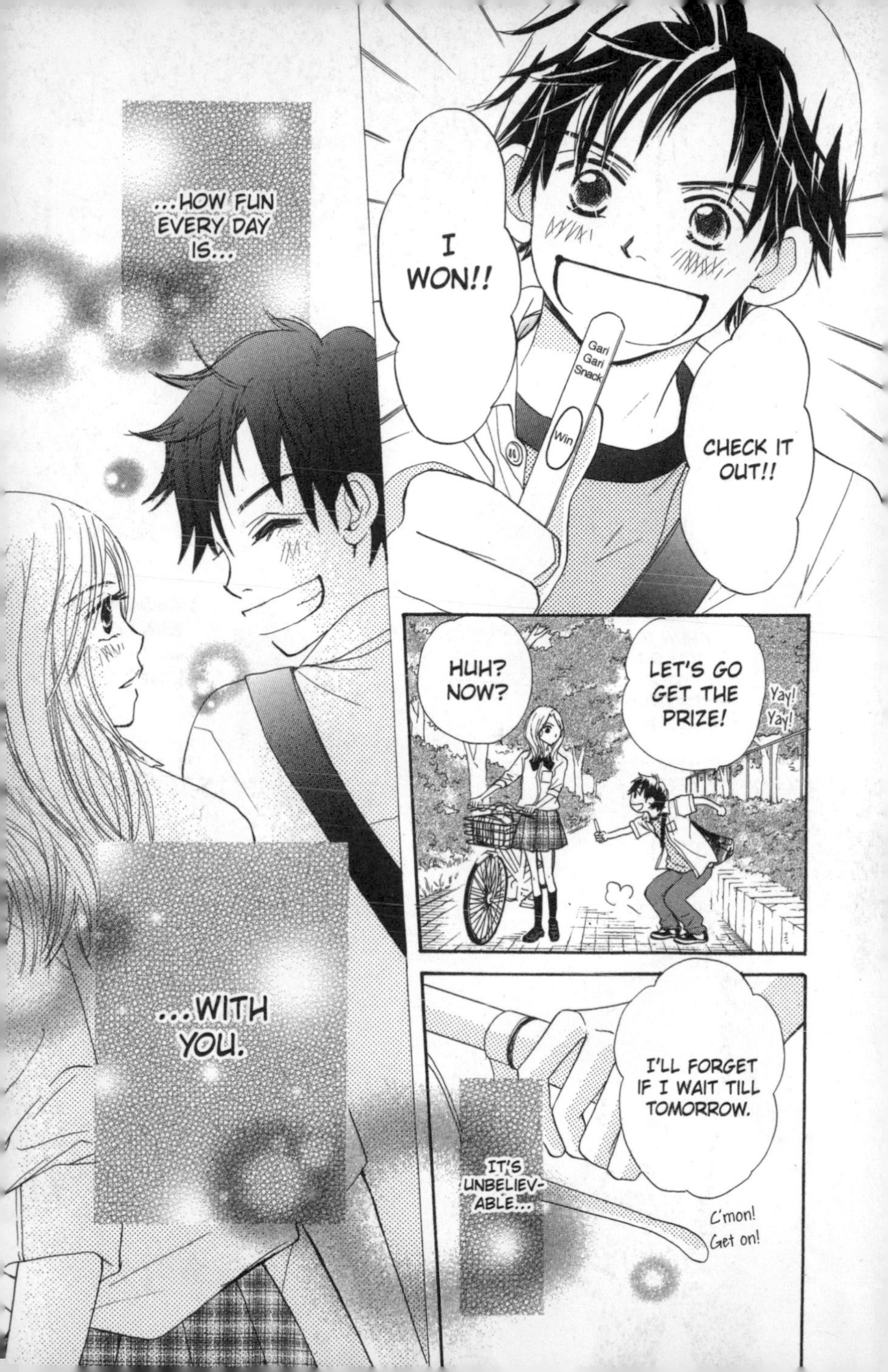
I WON!!
Gari Gari Snack
Win
CHECK IT OUT!!
LET'S GO GET THE PRIZE!
Yay! Yay!
HUH? NOW?
I'LL FORGET IF I WAIT TILL TOMORROW.
C'mon! Get on!
IT'S UNBELIEVABLE...
...HOW FUN EVERY DAY IS...
...WITH YOU.

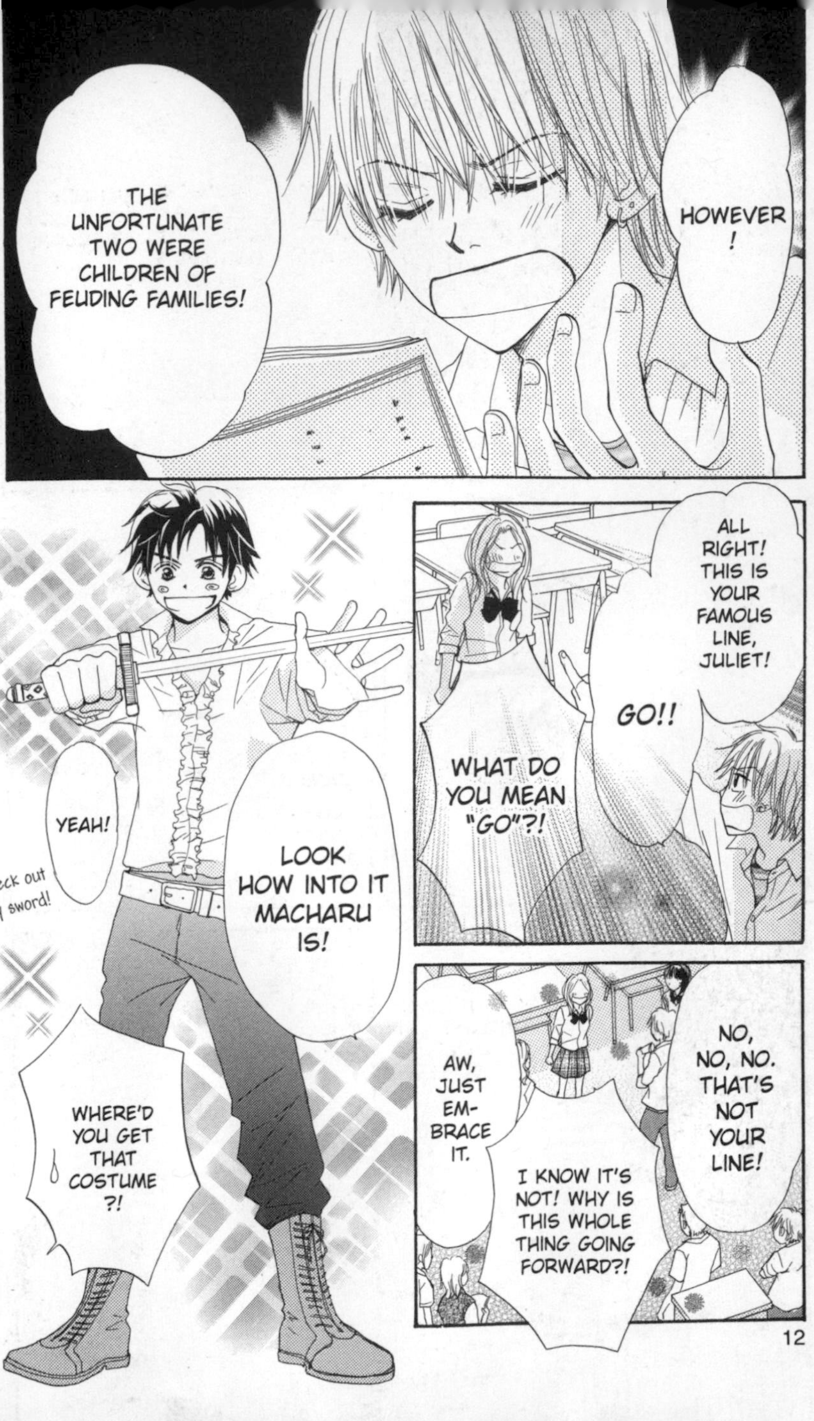
THE UNFORTUNATE TWO WERE CHILDREN OF FEUDING FAMILIES!
HOWEVER!
ALL RIGHT! THIS IS YOUR FAMOUS LINE, JULIET!
GO!!
WHAT DO YOU MEAN "GO"?!
NO, NO, NO. THAT'S NOT YOUR LINE!
AW, JUST EM-BRACE IT.
I KNOW IT'S NOT! WHY IS THIS WHOLE THING GOING FORWARD?!
LOOK HOW INTO IT MACHARU IS!
YEAH!
Check out my sword!
WHERE'D YOU GET THAT COSTUME?!

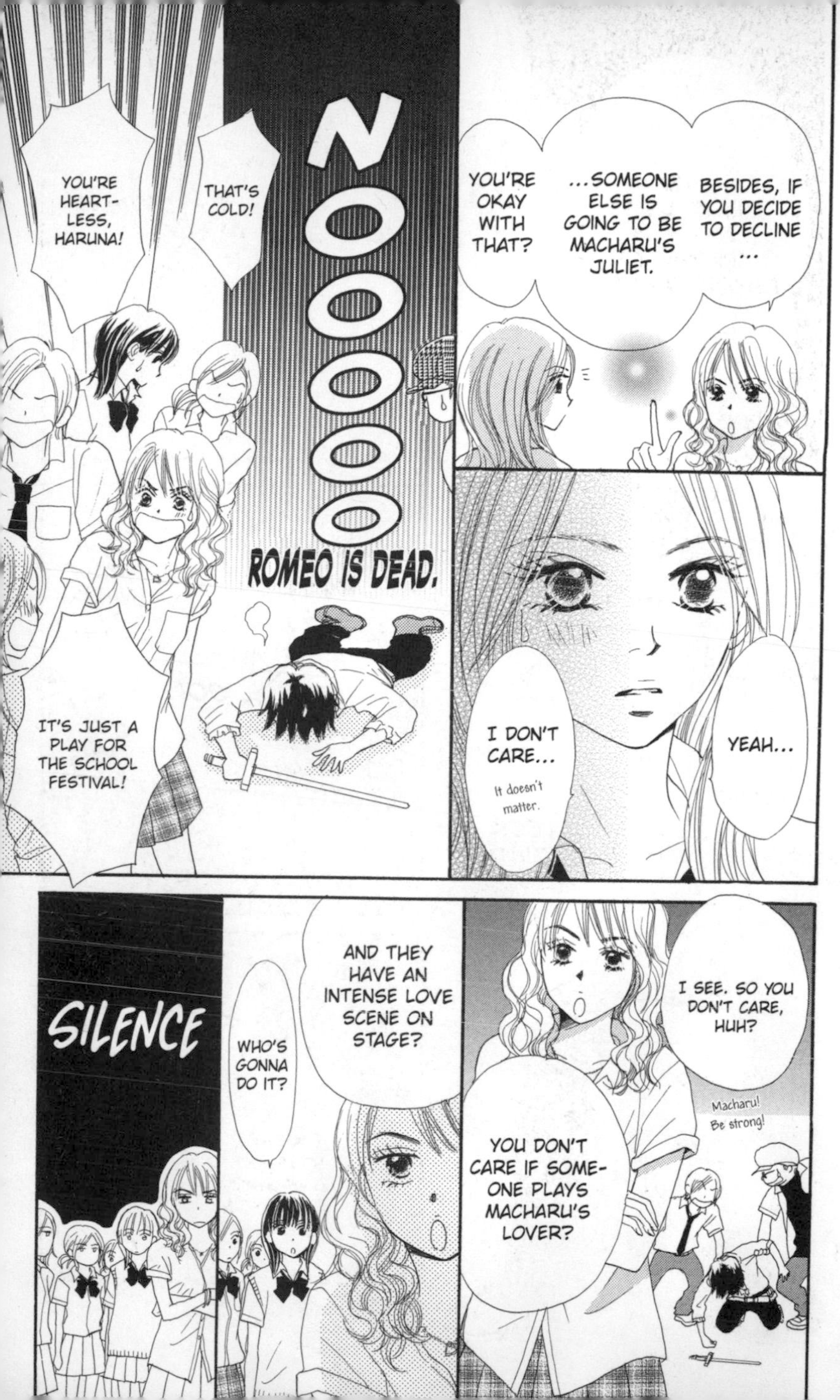
BESIDES, IF YOU DECIDE TO DECLINE ...
...SOMEONE ELSE IS GOING TO BE MACHARU'S JULIET.
YOU'RE OKAY WITH THAT?
YEAH...
I DON'T CARE...
It doesn't matter.
NOOOOOOO
THAT'S COLD!
YOU'RE HEART-LESS, HARUNA!
ROMEO IS DEAD.
IT'S JUST A PLAY FOR THE SCHOOL FESTIVAL!
I SEE. SO YOU DON'T CARE, HUH?
Macharu! Be strong!
YOU DON'T CARE IF SOME-ONE PLAYS MACHARU'S LOVER?
AND THEY HAVE AN INTENSE LOVE SCENE ON STAGE?
WHO'S GONNA DO IT?
SILENCE

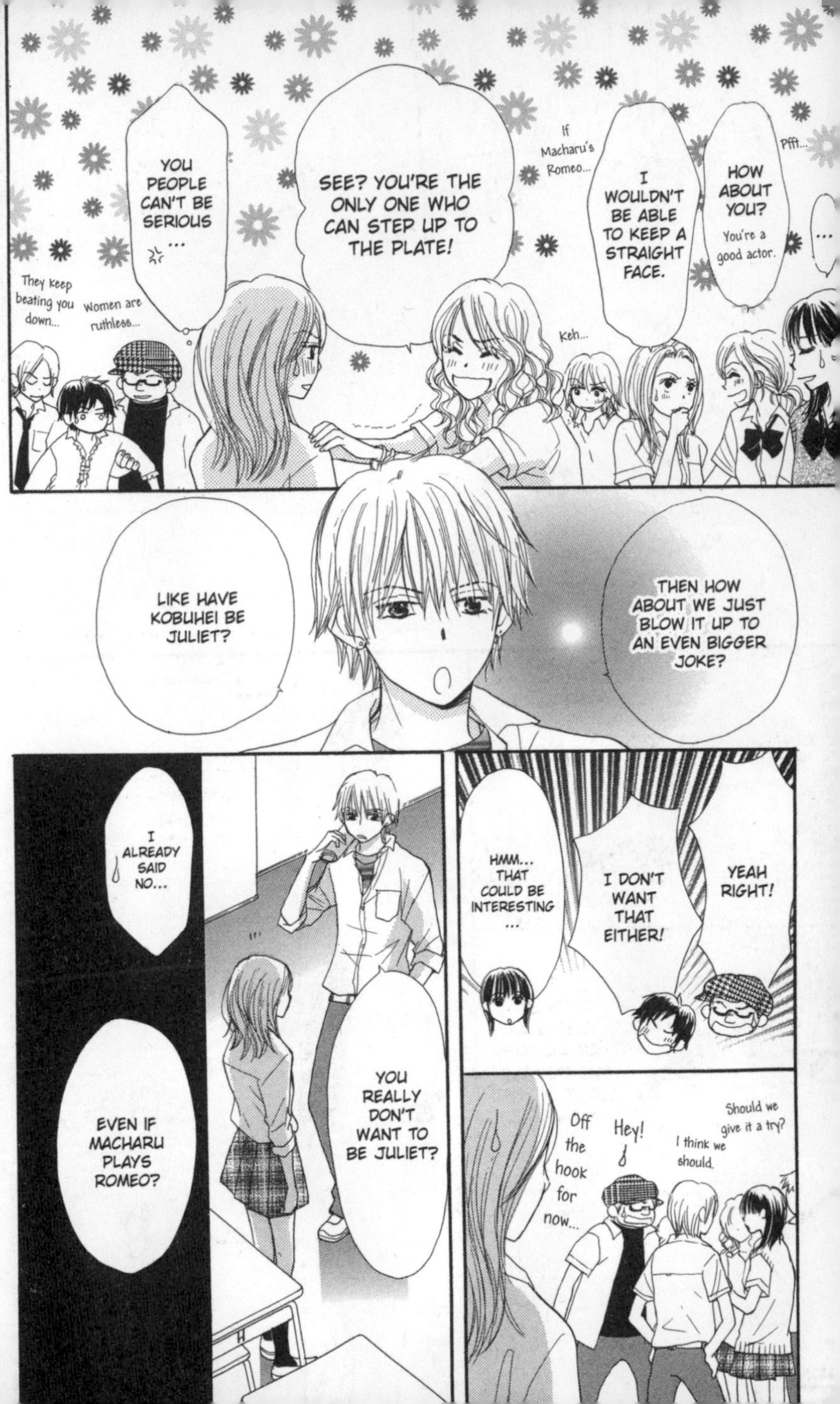
...
Pfft...
HOW ABOUT YOU?
You're a good actor.
I WOULDN'T BE ABLE TO KEEP A STRAIGHT FACE.
If Macharu's Romeo...
Keh...
SEE? YOU'RE THE ONLY ONE WHO CAN STEP UP TO THE PLATE!
YOU PEOPLE CAN'T BE SERIOUS...
Women are ruthless...
They keep beating you down...
THEN HOW ABOUT WE JUST BLOW IT UP TO AN EVEN BIGGER JOKE?
LIKE HAVE KOBUHEI BE JULIET?
YEAH RIGHT!
I DON'T WANT THAT EITHER!
HMM... THAT COULD BE INTERESTING...
Should we give it a try?
I think we should.
Hey!
Off the hook for now...
YOU REALLY DON'T WANT TO BE JULIET?
EVEN IF MACHARU PLAYS ROMEO?
I ALREADY SAID NO...

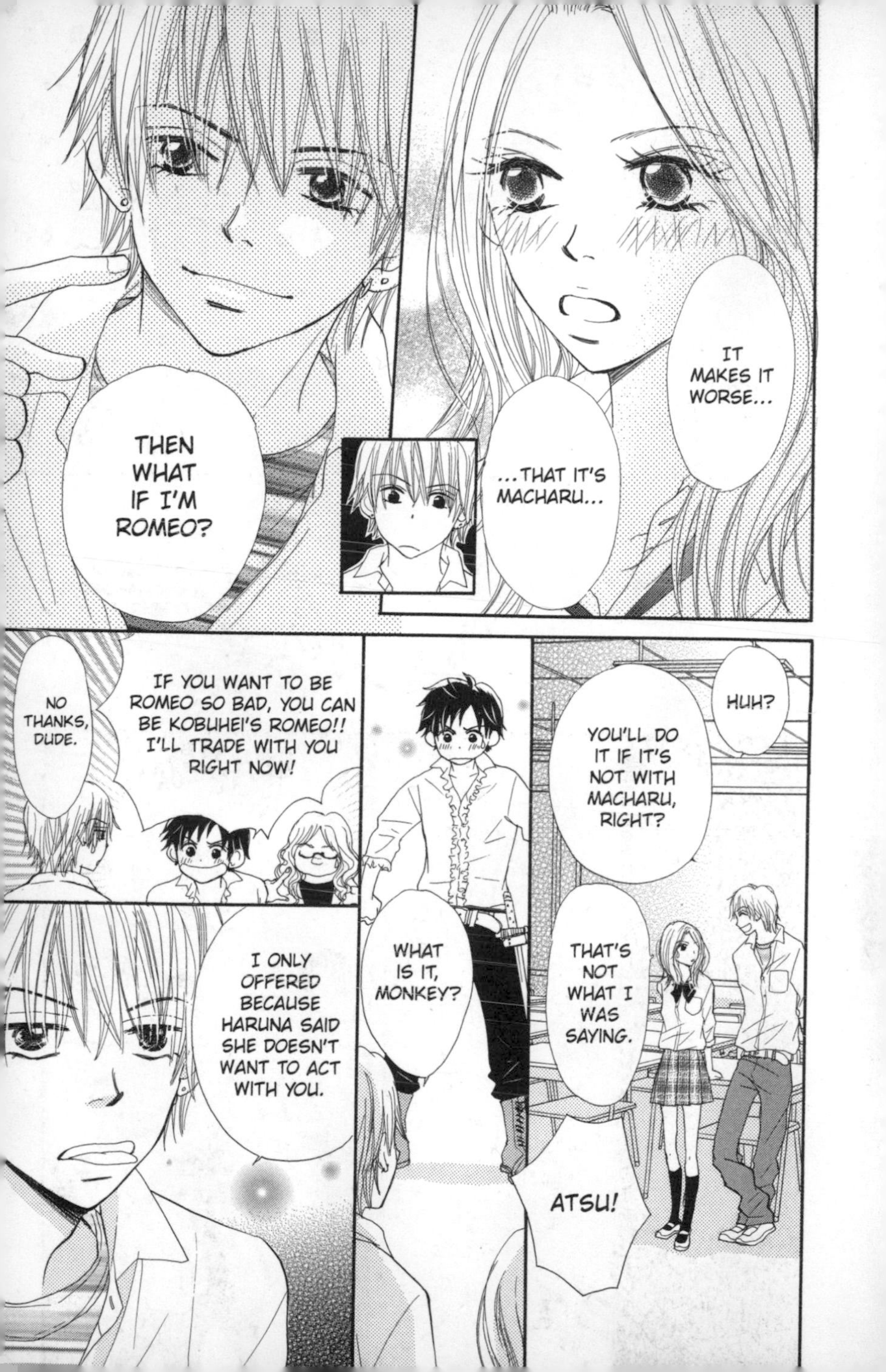
IT MAKES IT WORSE...
...THAT IT'S MACHARU...
THEN WHAT IF I'M ROMEO?
HUH?
YOU'LL DO IT IF IT'S NOT WITH MACHARU, RIGHT?
THAT'S NOT WHAT I WAS SAYING.
ATSU!
WHAT IS IT, MONKEY?
IF YOU WANT TO BE ROMEO SO BAD, YOU CAN BE KOBUHEI'S ROMEO!! I'LL TRADE WITH YOU RIGHT NOW!
NO THANKS, DUDE.
I ONLY OFFERED BECAUSE HARUNA SAID SHE DOESN'T WANT TO ACT WITH YOU.

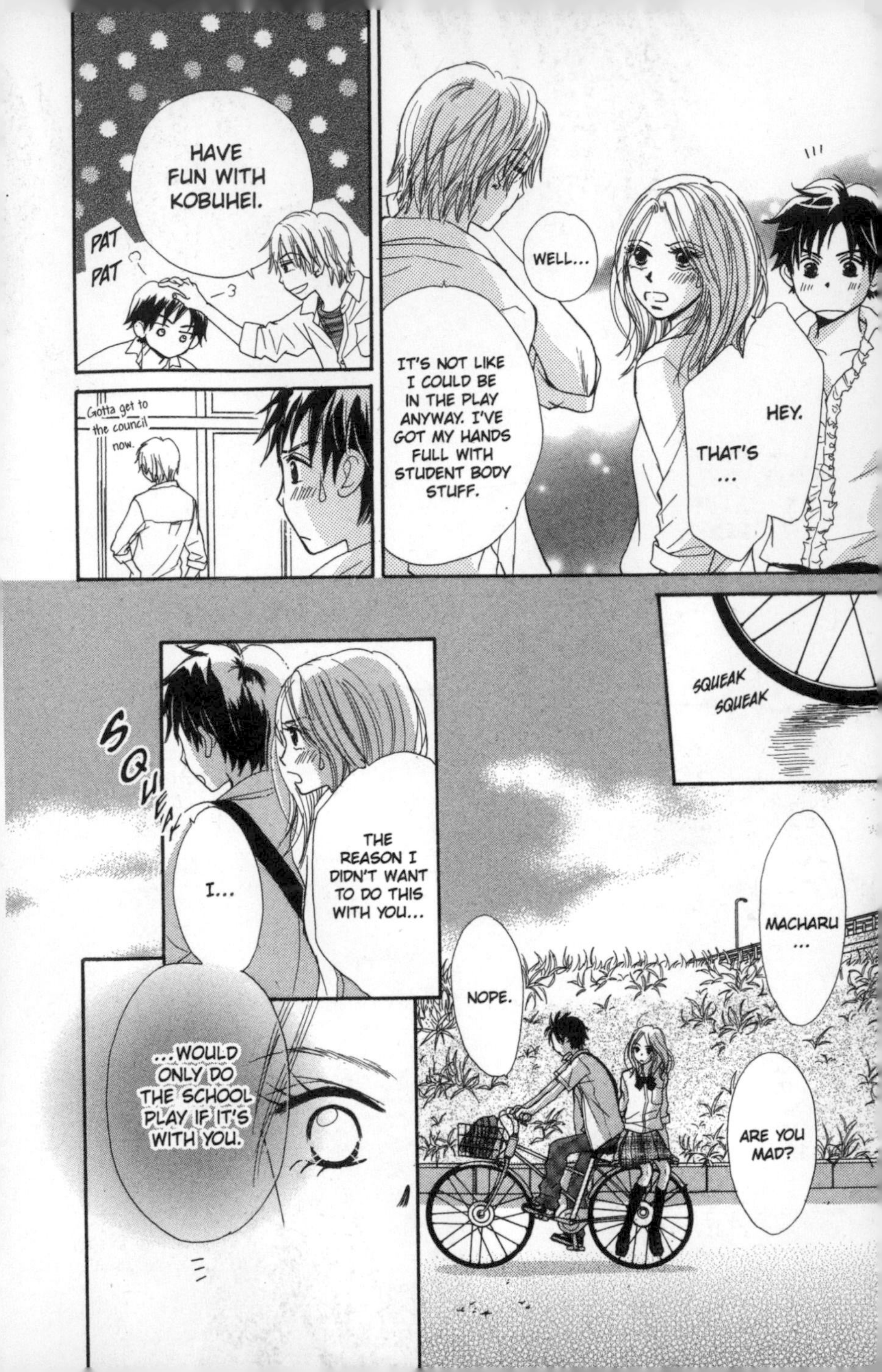
WELL...
IT'S NOT LIKE I COULD BE IN THE PLAY ANYWAY. I'VE GOT MY HANDS FULL WITH STUDENT BODY STUFF.
HEY.
THAT'S ...
HAVE FUN WITH KOBUHEI.
PAT PAT
Gotta get to the council now.
SQUEAK SQUEAK
MACHARU ...
ARE YOU MAD?
NOPE.
THE REASON I DIDN'T WANT TO DO THIS WITH YOU...
I...
SQUEAK
...WOULD ONLY DO THE SCHOOL PLAY IF IT'S WITH YOU.

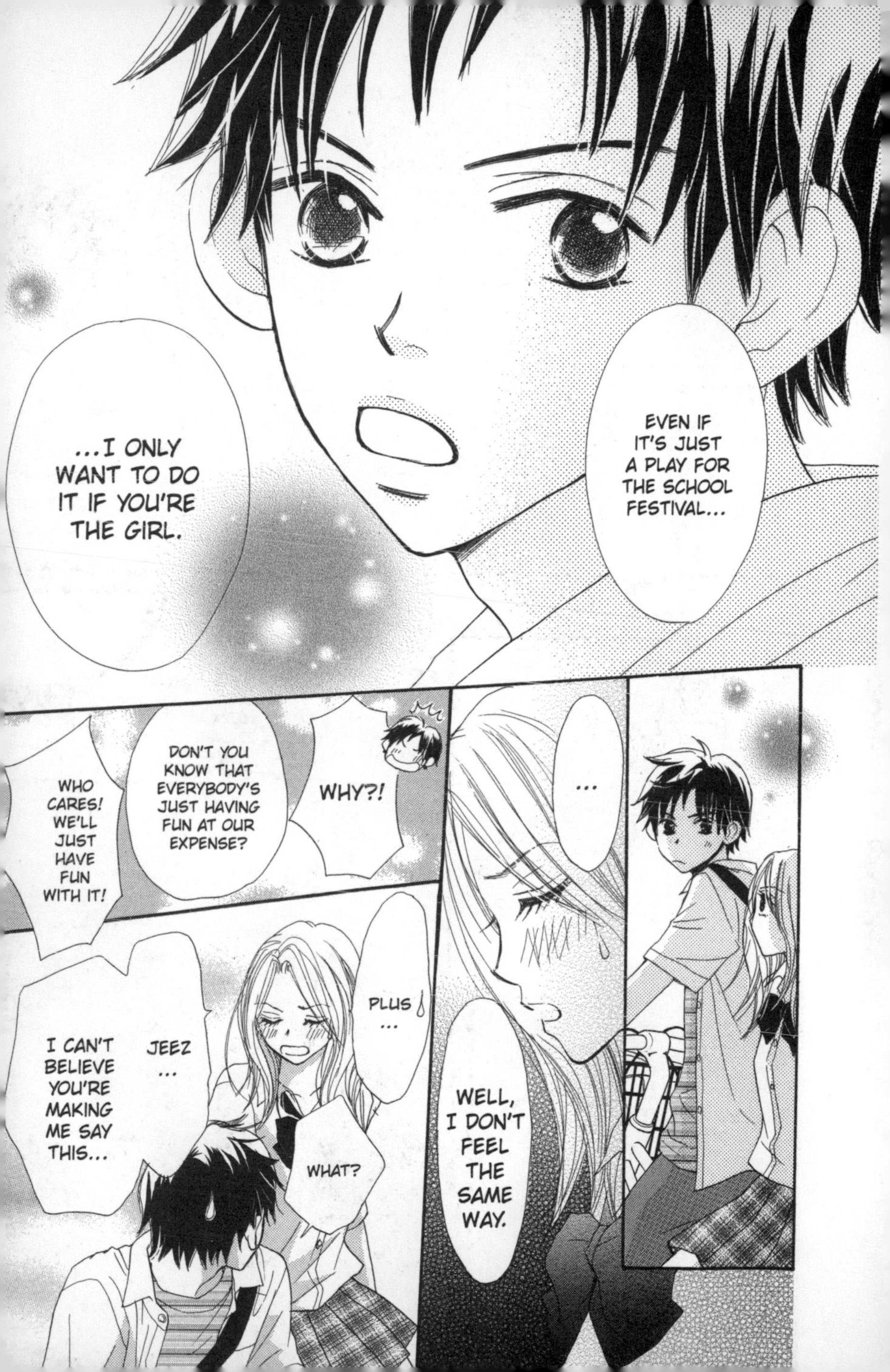
EVEN IF IT'S JUST A PLAY FOR THE SCHOOL FESTIVAL...
...I ONLY WANT TO DO IT IF YOU'RE THE GIRL.
...
WELL, I DON'T FEEL THE SAME WAY.
WHY?!
DON'T YOU KNOW THAT EVERYBODY'S JUST HAVING FUN AT OUR EXPENSE?
WHO CARES! WE'LL JUST HAVE FUN WITH IT!
PLUS ...
WHAT?
JEEZ ...
I CAN'T BELIEVE YOU'RE MAKING ME SAY THIS...

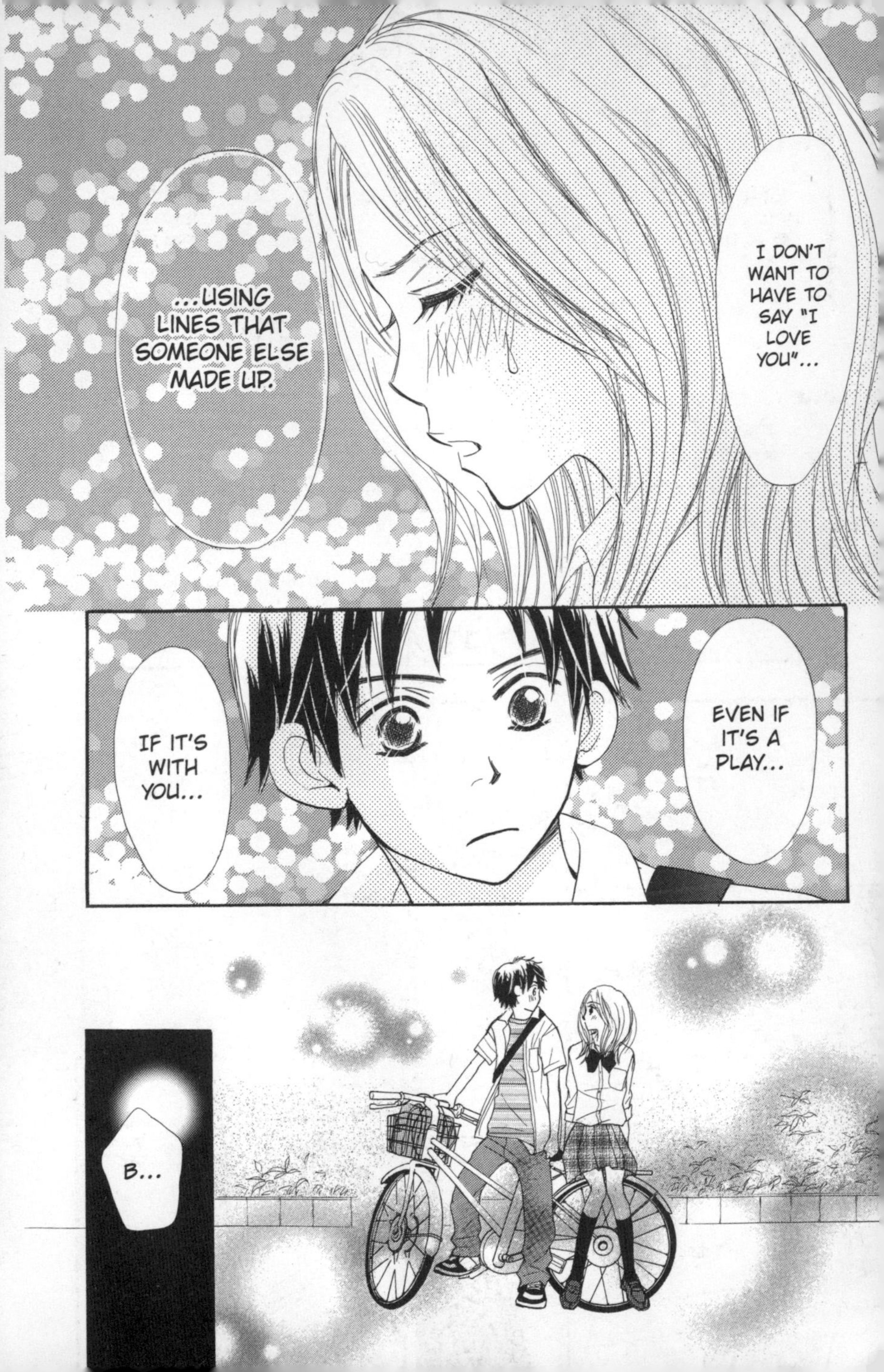
I DON'T WANT TO HAVE TO SAY "I LOVE YOU"...
...USING LINES THAT SOMEONE ELSE MADE UP.
EVEN IF IT'S A PLAY...
IF IT'S WITH YOU...
B...

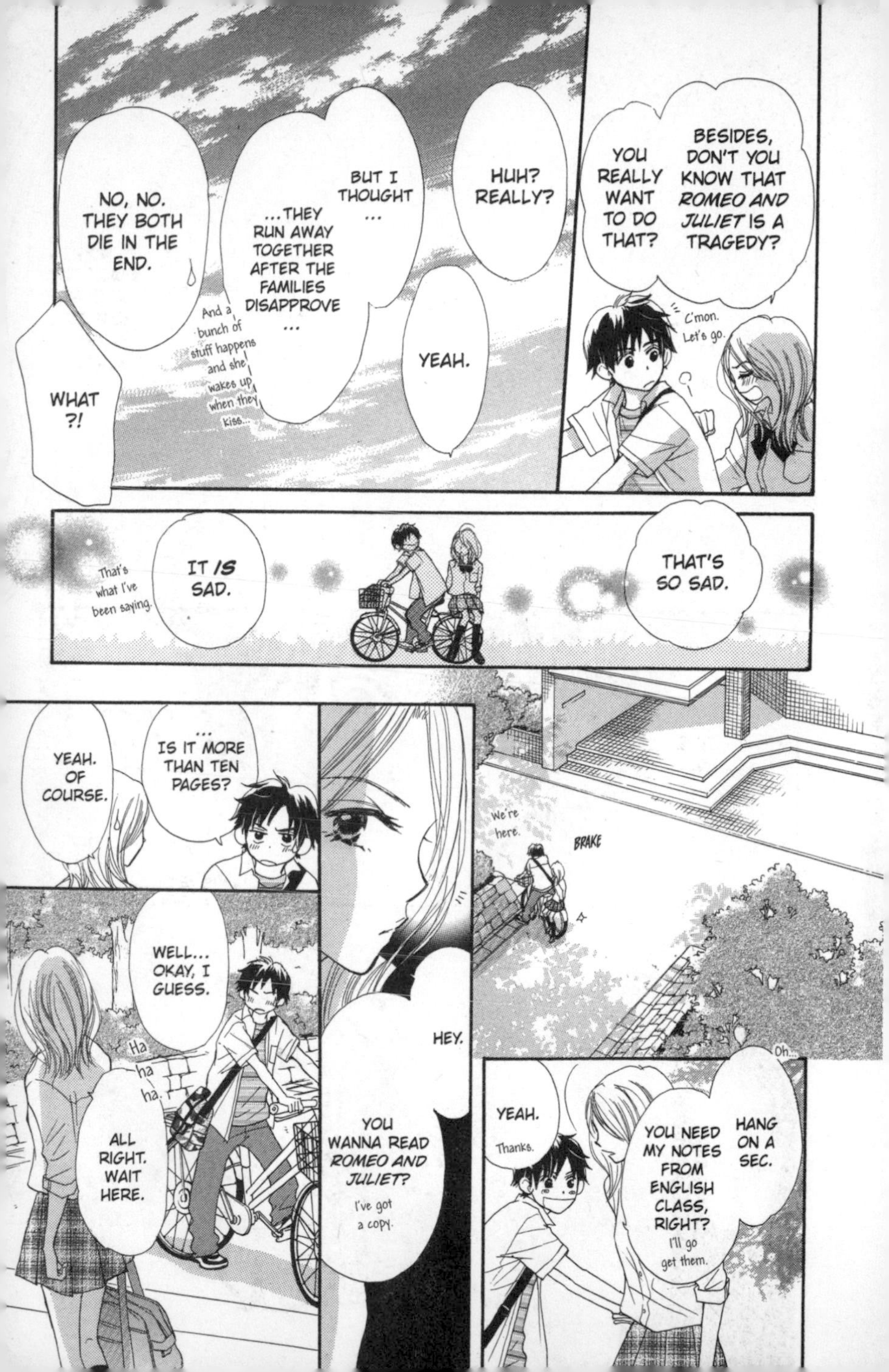
BESIDES, DON'T YOU KNOW THAT *ROMEO AND JULIET* IS A TRAGEDY?
C'mon. Let's go.
YOU REALLY WANT TO DO THAT?
HUH? REALLY?
YEAH.
BUT I THOUGHT...
...THEY RUN AWAY TOGETHER AFTER THE FAMILIES DISAPPROVE...
And a bunch of stuff happens and she wakes up when they kiss...
NO, NO. THEY BOTH DIE IN THE END.
WHAT?!
THAT'S SO SAD.
IT *IS* SAD.
That's what I've been saying.
BRAKE
We're here.
Oh...
HANG ON A SEC.
YOU NEED MY NOTES FROM ENGLISH CLASS, RIGHT?
I'll go get them.
YEAH.
Thanks.
HEY.
YOU WANNA READ *ROMEO AND JULIET?*
I've got a copy.
...IS IT MORE THAN TEN PAGES?
YEAH. OF COURSE.
WELL... OKAY, I GUESS.
Ha ha ha.
ALL RIGHT. WAIT HERE.

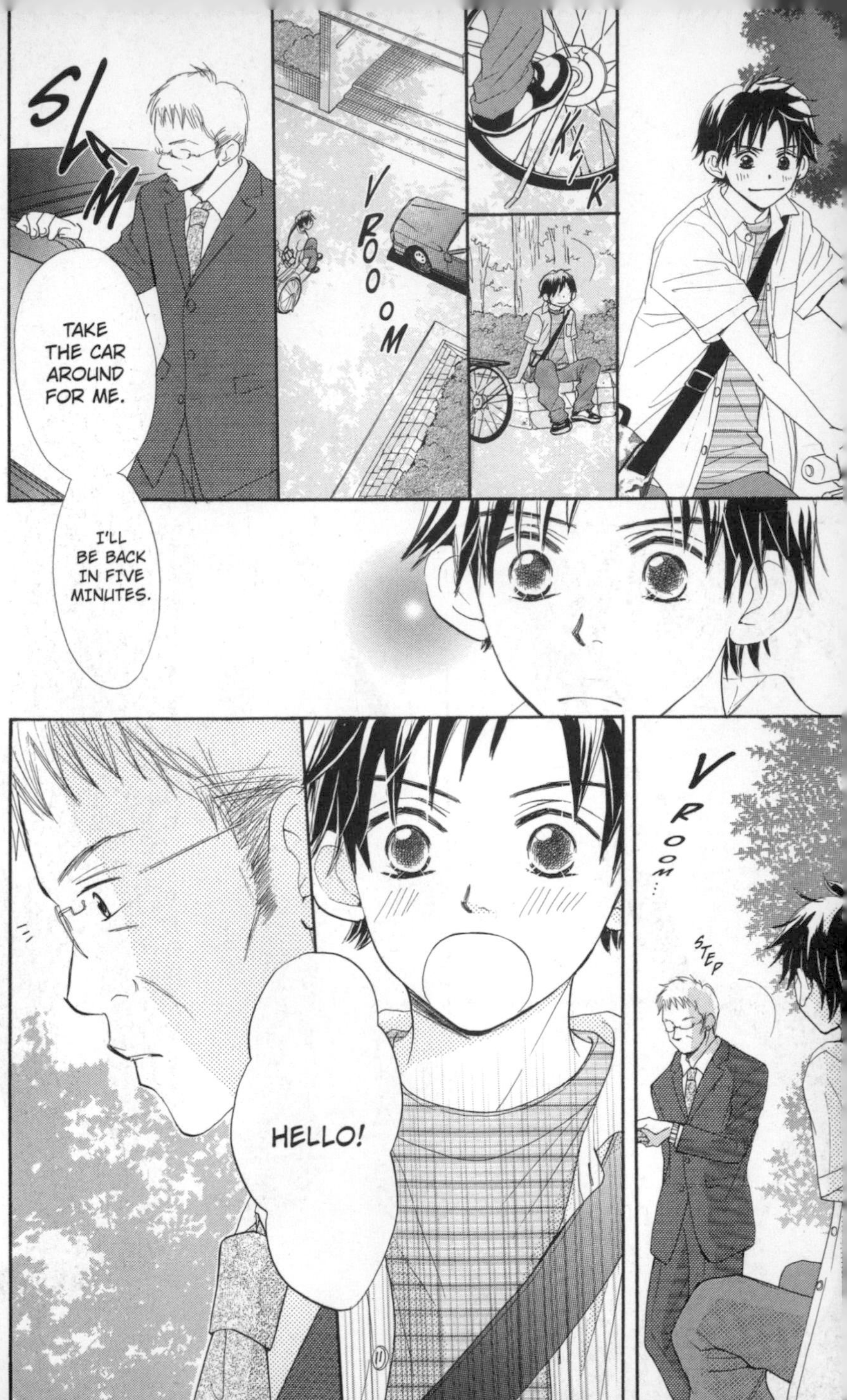
KLIK
VROOOOM
SLAM
TAKE THE CAR AROUND FOR ME.
I'LL BE BACK IN FIVE MINUTES.
VROOM...
STEP
HELLO!

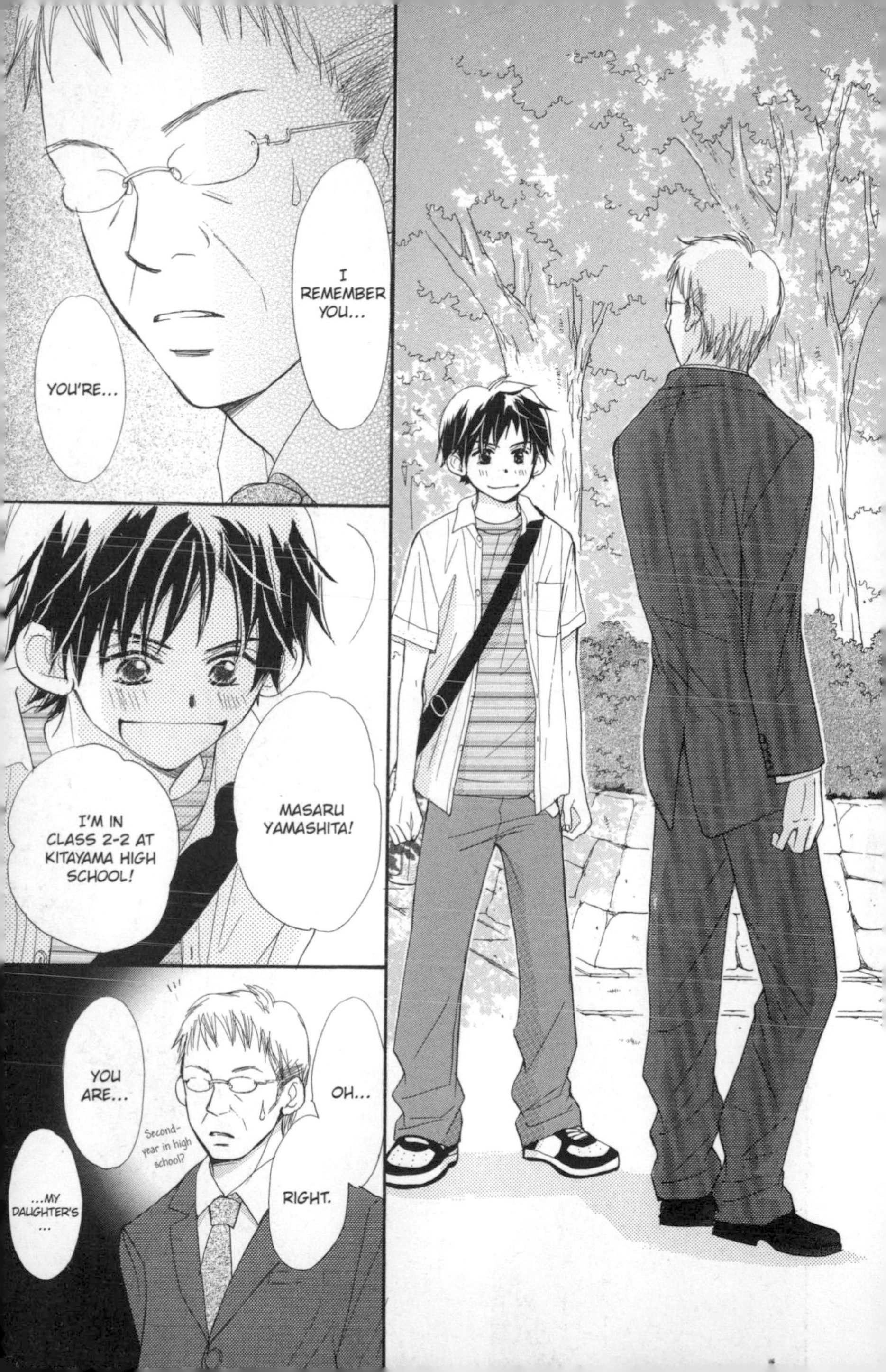
I REMEMBER YOU...
YOU'RE...
MASARU YAMASHITA!
I'M IN CLASS 2-2 AT KITAYAMA HIGH SCHOOL!
OH...
RIGHT.
YOU ARE...
Second-year in high school?
...MY DAUGHTER'S ...

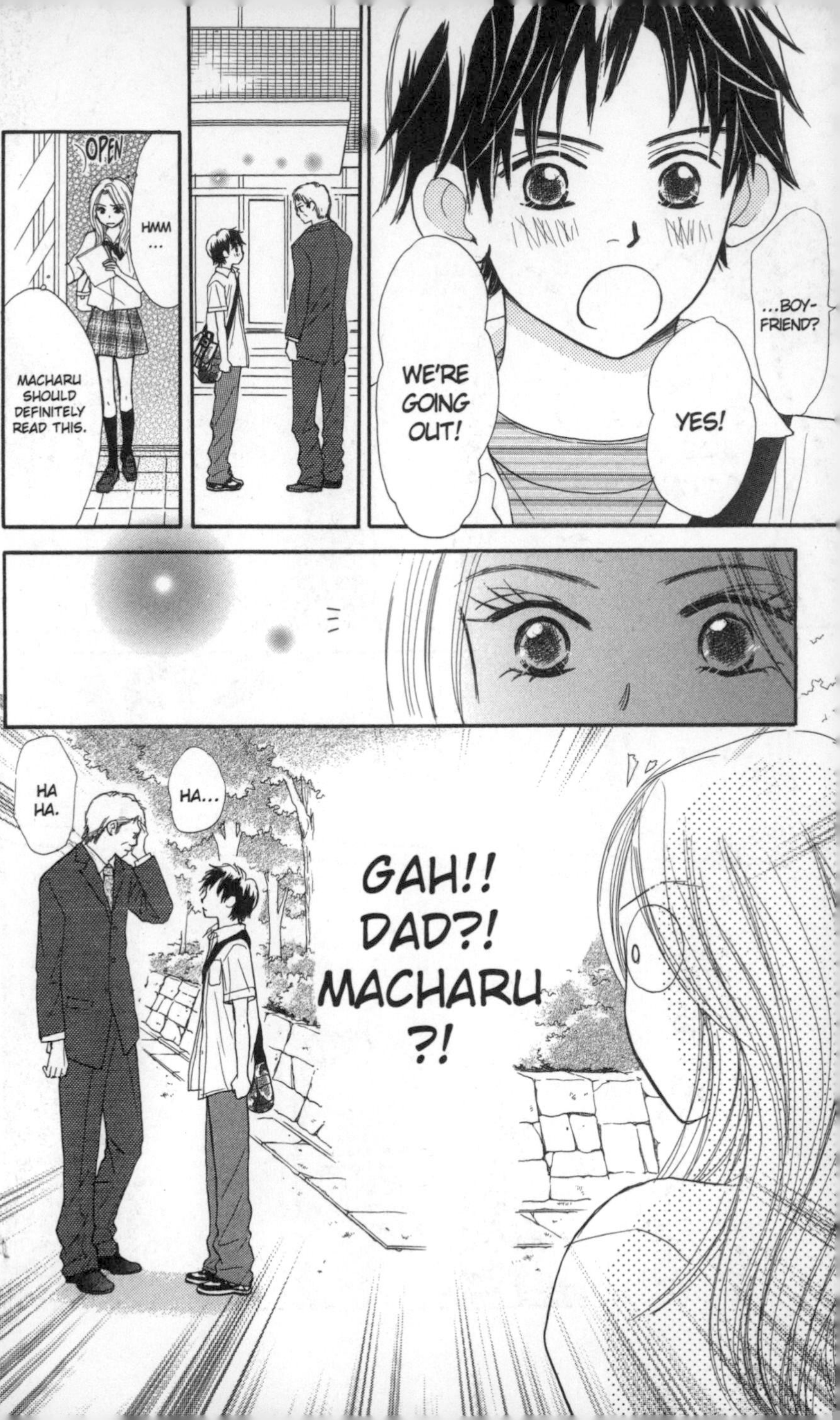

...BOY-FRIEND?
YES!
WE'RE GOING OUT!
OPEN
HMM ...
MACHARU SHOULD DEFINITELY READ THIS.
GAH!! DAD?! MACHARU ?!
HA...
HA HA.

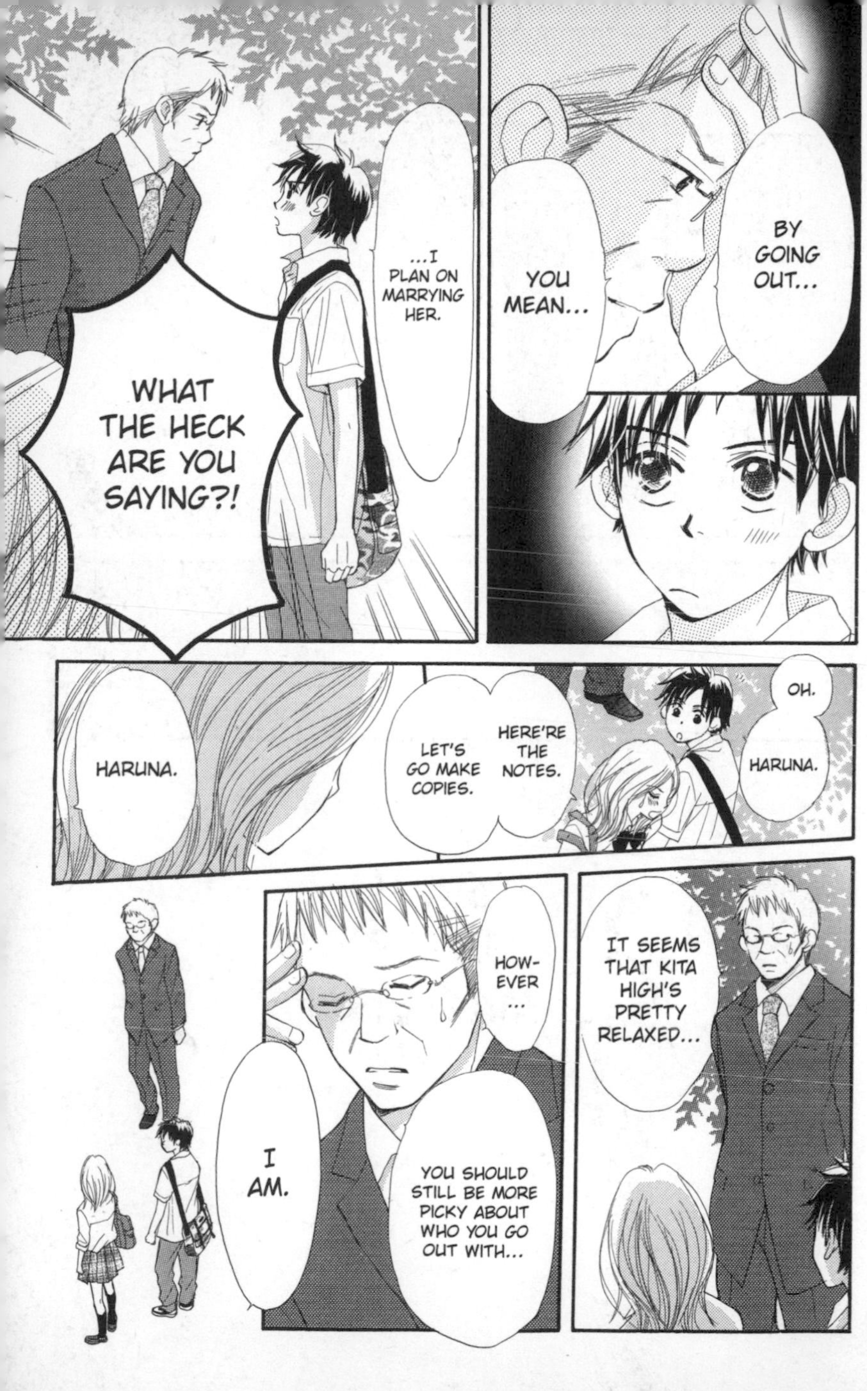
BY GOING OUT...
YOU MEAN...
...I PLAN ON MARRYING HER.
WHAT THE HECK ARE YOU SAYING?!
OH. HARUNA.
HERE'RE THE NOTES.
LET'S GO MAKE COPIES.
HARUNA.
IT SEEMS THAT KITA HIGH'S PRETTY RELAXED...
HOW-EVER...
YOU SHOULD STILL BE MORE PICKY ABOUT WHO YOU GO OUT WITH...
I AM.

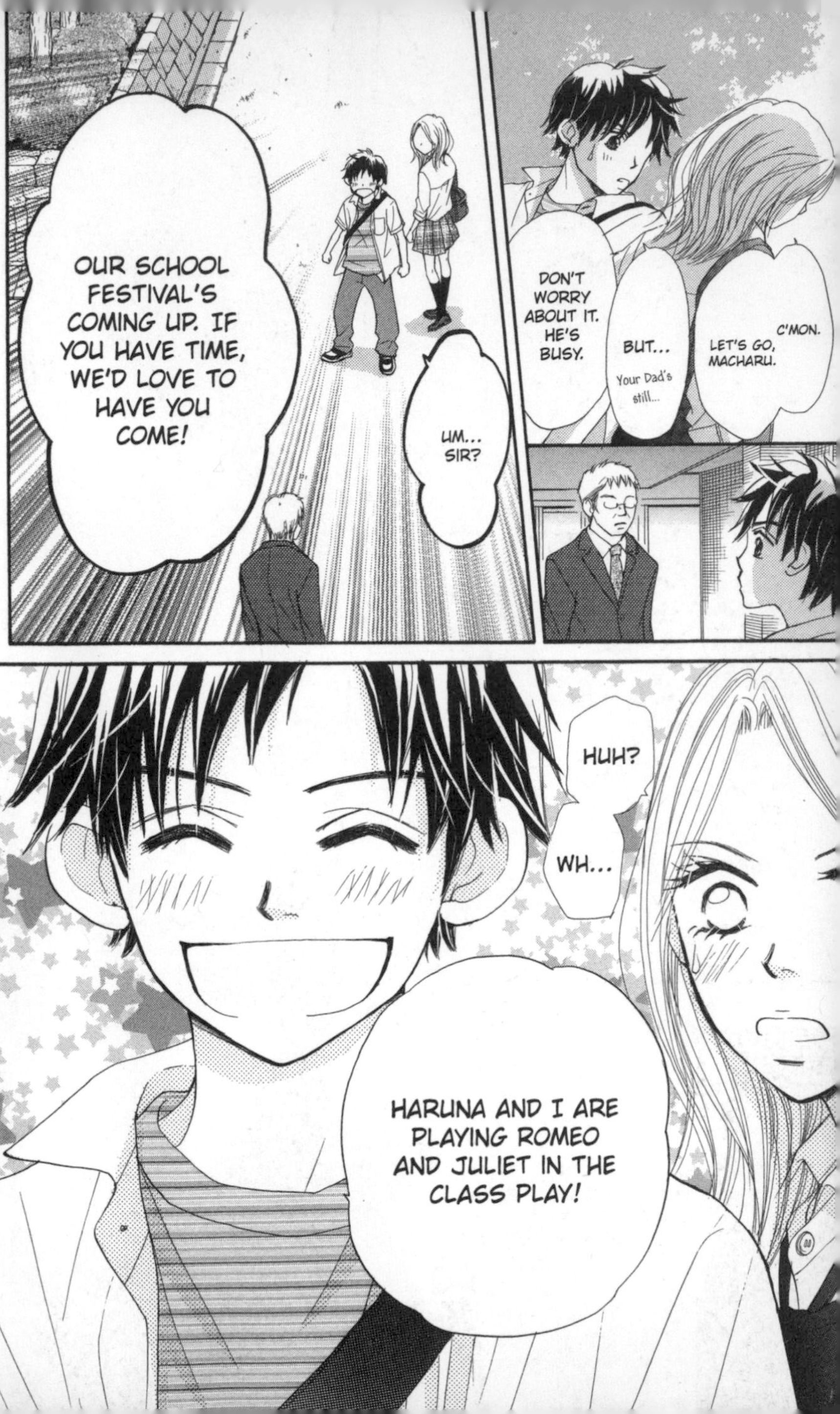
C'MON. LET'S GO, MACHARU.
BUT... Your Dad's still...
DON'T WORRY ABOUT IT. HE'S BUSY.
UM... SIR?
OUR SCHOOL FESTIVAL'S COMING UP. IF YOU HAVE TIME, WE'D LOVE TO HAVE YOU COME!
HUH?
WH...
HARUNA AND I ARE PLAYING ROMEO AND JULIET IN THE CLASS PLAY!

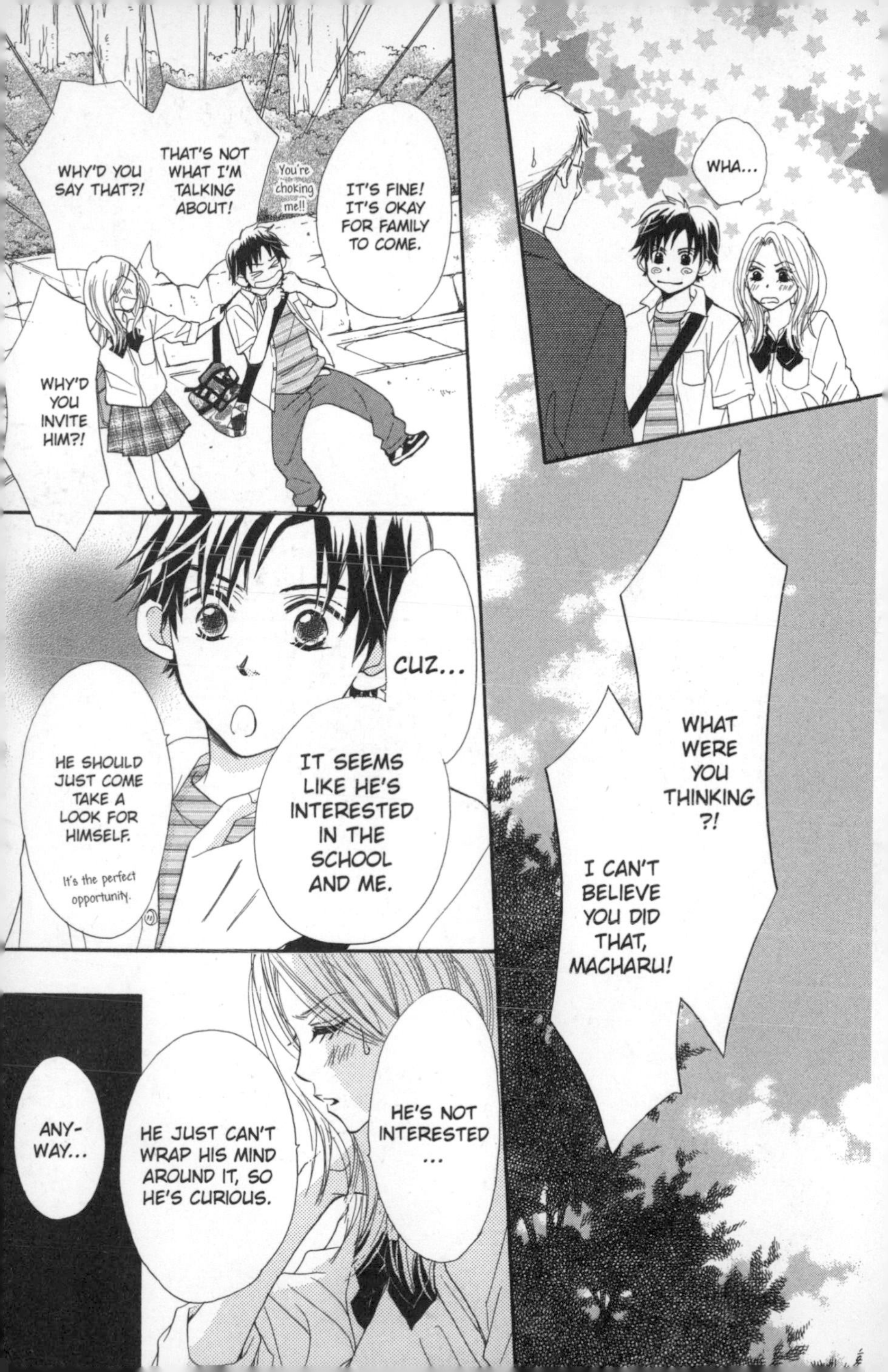
WHA...
WHAT WERE YOU THINKING?!
I CAN'T BELIEVE YOU DID THAT, MACHARU!
IT'S FINE! IT'S OKAY FOR FAMILY TO COME.
You're choking me!!
THAT'S NOT WHAT I'M TALKING ABOUT!
WHY'D YOU SAY THAT?!
WHY'D YOU INVITE HIM?!
CUZ...
IT SEEMS LIKE HE'S INTERESTED IN THE SCHOOL AND ME.
HE SHOULD JUST COME TAKE A LOOK FOR HIMSELF.
It's the perfect opportunity.
HE'S NOT INTERESTED...
HE JUST CAN'T WRAP HIS MIND AROUND IT, SO HE'S CURIOUS.
ANY-WAY...

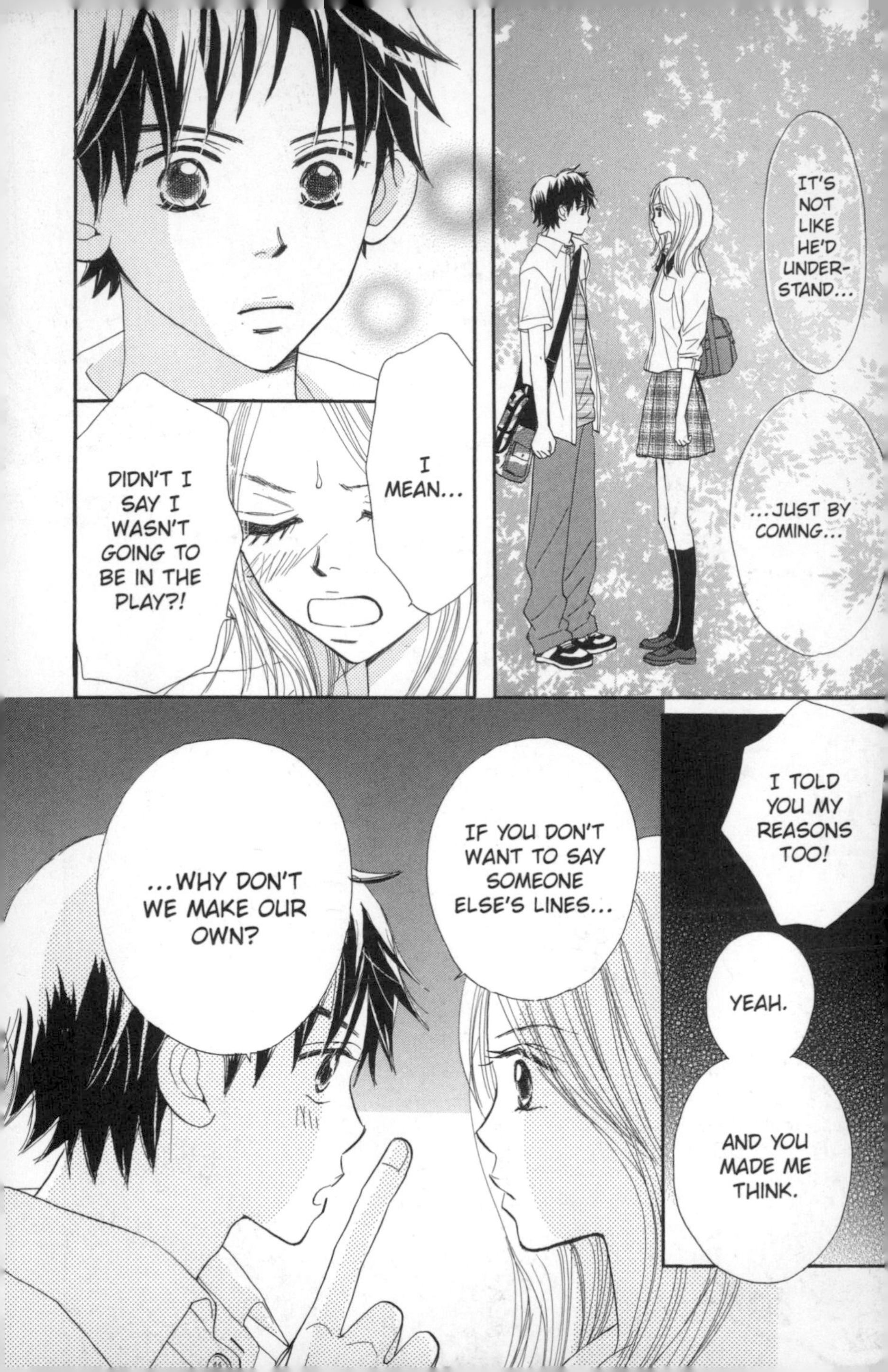
IT'S NOT LIKE HE'D UNDER-STAND...
...JUST BY COMING...
I MEAN...
DIDN'T I SAY I WASN'T GOING TO BE IN THE PLAY?!
I TOLD YOU MY REASONS TOO!
YEAH.
AND YOU MADE ME THINK.
IF YOU DON'T WANT TO SAY SOMEONE ELSE'S LINES...
...WHY DON'T WE MAKE OUR OWN?

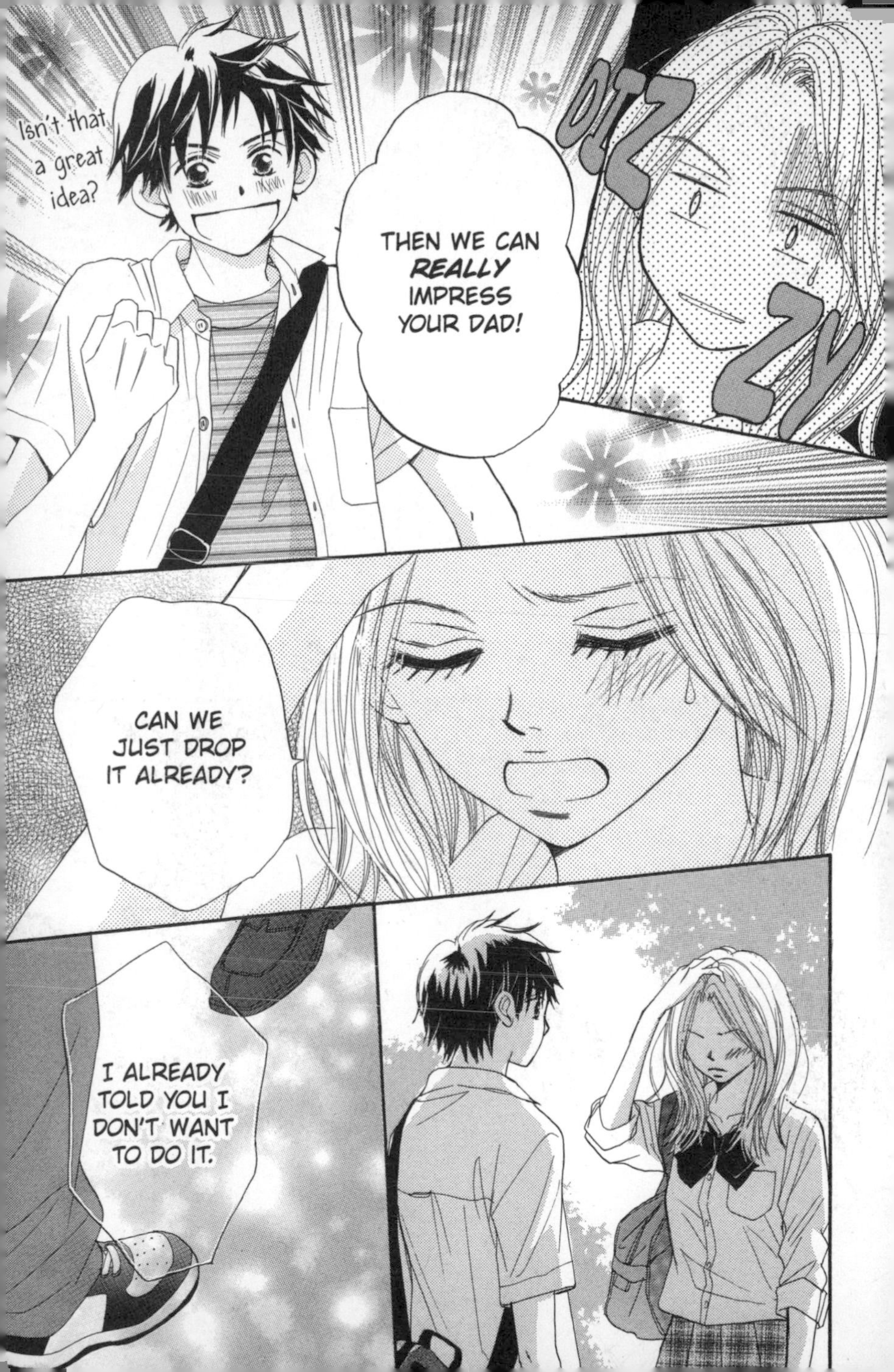
DIZZY
Isn't that a great idea?
THEN WE CAN *REALLY* IMPRESS YOUR DAD!
CAN WE JUST DROP IT ALREADY?
I ALREADY TOLD YOU I DON'T WANT TO DO IT.

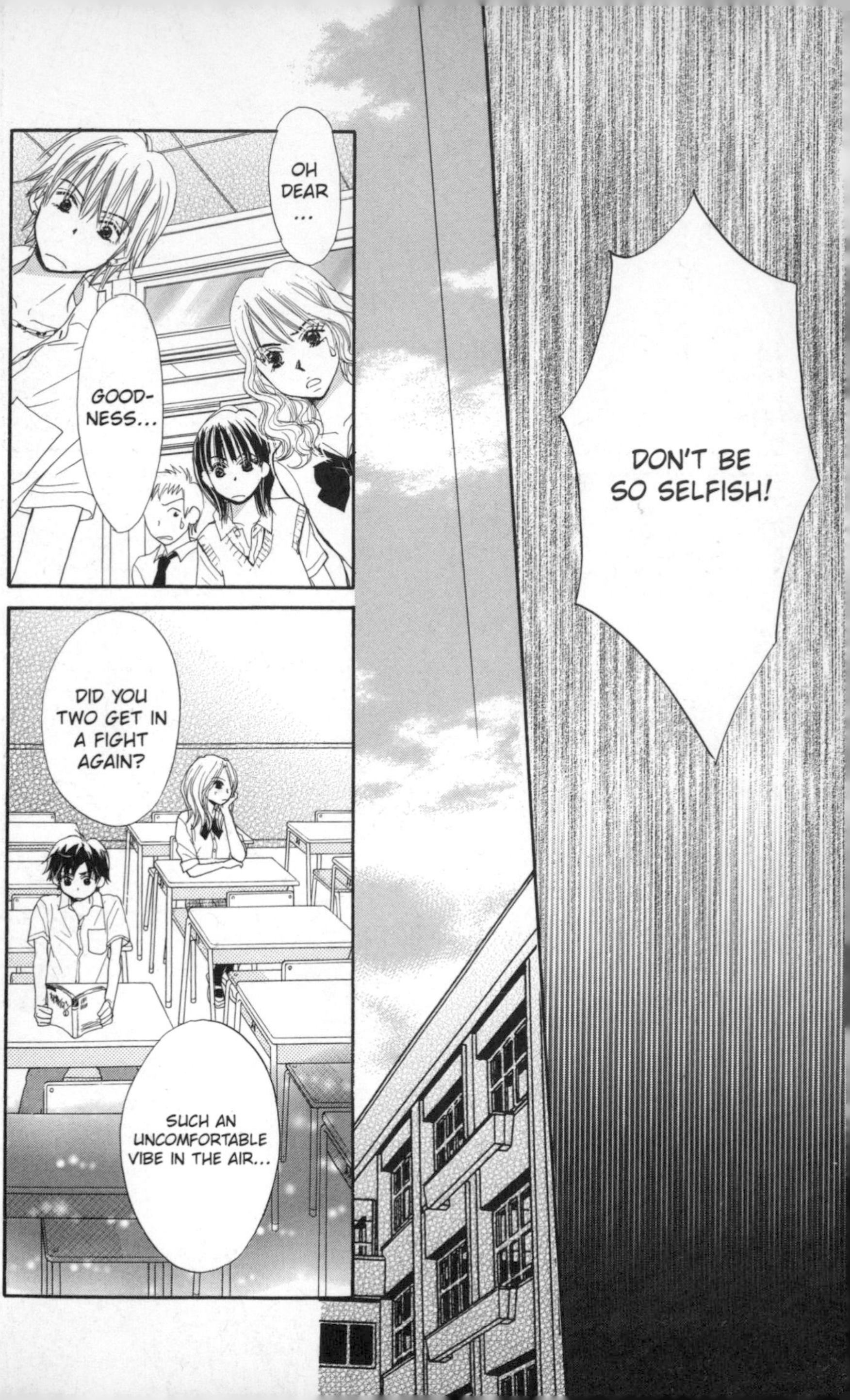
DON'T BE SO SELFISH!
OH DEAR ...
GOODNESS...
DID YOU TWO GET IN A FIGHT AGAIN?
SUCH AN UNCOMFORTABLE VIBE IN THE AIR...

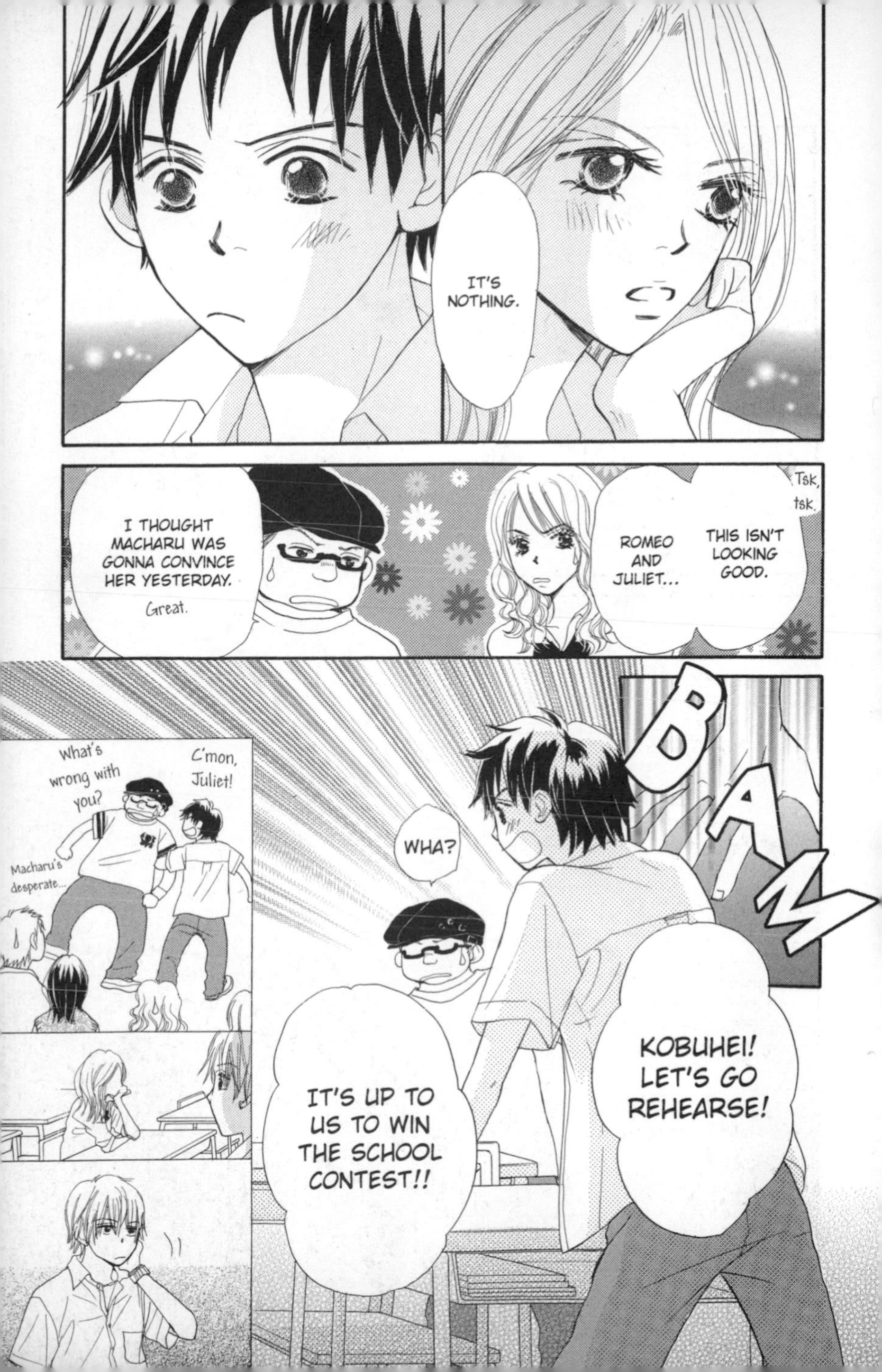
IT'S NOTHING.
Tsk, tsk.
THIS ISN'T LOOKING GOOD.
ROMEO AND JULIET...
I THOUGHT MACHARU WAS GONNA CONVINCE HER YESTERDAY.
Great.
BAM
KOBUHEI! LET'S GO REHEARSE!
IT'S UP TO US TO WIN THE SCHOOL CONTEST!!
WHA?
C'mon, Juliet!
What's wrong with you?
Macharu's desperate...

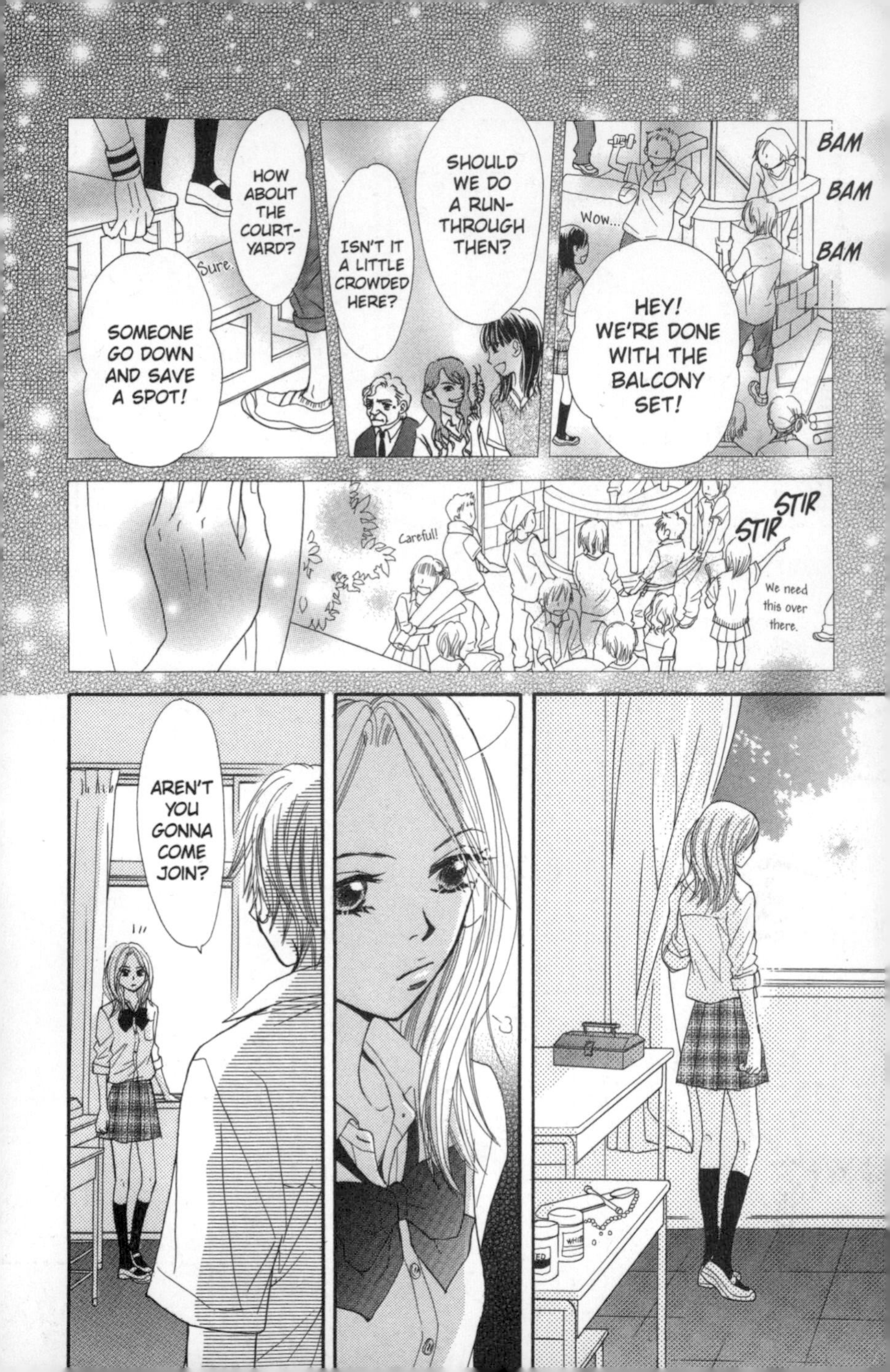
BAM
BAM
BAM
Wow...
HEY! WE'RE DONE WITH THE BALCONY SET!
SHOULD WE DO A RUN-THROUGH THEN?
ISN'T IT A LITTLE CROWDED HERE?
HOW ABOUT THE COURT-YARD?
Sure.
SOMEONE GO DOWN AND SAVE A SPOT!
STIR
STIR
We need this over there.
Careful!
AREN'T YOU GONNA COME JOIN?

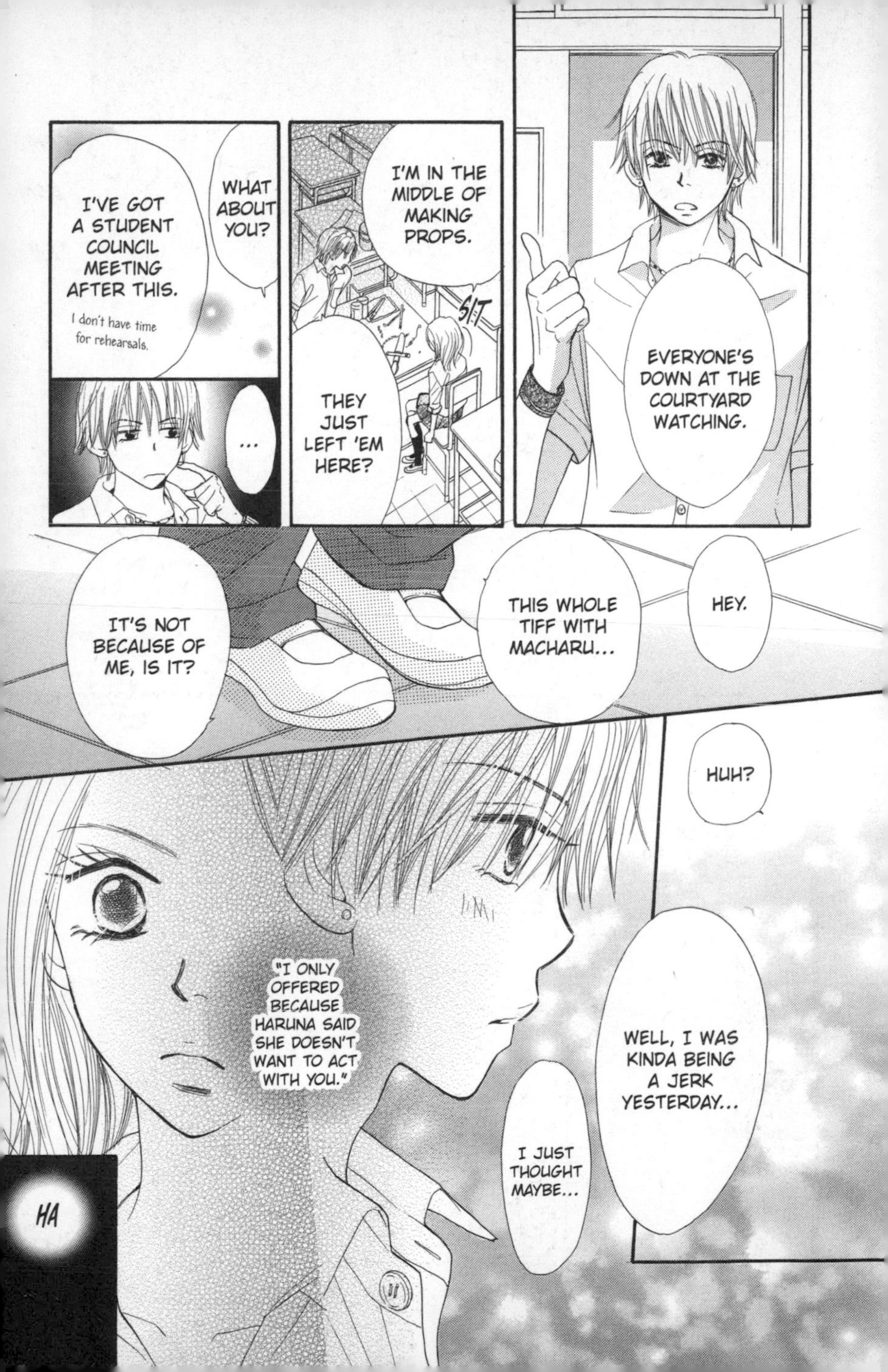
EVERYONE'S DOWN AT THE COURTYARD WATCHING.
I'M IN THE MIDDLE OF MAKING PROPS.
SIT
THEY JUST LEFT 'EM HERE?
WHAT ABOUT YOU?
I'VE GOT A STUDENT COUNCIL MEETING AFTER THIS.
I don't have time for rehearsals.
...
HEY.
THIS WHOLE TIFF WITH MACHARU...
IT'S NOT BECAUSE OF ME, IS IT?
HUH?
WELL, I WAS KINDA BEING A JERK YESTERDAY...
I JUST THOUGHT MAYBE...
"I ONLY OFFERED BECAUSE HARUNA SAID SHE DOESN'T WANT TO ACT WITH YOU."
HA

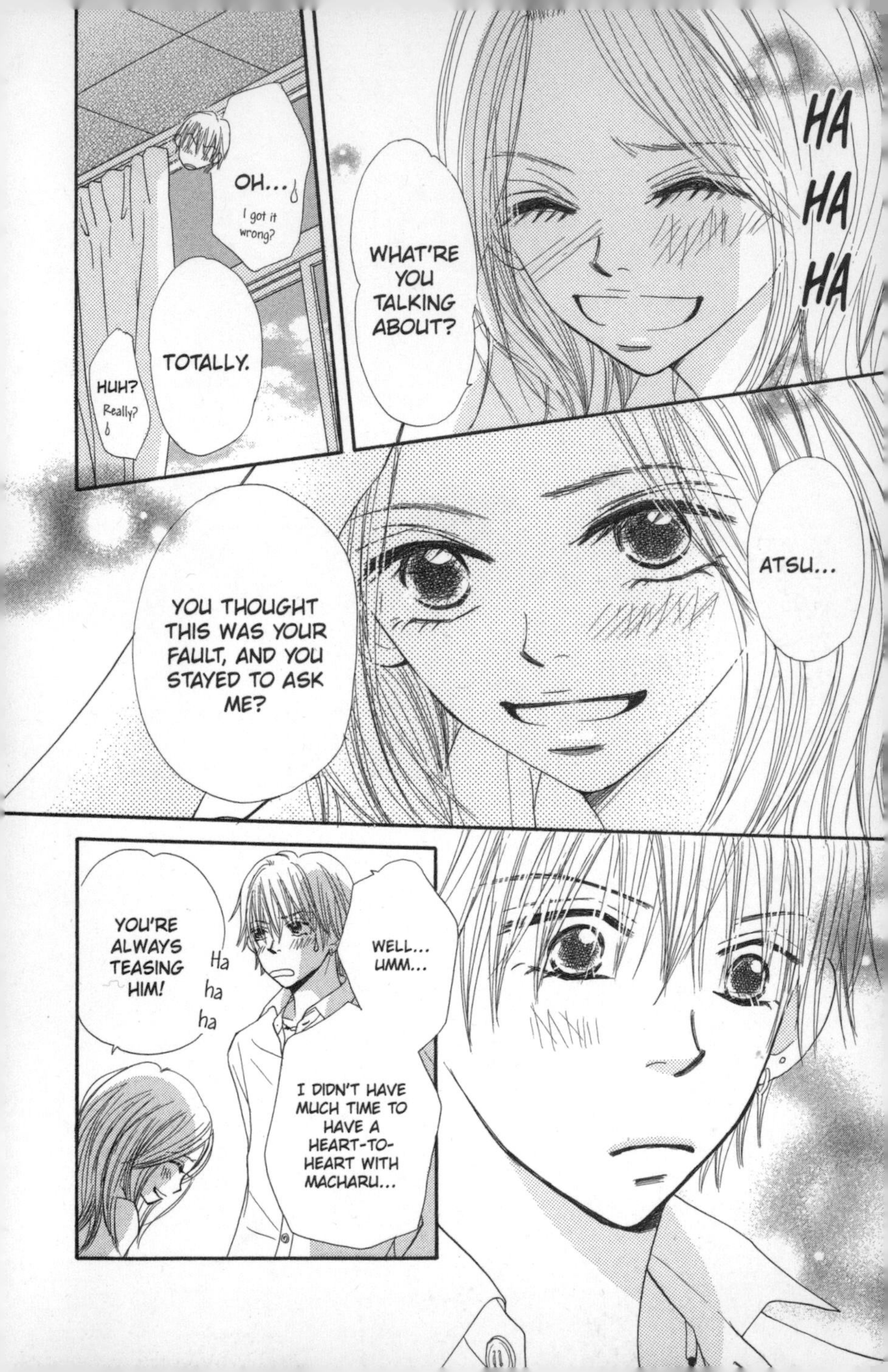

HA HA HA
WHAT'RE YOU TALKING ABOUT?
OH... I got it wrong?
TOTALLY.
HUH? Really?
ATSU...
YOU THOUGHT THIS WAS YOUR FAULT, AND YOU STAYED TO ASK ME?
WELL... UMM...
I DIDN'T HAVE MUCH TIME TO HAVE A HEART-TO-HEART WITH MACHARU...
YOU'RE ALWAYS TEASING HIM!
Ha ha ha

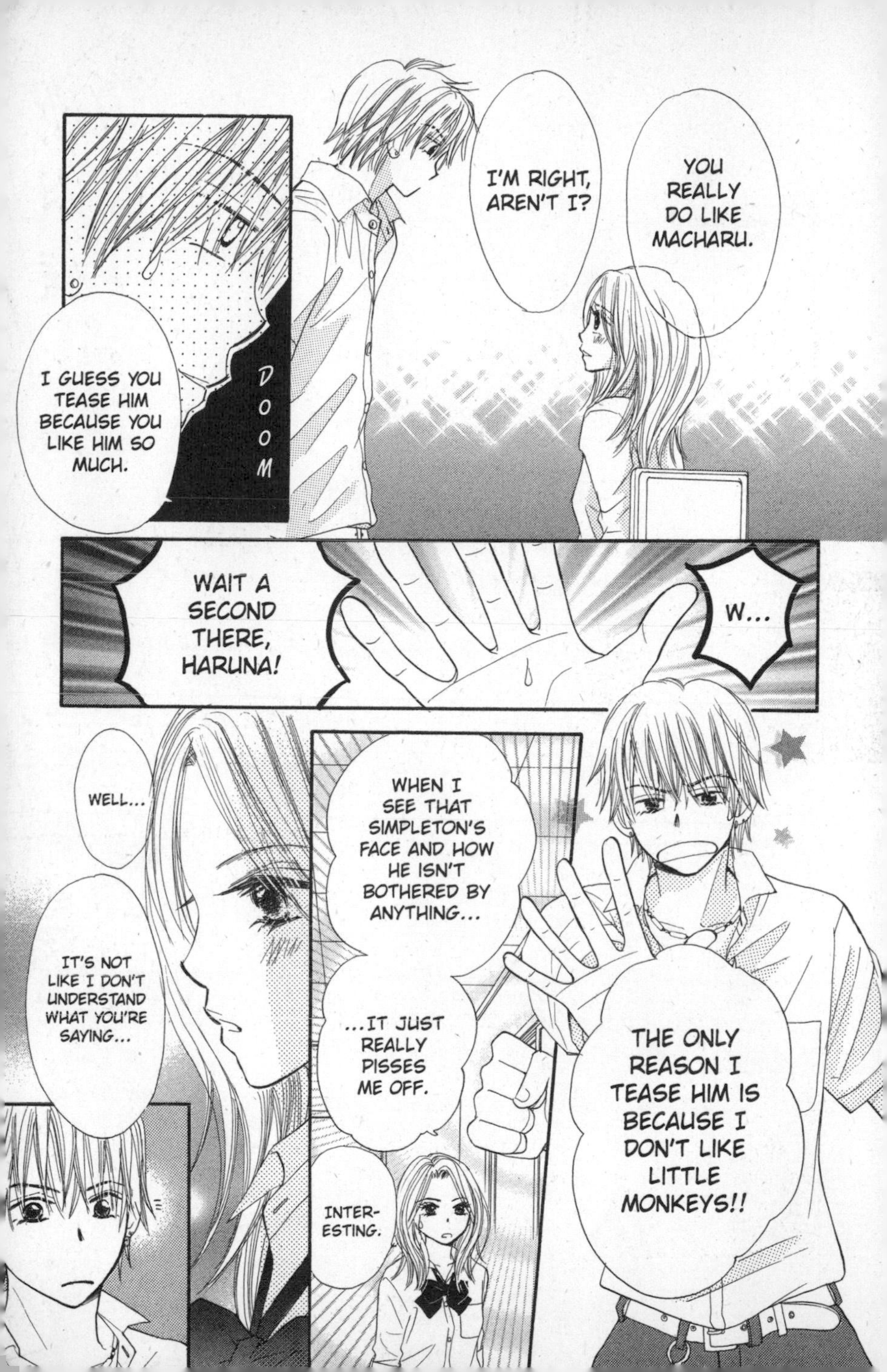
YOU REALLY DO LIKE MACHARU.
I'M RIGHT, AREN'T I?
I GUESS YOU TEASE HIM BECAUSE YOU LIKE HIM SO MUCH.
DOOOM
W...
WAIT A SECOND THERE, HARUNA!
THE ONLY REASON I TEASE HIM IS BECAUSE I DON'T LIKE LITTLE MONKEYS!!
WHEN I SEE THAT SIMPLETON'S FACE AND HOW HE ISN'T BOTHERED BY ANYTHING...
...IT JUST REALLY PISSES ME OFF.
INTER-ESTING.
WELL...
IT'S NOT LIKE I DON'T UNDERSTAND WHAT YOU'RE SAYING...

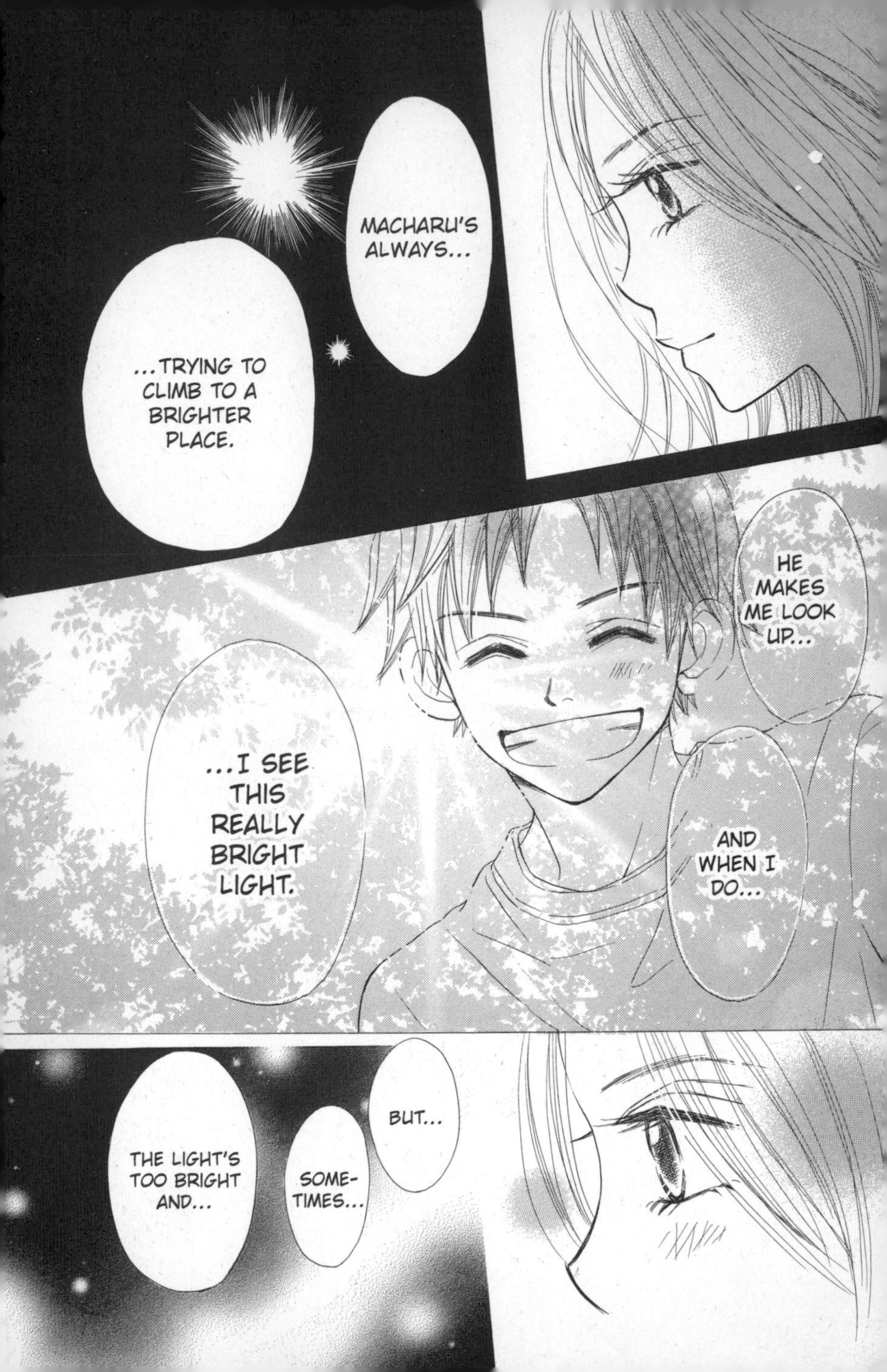
MACHARU'S ALWAYS...
...TRYING TO CLIMB TO A BRIGHTER PLACE.
HE MAKES ME LOOK UP...
AND WHEN I DO...
...I SEE THIS REALLY BRIGHT LIGHT.
BUT...
SOME-TIMES...
THE LIGHT'S TOO BRIGHT AND...

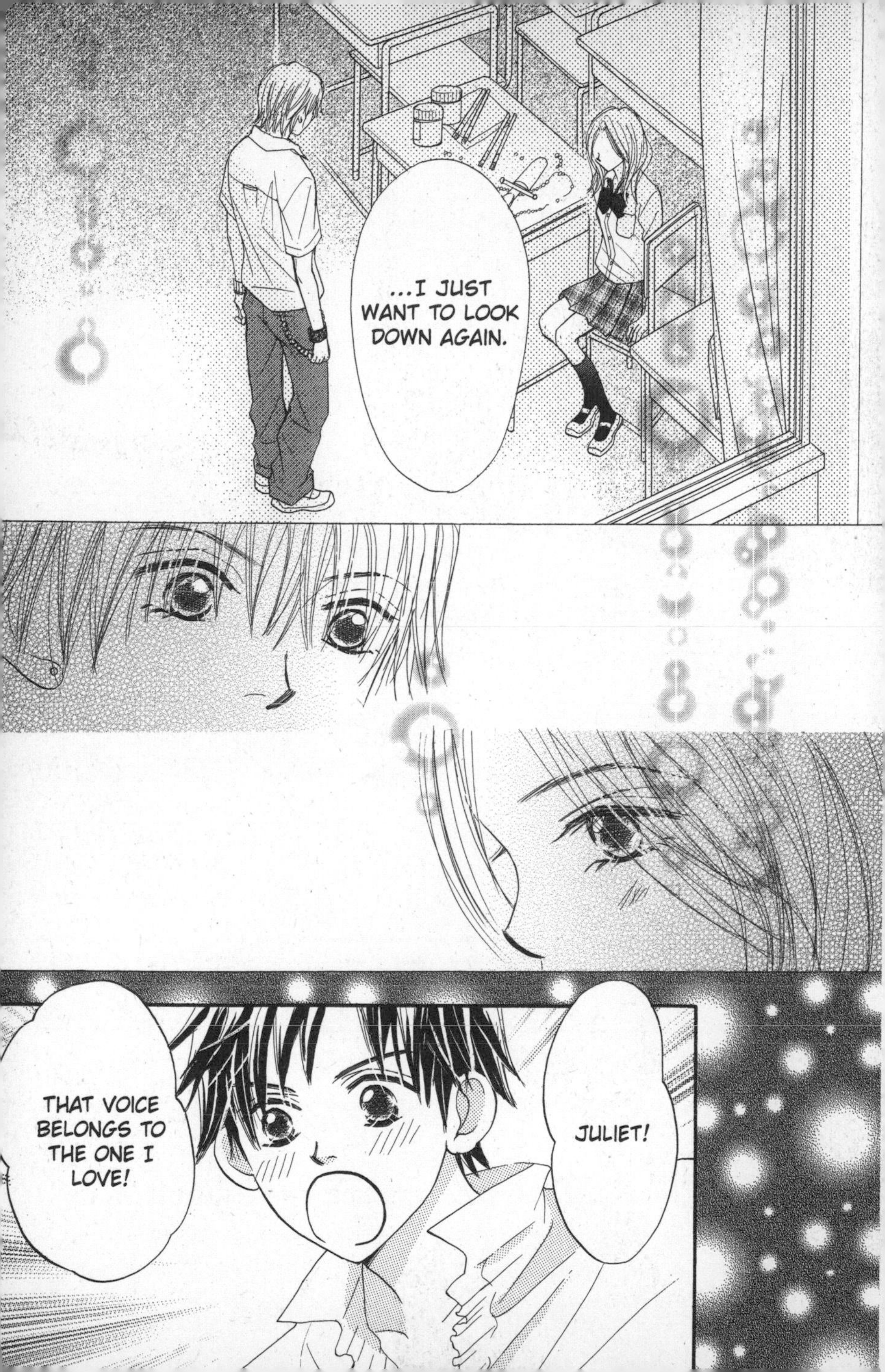
...I JUST WANT TO LOOK DOWN AGAIN.
JULIET!
THAT VOICE BELONGS TO THE ONE I LOVE!

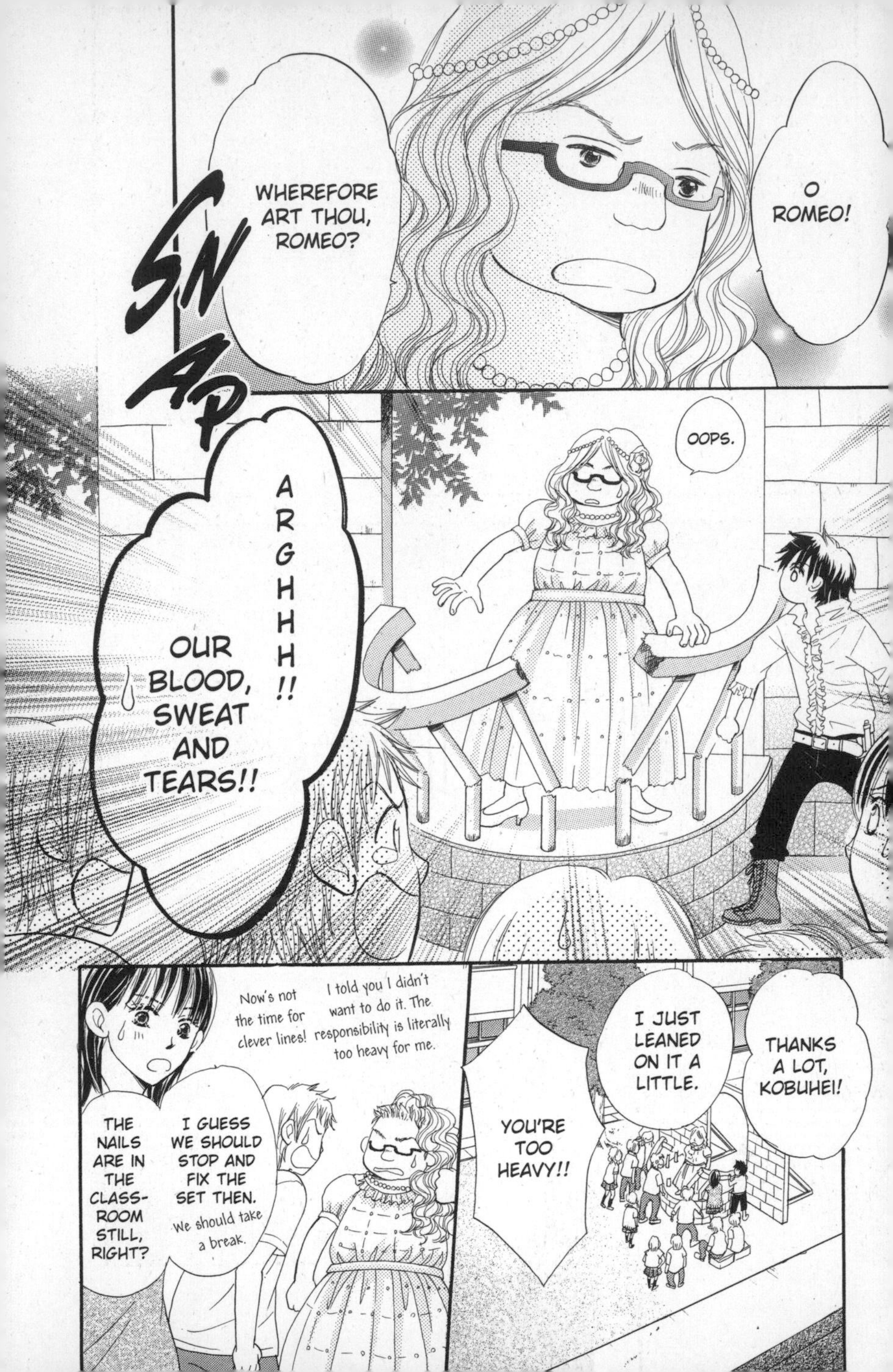
O ROMEO!
WHEREFORE ART THOU, ROMEO?
SNAP
OOPS.
ARGHHHH!!
OUR BLOOD, SWEAT AND TEARS!!
THANKS A LOT, KOBUHEI!
I JUST LEANED ON IT A LITTLE.
YOU'RE TOO HEAVY!!
I told you I didn't want to do it. The responsibility is literally too heavy for me.
Now's not the time for clever lines!
I GUESS WE SHOULD STOP AND FIX THE SET THEN. We should take a break.
THE NAILS ARE IN THE CLASS-ROOM STILL, RIGHT?

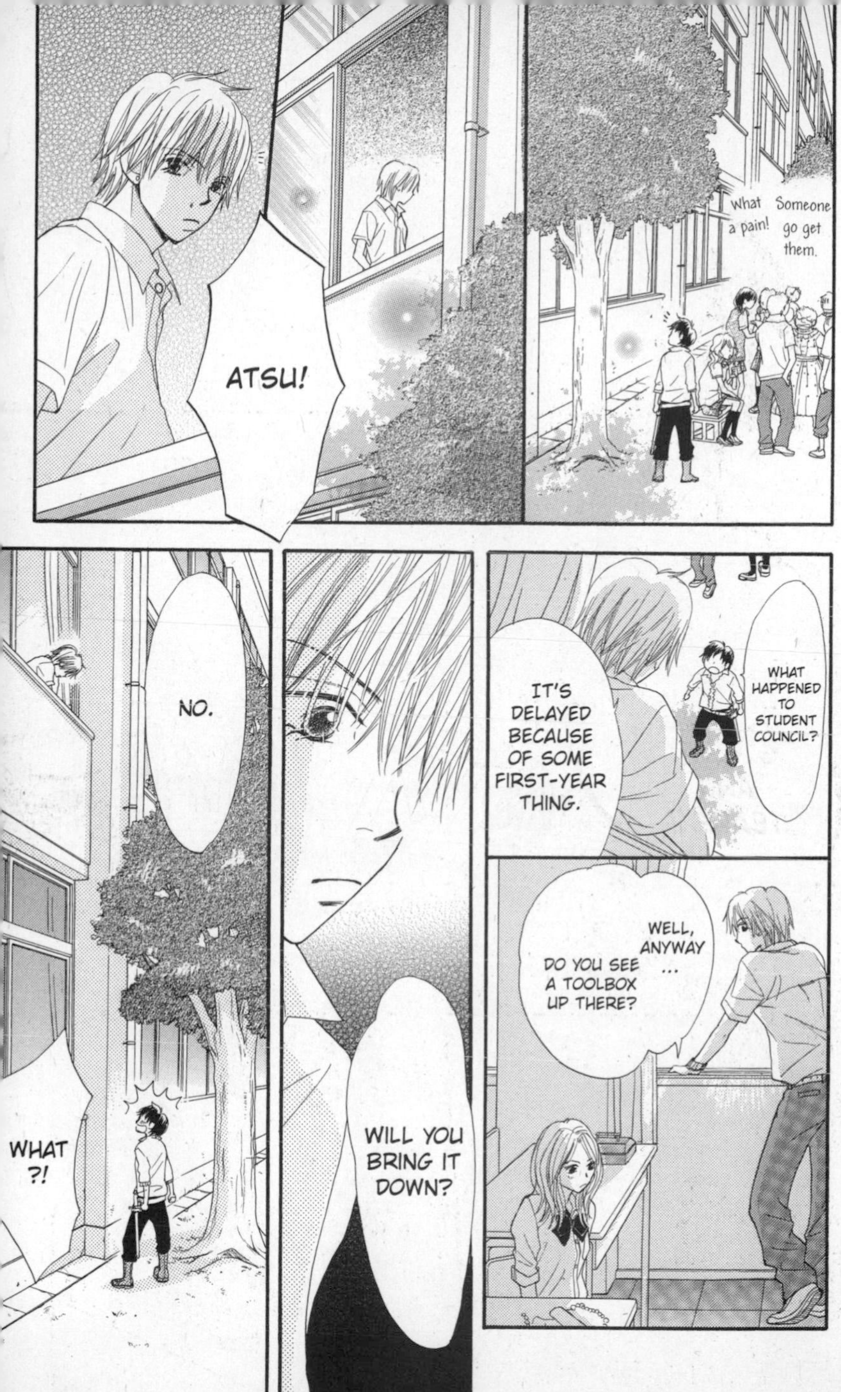
Someone go get them.
What a pain!
ATSU!
WHAT HAPPENED TO STUDENT COUNCIL?
IT'S DELAYED BECAUSE OF SOME FIRST-YEAR THING.
WELL, ANYWAY ...
DO YOU SEE A TOOLBOX UP THERE?
WILL YOU BRING IT DOWN?
NO.
WHAT ?!

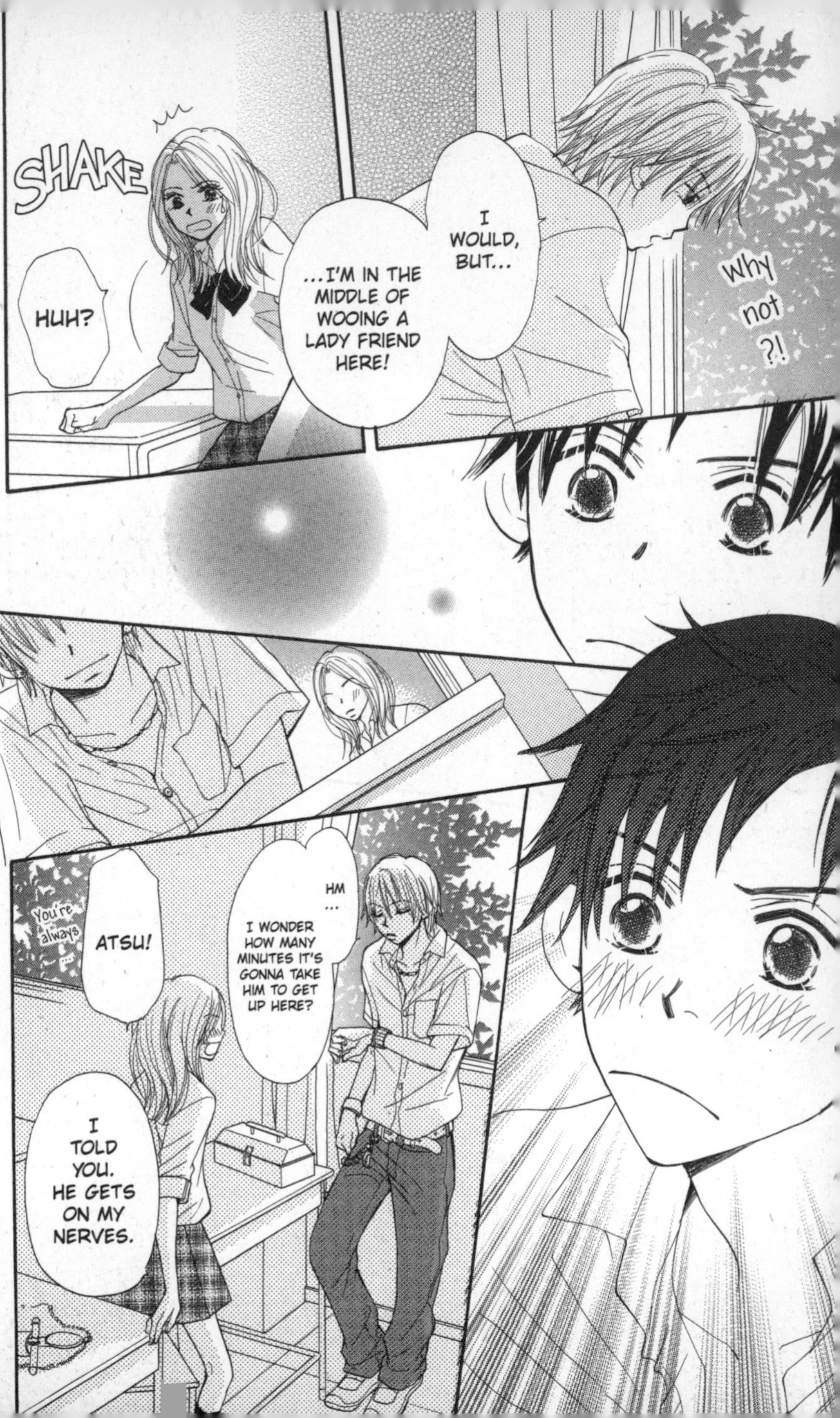
I WOULD, BUT...
...I'M IN THE MIDDLE OF WOOING A LADY FRIEND HERE!
Why not ?!
SHAKE
HUH?
HM ...
I WONDER HOW MANY MINUTES IT'S GONNA TAKE HIM TO GET UP HERE?
ATSU!
You're always ...
I TOLD YOU. HE GETS ON MY NERVES.

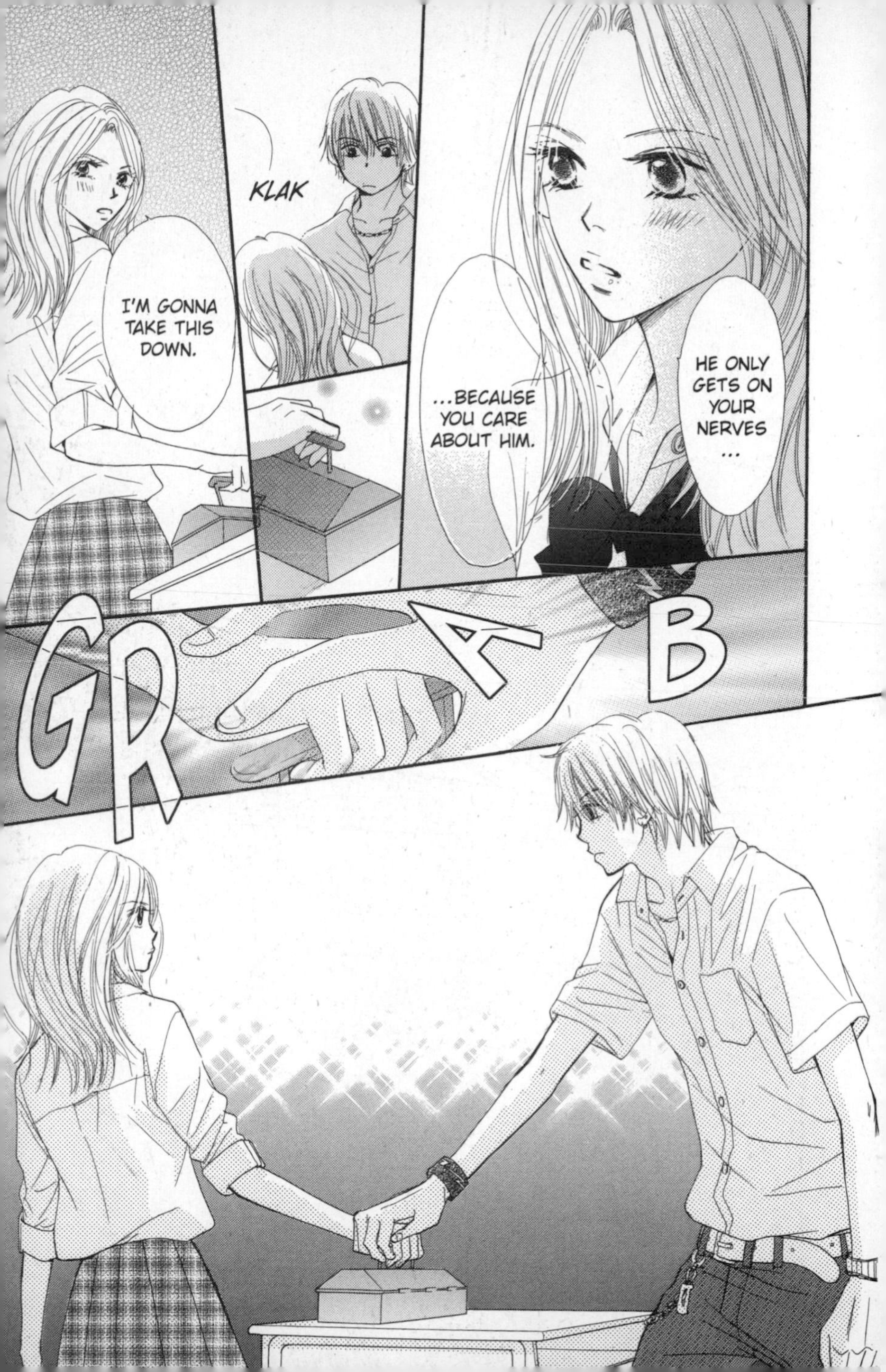
HE ONLY GETS ON YOUR NERVES ...
...BECAUSE YOU CARE ABOUT HIM.
KLAK
I'M GONNA TAKE THIS DOWN.
GRAB

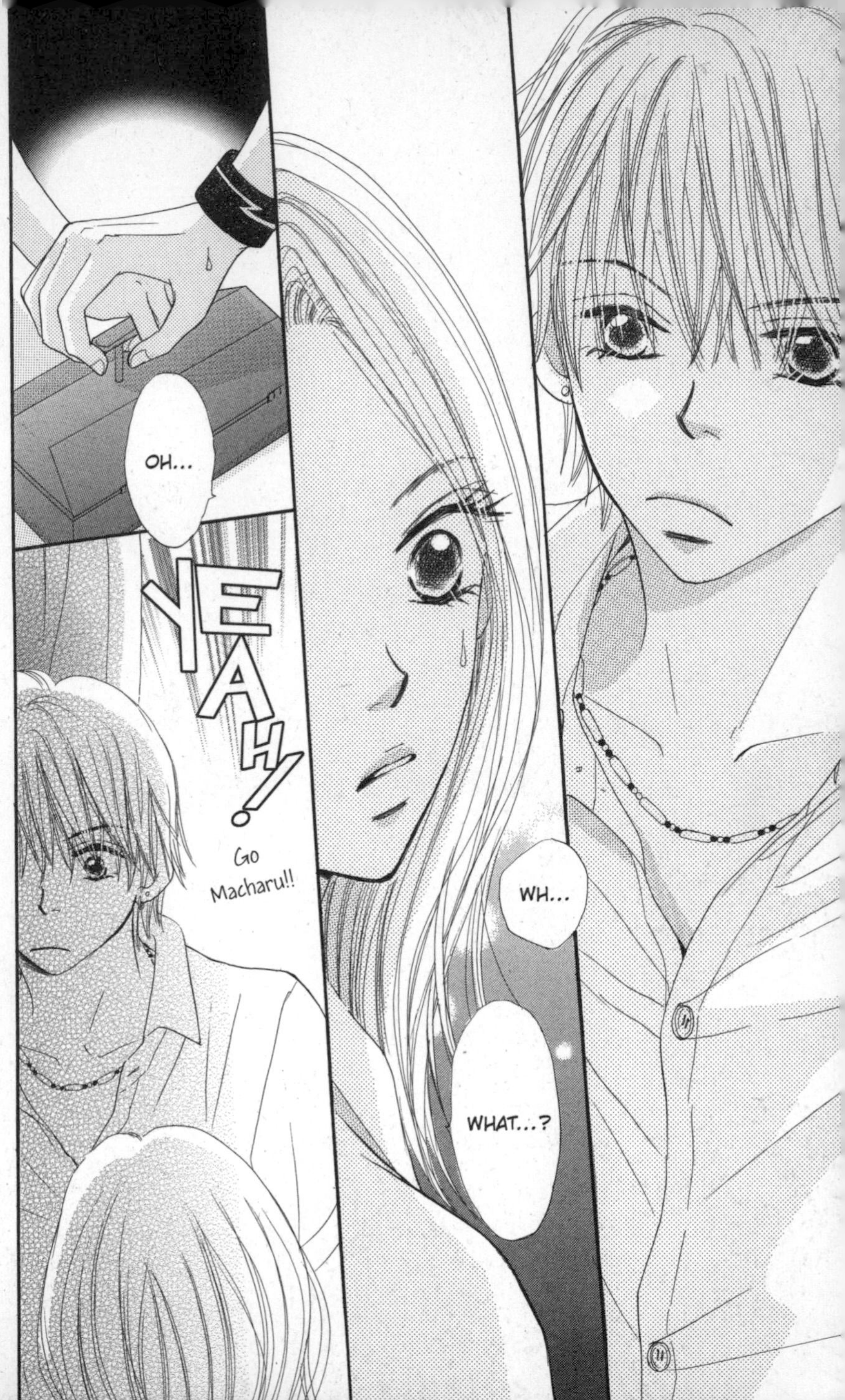
WH...
WHAT...?
OH...
YEAH!
Go Macharu!!

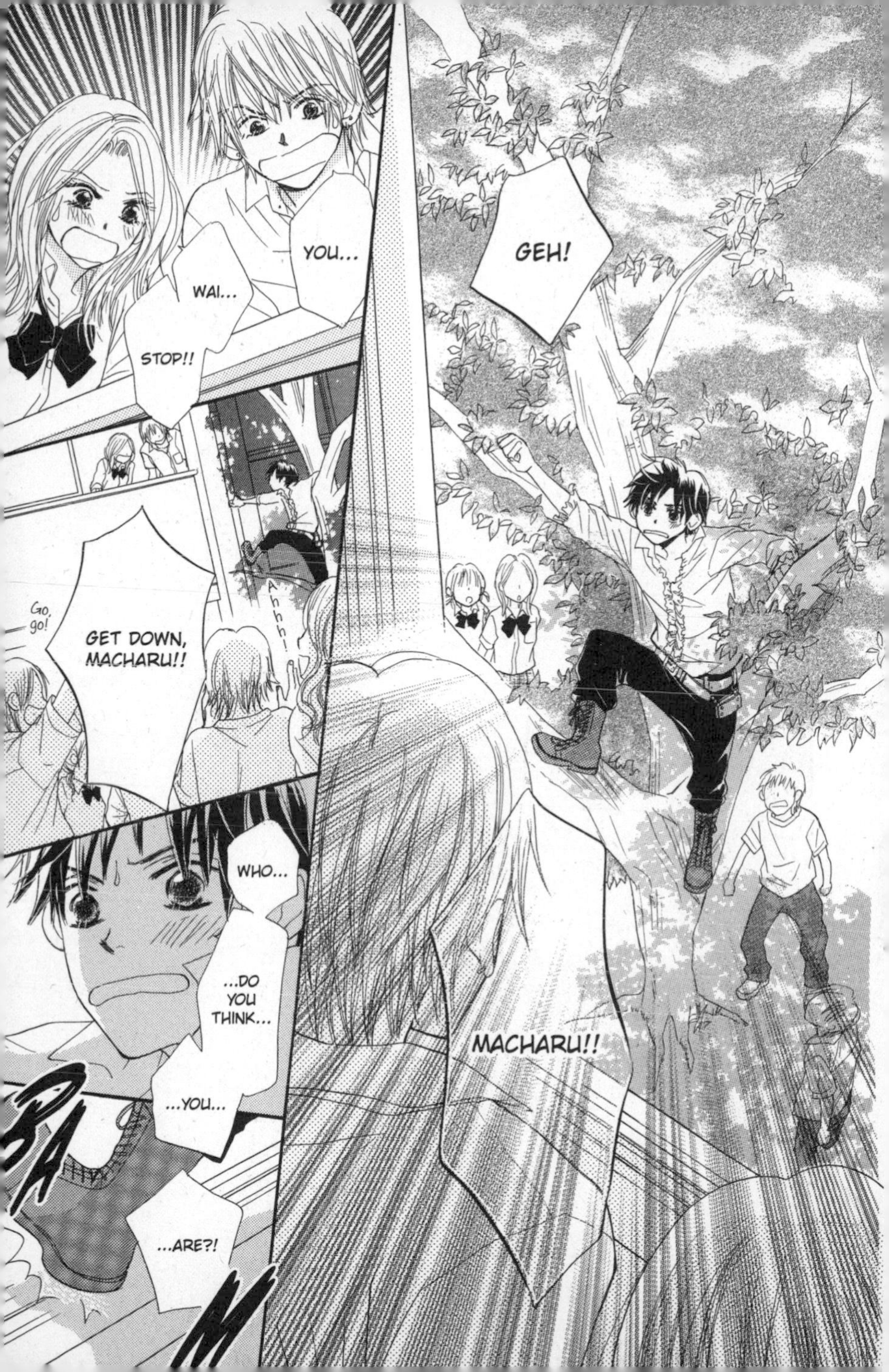
GEH!
MACHARU!!
YOU...
WAI...
STOP!!
GET DOWN, MACHARU!!
Go, go!
Ahhh!
WHO...
...DO YOU THINK...
...YOU...
...ARE?!

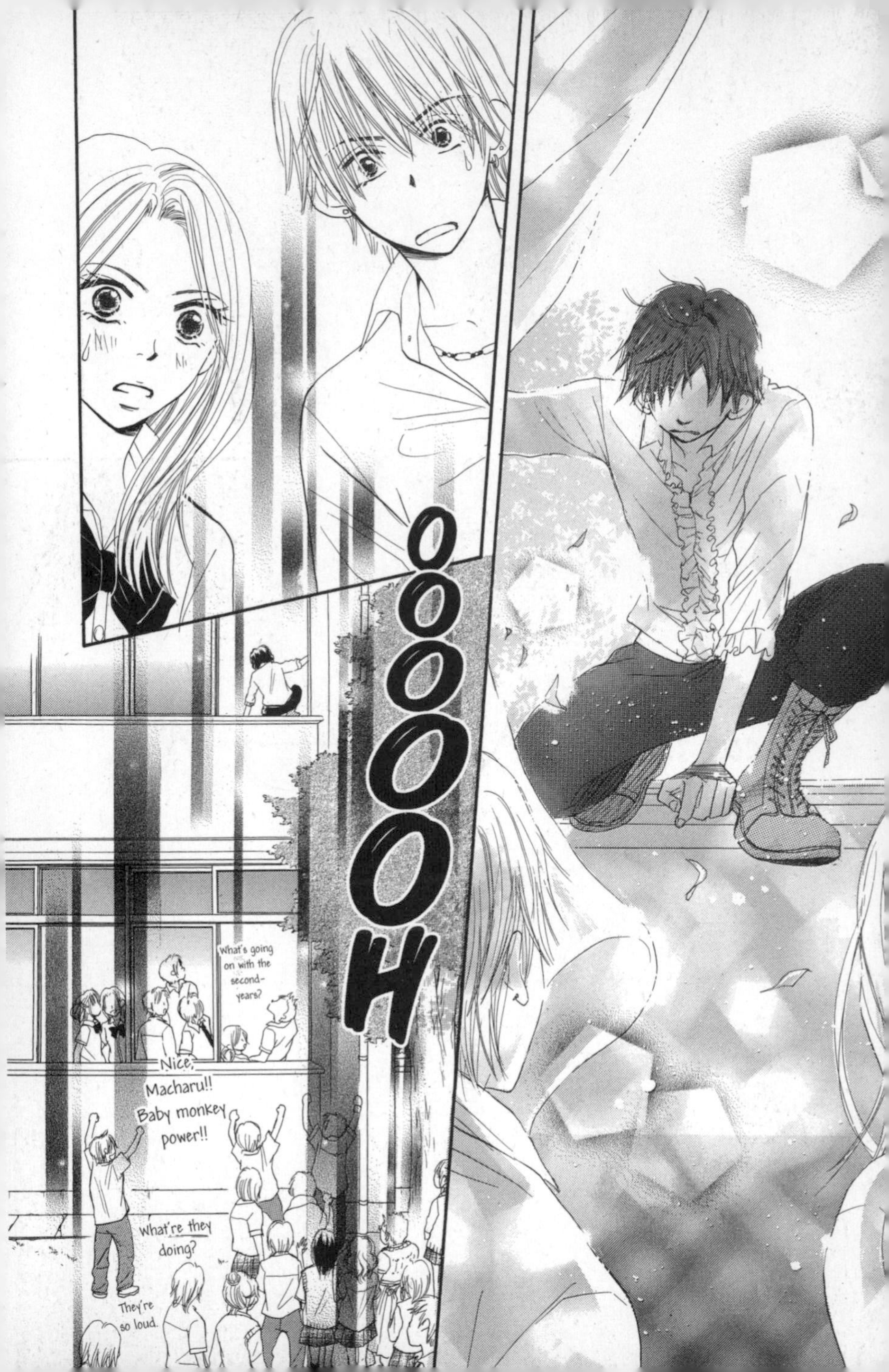
OOOOOOH
What's going on with the second-years?
Nice, Macharu!! Baby monkey power!!
What're they doing?
They're so loud.

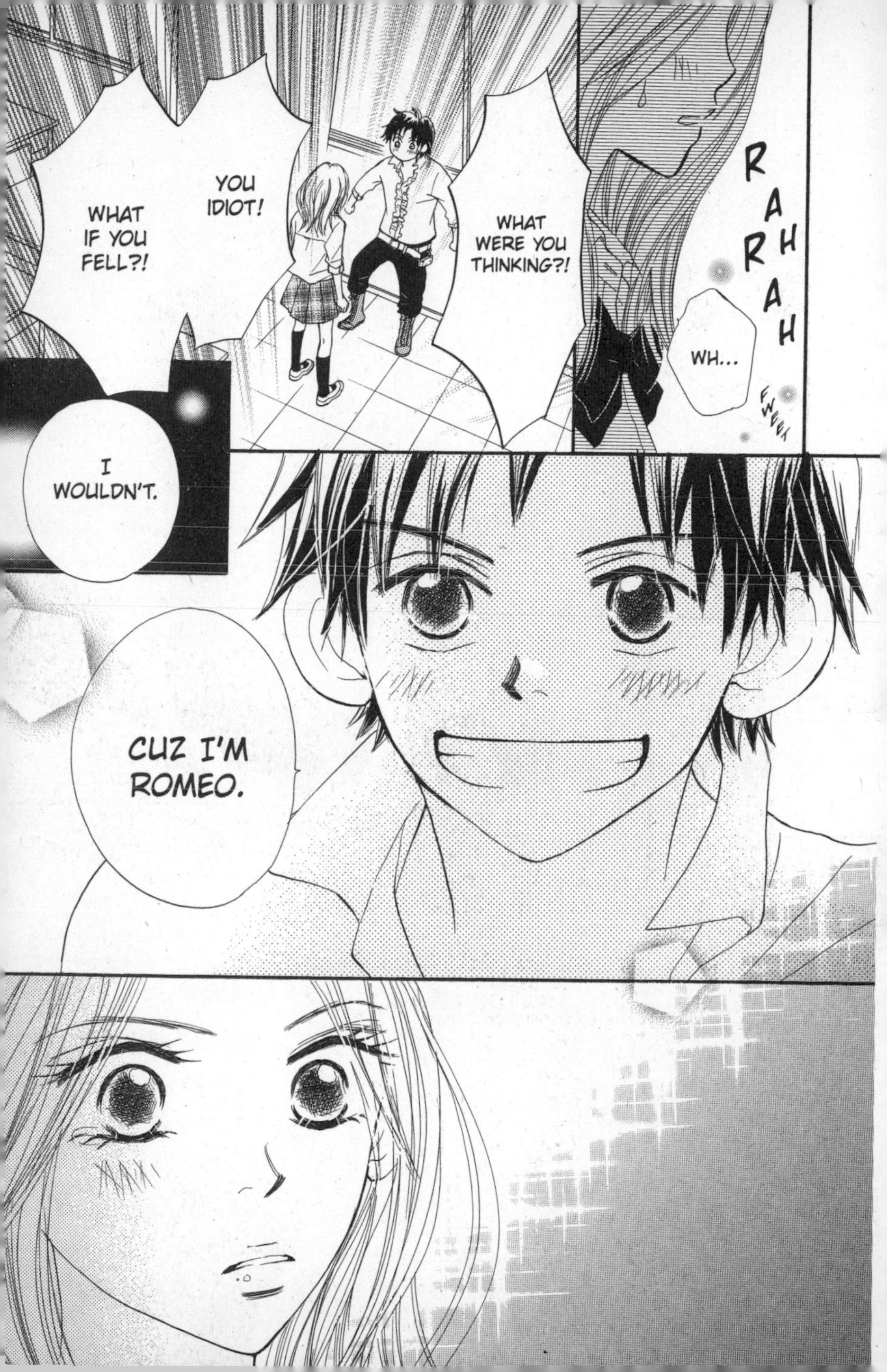
RAH RAH
WH...
WHAT WERE YOU THINKING?!
YOU IDIOT!
WHAT IF YOU FELL?!
I WOULDN'T.
CUZ I'M ROMEO.

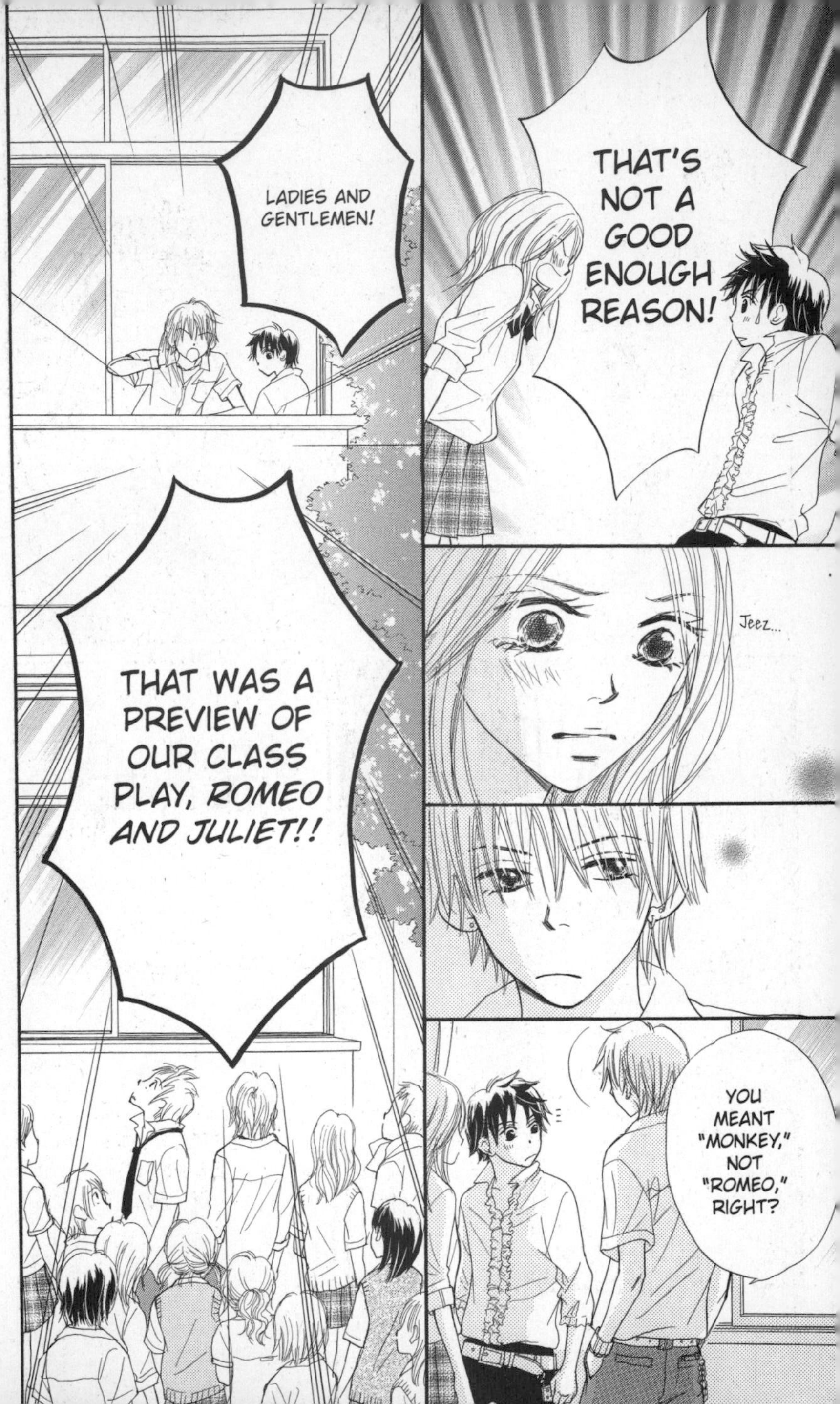
THAT'S NOT A GOOD ENOUGH REASON!
Jeez...
YOU MEANT "MONKEY," NOT "ROMEO," RIGHT?
LADIES AND GENTLEMEN!
THAT WAS A PREVIEW OF OUR CLASS PLAY, *ROMEO AND JULIET*!!

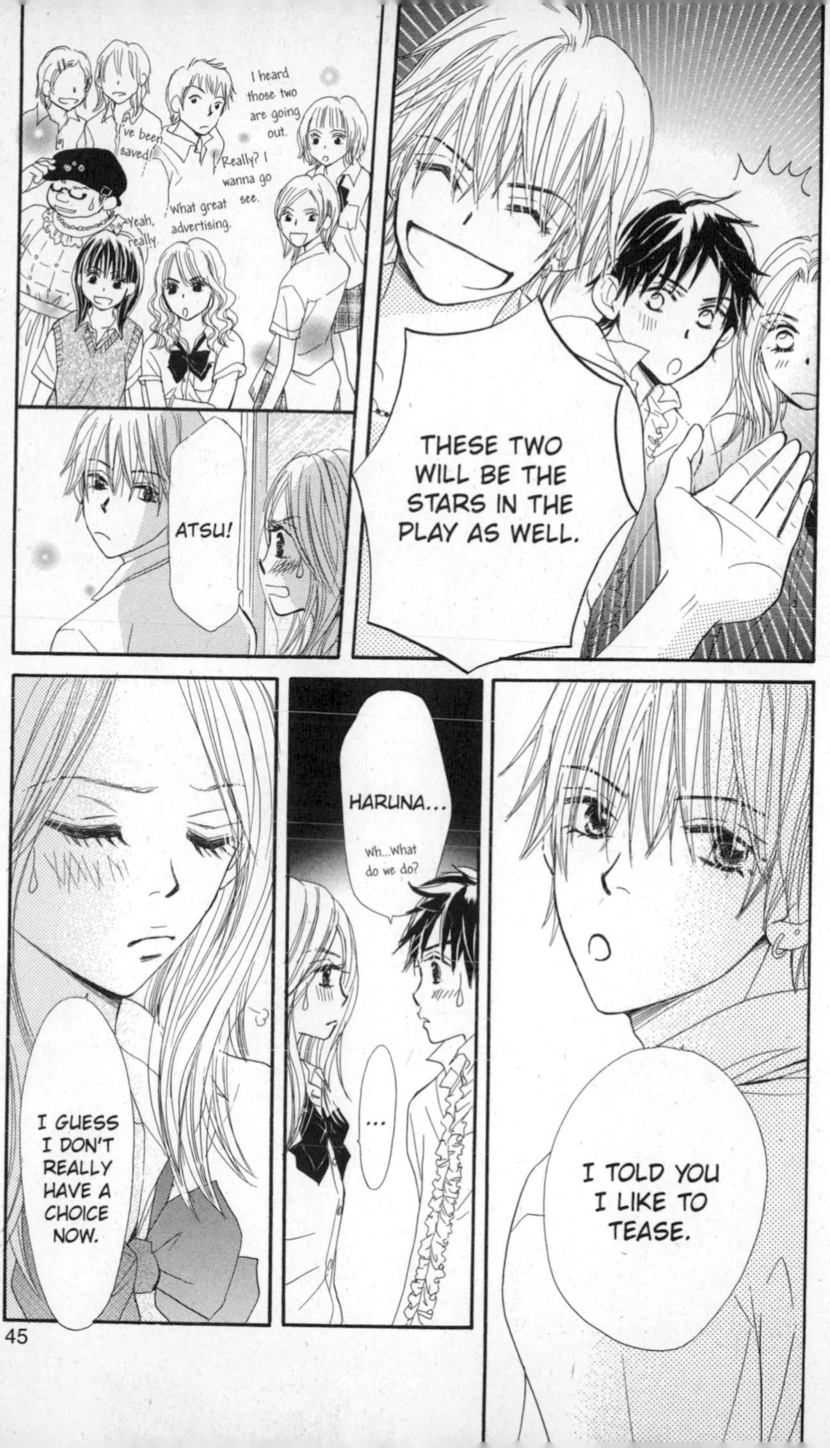
THESE TWO WILL BE THE STARS IN THE PLAY AS WELL.
I heard those two are going out.
Really? I wanna go see.
What great advertising.
I've been saved!
Yeah, really.
ATSU!
I TOLD YOU I LIKE TO TEASE.
HARUNA...
Wh...What do we do?
...
I GUESS I DON'T REALLY HAVE A CHOICE NOW.

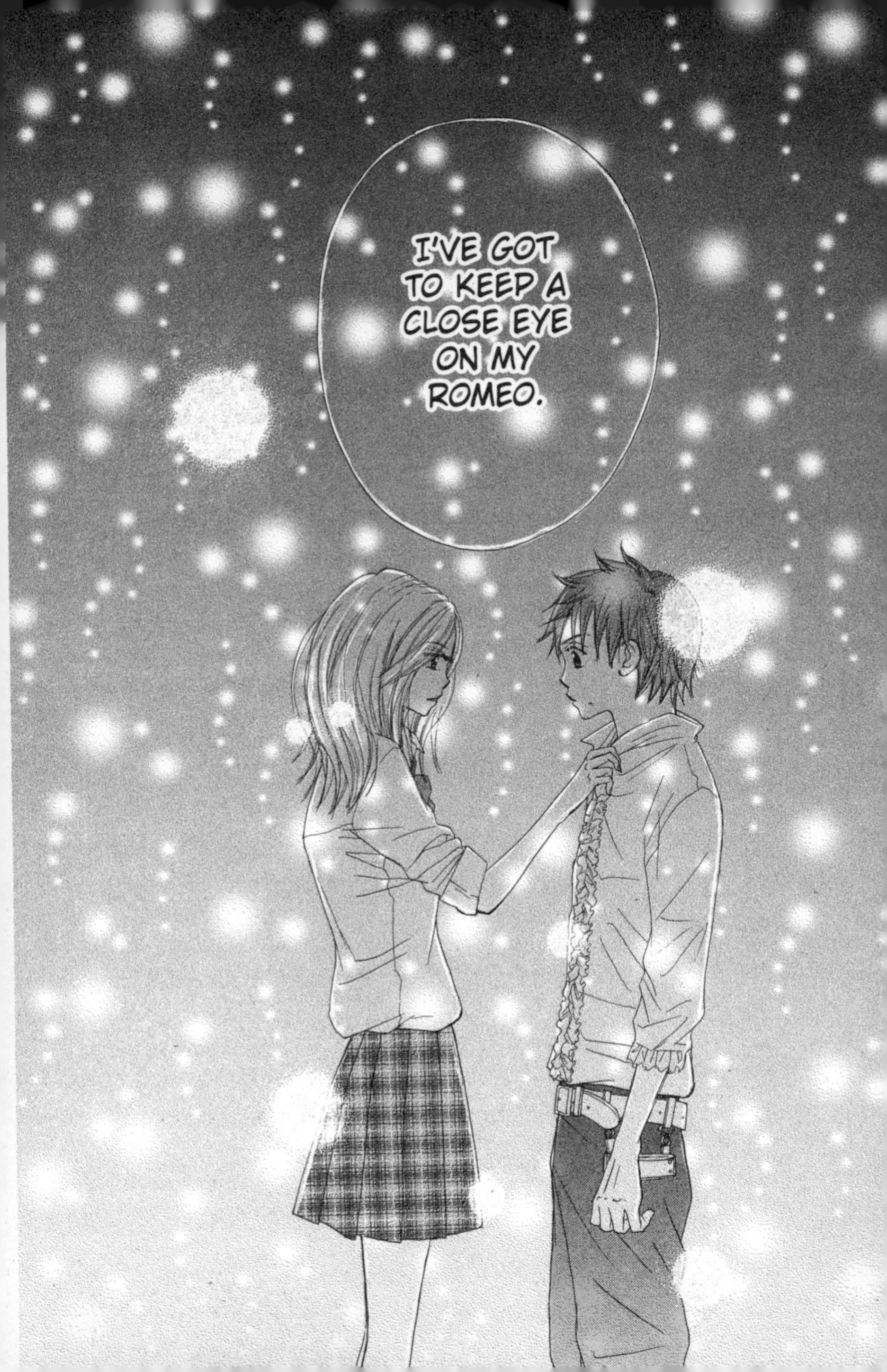
I'VE GOT TO KEEP A CLOSE EYE ON MY ROMEO.

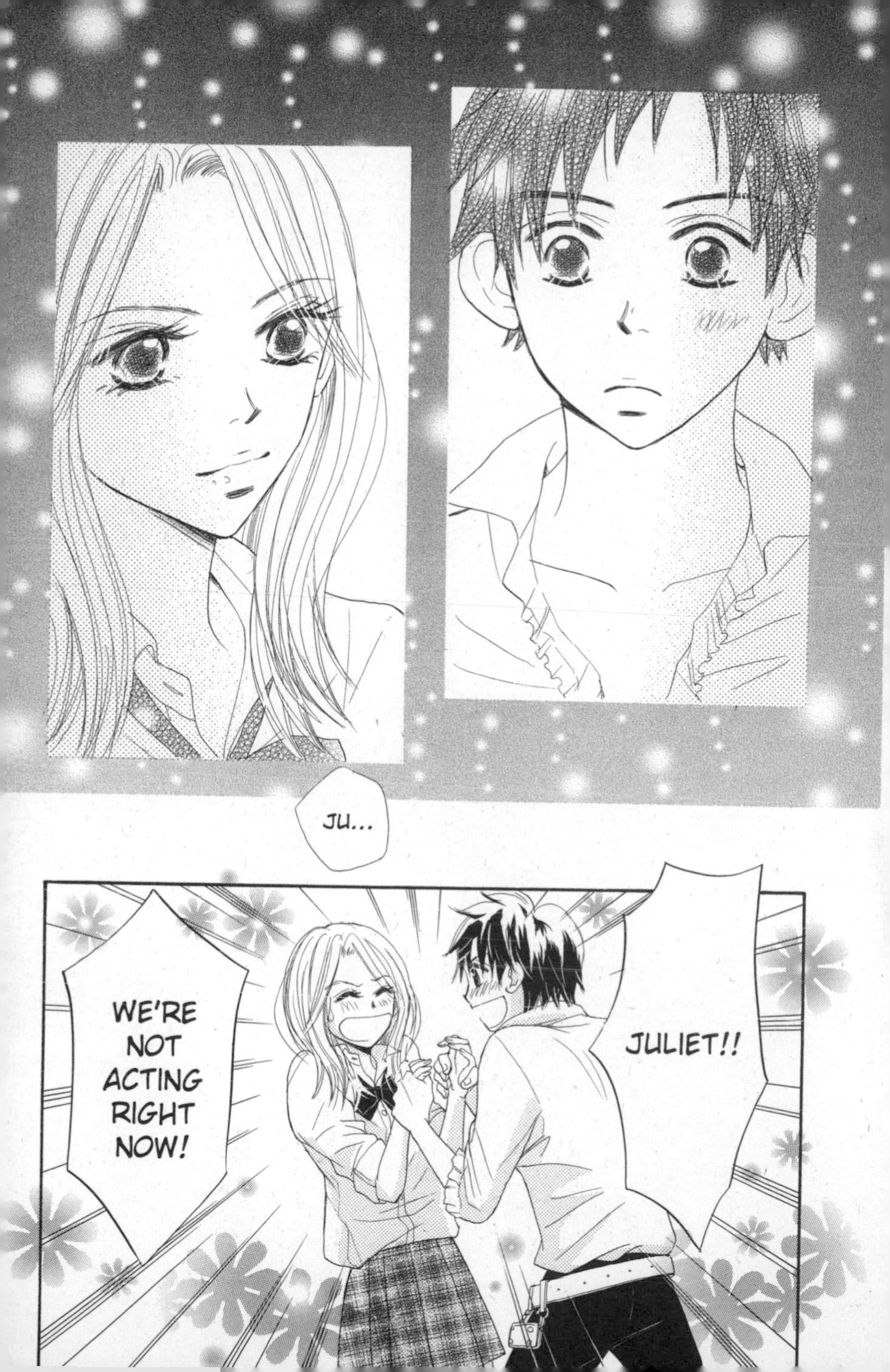
JU...
JULIET!!
WE'RE NOT ACTING RIGHT NOW!

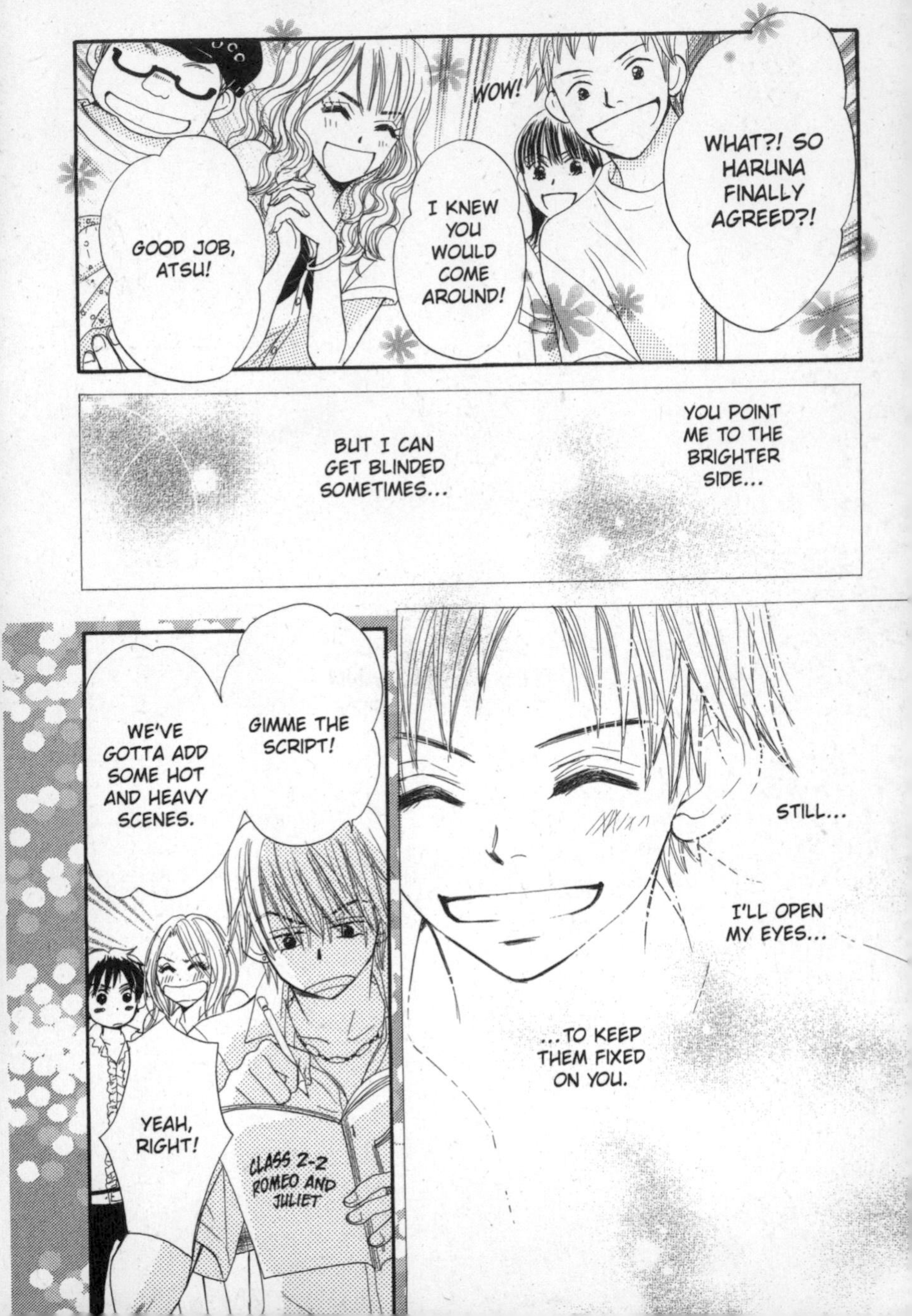
WHAT?! SO HARUNA FINALLY AGREED?!
WOW!
I KNEW YOU WOULD COME AROUND!
GOOD JOB, ATSU!
YOU POINT ME TO THE BRIGHTER SIDE...
BUT I CAN GET BLINDED SOMETIMES...
STILL...
I'LL OPEN MY EYES...
...TO KEEP THEM FIXED ON YOU.
GIMME THE SCRIPT!
WE'VE GOTTA ADD SOME HOT AND HEAVY SCENES.
YEAH, RIGHT!
CLASS 2-2 ROMEO AND JULIET

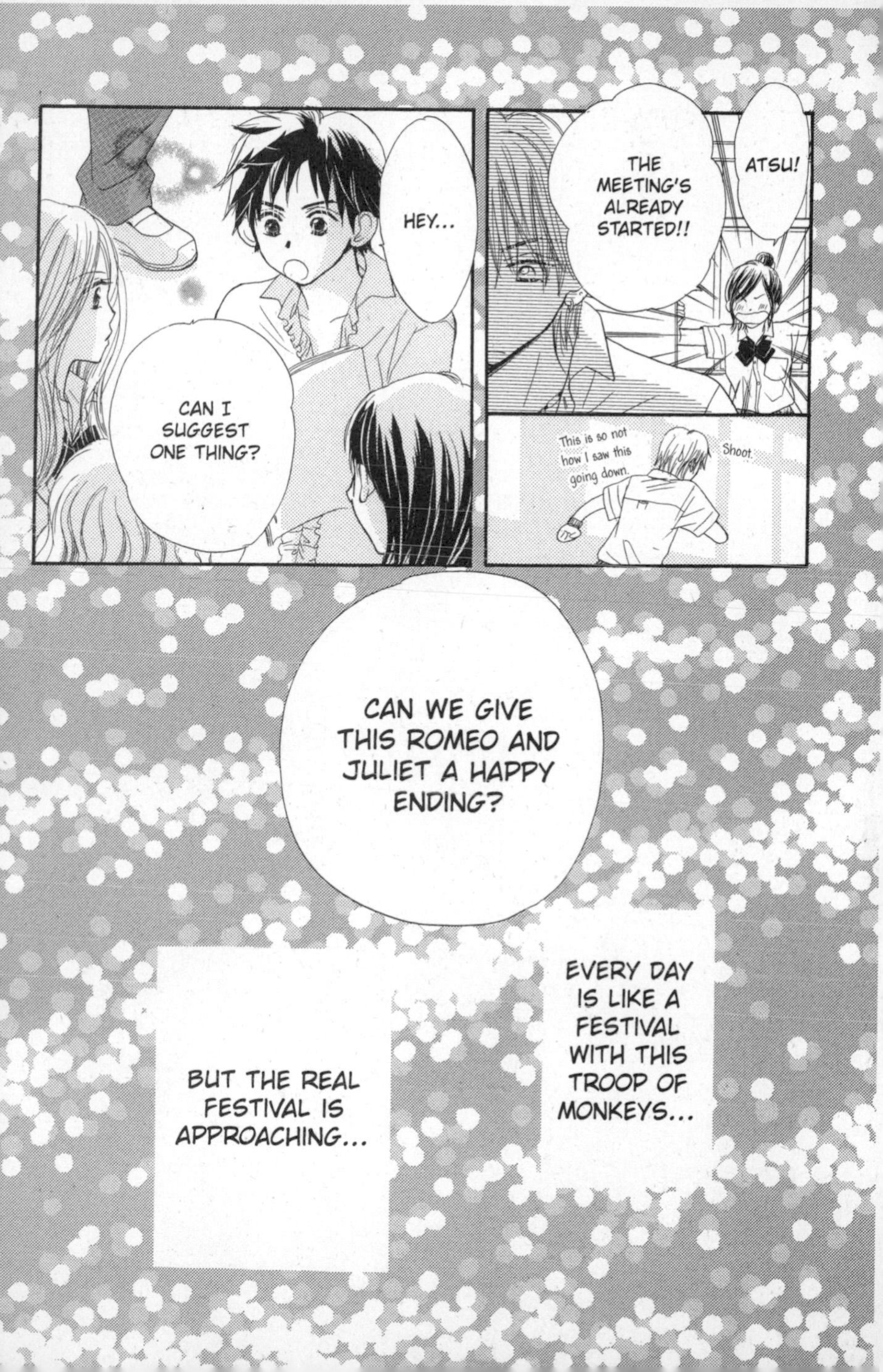
ATSU!
THE MEETING'S ALREADY STARTED!!
Shoot.
This is so not how I saw this going down.
HEY...
CAN I SUGGEST ONE THING?
CAN WE GIVE THIS ROMEO AND JULIET A HAPPY ENDING?
EVERY DAY IS LIKE A FESTIVAL WITH THIS TROOP OF MONKEYS...
BUT THE REAL FESTIVAL IS APPROACHING...

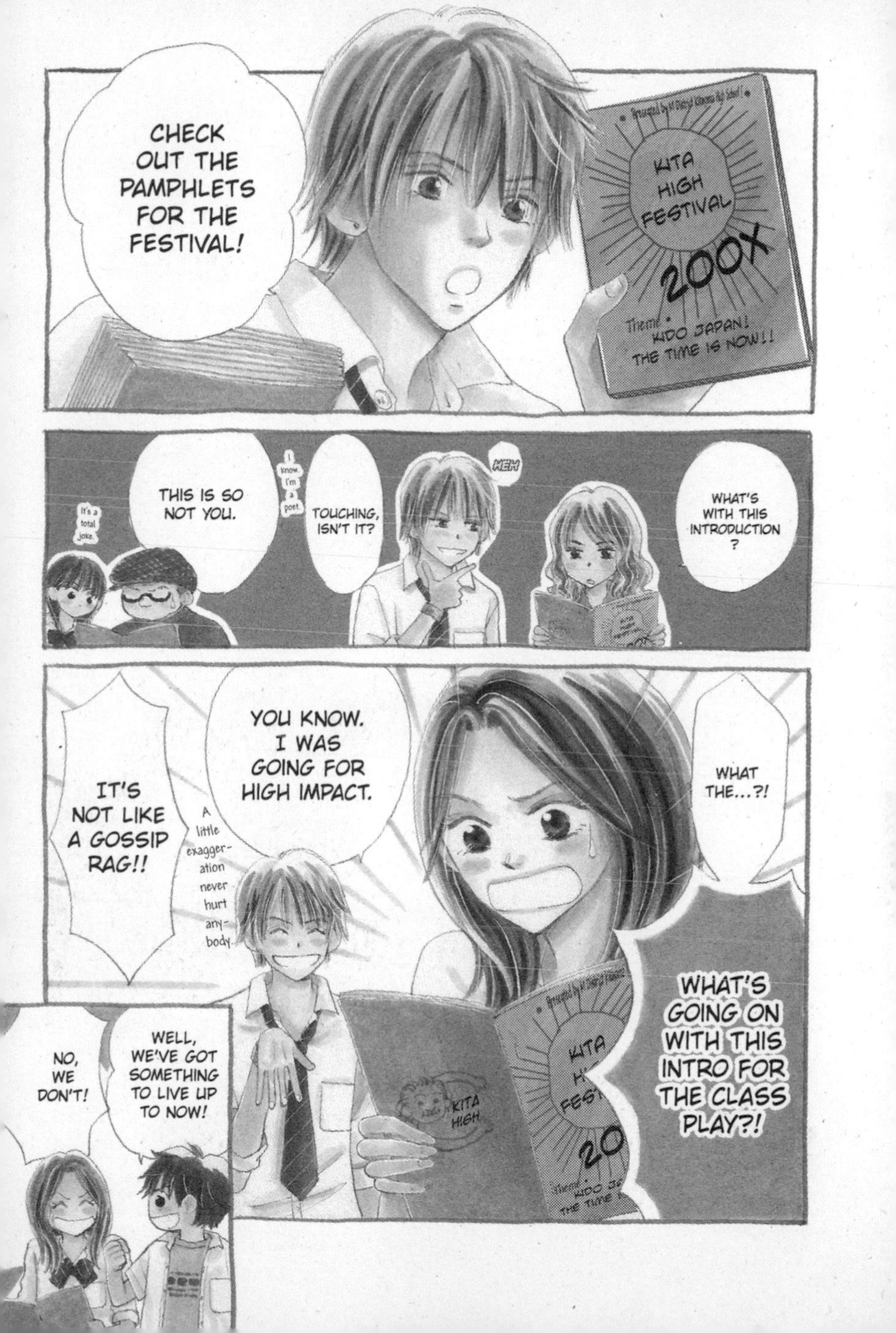
KITA HIGH FESTIVAL
200X
Theme • KDO JAPAN! THE TIME IS NOW!!
CHECK OUT THE PAMPHLETS FOR THE FESTIVAL!
WHAT'S WITH THIS INTRODUCTION ?
HEH
TOUCHING, ISN'T IT?
I know. I'm a poet.
THIS IS SO NOT YOU.
It's a total joke.
WHAT THE...?!
YOU KNOW. I WAS GOING FOR HIGH IMPACT.
A little exagger-ation never hurt any-body.
IT'S NOT LIKE A GOSSIP RAG!!
WHAT'S GOING ON WITH THIS INTRO FOR THE CLASS PLAY?!
KITA HIGH
WELL, WE'VE GOT SOMETHING TO LIVE UP TO NOW!
NO, WE DON'T!

FESTIVAL!!

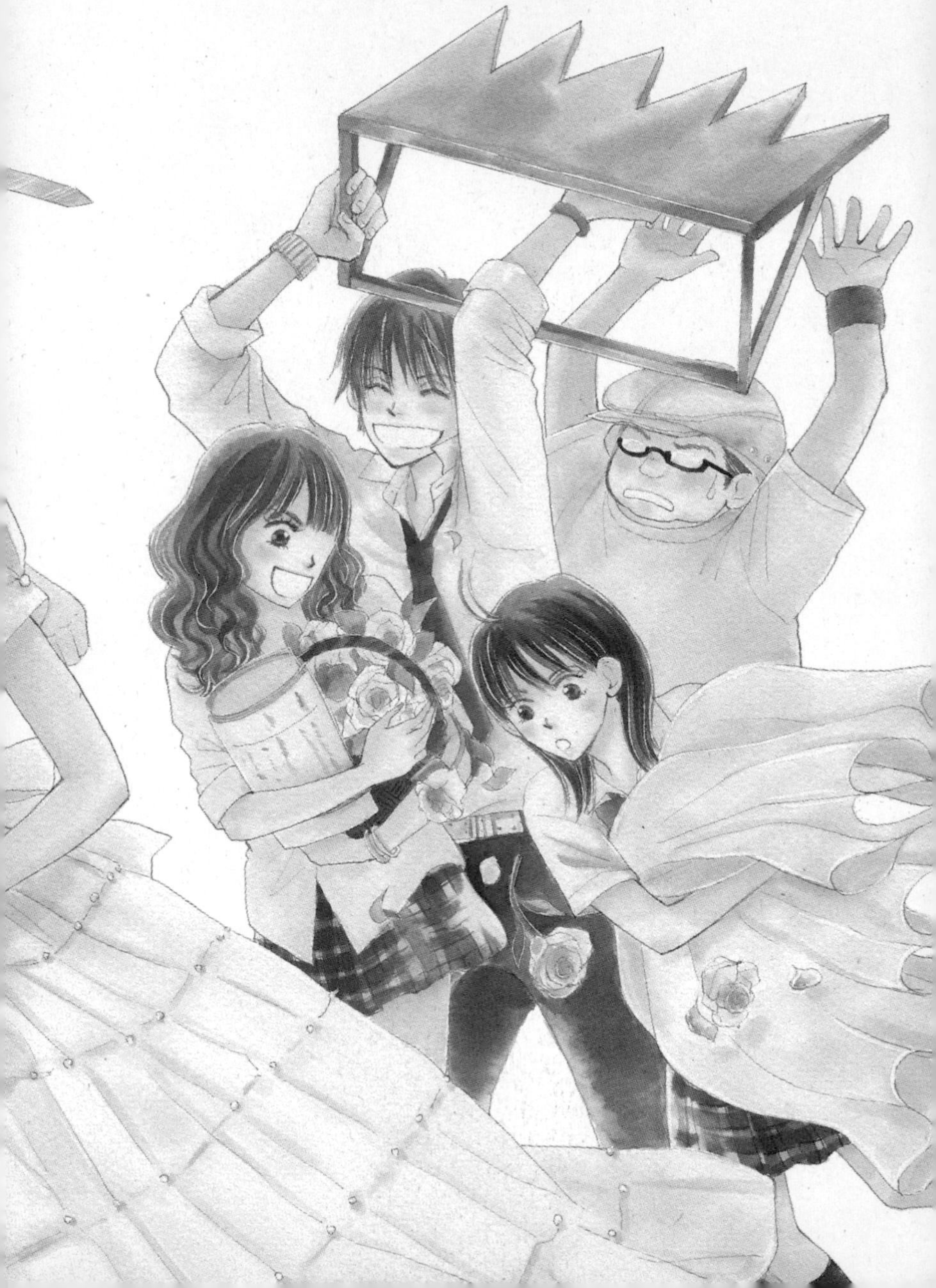

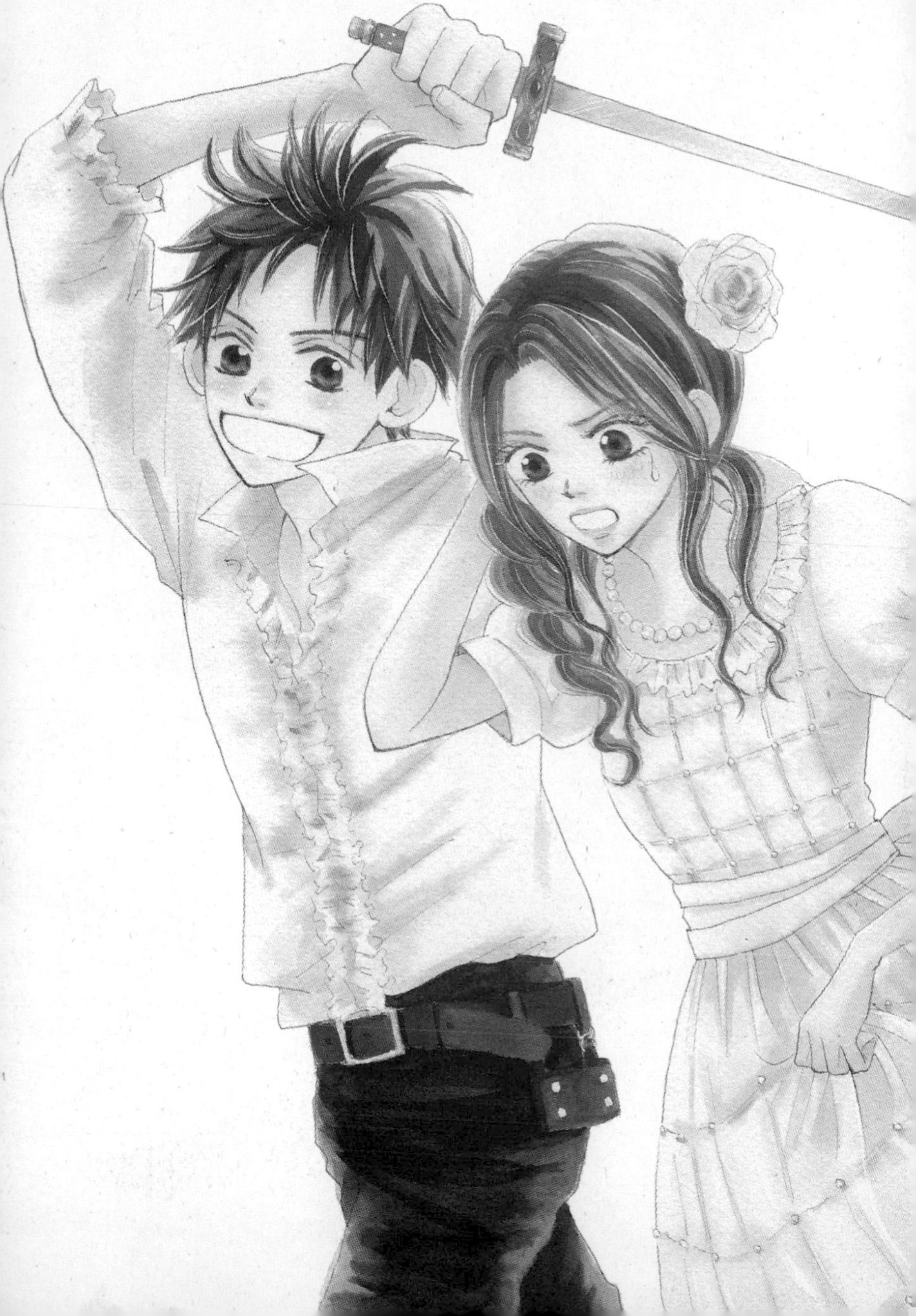

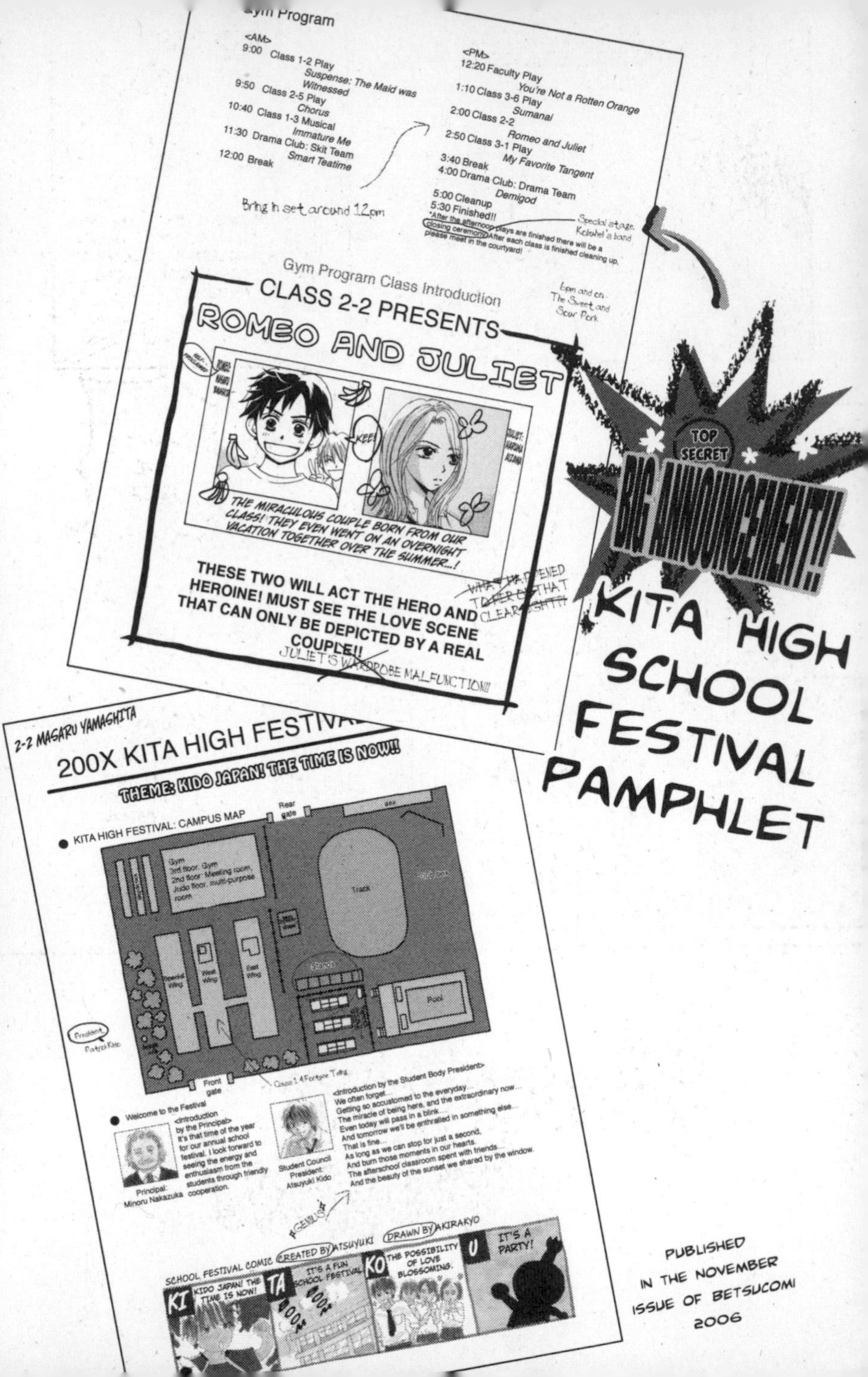
Gym Program
<AM>
9:00 Class 1-2 Play
Suspense: The Maid was Witnessed
9:50 Class 2-5 Play
Chorus
10:40 Class 1-3 Musical
Immature Me
11:30 Drama Club: Skit Team
Smart Teatime
12:00 Break
<PM>
12:20 Faculty Play
You're Not a Rotten Orange
1:10 Class 3-6 Play
Sumanai
2:00 Class 2-2
Romeo and Juliet
2:50 Class 3-1 Play
My Favorite Tangent
3:40 Break
4:00 Drama Club: Drama Team
Demigod
5:00 Cleanup
5:30 Finished!!
*After the afternoon plays are finished there will be a closing ceremony. After each class is finished cleaning up, please meet in the courtyard!
Bring in set around 12pm
Special stage. Kohei's band
6pm and on. The Sweet and Sour Pork
Gym Program Class Introduction
CLASS 2-2 PRESENTS
ROMEO AND JULIET
ROMEO: MASARU YAMASHITA
JULIET: MARINA AIZAWA
KEE!
THE MIRACULOUS COUPLE BORN FROM OUR CLASS! THEY EVEN WENT ON AN OVERNIGHT VACATION TOGETHER OVER THE SUMMER...!
THESE TWO WILL ACT THE HERO AND HEROINE! MUST SEE THE LOVE SCENE THAT CAN ONLY BE DEPICTED BY A REAL COUPLE!!
WHAT HAPPENED TO HER ON THAT CLEAR NIGHT!!
JULIET'S WARDROBE MALFUNCTION!!
TOP SECRET
BIG ANNOUNCEMENT!!
KITA HIGH SCHOOL FESTIVAL PAMPHLET
2-2 MASARU YAMASHITA
200X KITA HIGH FESTIVAL
THEME: KIDO JAPAN! THE TIME IS NOW!!
KITA HIGH FESTIVAL: CAMPUS MAP
Rear gate
Gym
3rd floor: Gym
2nd floor: Meeting room, Judo floor, multi-purpose room
Track
Special Wing
West Wing
East Wing
Pool
Front gate
President
Patrol Kido
Class 1-4 Fortune Telling
Welcome to the Festival
<Introduction by the Principal>
It's that time of the year for our annual school festival. I look forward to seeing the energy and enthusiasm from the students through friendly cooperation.
Principal: Minoru Nakazuka
Student Council President: Atsuyuki Kido
<Introduction by the Student Body President>
We often forget...
Getting so accustomed to the everyday...
The miracle of being here, and the extraordinary now...
Even today will pass in a blink...
And tomorrow we'll be enthralled in something else...
That is fine...
As long as we can stop for just a second,
And burn those moments in our hearts.
The afterschool classroom spent with friends...
And the beauty of the sunset we shared by the window.
GENIUS
SCHOOL FESTIVAL COMIC CREATED BY ATSUYUKI DRAWN BY AKIRAKYO
KI
KIDO JAPAN! THE TIME IS NOW!
TA
IT'S A FUN SCHOOL FESTIVAL
KO
THE POSSIBILITY OF LOVE BLOSSOMING.
U
IT'S A PARTY!

PUBLISHED IN THE NOVEMBER ISSUE OF BETSUCOMI 2006

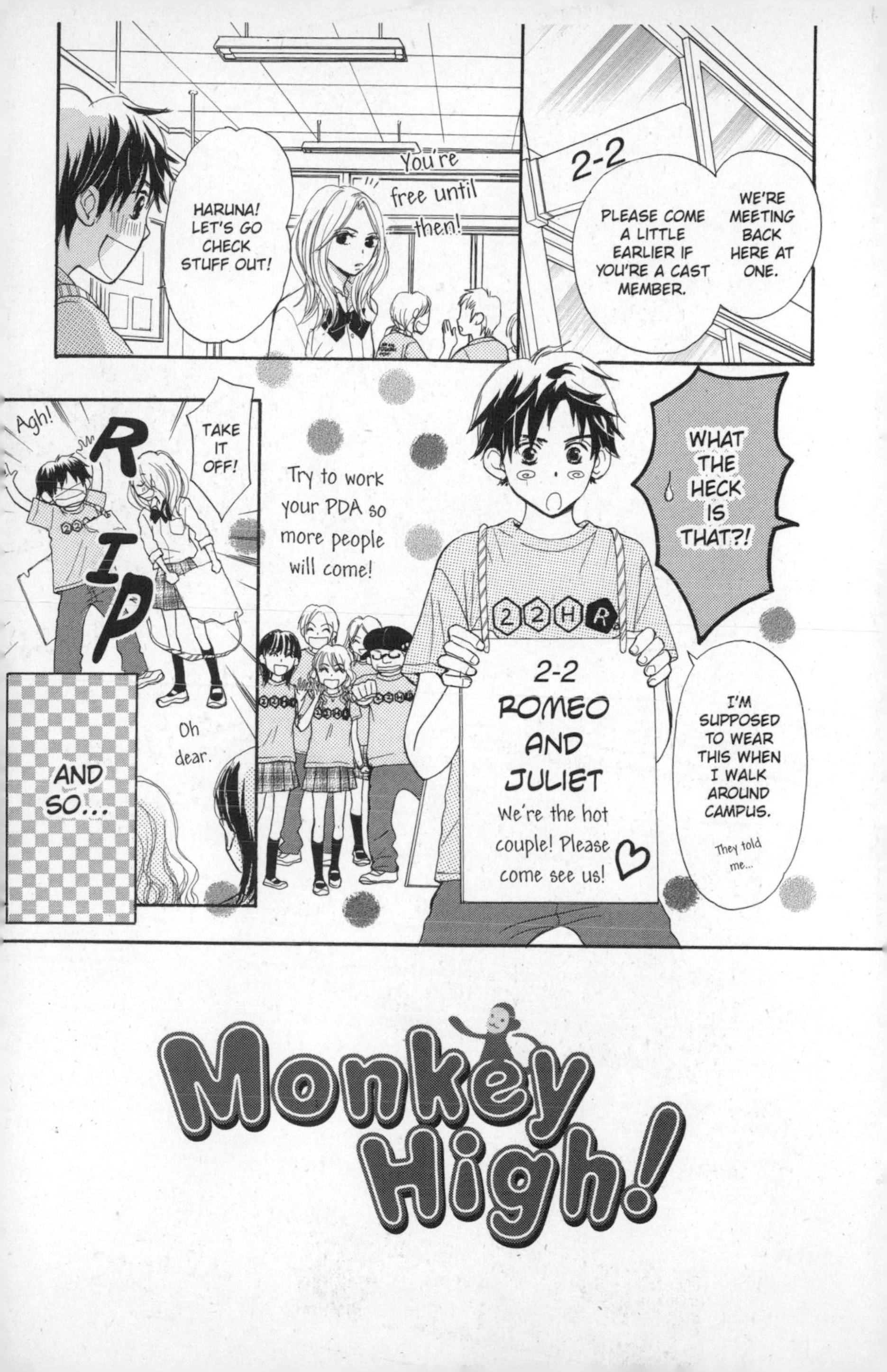
2-2
WE'RE MEETING BACK HERE AT ONE.
PLEASE COME A LITTLE EARLIER IF YOU'RE A CAST MEMBER.
You're free until then!
HARUNA! LET'S GO CHECK STUFF OUT!
WHAT THE HECK IS THAT?!
22HR
2-2 ROMEO AND JULIET
We're the hot couple! Please come see us!
I'M SUPPOSED TO WEAR THIS WHEN I WALK AROUND CAMPUS.
They told me...
Try to work your PDA so more people will come!
TAKE IT OFF!
RIP
Agh!
Oh dear.
AND SO...
Monkey High!

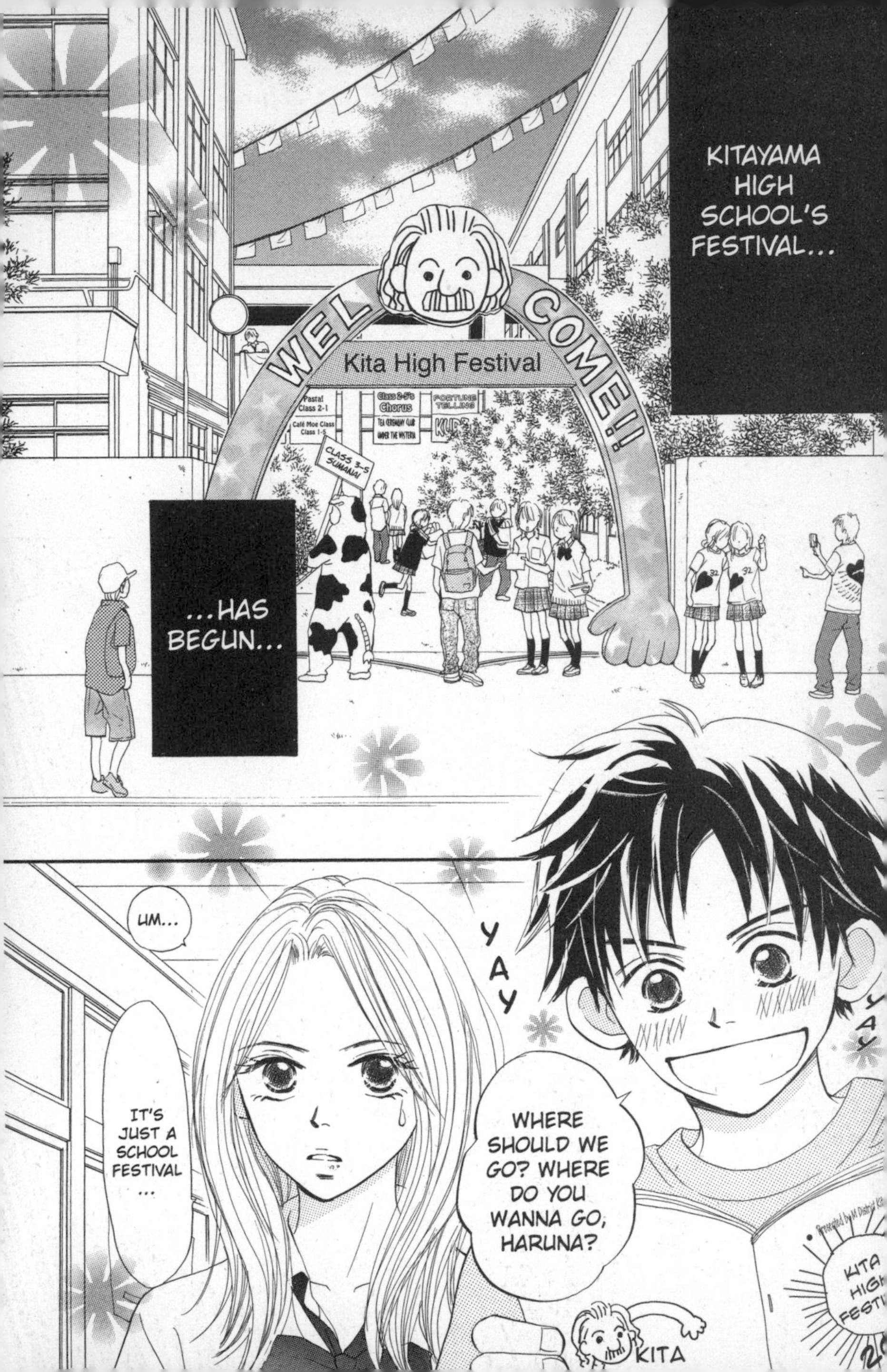
KITAYAMA HIGH SCHOOL'S FESTIVAL...
WEL COME!!
Kita High Festival
Class 2-5's Chorus
FORTUNE TELLING
TEA CEREMONY CLUB UNDER THE WISTERIA
Pasta! Class 2-1
Café Moe Class Class 1-5
CLASS 3-5 SUMANAI
...HAS BEGUN...
YAY
WHERE SHOULD WE GO? WHERE DO YOU WANNA GO, HARUNA?
KITA
YAY
UM...
IT'S JUST A SCHOOL FESTIVAL ...

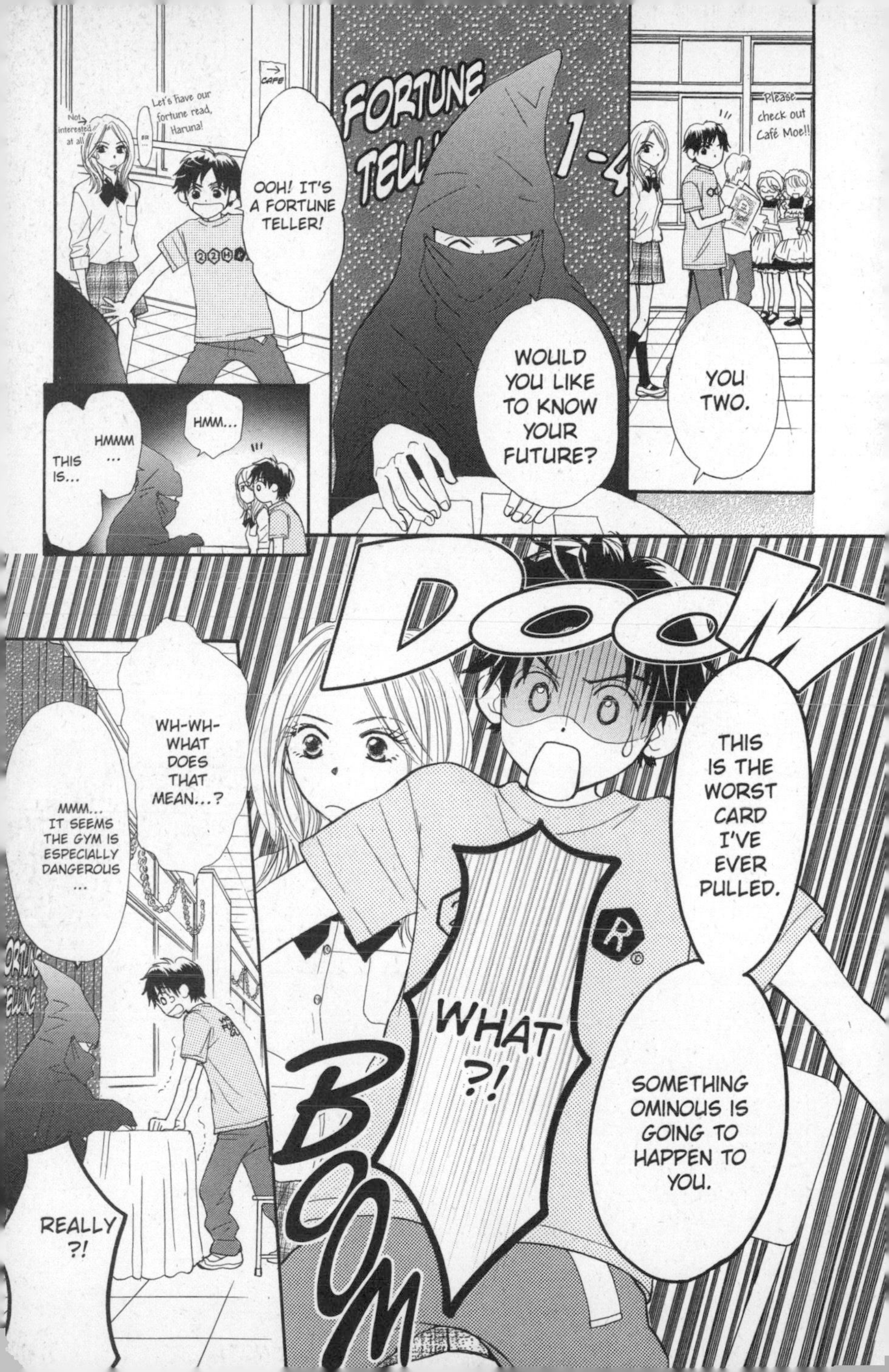
Please check out Café Moe!!
YOU TWO.
1-4
WOULD YOU LIKE TO KNOW YOUR FUTURE?
CAFE
Let's have our fortune read, Haruna!
Not interested at all
OOH! IT'S A FORTUNE TELLER!
HMM...
HMMM...
THIS IS...
DOOM
THIS IS THE WORST CARD I'VE EVER PULLED.
SOMETHING OMINOUS IS GOING TO HAPPEN TO YOU.
WHAT?!
BOOM
WH-WH-WHAT DOES THAT MEAN...?
MMM... IT SEEMS THE GYM IS ESPECIALLY DANGEROUS...
REALLY?!

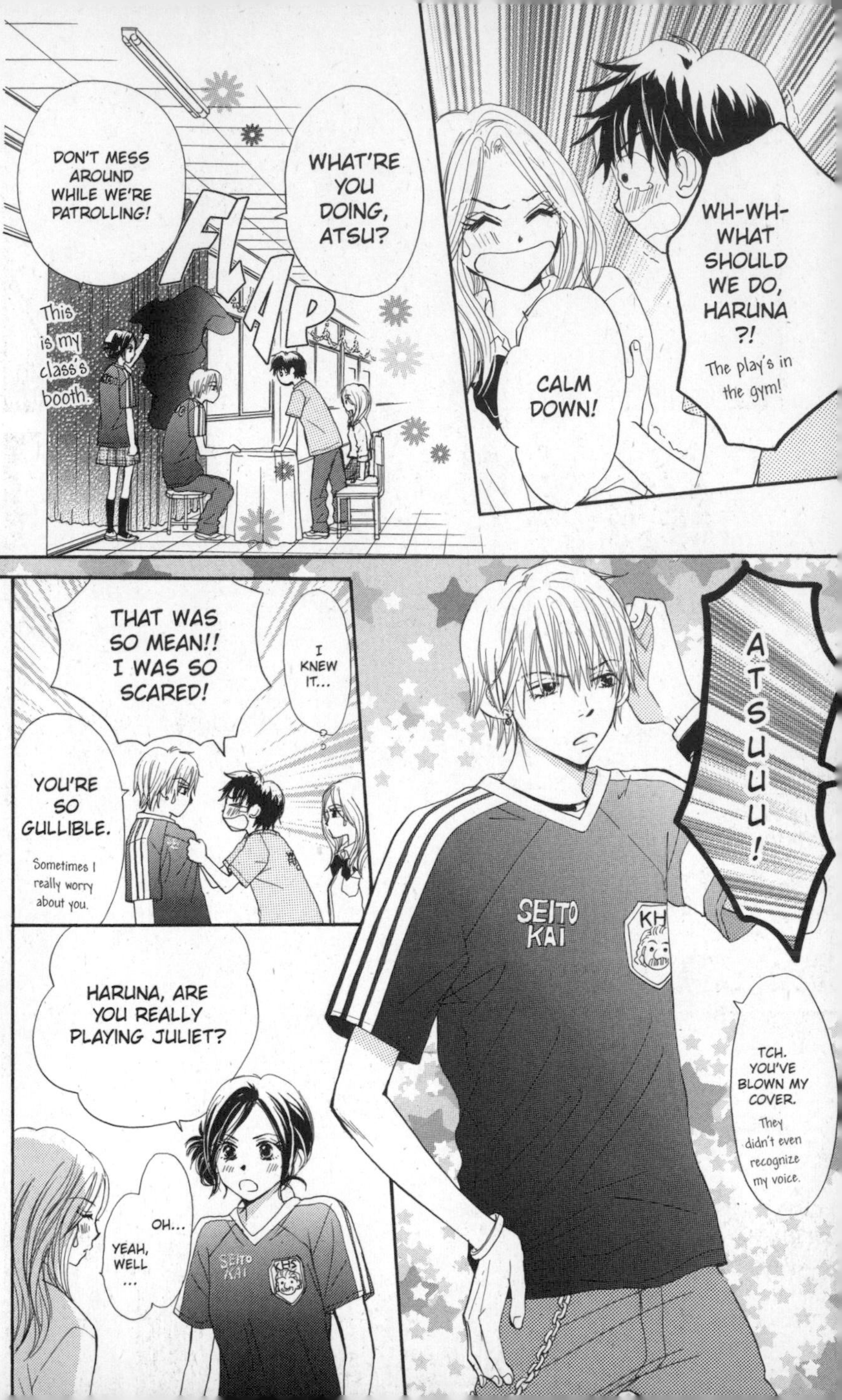
WH-WH-WHAT SHOULD WE DO, HARUNA?!
The play's in the gym!
CALM DOWN!
WHAT'RE YOU DOING, ATSU?
DON'T MESS AROUND WHILE WE'RE PATROLLING!
FLAP
This is my class's booth.
ATSUUU!
TCH. YOU'VE BLOWN MY COVER.
They didn't even recognize my voice.
I KNEW IT...
THAT WAS SO MEAN!! I WAS SO SCARED!
YOU'RE SO GULLIBLE.
Sometimes I really worry about you.
SEITO KAI
HARUNA, ARE YOU REALLY PLAYING JULIET?
OH... YEAH, WELL ...

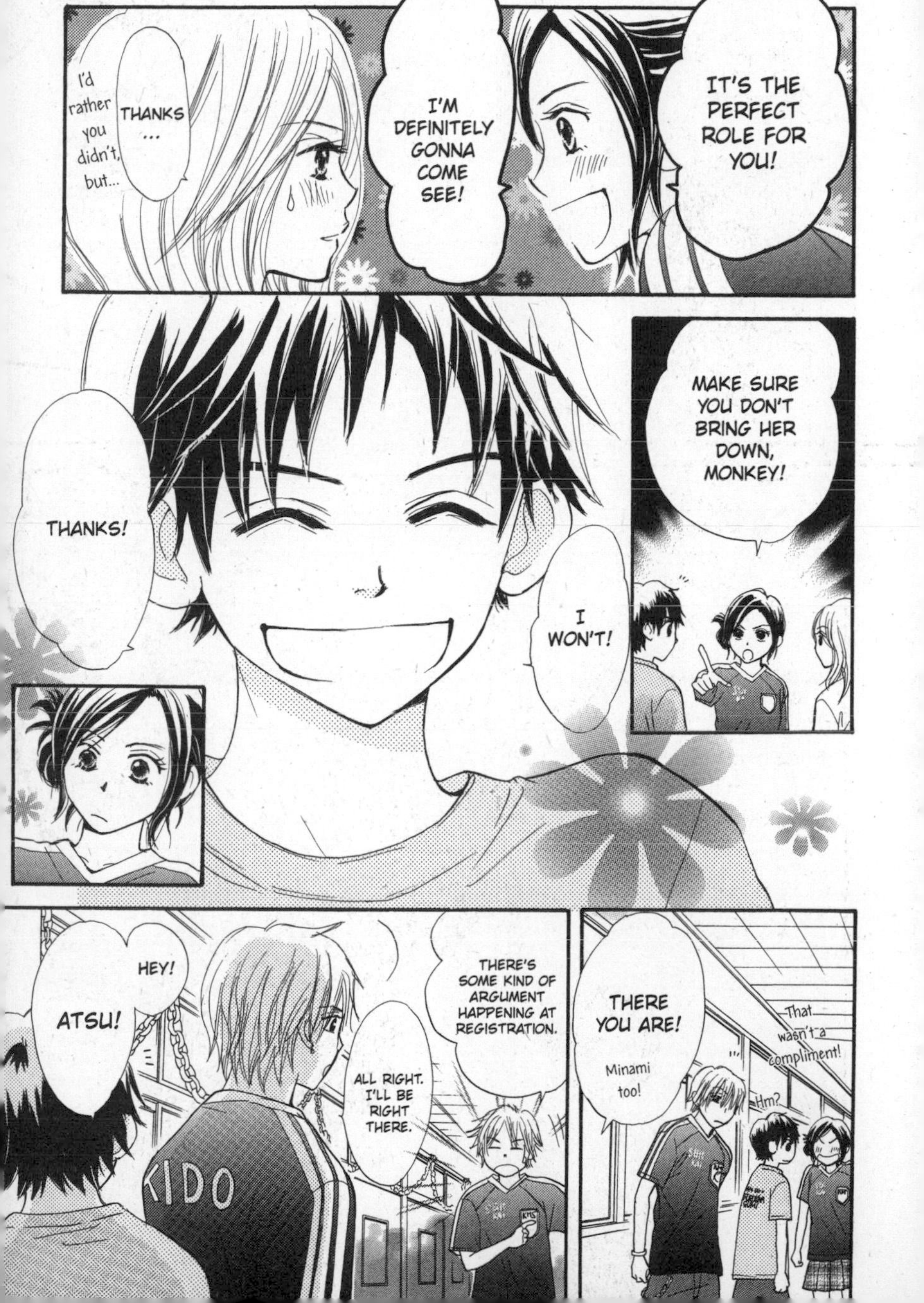
IT'S THE PERFECT ROLE FOR YOU!
I'M DEFINITELY GONNA COME SEE!
THANKS ...
I'd rather you didn't, but...
MAKE SURE YOU DON'T BRING HER DOWN, MONKEY!
I WON'T!
THANKS!
That wasn't a compliment!
THERE YOU ARE!
Minami too!
Hm?
THERE'S SOME KIND OF ARGUMENT HAPPENING AT REGISTRATION.
ALL RIGHT. I'LL BE RIGHT THERE.
HEY!
ATSU!
KIDO

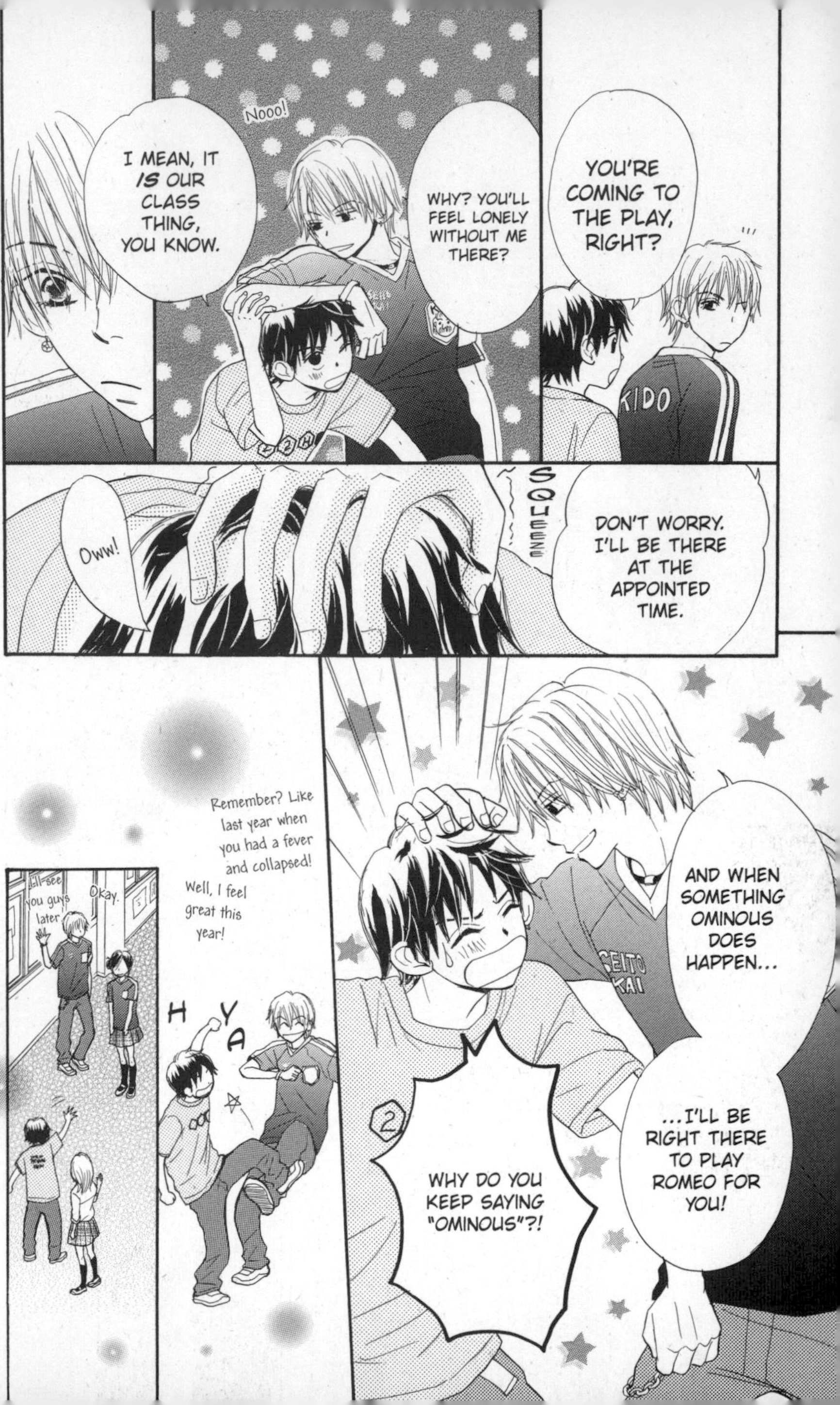
YOU'RE COMING TO THE PLAY, RIGHT?
WHY? YOU'LL FEEL LONELY WITHOUT ME THERE?
Nooo!
I MEAN, IT *IS* OUR CLASS THING, YOU KNOW.
DON'T WORRY. I'LL BE THERE AT THE APPOINTED TIME.
SQUEEZE
Oww!
AND WHEN SOMETHING OMINOUS DOES HAPPEN...
...I'LL BE RIGHT THERE TO PLAY ROMEO FOR YOU!
WHY DO YOU KEEP SAYING "OMINOUS"?!
Remember? Like last year when you had a fever and collapsed!
Well, I feel great this year!
HYA
I'll see you guys later.
Okay.

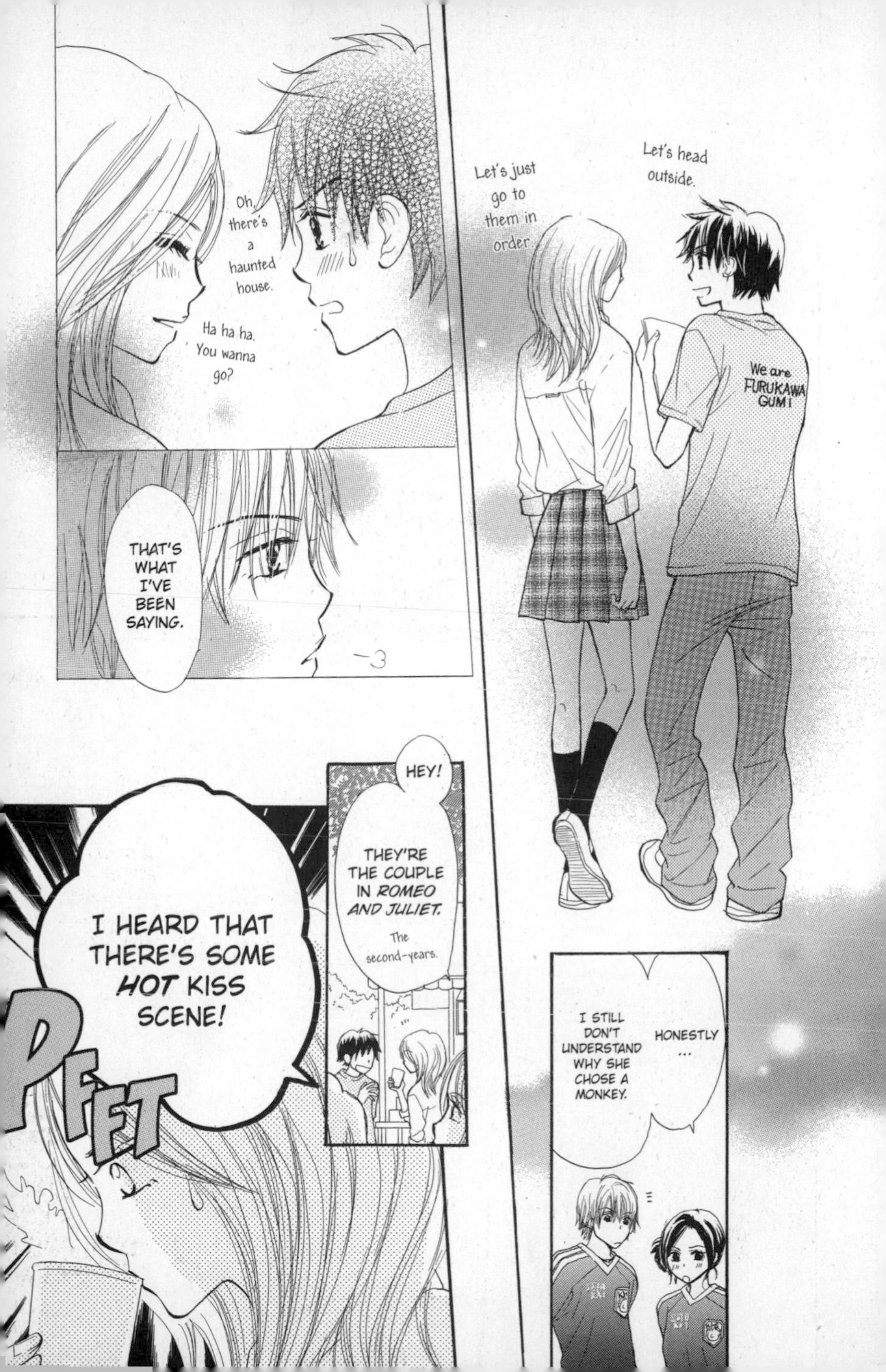

Let's head outside.
Let's just go to them in order.
We are FURUKAWA GUMI
Oh, there's a haunted house.
Ha ha ha. You wanna go?
THAT'S WHAT I'VE BEEN SAYING.
HONESTLY...
I STILL DON'T UNDERSTAND WHY SHE CHOSE A MONKEY.
HEY!
THEY'RE THE COUPLE IN *ROMEO AND JULIET.*
The second-years.
I HEARD THAT THERE'S SOME *HOT* KISS SCENE!
PFFT

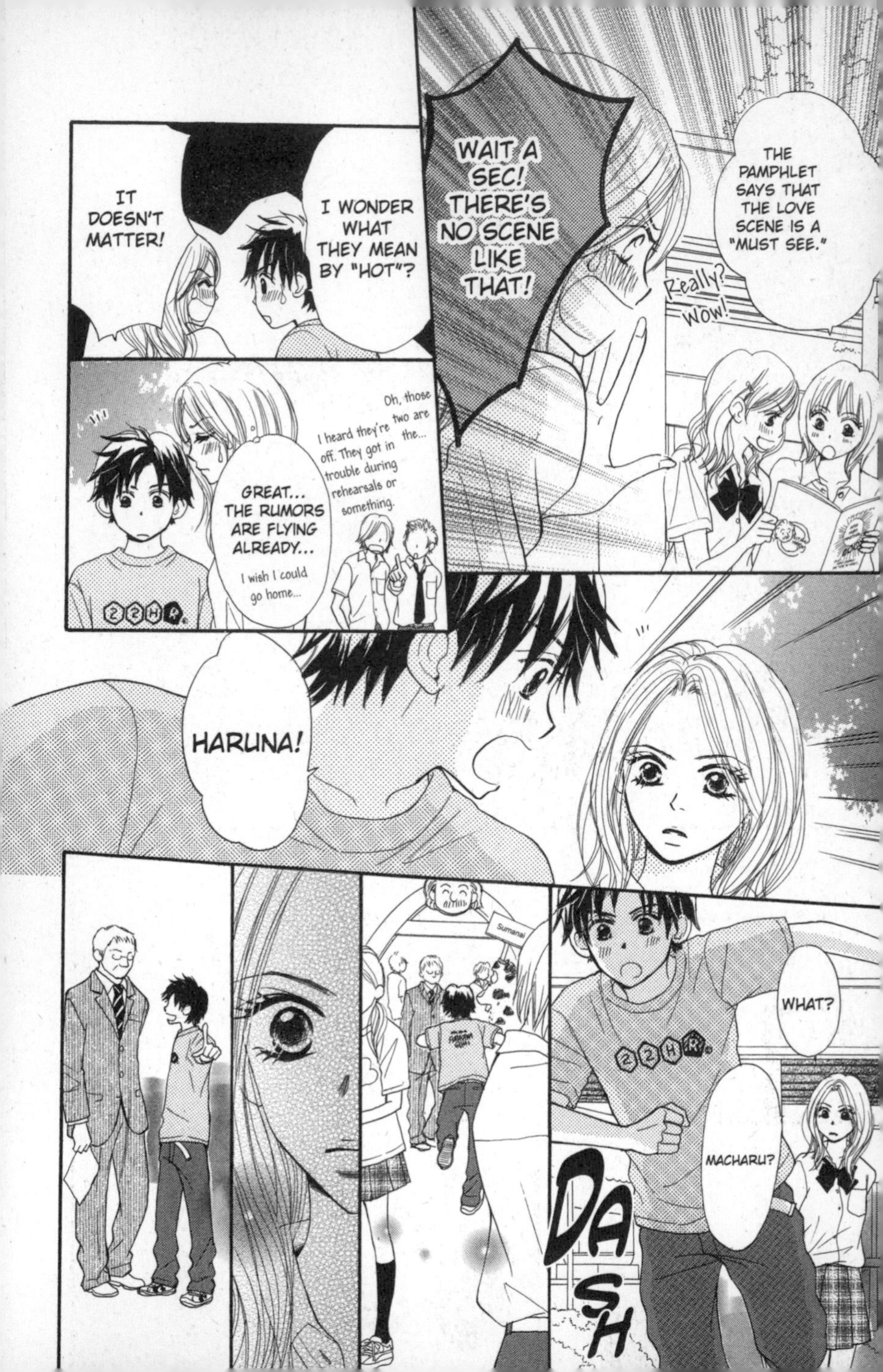
THE PAMPHLET SAYS THAT THE LOVE SCENE IS A "MUST SEE."
Really? Wow!
WAIT A SEC! THERE'S NO SCENE LIKE THAT!
I WONDER WHAT THEY MEAN BY "HOT"?
IT DOESN'T MATTER!
Oh, those two are the...
I heard they're off. They got in trouble during rehearsals or something.
GREAT... THE RUMORS ARE FLYING ALREADY...
I wish I could go home...
HARUNA!
WHAT?
MACHARU?
DASH
Sumanai

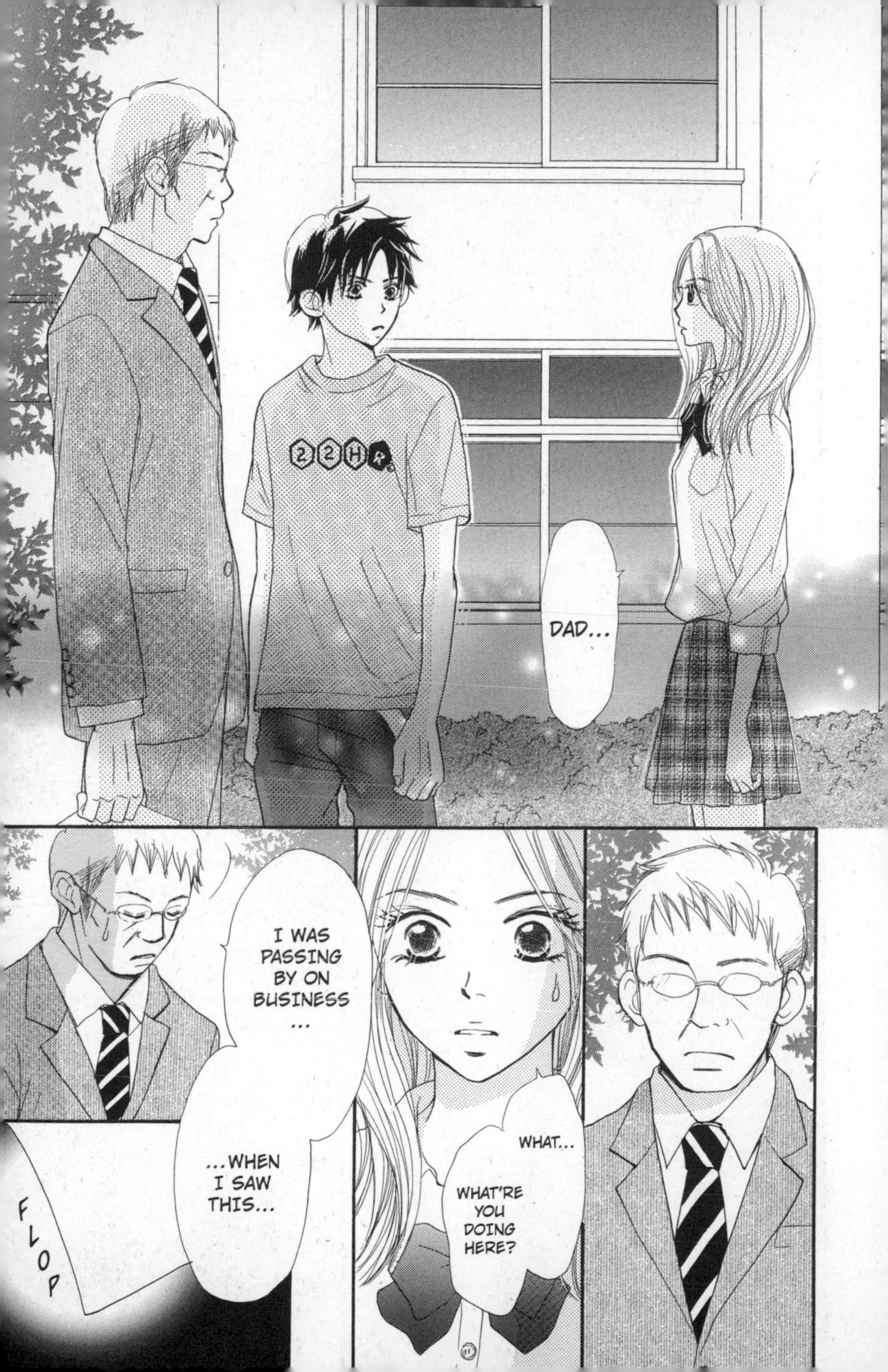
DAD...
WHAT...
WHAT'RE YOU DOING HERE?
I WAS PASSING BY ON BUSINESS ...
...WHEN I SAW THIS...
FLOP

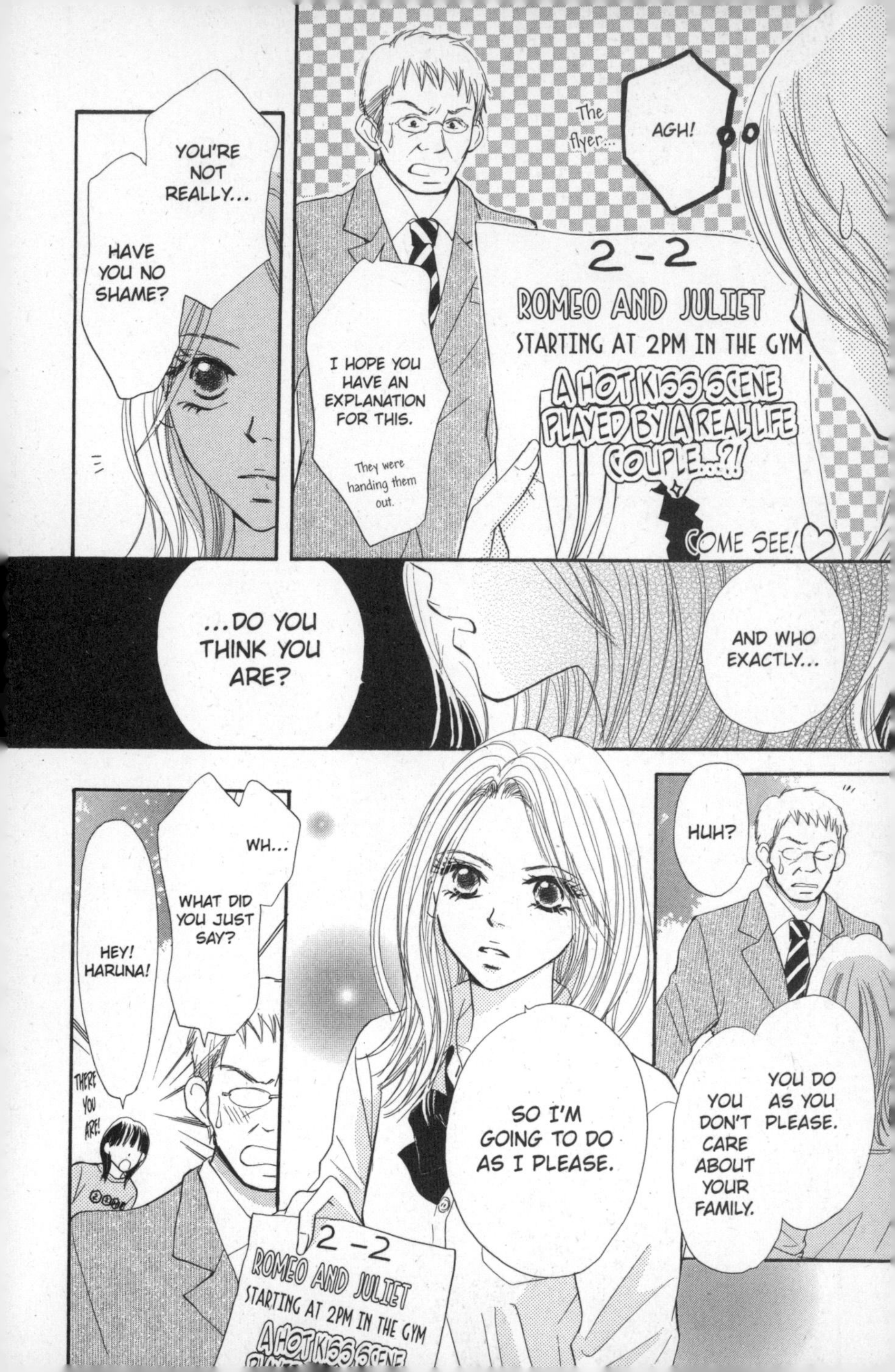
AGH!
The flyer...
2-2
ROMEO AND JULIET
STARTING AT 2PM IN THE GYM
A HOT KISS SCENE PLAYED BY A REAL LIFE COUPLE...?!
COME SEE!
I HOPE YOU HAVE AN EXPLANATION FOR THIS.
They were handing them out.
YOU'RE NOT REALLY...
HAVE YOU NO SHAME?
AND WHO EXACTLY...
...DO YOU THINK YOU ARE?
HUH?
YOU DO AS YOU PLEASE.
YOU DON'T CARE ABOUT YOUR FAMILY.
SO I'M GOING TO DO AS I PLEASE.
2-2
ROMEO AND JULIET
STARTING AT 2PM IN THE GYM
A HOT KISS SCENE
WH...
WHAT DID YOU JUST SAY?
HEY! HARUNA!
THERE YOU ARE!

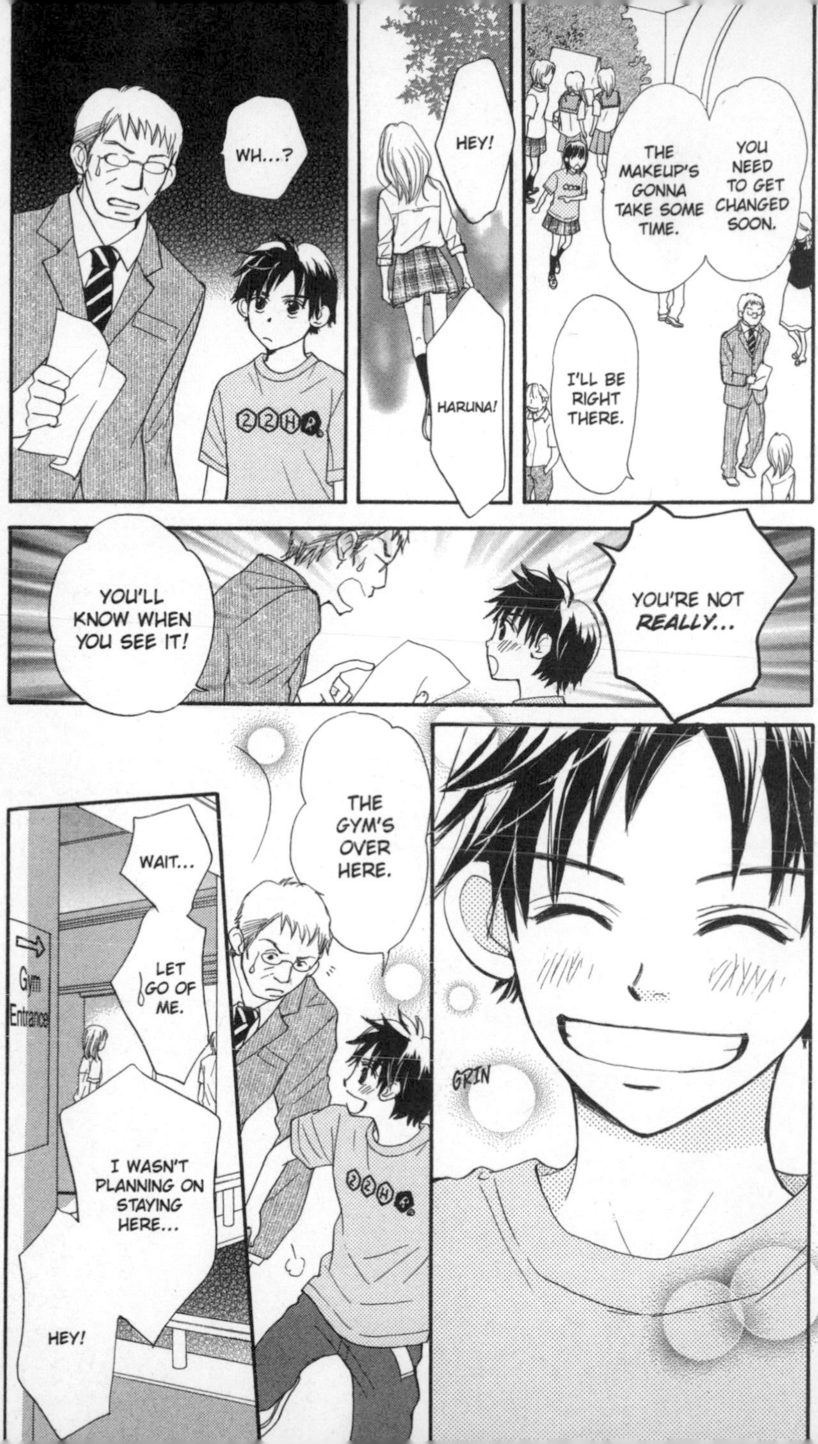
YOU NEED TO GET CHANGED SOON.
THE MAKEUP'S GONNA TAKE SOME TIME.
I'LL BE RIGHT THERE.
HEY!
HARUNA!
WH...?
YOU'RE NOT **REALLY...**
YOU'LL KNOW WHEN YOU SEE IT!
THE GYM'S OVER HERE.
GRIN
WAIT...
LET GO OF ME.
Gym Entrance
I WASN'T PLANNING ON STAYING HERE...
HEY!

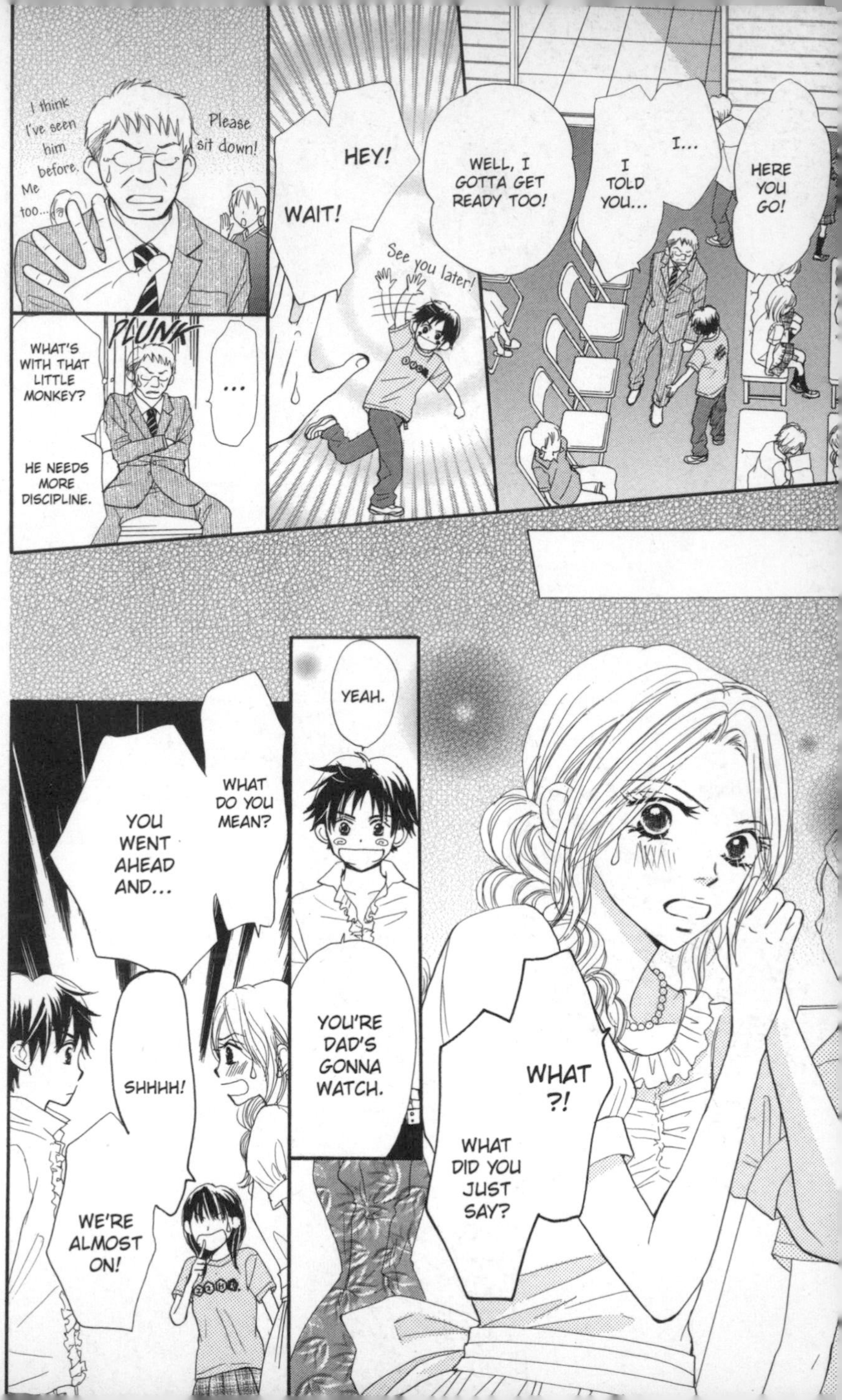
HERE YOU GO!
I... I TOLD YOU...
WELL, I GOTTA GET READY TOO!
HEY!
WAIT!
See you later!
Please sit down!
I think I've seen him before.
Me too...
PLUNK
...
WHAT'S WITH THAT LITTLE MONKEY?
HE NEEDS MORE DISCIPLINE.
YEAH.
YOU'RE DAD'S GONNA WATCH.
WHAT ?!
WHAT DID YOU JUST SAY?
WHAT DO YOU MEAN?
YOU WENT AHEAD AND...
SHHHH!
WE'RE ALMOST ON!

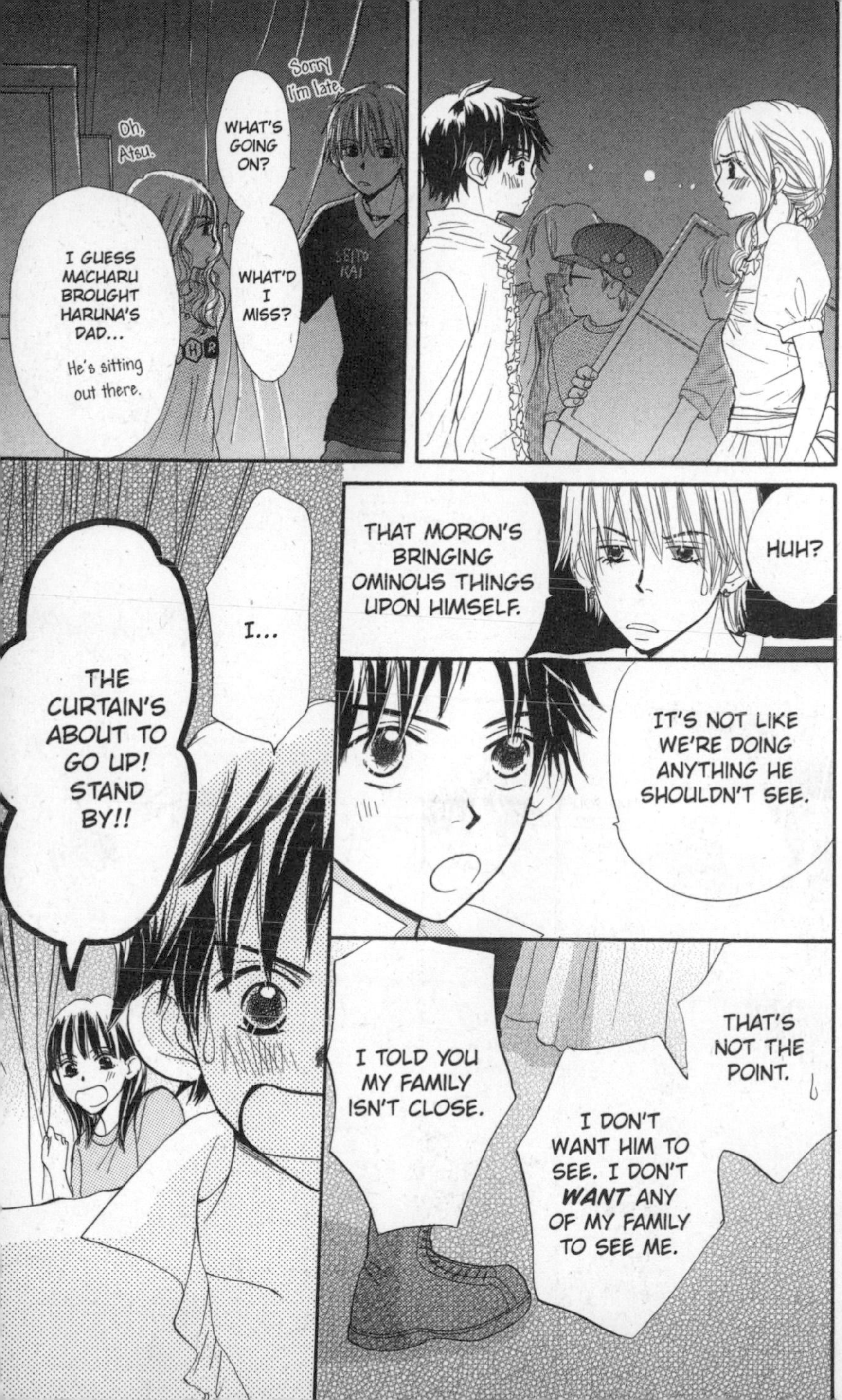
Sorry I'm late.
WHAT'S GOING ON?
Oh, Atsu.
WHAT'D I MISS?
I GUESS MACHARU BROUGHT HARUNA'S DAD...
He's sitting out there.
HUH?
THAT MORON'S BRINGING OMINOUS THINGS UPON HIMSELF.
IT'S NOT LIKE WE'RE DOING ANYTHING HE SHOULDN'T SEE.
THAT'S NOT THE POINT.
I TOLD YOU MY FAMILY ISN'T CLOSE.
I DON'T WANT HIM TO SEE. I DON'T *WANT* ANY OF MY FAMILY TO SEE ME.
I...
THE CURTAIN'S ABOUT TO GO UP! STAND BY!!

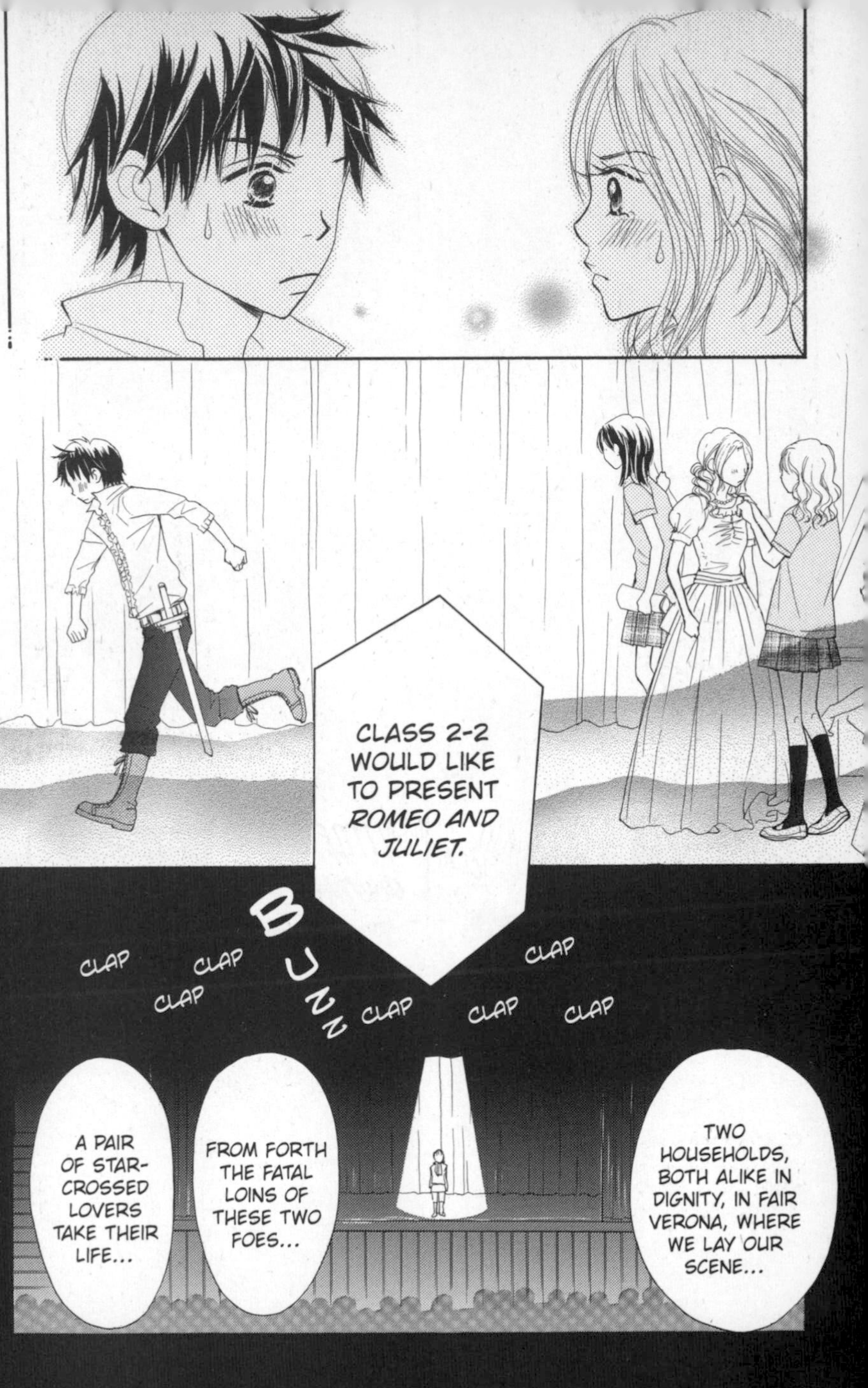
CLASS 2-2 WOULD LIKE TO PRESENT *ROMEO AND JULIET.*
BUNN
CLAP
CLAP
CLAP
CLAP
CLAP
CLAP
CLAP
CLAP
TWO HOUSEHOLDS, BOTH ALIKE IN DIGNITY, IN FAIR VERONA, WHERE WE LAY OUR SCENE...
FROM FORTH THE FATAL LOINS OF THESE TWO FOES...
A PAIR OF STAR-CROSSED LOVERS TAKE THEIR LIFE...

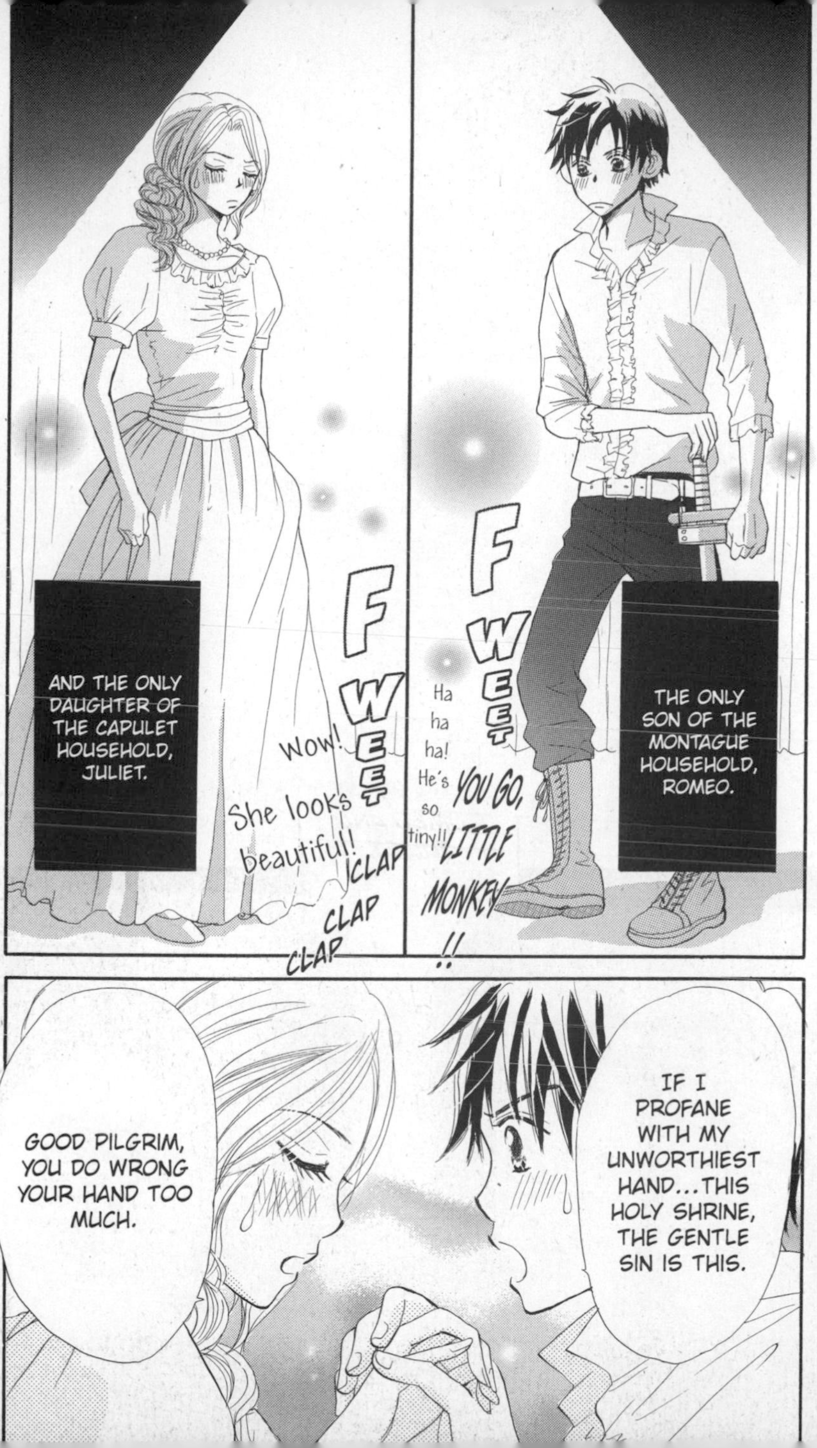
THE ONLY SON OF THE MONTAGUE HOUSEHOLD, ROMEO.
FWEET
YOU GO, LITTLE MONKEY!!
Ha ha ha! He's so tiny!!
AND THE ONLY DAUGHTER OF THE CAPULET HOUSEHOLD, JULIET.
FWEET
Wow! She looks beautiful!
CLAP CLAP CLAP
IF I PROFANE WITH MY UNWORTHIEST HAND...THIS HOLY SHRINE, THE GENTLE SIN IS THIS.
GOOD PILGRIM, YOU DO WRONG YOUR HAND TOO MUCH.

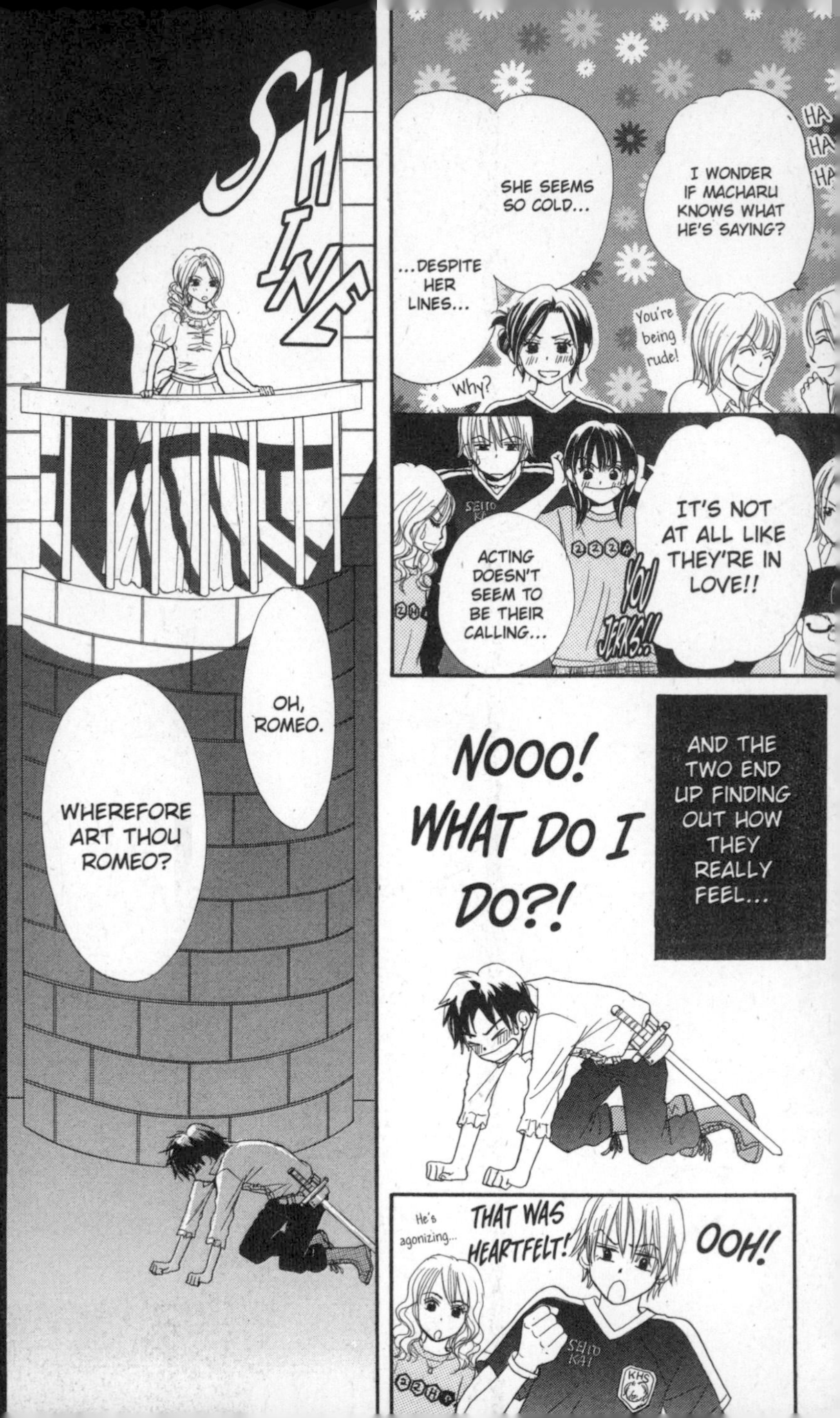
HA HA HA
I WONDER IF MACHARU KNOWS WHAT HE'S SAYING?
You're being rude!
SHE SEEMS SO COLD...
...DESPITE HER LINES...
Why?
IT'S NOT AT ALL LIKE THEY'RE IN LOVE!!
YOU JERKS!!
ACTING DOESN'T SEEM TO BE THEIR CALLING...
AND THE TWO END UP FINDING OUT HOW THEY REALLY FEEL...
NOOO! WHAT DO I DO?!
OOH!
THAT WAS HEARTFELT!
He's agonizing...
SHINE
OH, ROMEO.
WHEREFORE ART THOU ROMEO?

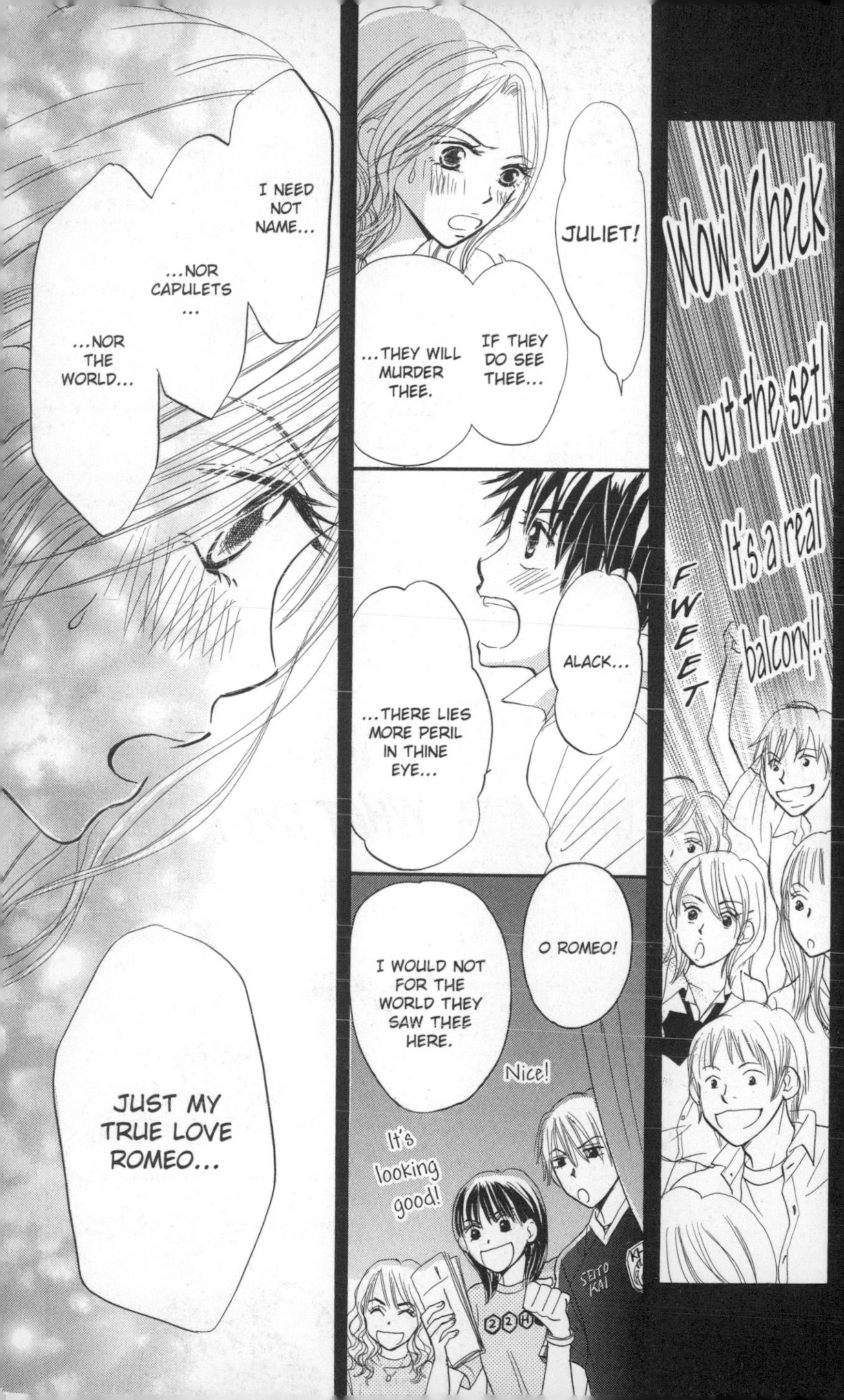
Wow! Check out the set! It's a real balcony!!
FWEET
JULIET!
IF THEY DO SEE THEE...
...THEY WILL MURDER THEE.
ALACK...
...THERE LIES MORE PERIL IN THINE EYE...
O ROMEO!
I WOULD NOT FOR THE WORLD THEY SAW THEE HERE.
Nice!
It's looking good!
I NEED NOT NAME...
...NOR CAPULETS...
...NOR THE WORLD...
JUST MY TRUE LOVE ROMEO...

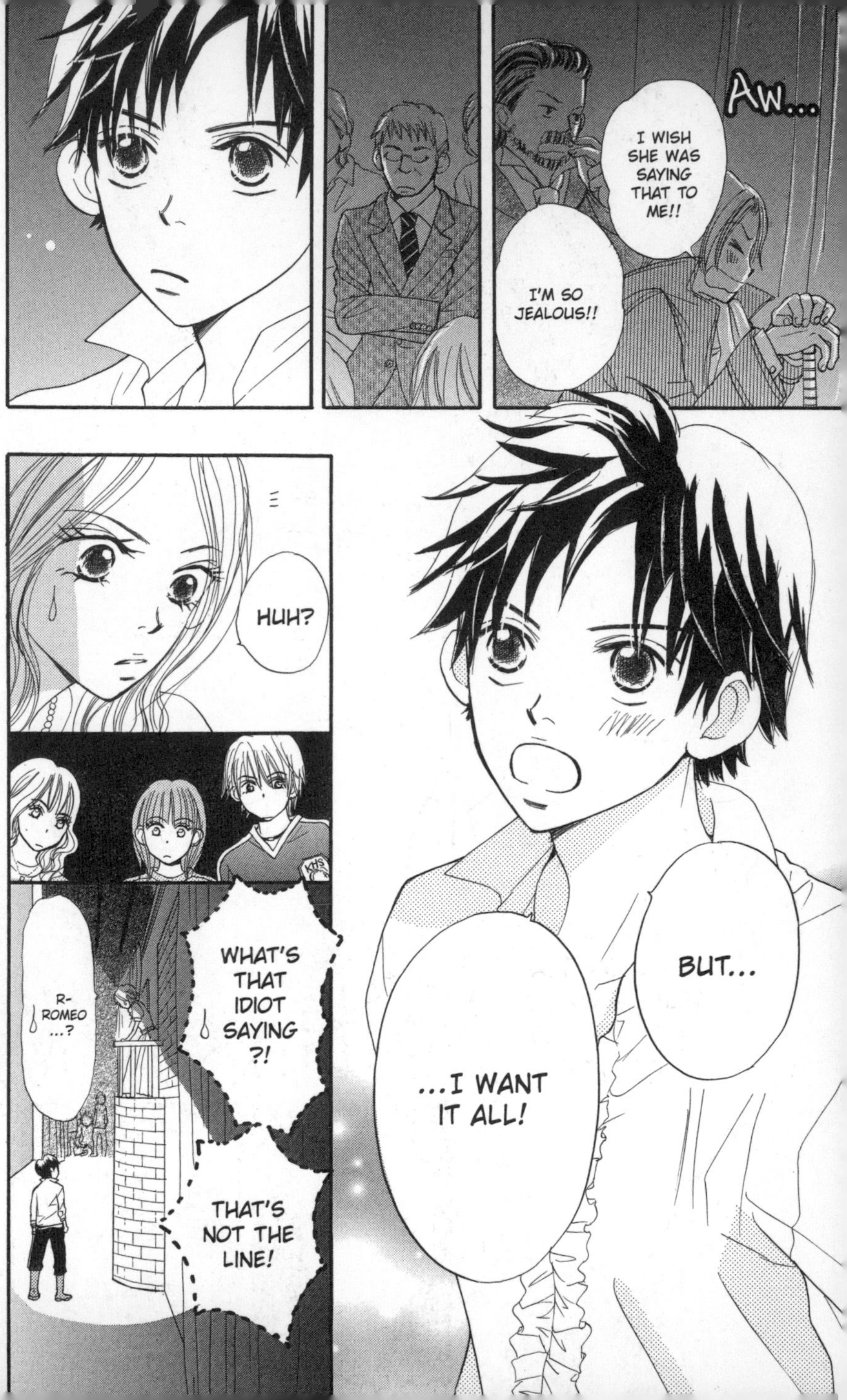
AW...
I WISH SHE WAS SAYING THAT TO ME!!
I'M SO JEALOUS!!
BUT...
...I WANT IT ALL!
HUH?
WHAT'S THAT IDIOT SAYING?!
THAT'S NOT THE LINE!
R-ROMEO...?

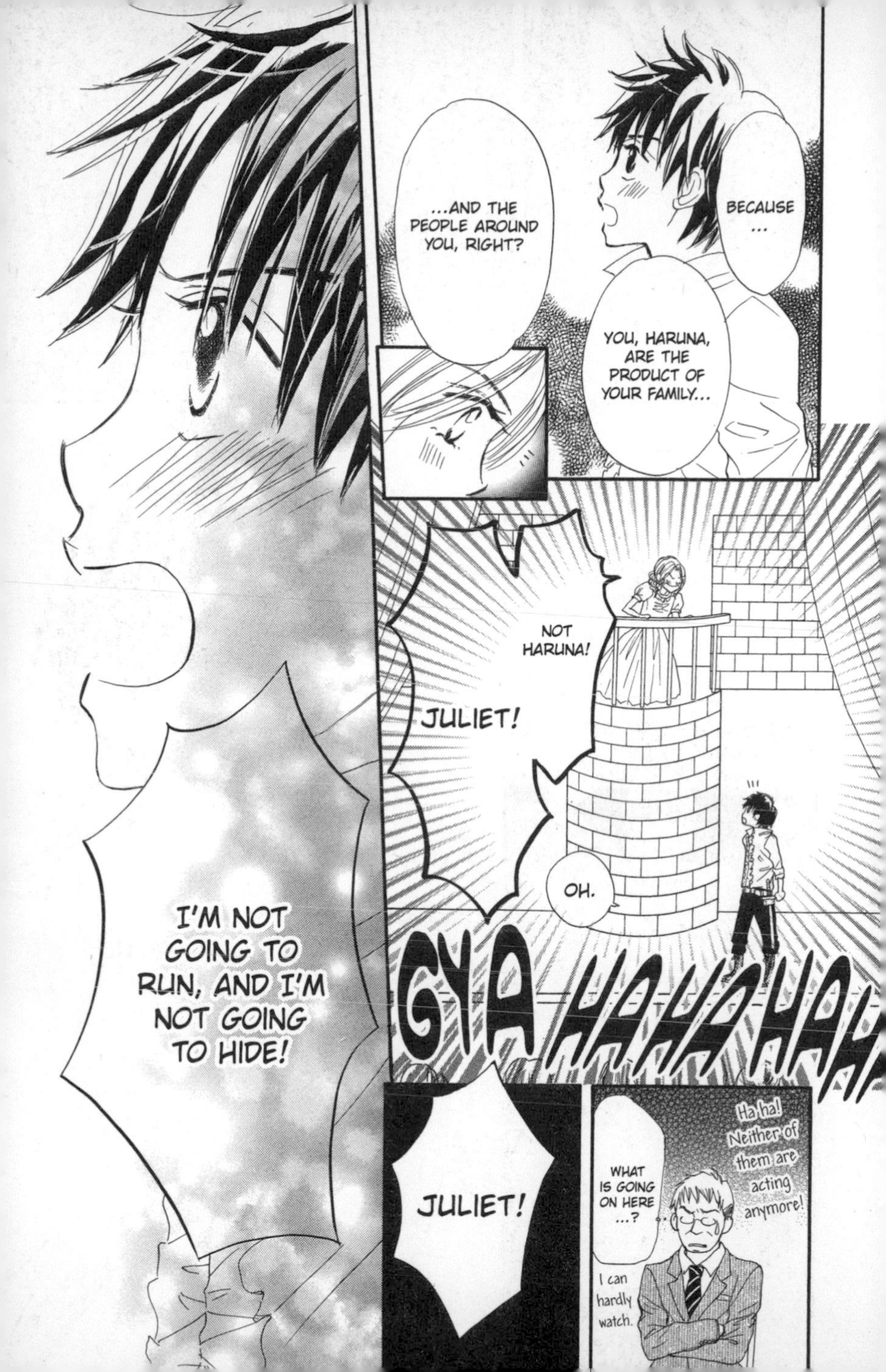
BECAUSE ...
YOU, HARUNA, ARE THE PRODUCT OF YOUR FAMILY...
...AND THE PEOPLE AROUND YOU, RIGHT?
NOT HARUNA!
JULIET!
OH.
GYAHAHAHAHAH
Ha ha! Neither of them are acting anymore!
WHAT IS GOING ON HERE ...?
I can hardly watch.
JULIET!
I'M NOT GOING TO RUN, AND I'M NOT GOING TO HIDE!

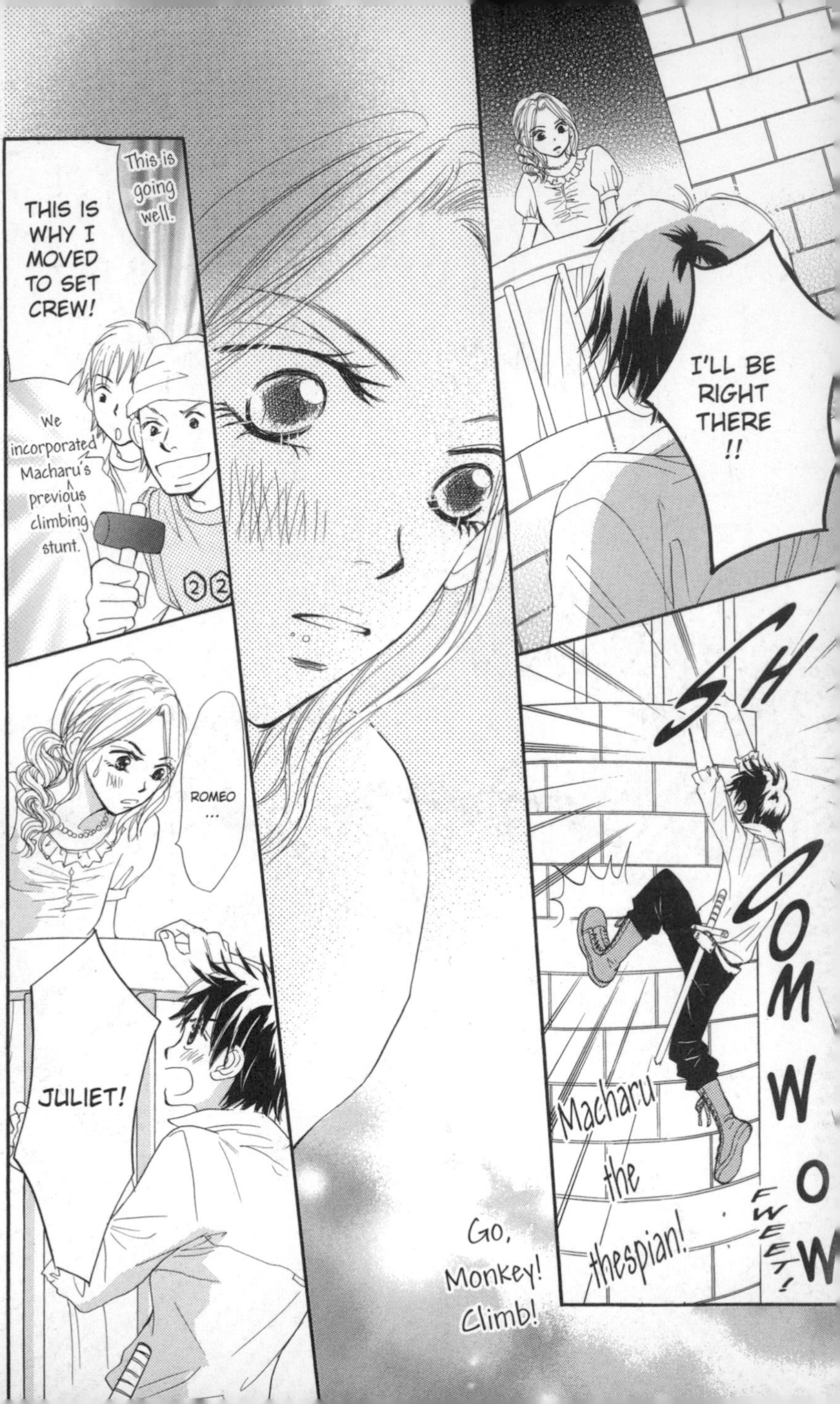

I'LL BE RIGHT THERE !!
SHOOMWOW
FWEET!
Macharu the thespian!
Go, Monkey! Climb!
This is going well.
THIS IS WHY I MOVED TO SET CREW!
We incorporated Macharu's previous climbing stunt.
ROMEO ...
JULIET!

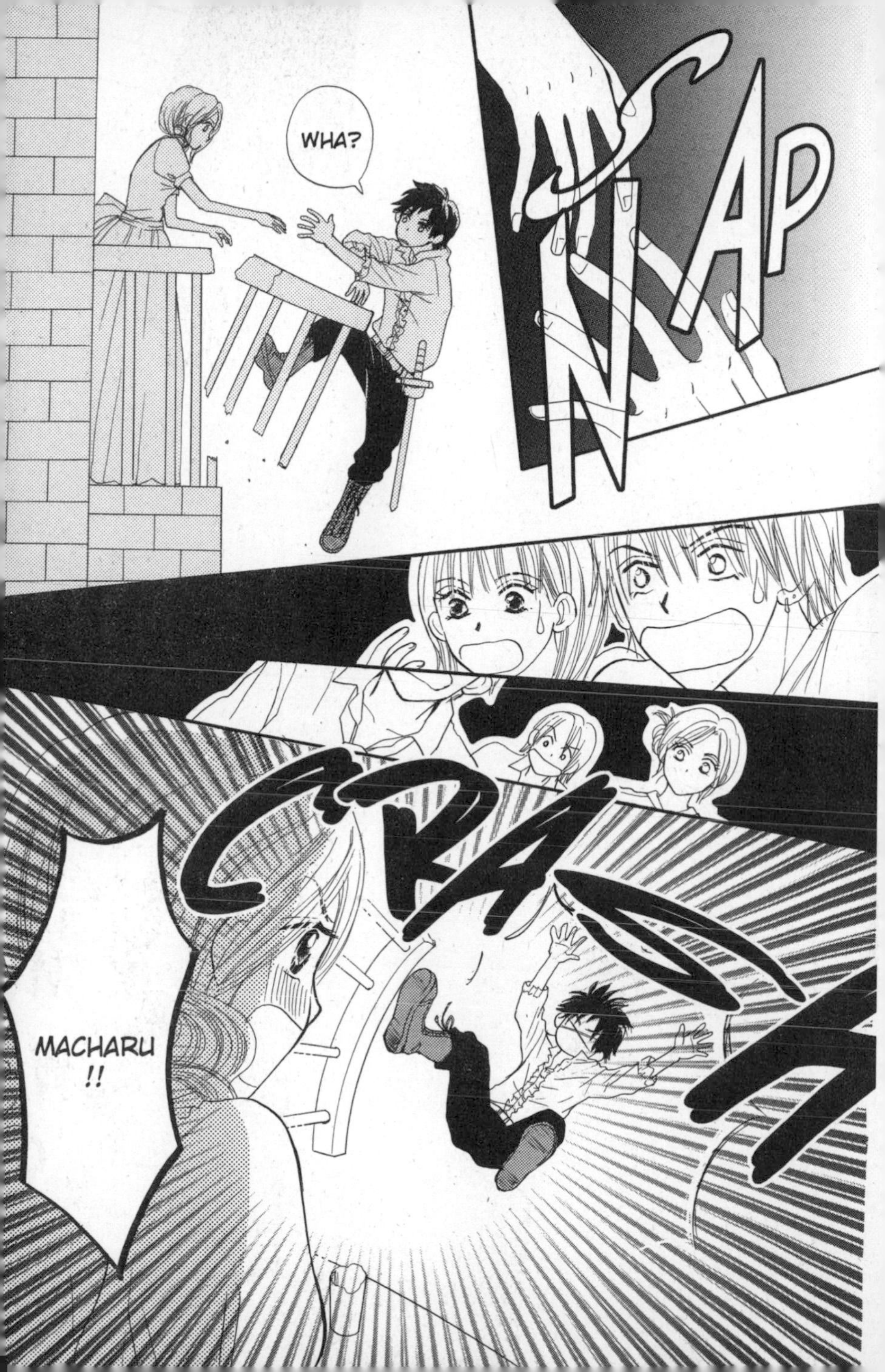
SNAP
WHA?
MACHARU !!

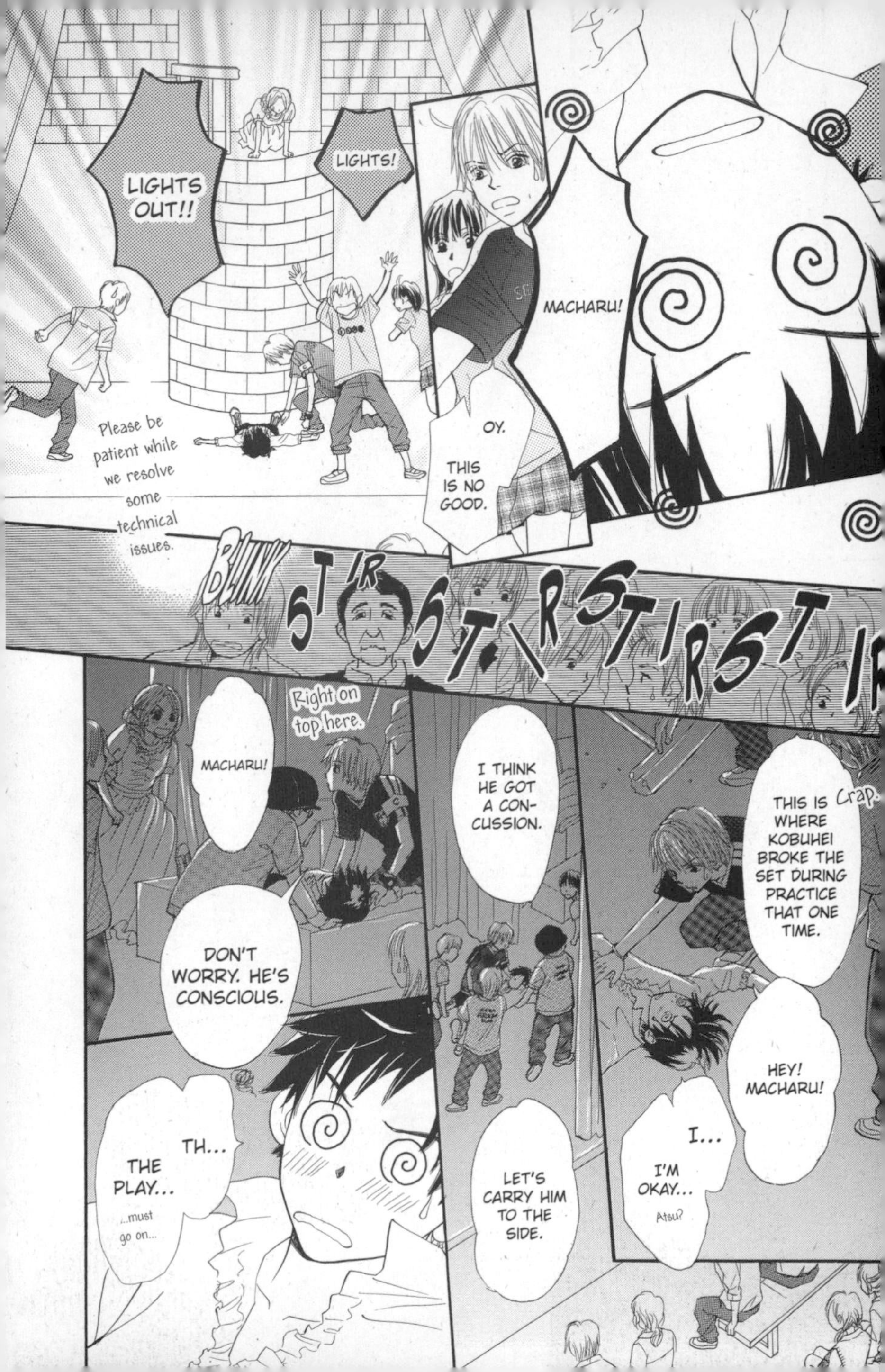
MACHARU!
OY.
THIS IS NO GOOD.
LIGHTS!
LIGHTS OUT!!
Please be patient while we resolve some technical issues.
STIR STIR STIR STIR STIR
BLINK
THIS IS WHERE KOBUHEI BROKE THE SET DURING PRACTICE THAT ONE TIME.
Crap.
HEY! MACHARU!
I... I'M OKAY...
Atsu?
I THINK HE GOT A CONCUSSION.
LET'S CARRY HIM TO THE SIDE.
Right on top here.
MACHARU!
DON'T WORRY. HE'S CONSCIOUS.
TH... THE PLAY...
...must go on...

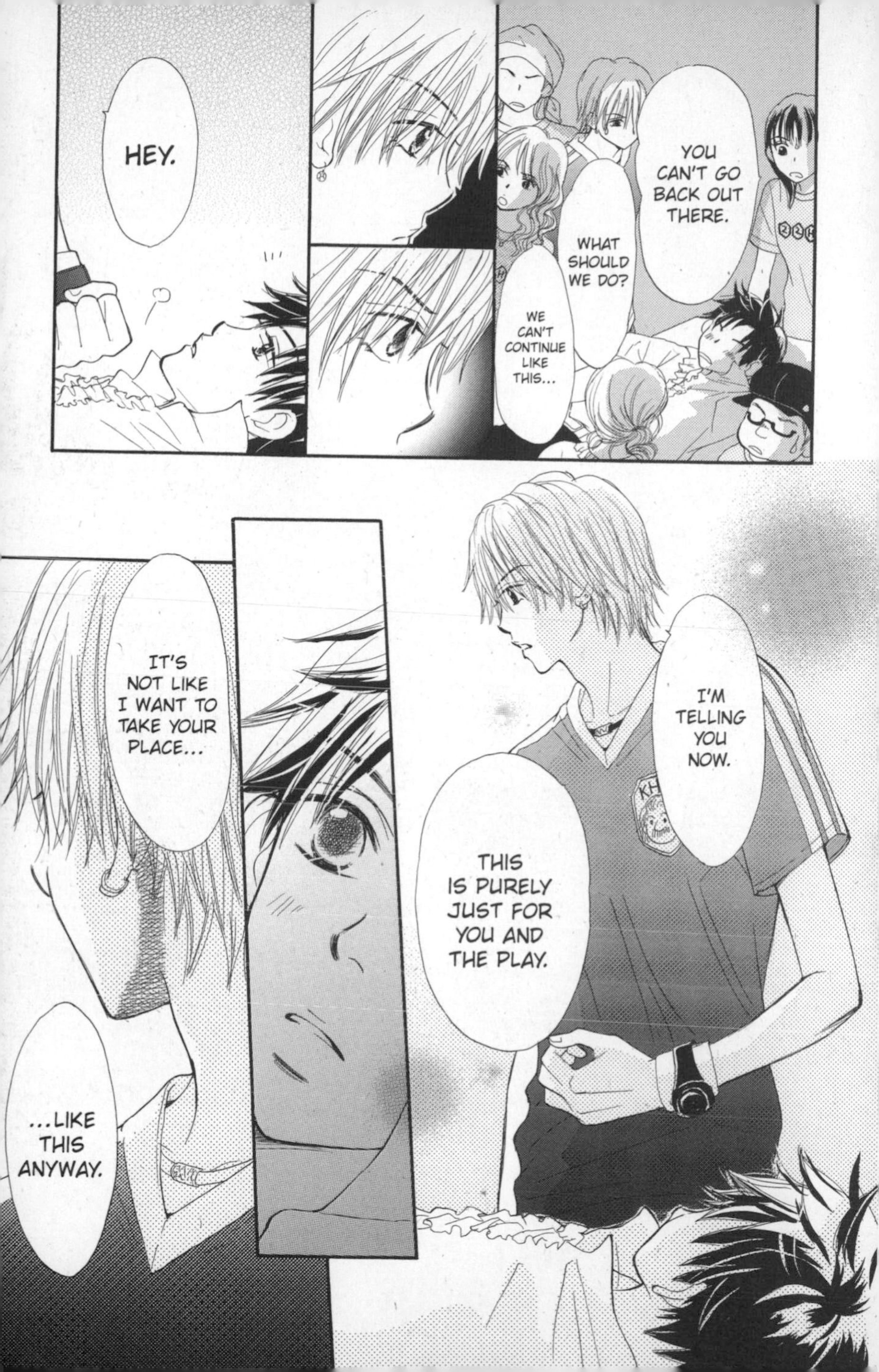
YOU CAN'T GO BACK OUT THERE.
WHAT SHOULD WE DO?
WE CAN'T CONTINUE LIKE THIS...
HEY.
I'M TELLING YOU NOW.
THIS IS PURELY JUST FOR YOU AND THE PLAY.
IT'S NOT LIKE I WANT TO TAKE YOUR PLACE...
...LIKE THIS ANYWAY.

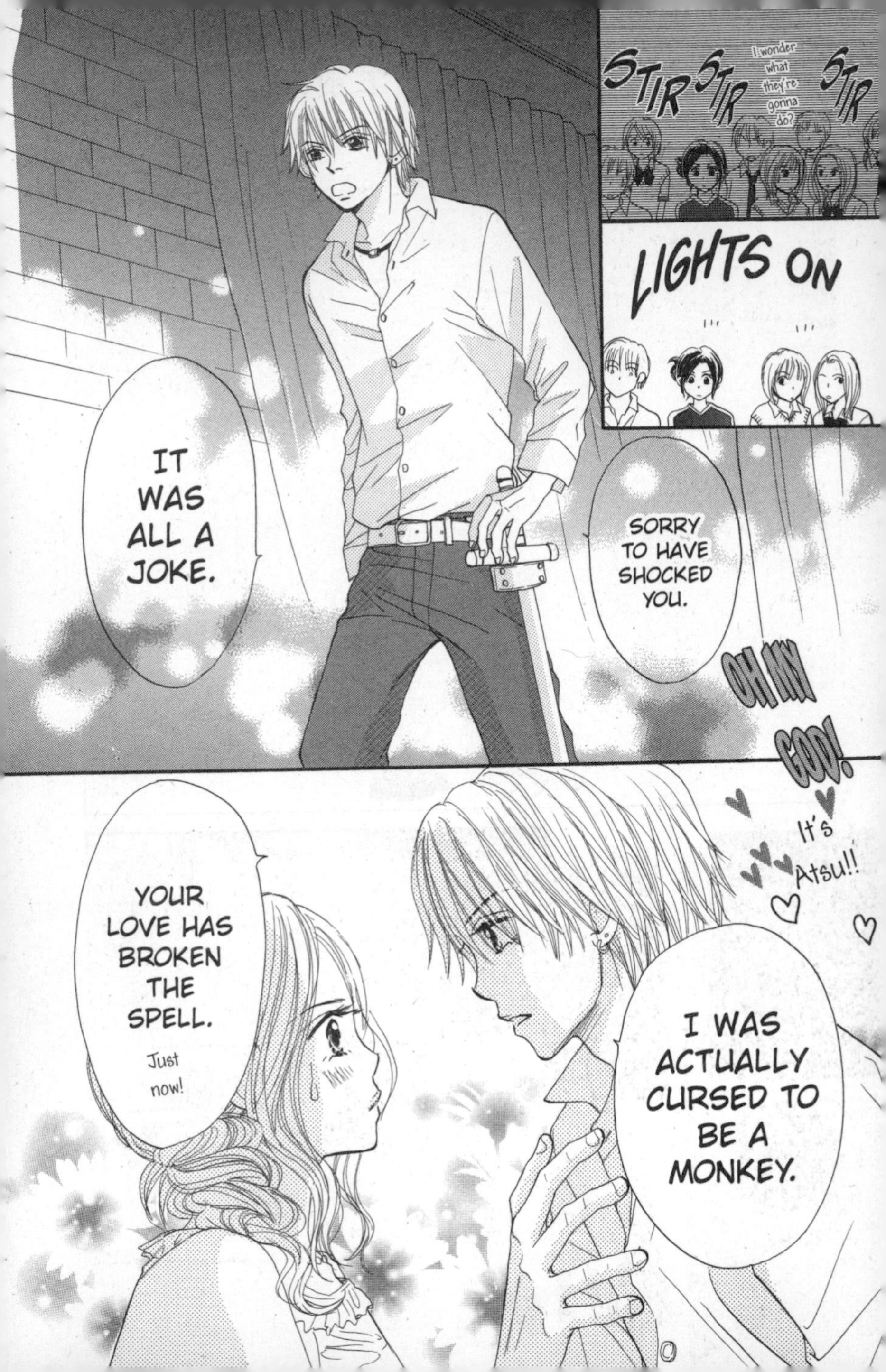
STIR STIR STIR
I wonder what they're gonna do?
LIGHTS ON
!!!
!!
IT WAS ALL A JOKE.
SORRY TO HAVE SHOCKED YOU.
OH MY GOD!
It's Atsu!!
I WAS ACTUALLY CURSED TO BE A MONKEY.
YOUR LOVE HAS BROKEN THE SPELL.
Just now!

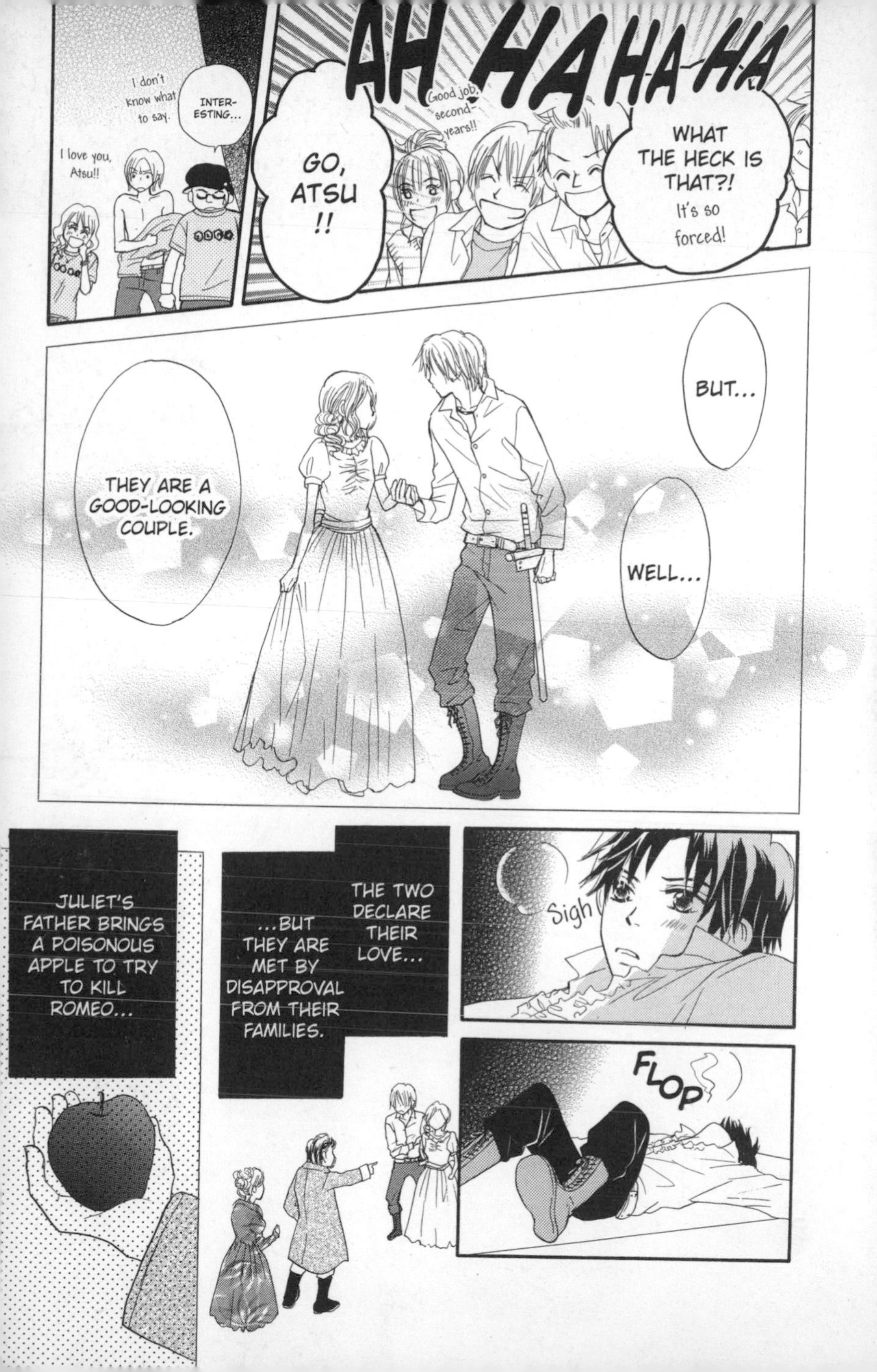
AH HAHA-HA-HA
WHAT THE HECK IS THAT?! It's so forced!
Good job, second-years!!
GO, ATSU!!
INTER-ESTING...
I don't know what to say.
I love you, Atsu!!
BUT...
WELL...
THEY ARE A GOOD-LOOKING COUPLE.
Sigh
FLOP
THE TWO DECLARE THEIR LOVE...
...BUT THEY ARE MET BY DISAPPROVAL FROM THEIR FAMILIES.
JULIET'S FATHER BRINGS A POISONOUS APPLE TO TRY TO KILL ROMEO...

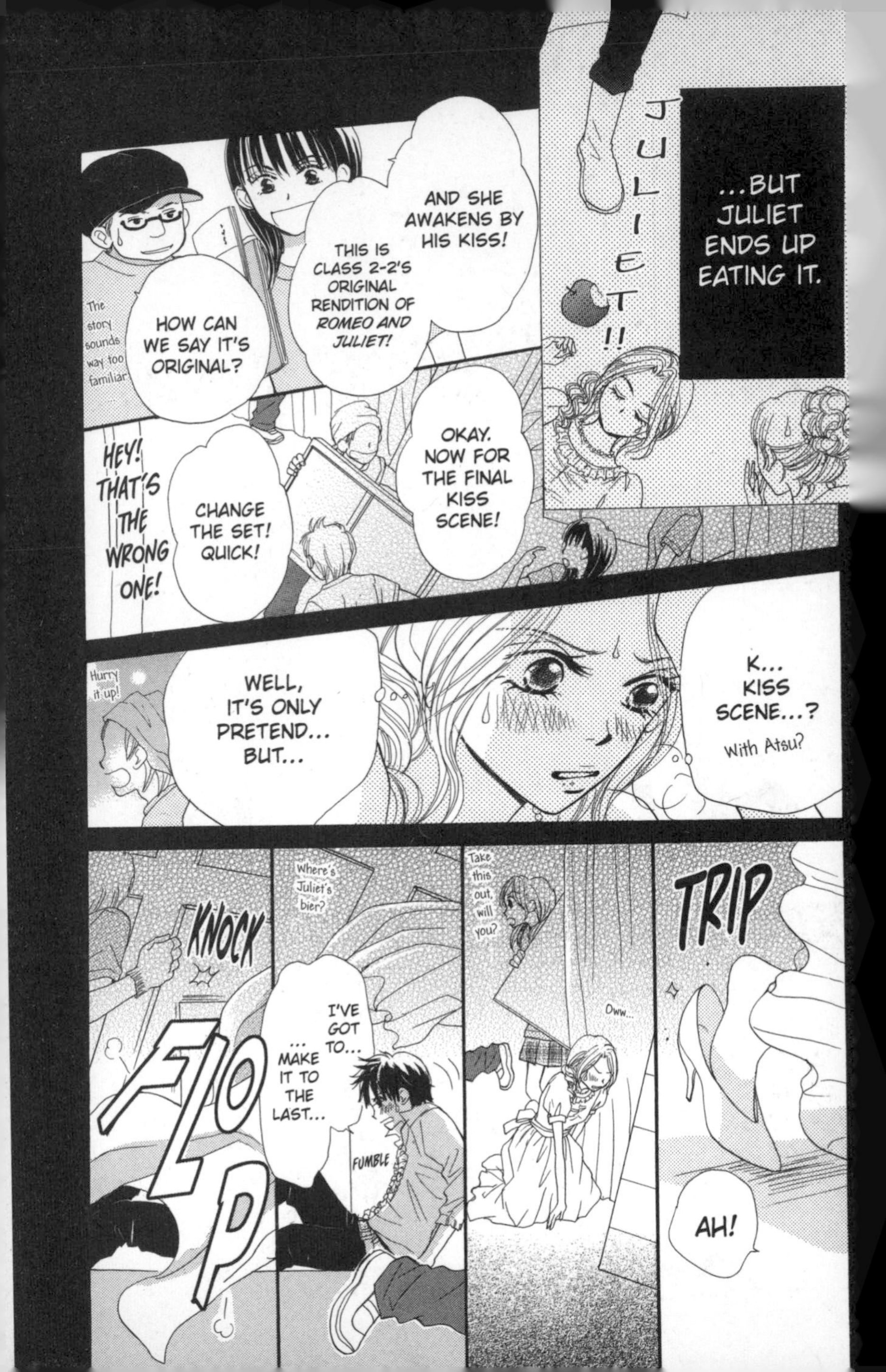
...BUT JULIET ENDS UP EATING IT.
JULIET!!
AND SHE AWAKENS BY HIS KISS!
THIS IS CLASS 2-2'S ORIGINAL RENDITION OF *ROMEO AND JULIET!*
HOW CAN WE SAY IT'S ORIGINAL?
The story sounds way too familiar...
OKAY. NOW FOR THE FINAL KISS SCENE!
CHANGE THE SET! QUICK!
HEY! THAT'S THE WRONG ONE!
K... KISS SCENE...?
With Atsu?
WELL, IT'S ONLY PRETEND... BUT...
Hurry it up!
TRIP
AH!
Take this out, will you?
Oww...
Where's Juliet's bier?
KNOCK
I'VE GOT TO...
...MAKE IT TO THE LAST...
FUMBLE
FLOP

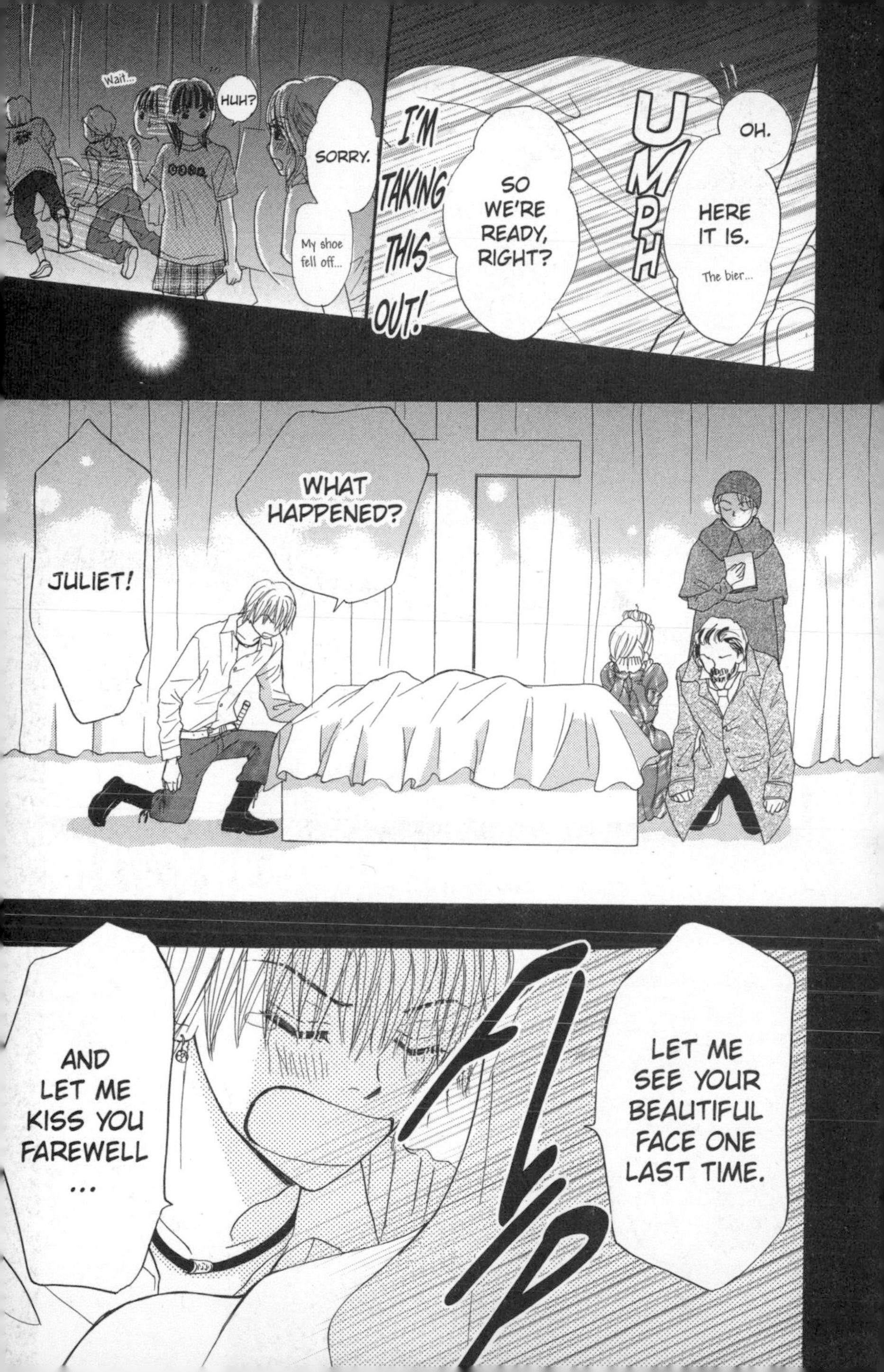
OH.
HERE IT IS.
The bier...
UMPH
SO WE'RE READY, RIGHT?
I'M TAKING THIS OUT!
SORRY.
My shoe fell off...
HUH?
Wait...
WHAT HAPPENED?
JULIET!
LET ME SEE YOUR BEAUTIFUL FACE ONE LAST TIME.
AND LET ME KISS YOU FAREWELL ...

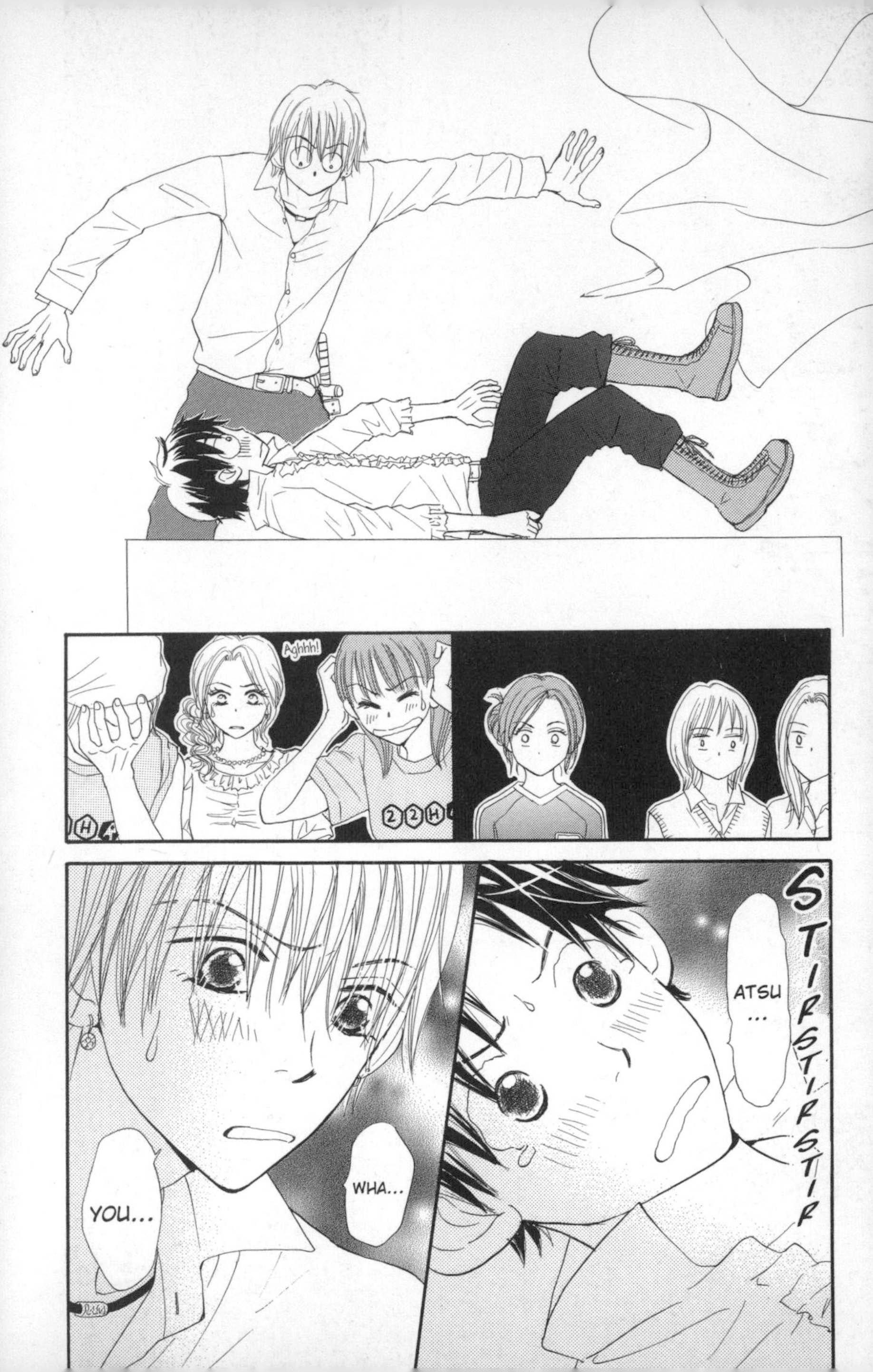
Aghhh!
STIRSTIRSTIR
ATSU ...
WHA...
YOU...

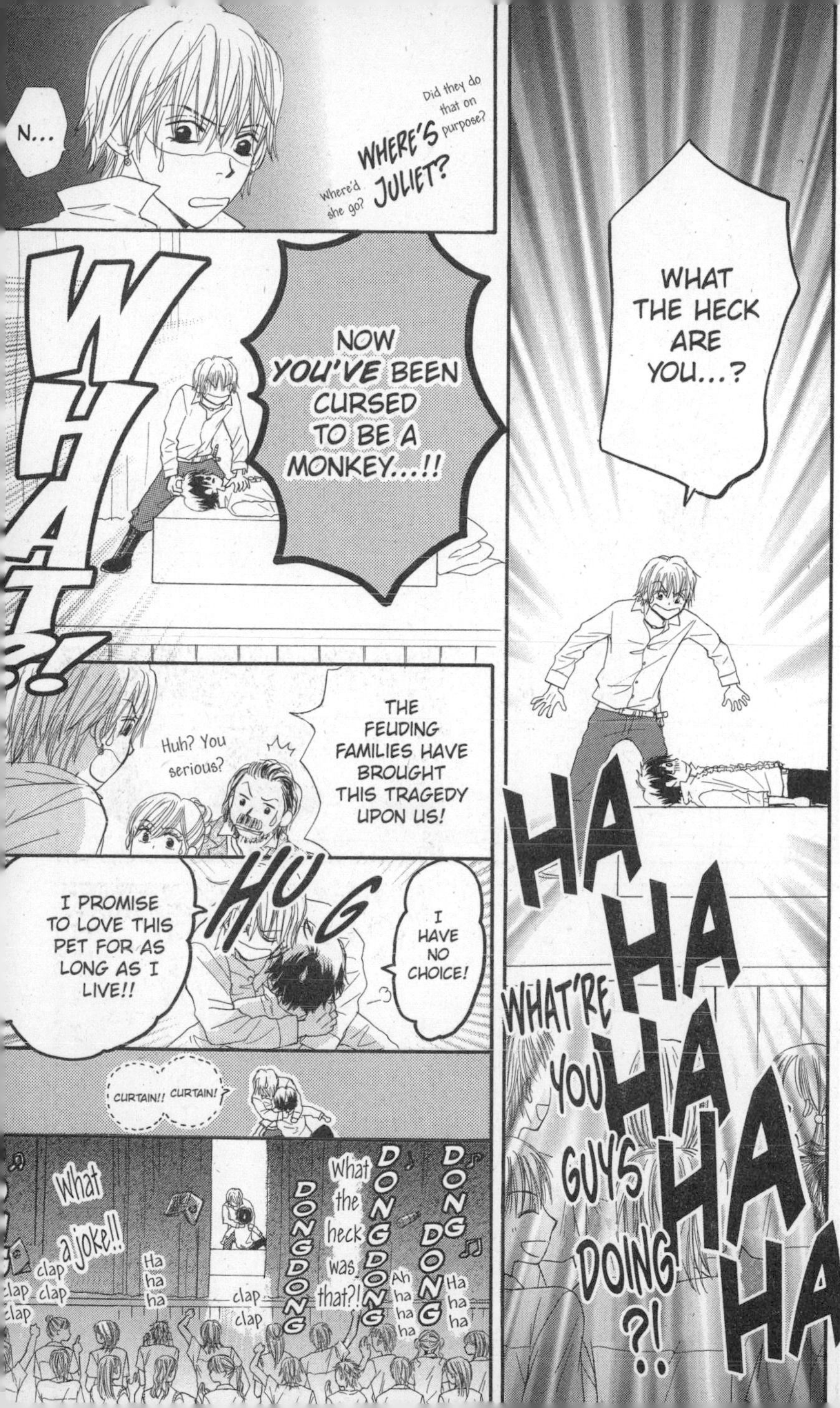
WHAT THE HECK ARE YOU...?
HA HA HA HA HA HA HA
WHAT'RE YOU GUYS DOING?!
Did they do that on purpose?
WHERE'S JULIET?
Where'd she go?
N...
NOW YOU'VE BEEN CURSED TO BE A MONKEY...!!
WHAT?!
THE FEUDING FAMILIES HAVE BROUGHT THIS TRAGEDY UPON US!
Huh? You serious?
I HAVE NO CHOICE!
HUG
I PROMISE TO LOVE THIS PET FOR AS LONG AS I LIVE!!
CURTAIN!
CURTAIN!!
DONG DONG DONG
Ha ha ha
DONG DONG DONG
Ah ha ha ha
What the heck was that?!
DONG DONG DONG
clap clap
Ha ha ha
What a joke!!
clap clap
clap clap

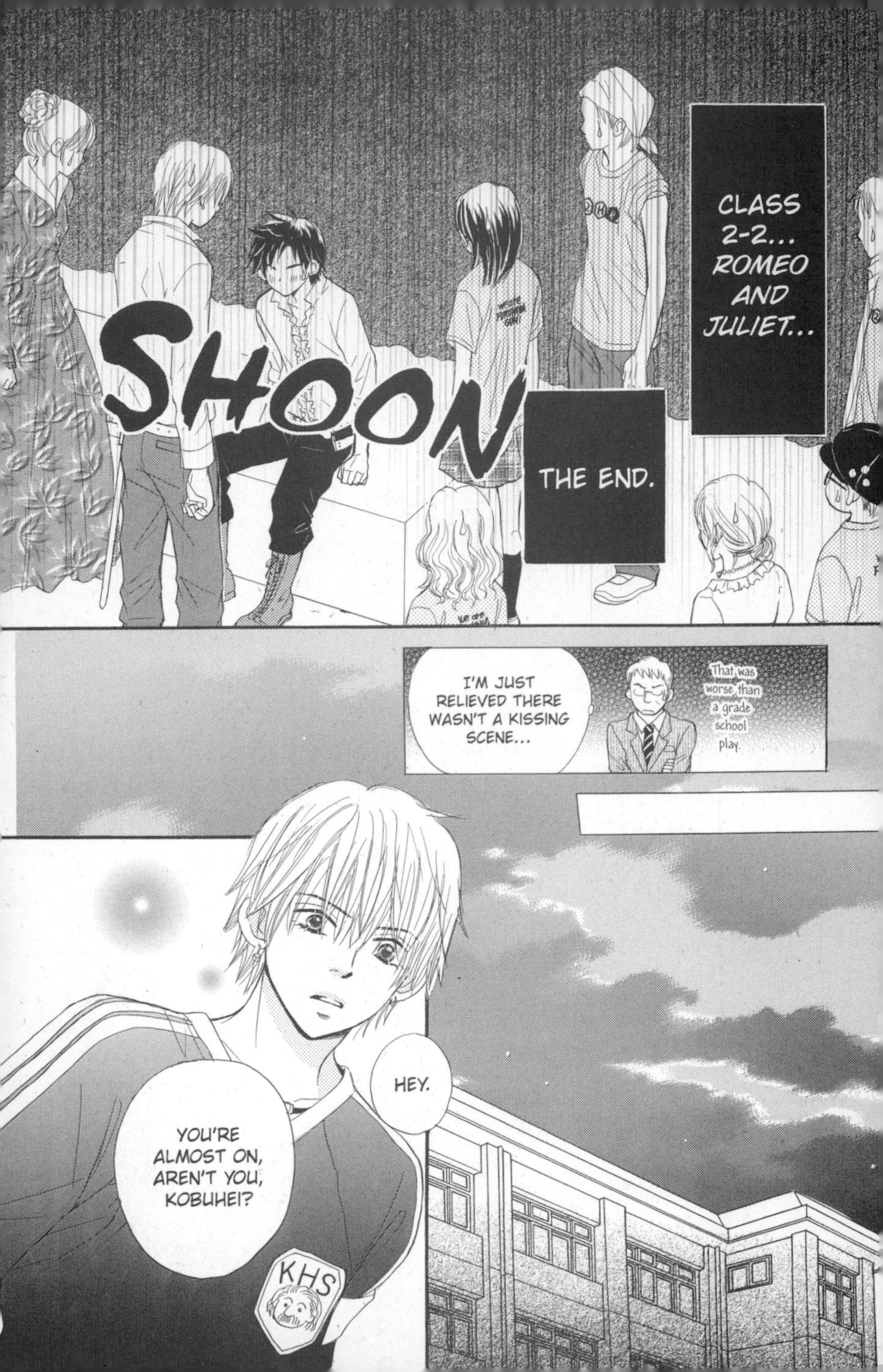
CLASS 2-2... ROMEO AND JULIET...
THE END.
SHOON
That was worse than a grade school play.
I'M JUST RELIEVED THERE WASN'T A KISSING SCENE...
HEY.
YOU'RE ALMOST ON, AREN'T YOU, KOBUHEI?
KHS

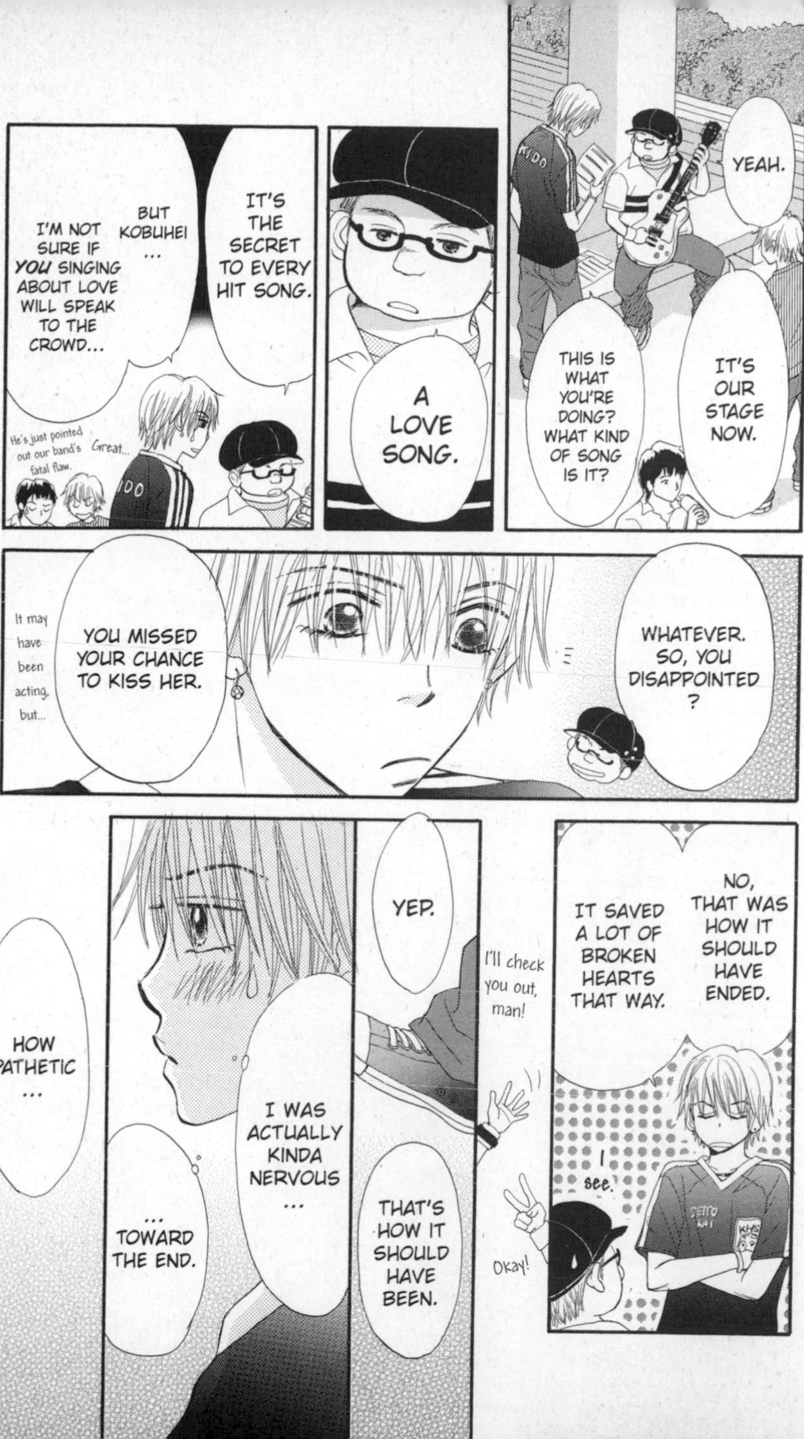
YEAH.
IT'S OUR STAGE NOW.
THIS IS WHAT YOU'RE DOING? WHAT KIND OF SONG IS IT?
A LOVE SONG.
IT'S THE SECRET TO EVERY HIT SONG.
BUT KOBUHEI...
I'M NOT SURE IF *YOU* SINGING ABOUT LOVE WILL SPEAK TO THE CROWD...
Great...
He's just pointed out our band's fatal flaw.
WHATEVER. SO, YOU DISAPPOINTED?
YOU MISSED YOUR CHANCE TO KISS HER.
It may have been acting, but...
NO, THAT WAS HOW IT SHOULD HAVE ENDED.
IT SAVED A LOT OF BROKEN HEARTS THAT WAY.
I see.
I'll check you out, man!
Okay!
YEP.
THAT'S HOW IT SHOULD HAVE BEEN.
I WAS ACTUALLY KINDA NERVOUS...
...TOWARD THE END.
HOW PATHETIC...

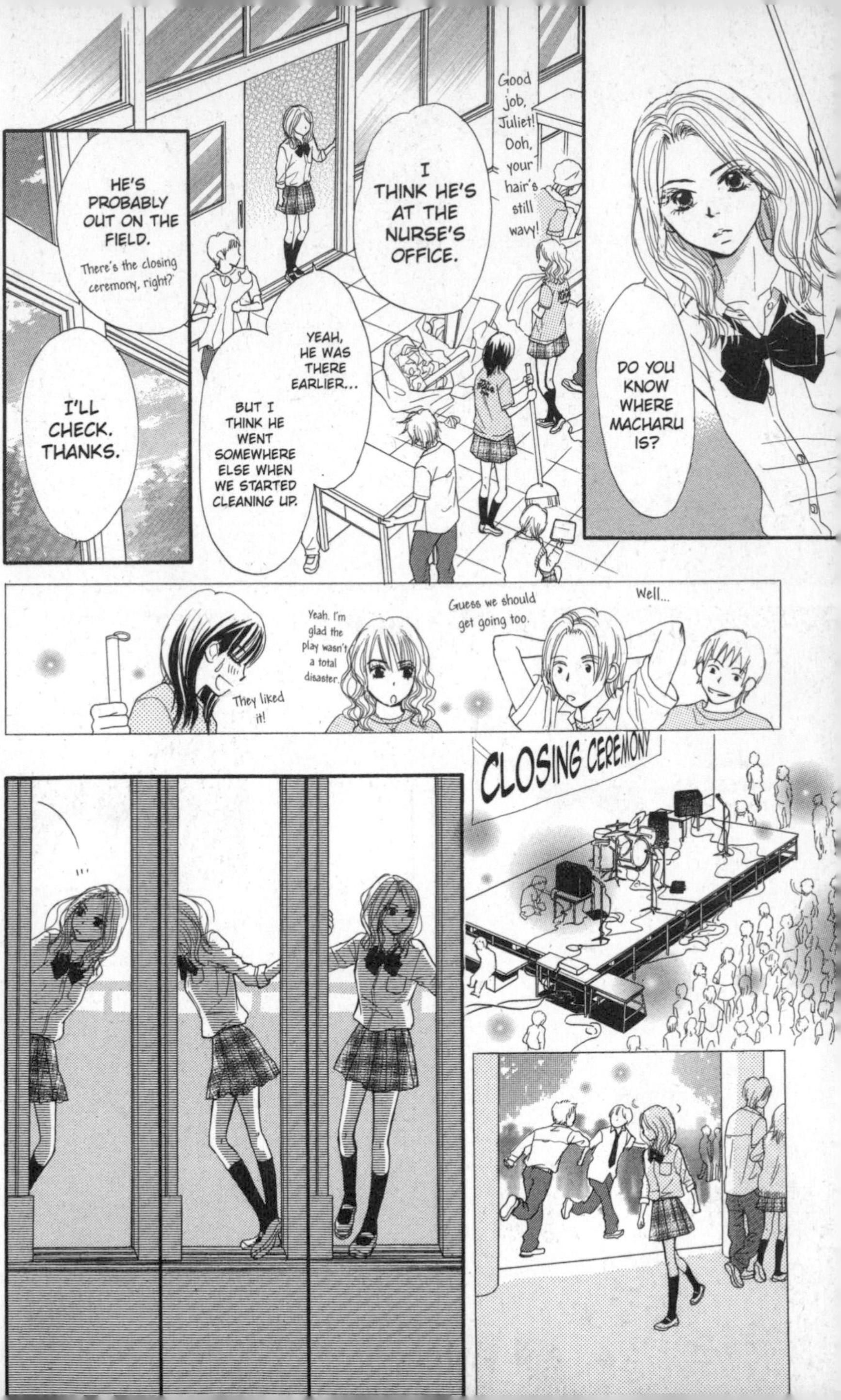
DO YOU KNOW WHERE MACHARU IS?
Good job, Juliet! Ooh, your hair's still wavy!
I THINK HE'S AT THE NURSE'S OFFICE.
YEAH, HE WAS THERE EARLIER...
BUT I THINK HE WENT SOMEWHERE ELSE WHEN WE STARTED CLEANING UP.
HE'S PROBABLY OUT ON THE FIELD.
There's the closing ceremony, right?
I'LL CHECK. THANKS.
Well...
Guess we should get going too.
Yeah. I'm glad the play wasn't a total disaster.
They liked it!
CLOSING CEREMONY

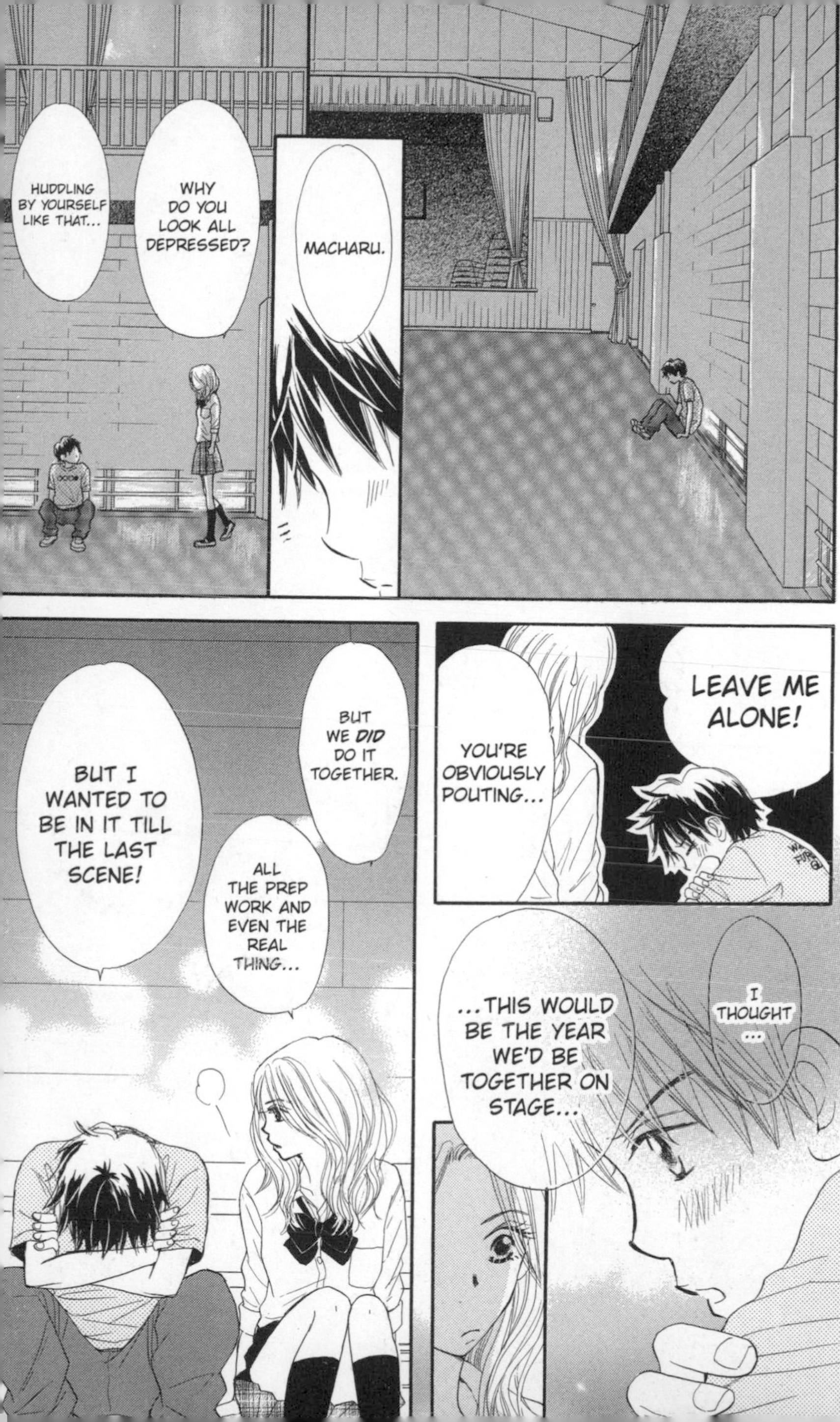
MACHARU.
WHY DO YOU LOOK ALL DEPRESSED?
HUDDLING BY YOURSELF LIKE THAT...
LEAVE ME ALONE!
YOU'RE OBVIOUSLY POUTING...
I THOUGHT...
...THIS WOULD BE THE YEAR WE'D BE TOGETHER ON STAGE...
BUT WE *DID* DO IT TOGETHER.
ALL THE PREP WORK AND EVEN THE REAL THING...
BUT I WANTED TO BE IN IT TILL THE LAST SCENE!

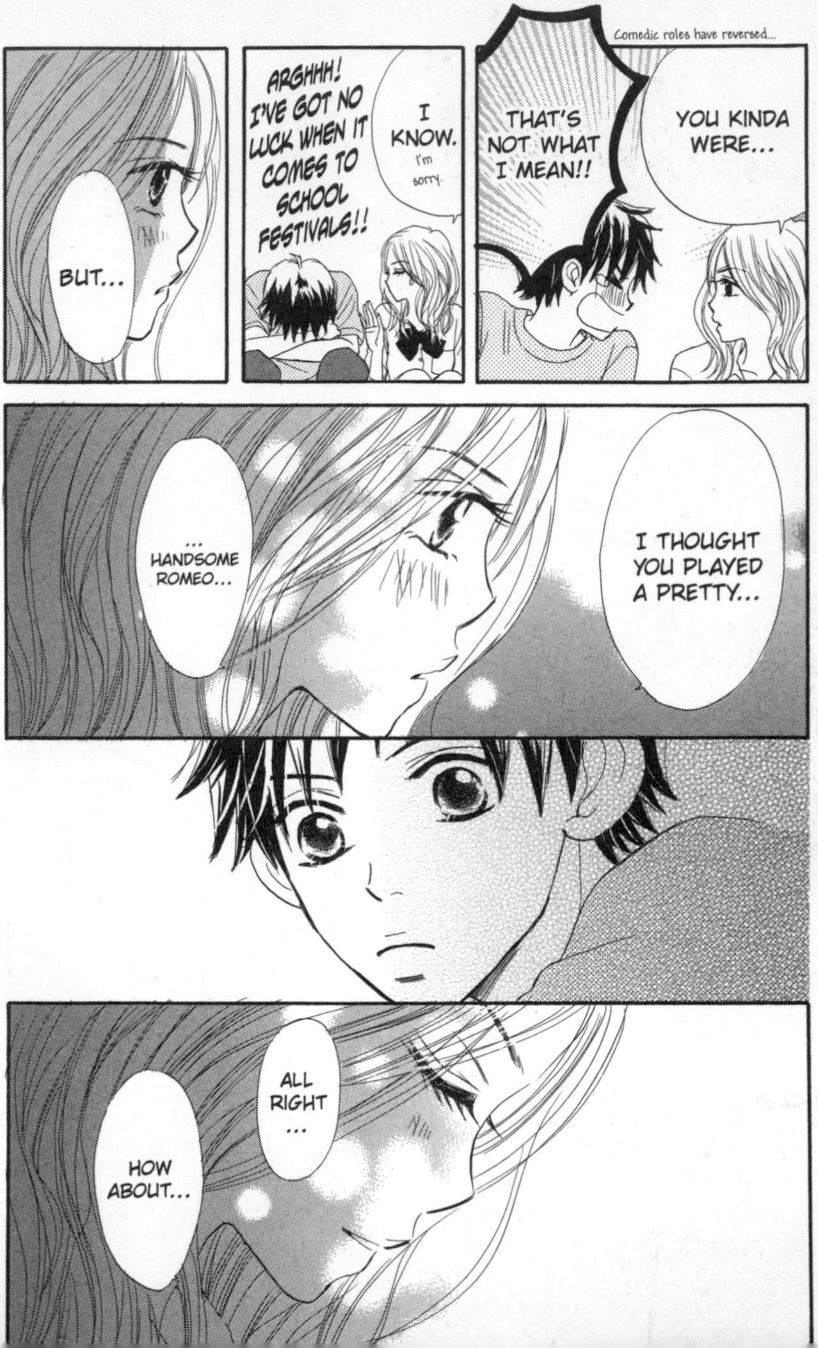
Comedic roles have reversed...
YOU KINDA WERE...
THAT'S NOT WHAT I MEAN!!
I KNOW.
I'm sorry.
ARGHHH! I'VE GOT NO LUCK WHEN IT COMES TO SCHOOL FESTIVALS!!
BUT...
I THOUGHT YOU PLAYED A PRETTY...
... HANDSOME ROMEO...
ALL RIGHT ...
HOW ABOUT...

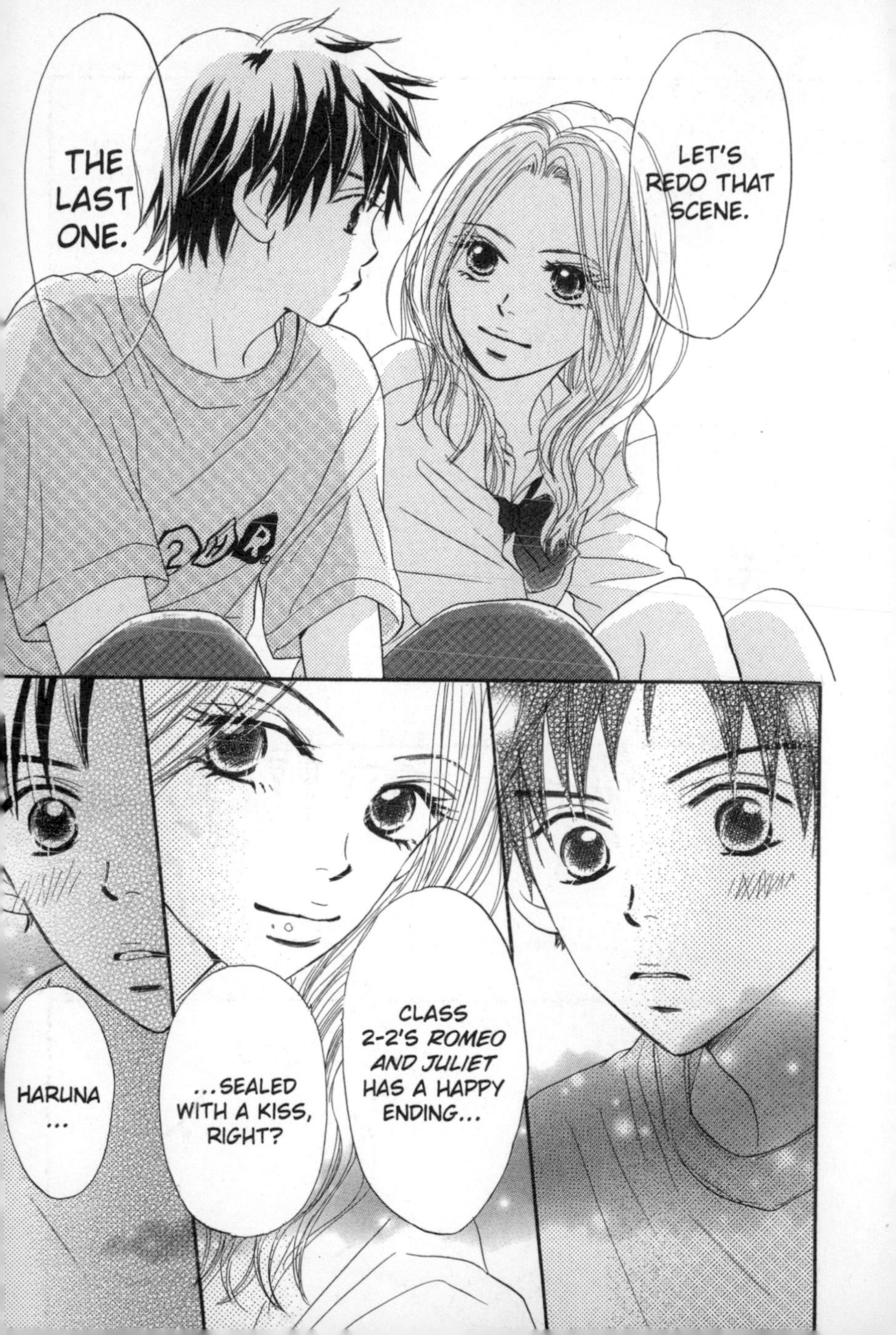
LET'S REDO THAT SCENE.
THE LAST ONE.
CLASS 2-2'S *ROMEO AND JULIET* HAS A HAPPY ENDING...
...SEALED WITH A KISS, RIGHT?
HARUNA ...

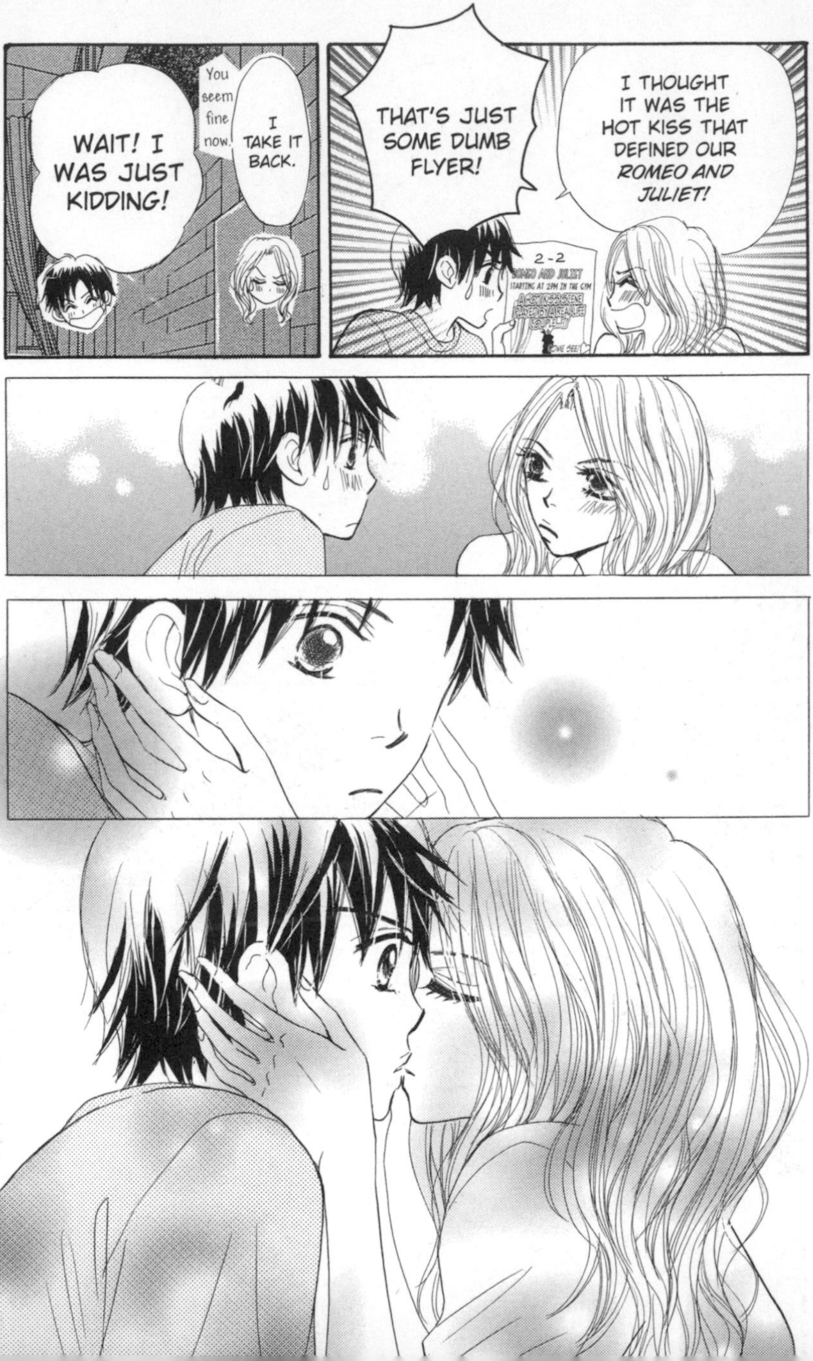
I THOUGHT IT WAS THE HOT KISS THAT DEFINED OUR *ROMEO AND JULIET!*
THAT'S JUST SOME DUMB FLYER!
2-2
ROMEO AND JULIET
STARTING AT 2PM IN THE GYM
I TAKE IT BACK.
You seem fine now.
WAIT! I WAS JUST KIDDING!

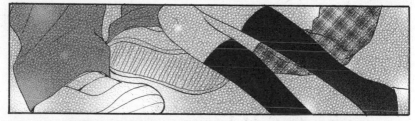

TH...

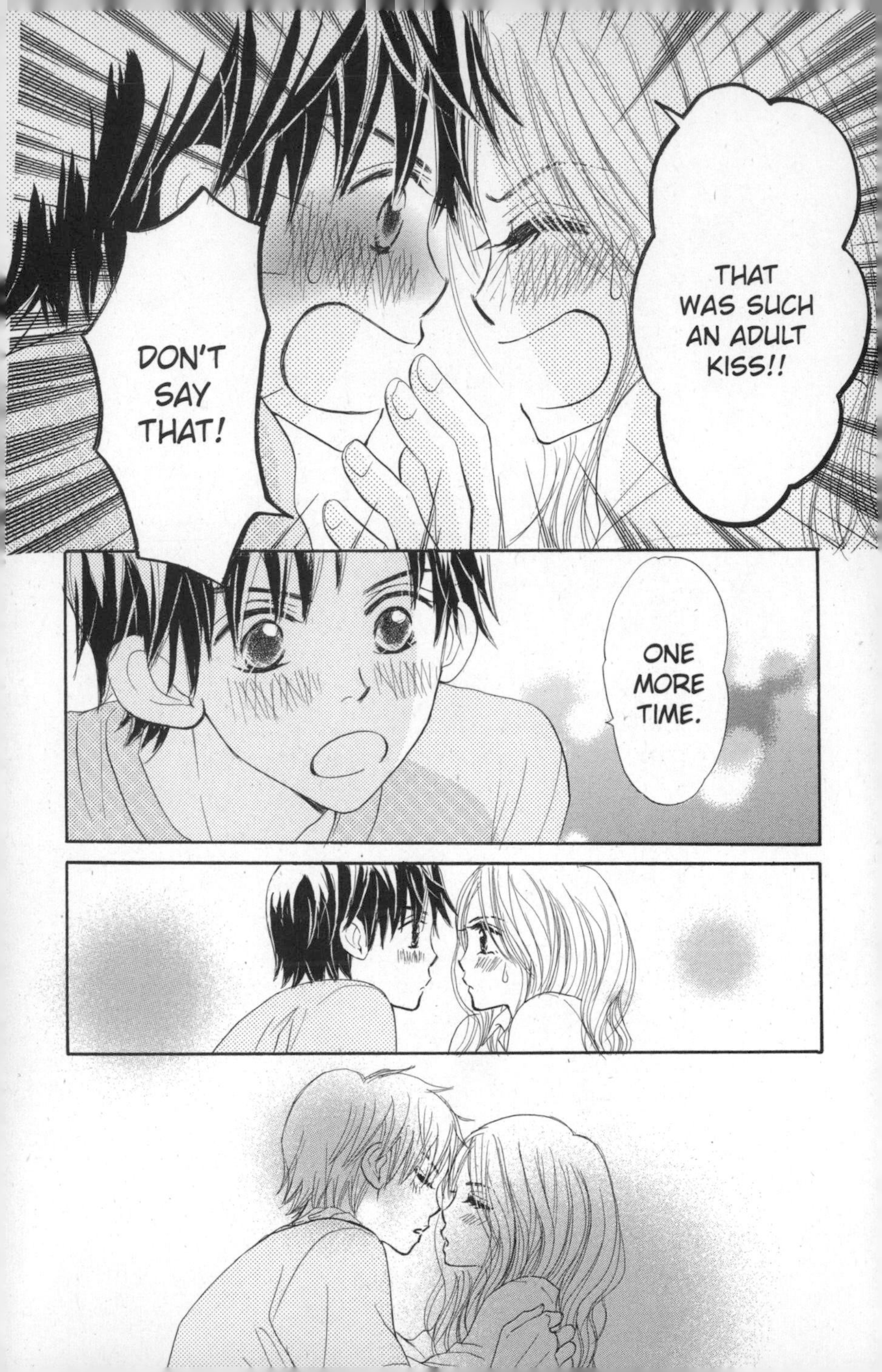
THAT WAS SUCH AN ADULT KISS!!
DON'T SAY THAT!
ONE MORE TIME.

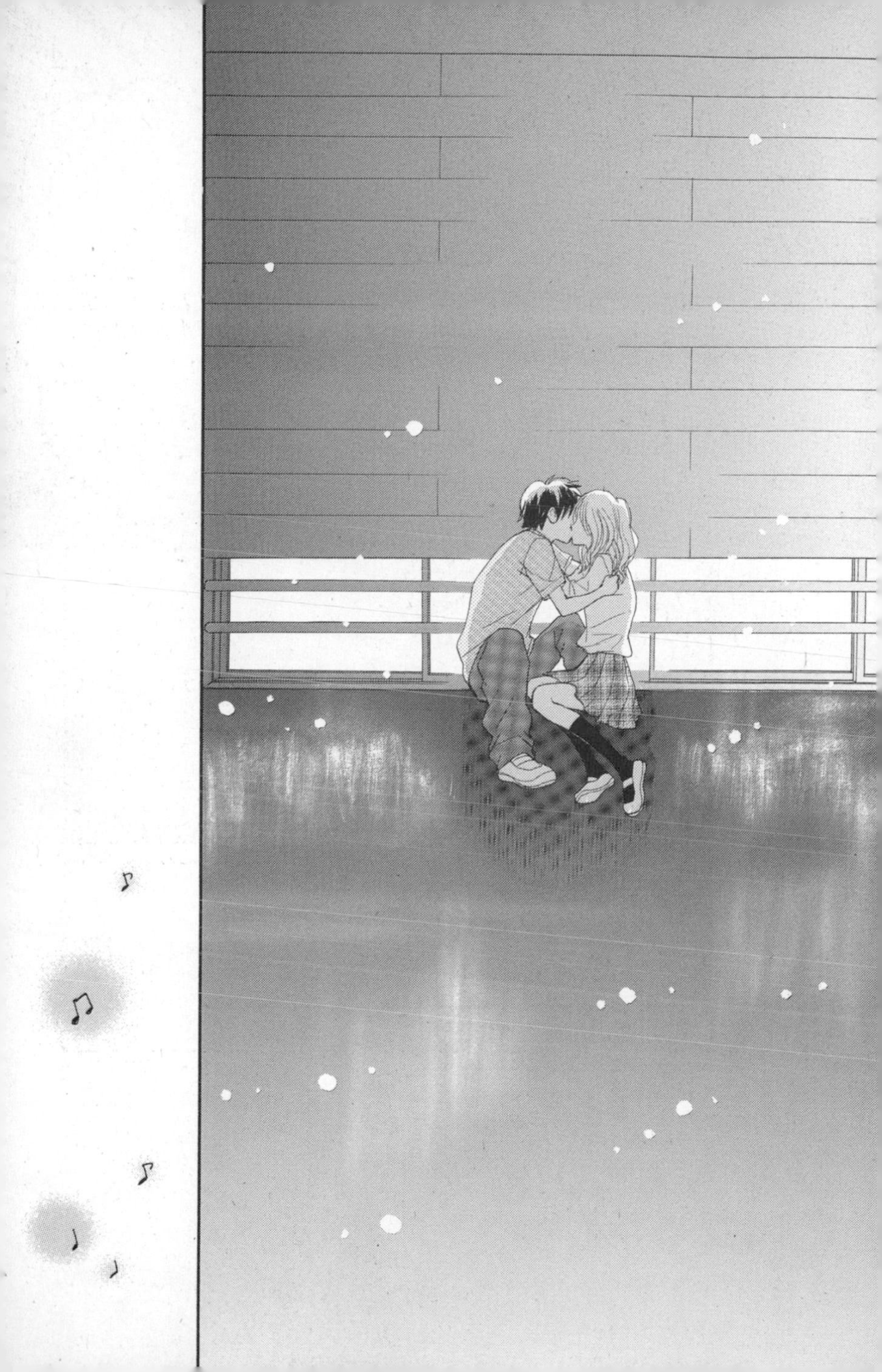

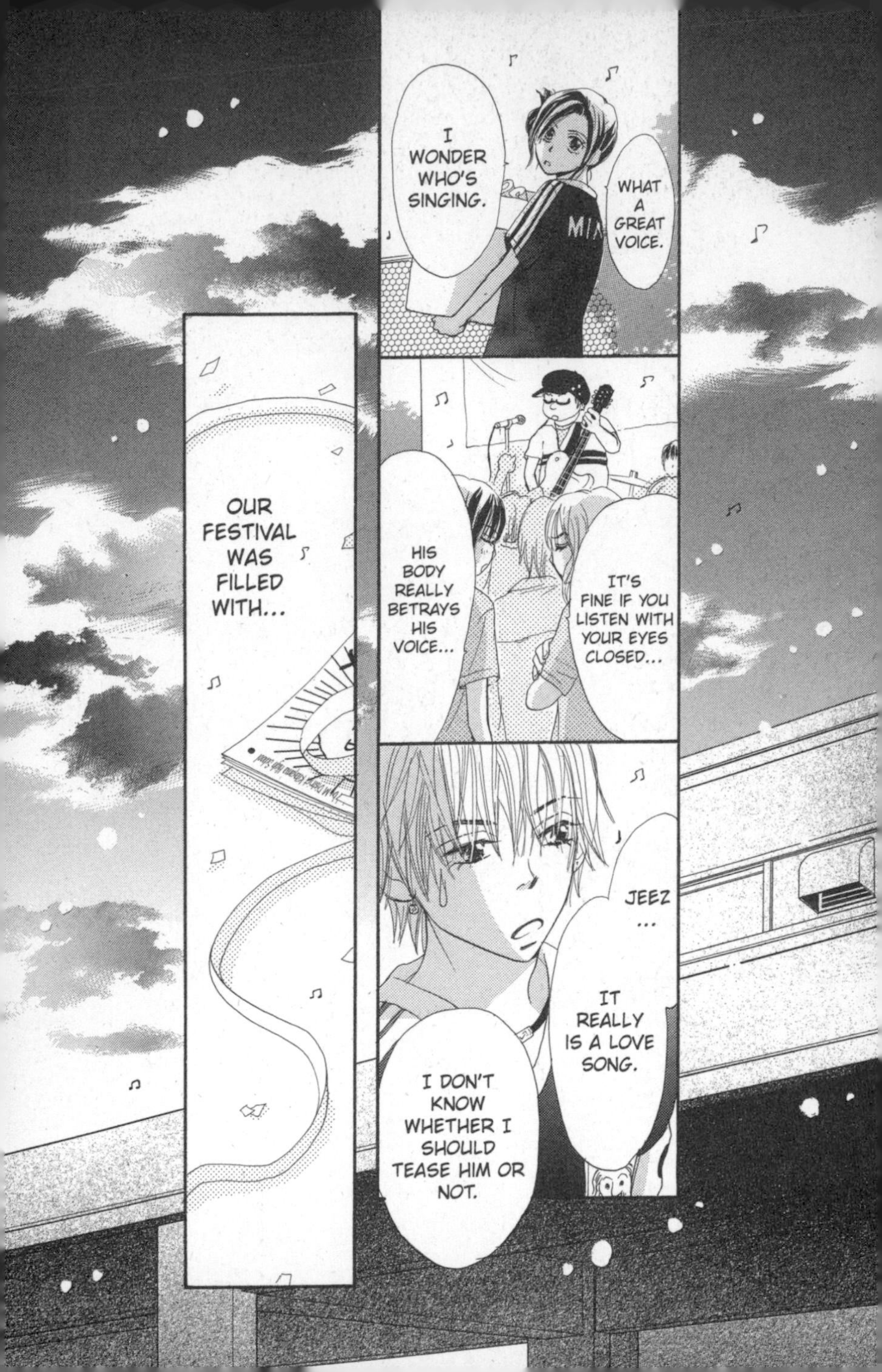
WHAT A GREAT VOICE.
I WONDER WHO'S SINGING.
IT'S FINE IF YOU LISTEN WITH YOUR EYES CLOSED...
HIS BODY REALLY BETRAYS HIS VOICE...
JEEZ...
IT REALLY IS A LOVE SONG.
I DON'T KNOW WHETHER I SHOULD TEASE HIM OR NOT.
OUR FESTIVAL WAS FILLED WITH...

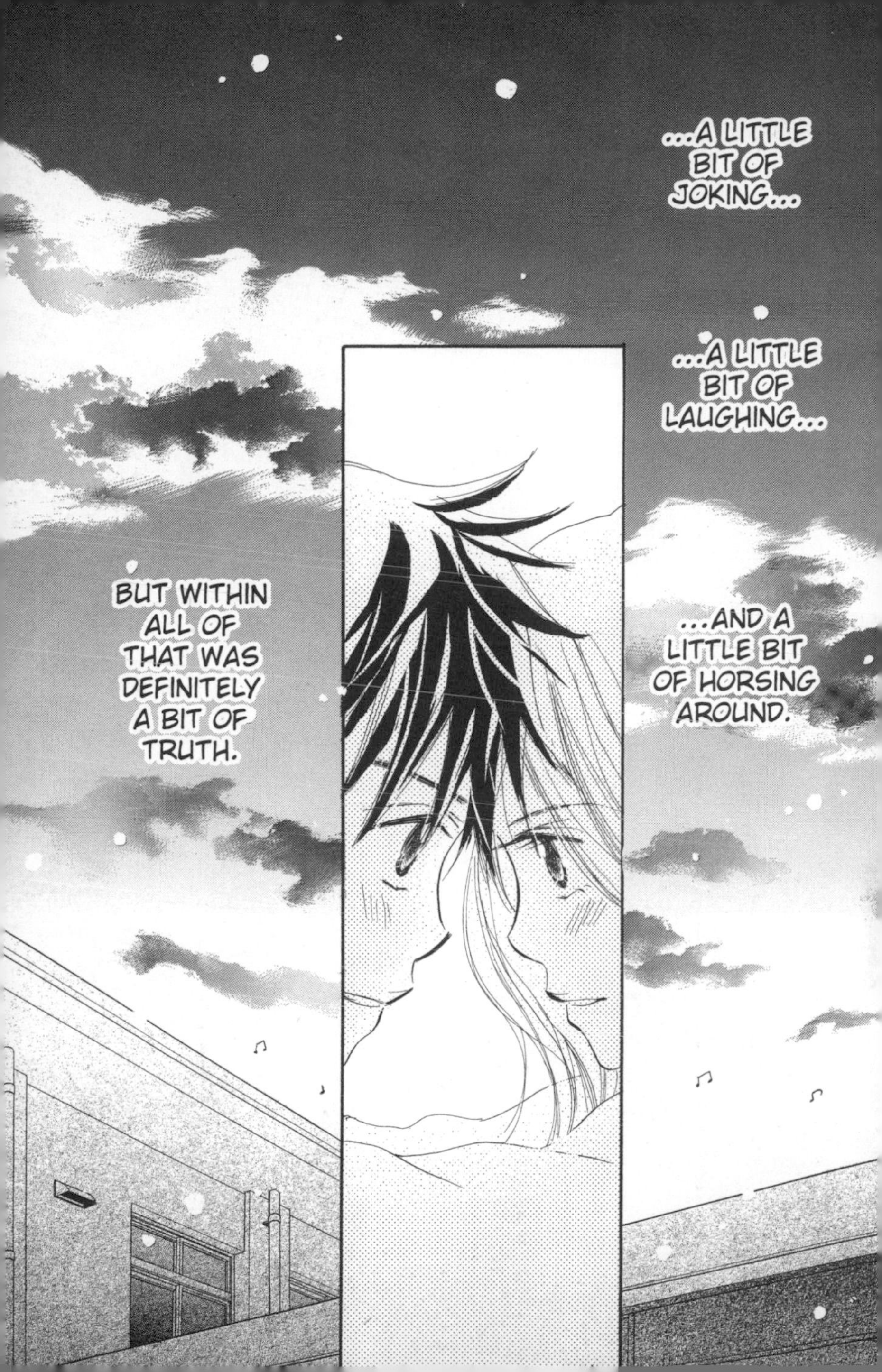
...A LITTLE BIT OF JOKING...
...A LITTLE BIT OF LAUGHING...
...AND A LITTLE BIT OF HORSING AROUND.
BUT WITHIN ALL OF THAT WAS DEFINITELY A BIT OF TRUTH.

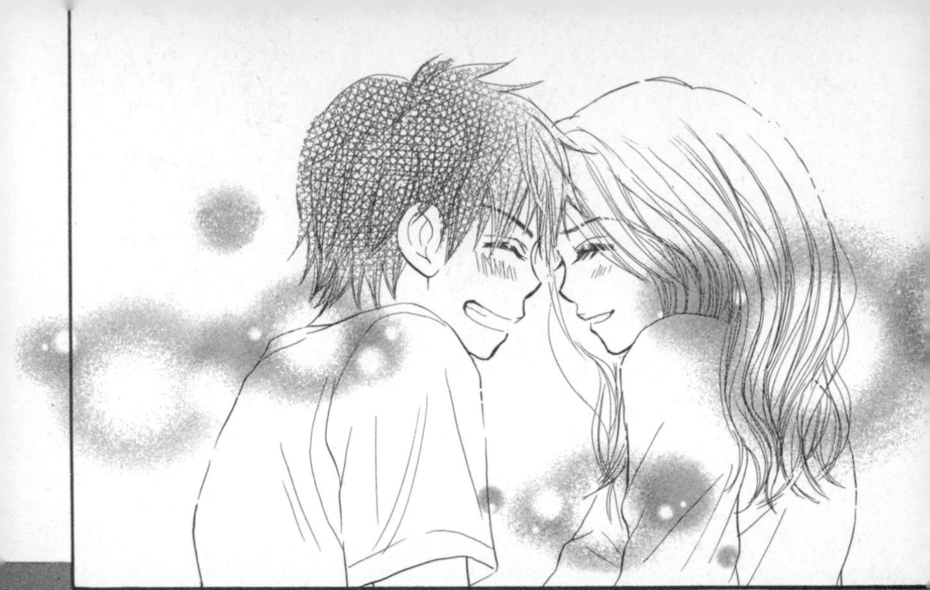

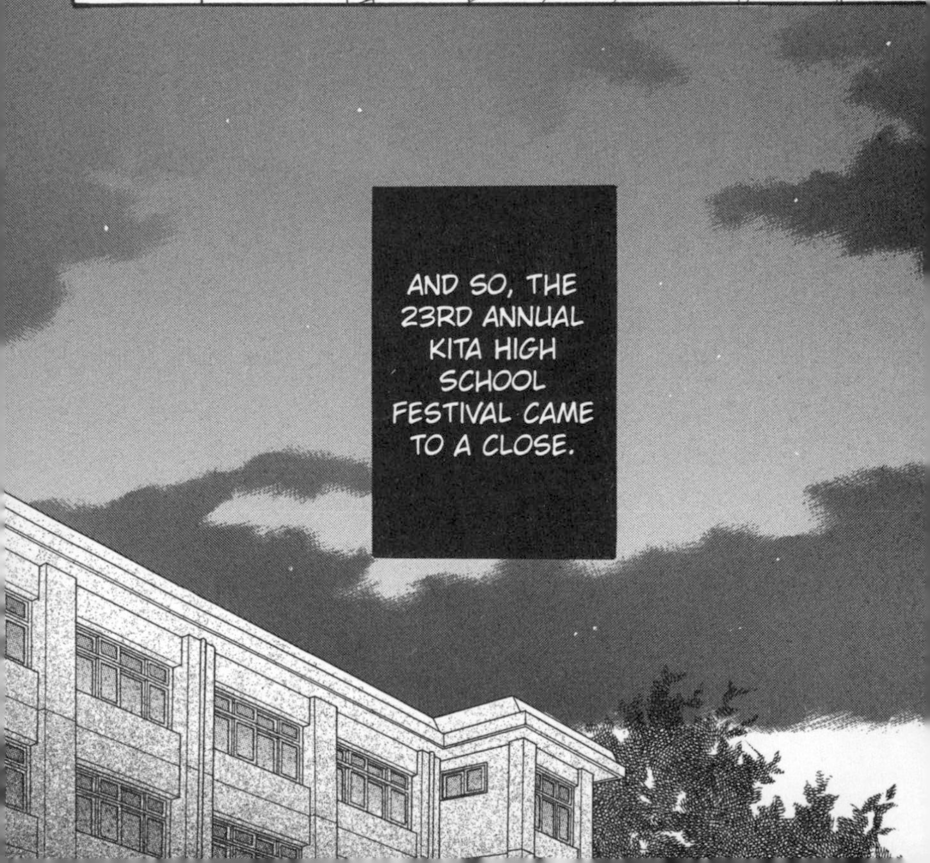
AND SO, THE 23RD ANNUAL KITA HIGH SCHOOL FESTIVAL CAME TO A CLOSE.

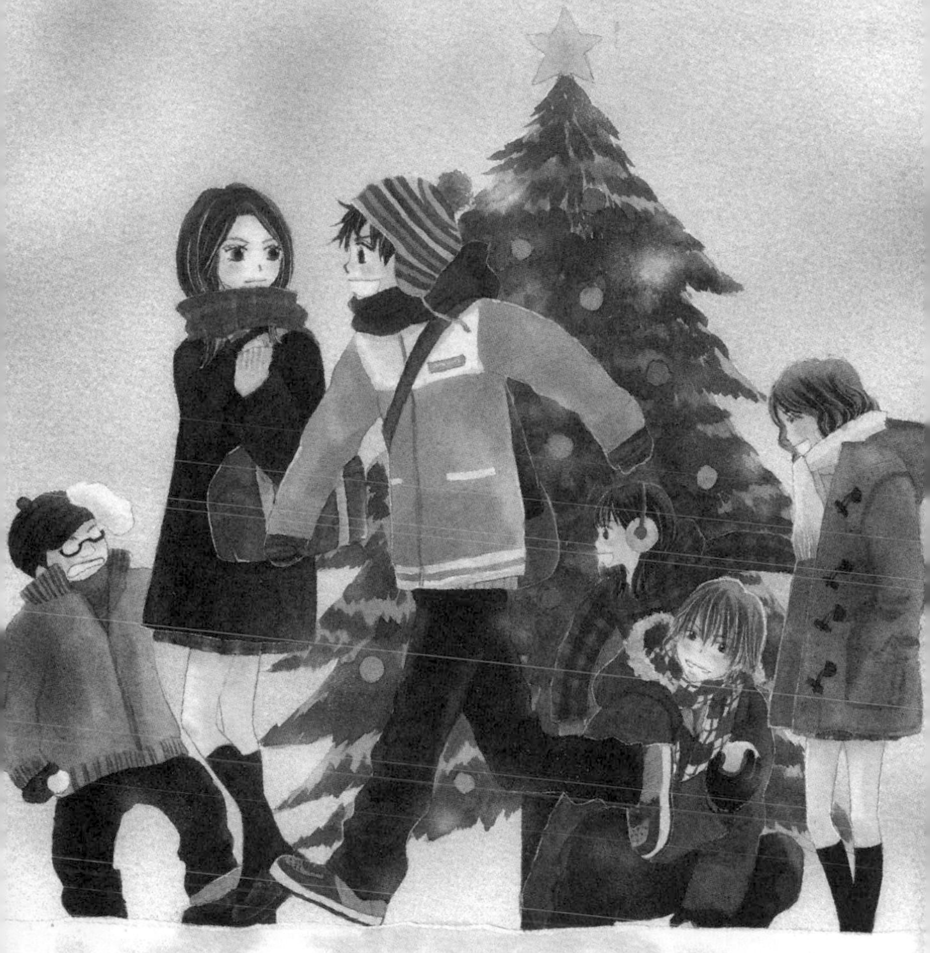

WINTER'S BEGINNING: SECOND YEAR EDITION

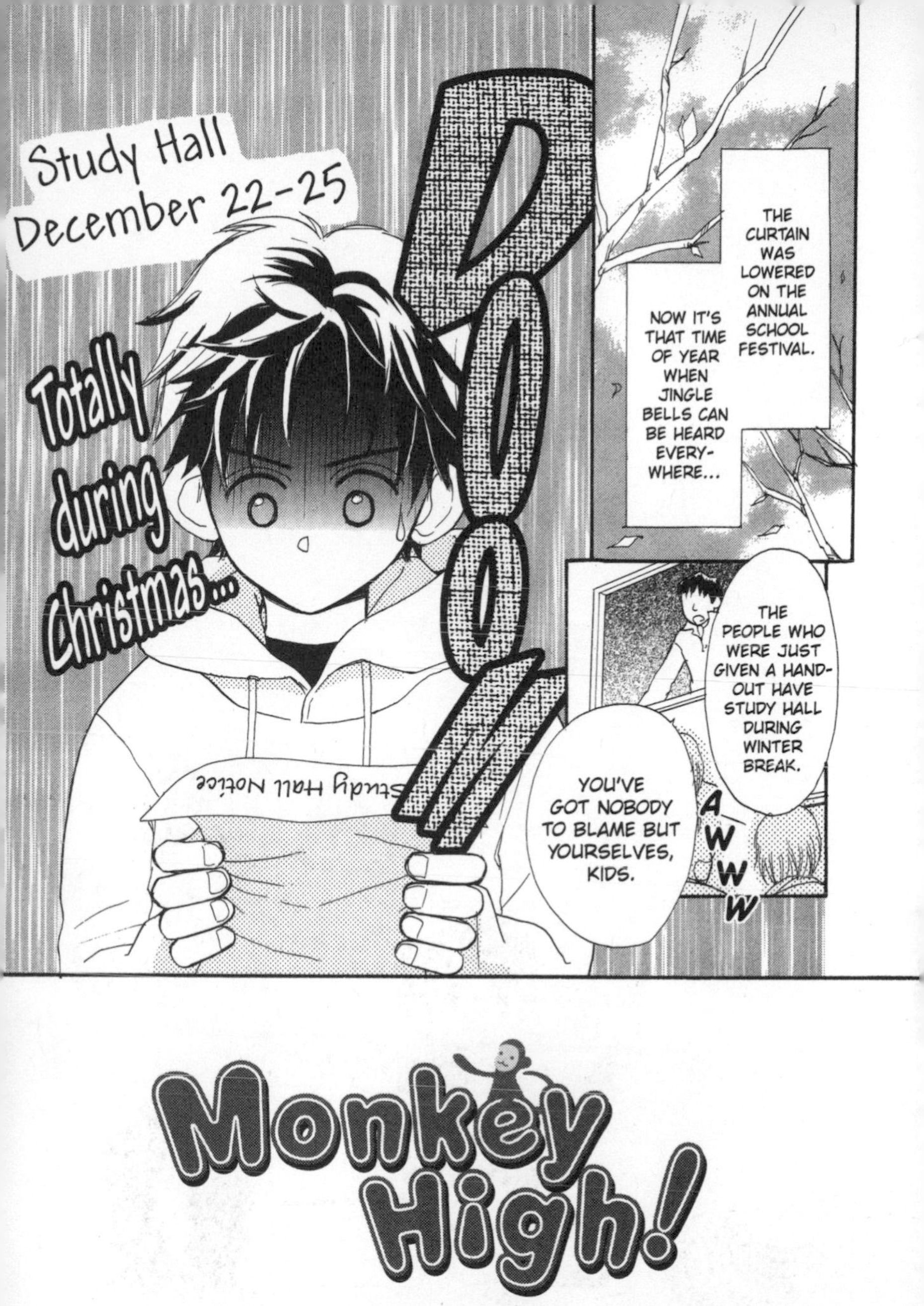
THE CURTAIN WAS LOWERED ON THE ANNUAL SCHOOL FESTIVAL.
NOW IT'S THAT TIME OF YEAR WHEN JINGLE BELLS CAN BE HEARD EVERY-WHERE...
THE PEOPLE WHO WERE JUST GIVEN A HAND-OUT HAVE STUDY HALL DURING WINTER BREAK.
AWWW
YOU'VE GOT NOBODY TO BLAME BUT YOURSELVES, KIDS.
Study Hall Notice
DOOM
Study Hall December 22-25
Totally during Christmas...

Monkey High!

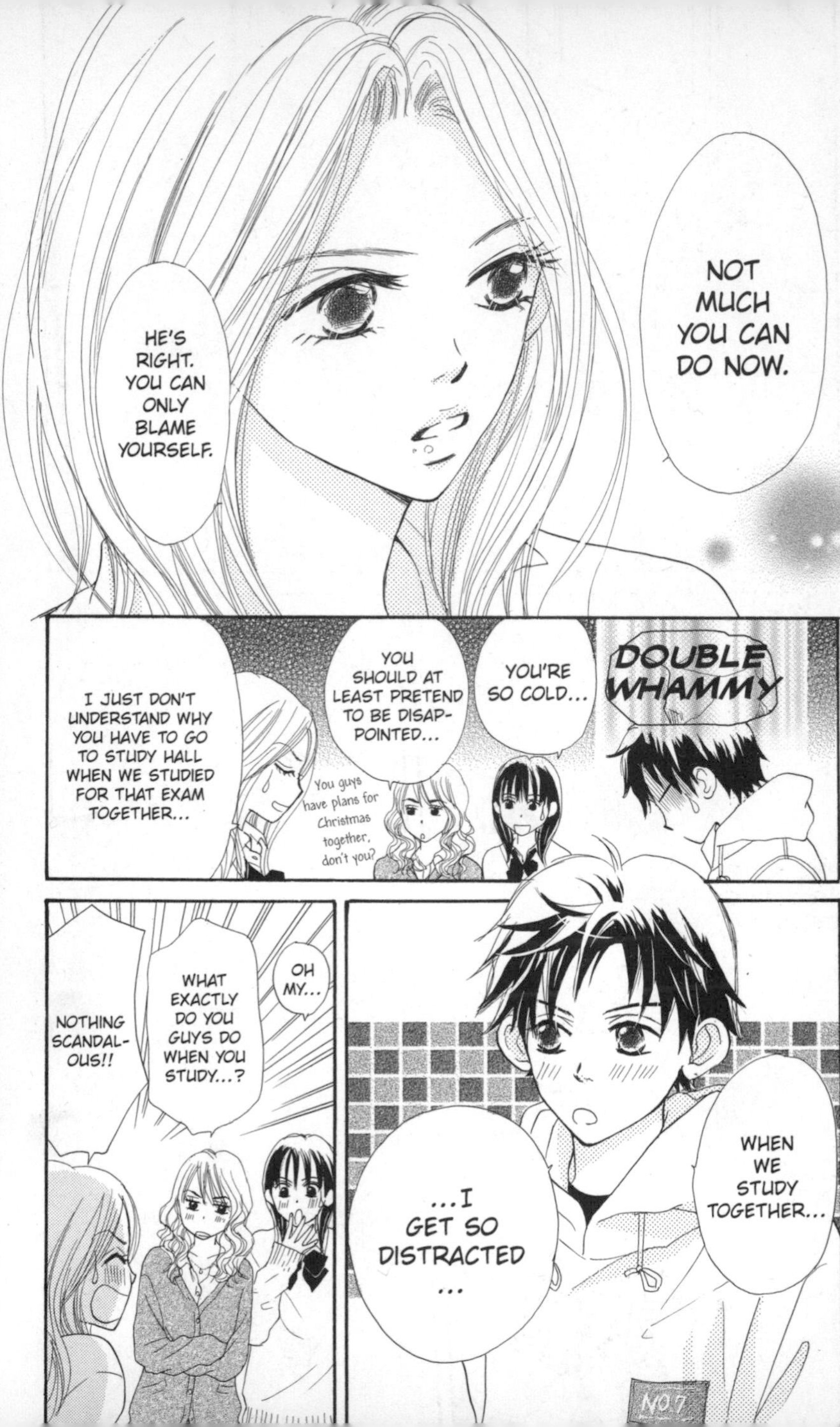
NOT MUCH YOU CAN DO NOW.
HE'S RIGHT. YOU CAN ONLY BLAME YOURSELF.
DOUBLE WHAMMY
YOU'RE SO COLD...
YOU SHOULD AT LEAST PRETEND TO BE DISAP-POINTED...
You guys have plans for Christmas together, don't you?
I JUST DON'T UNDERSTAND WHY YOU HAVE TO GO TO STUDY HALL WHEN WE STUDIED FOR THAT EXAM TOGETHER...
WHEN WE STUDY TOGETHER...
...I GET SO DISTRACTED...
NO 7
OH MY...
WHAT EXACTLY DO YOU GUYS DO WHEN YOU STUDY...?
NOTHING SCANDAL-OUS!!

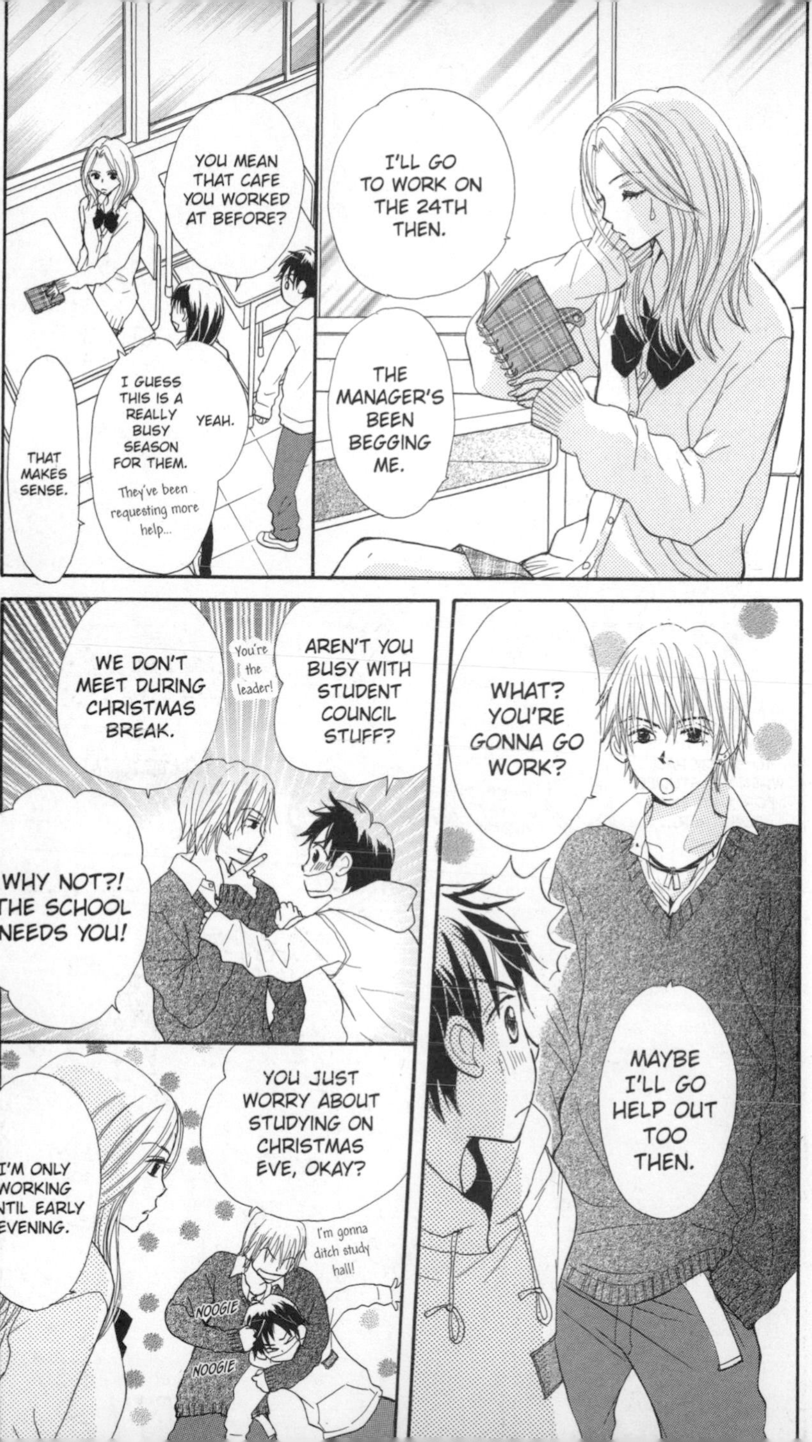
I'LL GO TO WORK ON THE 24TH THEN.
THE MANAGER'S BEEN BEGGING ME.
YOU MEAN THAT CAFE YOU WORKED AT BEFORE?
YEAH.
I GUESS THIS IS A REALLY BUSY SEASON FOR THEM.
They've been requesting more help...
THAT MAKES SENSE.
WHAT? YOU'RE GONNA GO WORK?
MAYBE I'LL GO HELP OUT TOO THEN.
AREN'T YOU BUSY WITH STUDENT COUNCIL STUFF?
You're the leader!
WE DON'T MEET DURING CHRISTMAS BREAK.
WHY NOT?! THE SCHOOL NEEDS YOU!
YOU JUST WORRY ABOUT STUDYING ON CHRISTMAS EVE, OKAY?
I'm gonna ditch study hall!
NOOGIE
NOOGIE
I'M ONLY WORKING UNTIL EARLY EVENING.

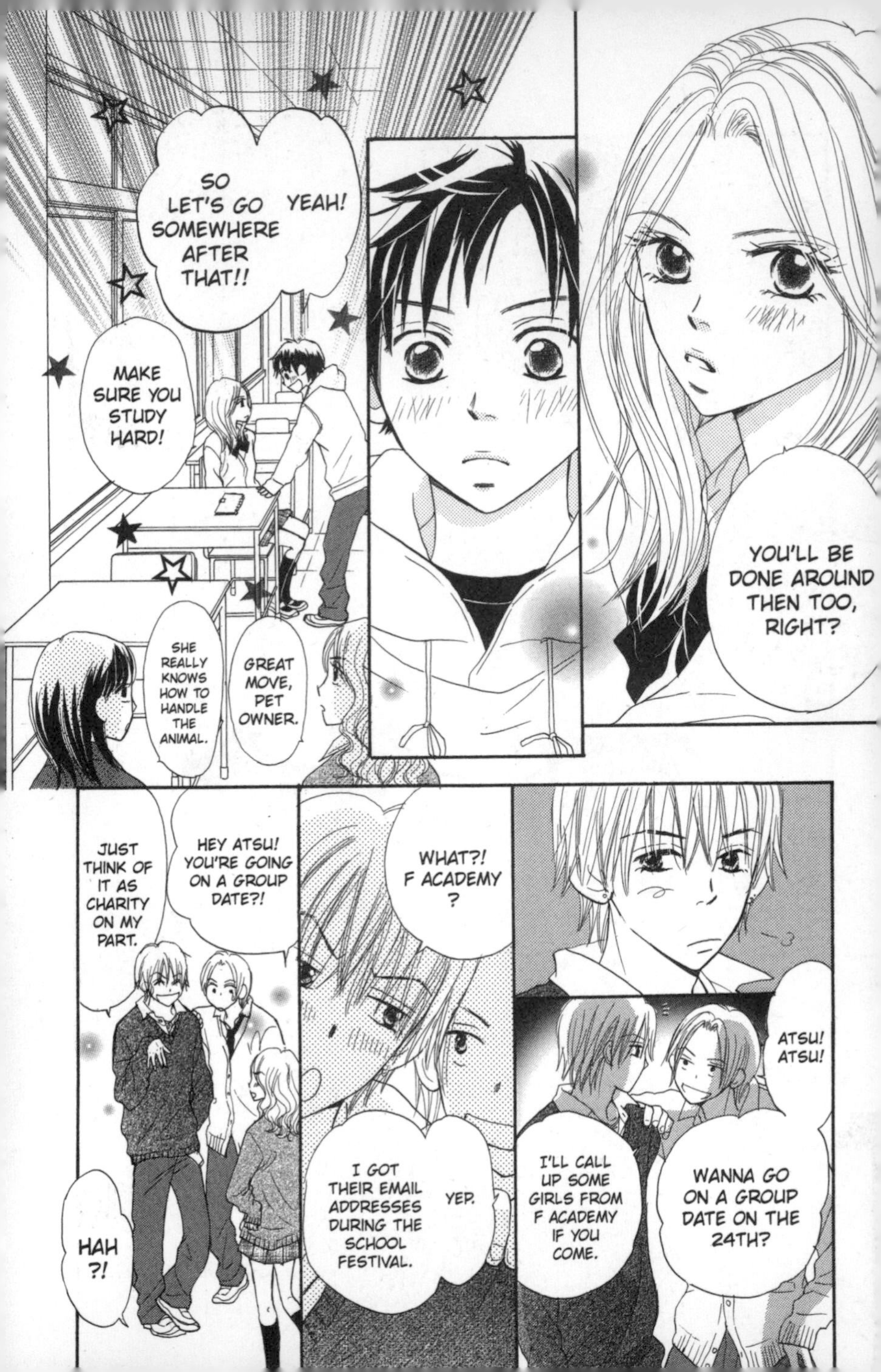
YOU'LL BE DONE AROUND THEN TOO, RIGHT?
SO LET'S GO SOMEWHERE AFTER THAT!!
YEAH!
MAKE SURE YOU STUDY HARD!
GREAT MOVE, PET OWNER.
SHE REALLY KNOWS HOW TO HANDLE THE ANIMAL.
ATSU! ATSU!
WANNA GO ON A GROUP DATE ON THE 24TH?
I'LL CALL UP SOME GIRLS FROM F ACADEMY IF YOU COME.
WHAT?! F ACADEMY ?
YEP.
I GOT THEIR EMAIL ADDRESSES DURING THE SCHOOL FESTIVAL.
HEY ATSU! YOU'RE GOING ON A GROUP DATE?!
JUST THINK OF IT AS CHARITY ON MY PART.
HAH ?!

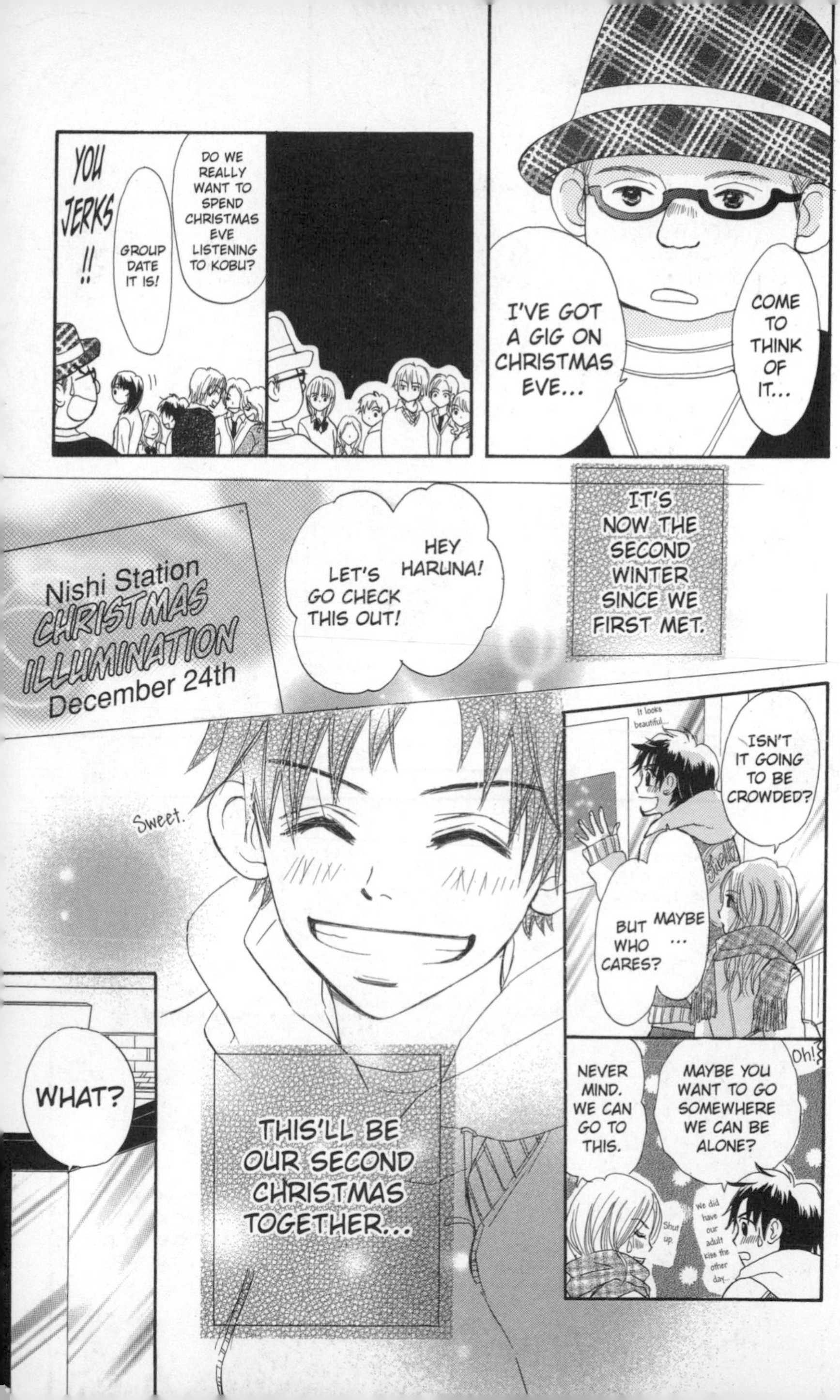
COME TO THINK OF IT...
I'VE GOT A GIG ON CHRISTMAS EVE...
DO WE REALLY WANT TO SPEND CHRISTMAS EVE LISTENING TO KOBU?
GROUP DATE IT IS!
YOU JERKS!!
IT'S NOW THE SECOND WINTER SINCE WE FIRST MET.
HEY HARUNA!
LET'S GO CHECK THIS OUT!
Nishi Station
CHRISTMAS ILLUMINATION
December 24th
It looks beautiful...
ISN'T IT GOING TO BE CROWDED?
MAYBE...
BUT WHO CARES?
Oh!
MAYBE YOU WANT TO GO SOMEWHERE WE CAN BE ALONE?
NEVER MIND. WE CAN GO TO THIS.
We did have our adult kiss the other day...
Shut up.
Sweet.
THIS'LL BE OUR SECOND CHRISTMAS TOGETHER...
WHAT?

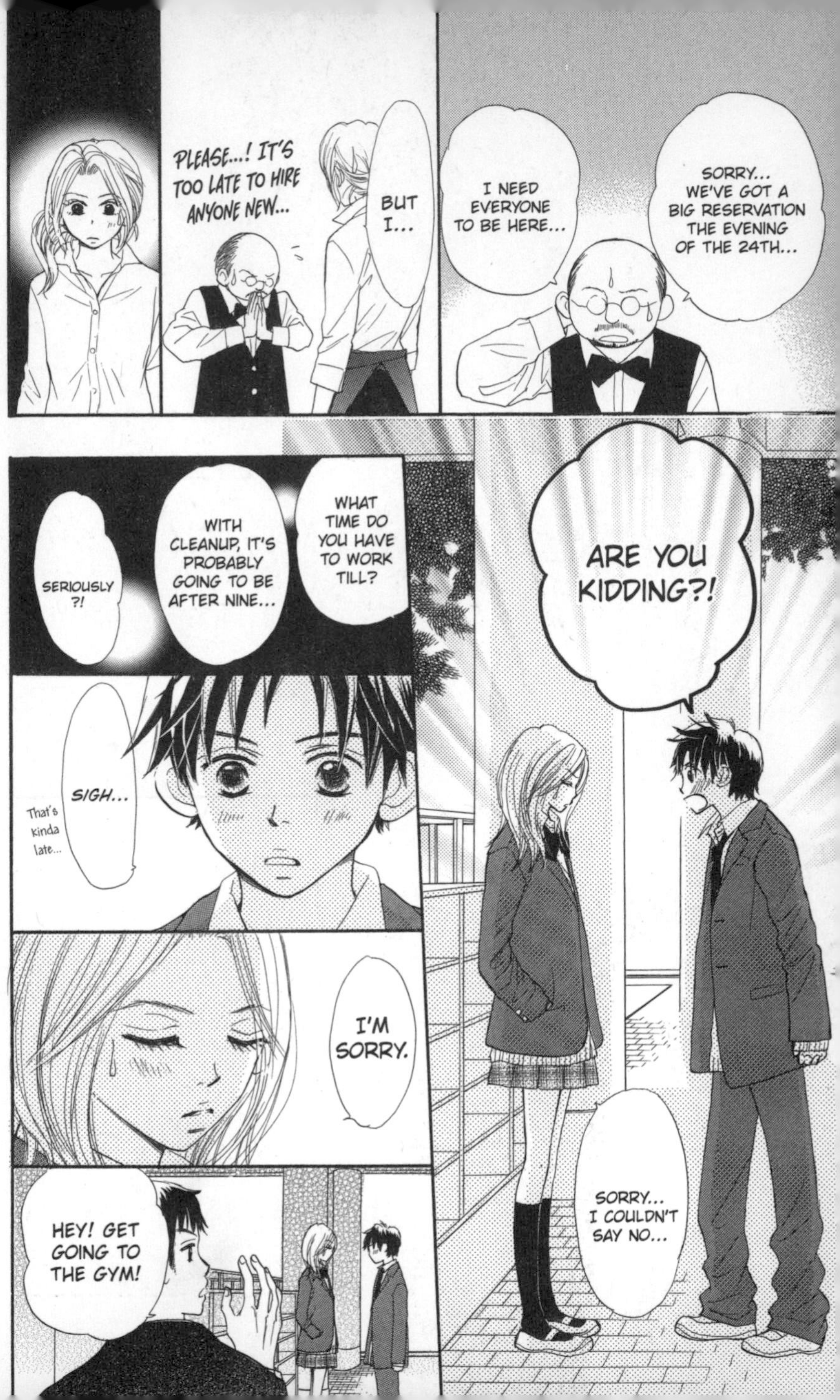

SORRY... WE'VE GOT A BIG RESERVATION THE EVENING OF THE 24TH...
I NEED EVERYONE TO BE HERE...
BUT I...
PLEASE...! IT'S TOO LATE TO HIRE ANYONE NEW...
ARE YOU KIDDING?!
SORRY... I COULDN'T SAY NO...
WHAT TIME DO YOU HAVE TO WORK TILL?
WITH CLEANUP, IT'S PROBABLY GOING TO BE AFTER NINE...
SERIOUSLY?!
SIGH...
That's kinda late...
I'M SORRY.
HEY! GET GOING TO THE GYM!

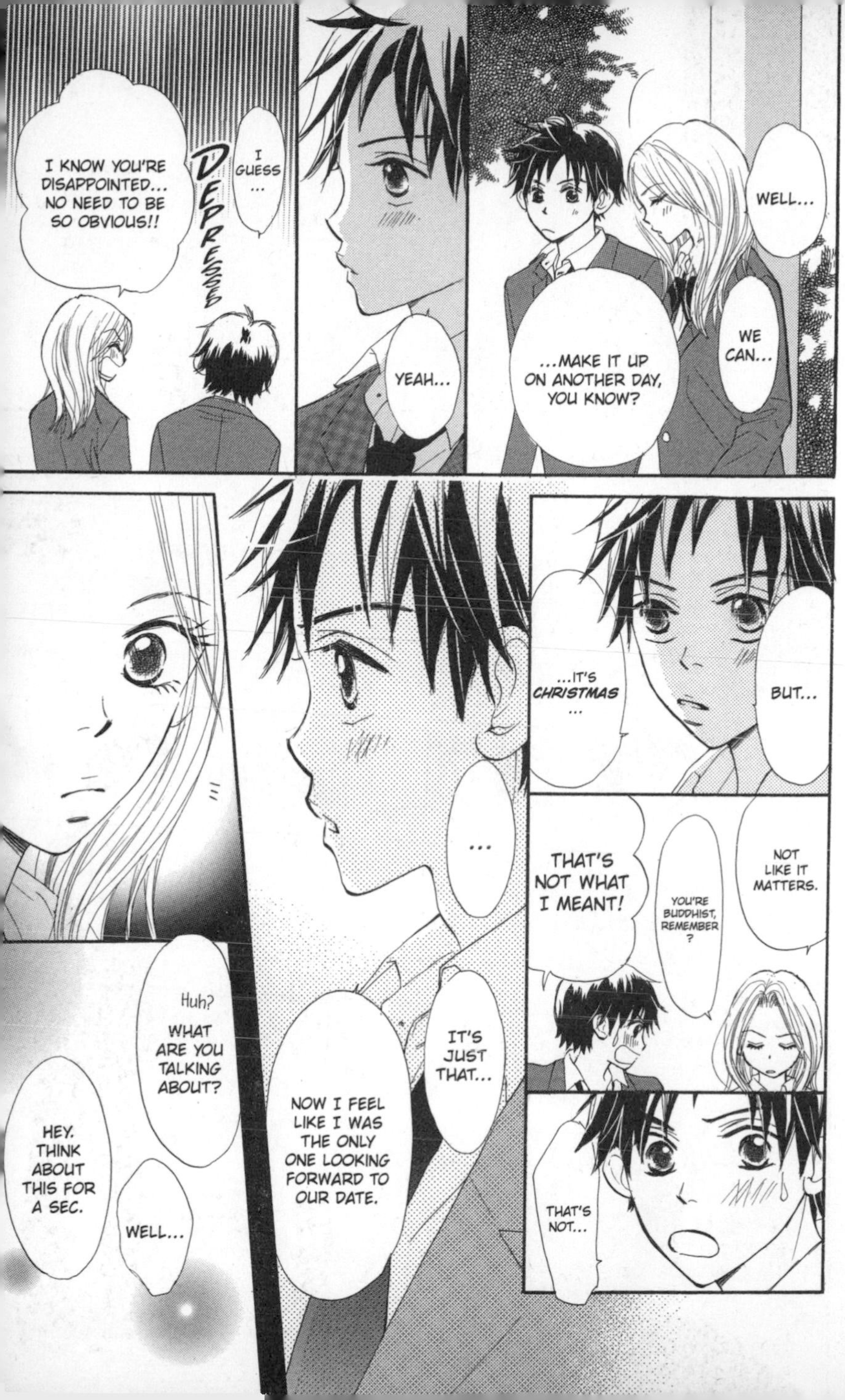
WELL...
WE CAN...
...MAKE IT UP ON ANOTHER DAY, YOU KNOW?
YEAH...
I GUESS...
DEPRESS
I KNOW YOU'RE DISAPPOINTED... NO NEED TO BE SO OBVIOUS!!
BUT...
...IT'S CHRISTMAS...
NOT LIKE IT MATTERS.
YOU'RE BUDDHIST, REMEMBER?
THAT'S NOT WHAT I MEANT!
THAT'S NOT...
...
IT'S JUST THAT...
NOW I FEEL LIKE I WAS THE ONLY ONE LOOKING FORWARD TO OUR DATE.
Huh? WHAT ARE YOU TALKING ABOUT?
WELL...
HEY. THINK ABOUT THIS FOR A SEC.

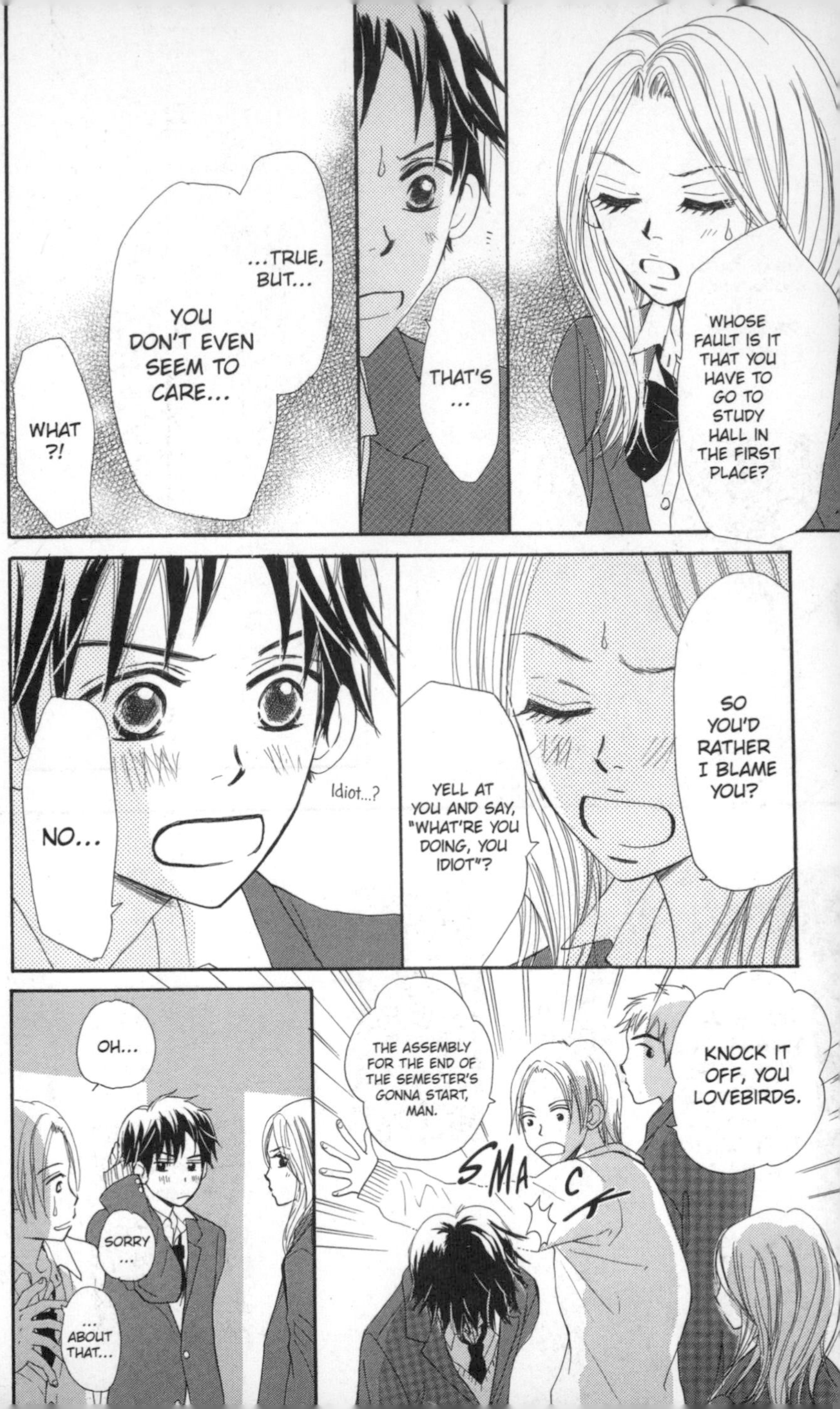
WHOSE FAULT IS IT THAT YOU HAVE TO GO TO STUDY HALL IN THE FIRST PLACE?
THAT'S ...
...TRUE, BUT...
YOU DON'T EVEN SEEM TO CARE...
WHAT ?!
SO YOU'D RATHER I BLAME YOU?
YELL AT YOU AND SAY, "WHAT'RE YOU DOING, YOU IDIOT"?
Idiot...?
NO...
KNOCK IT OFF, YOU LOVEBIRDS.
THE ASSEMBLY FOR THE END OF THE SEMESTER'S GONNA START, MAN.
SMACK
OH...
SORRY ...
... ABOUT THAT...

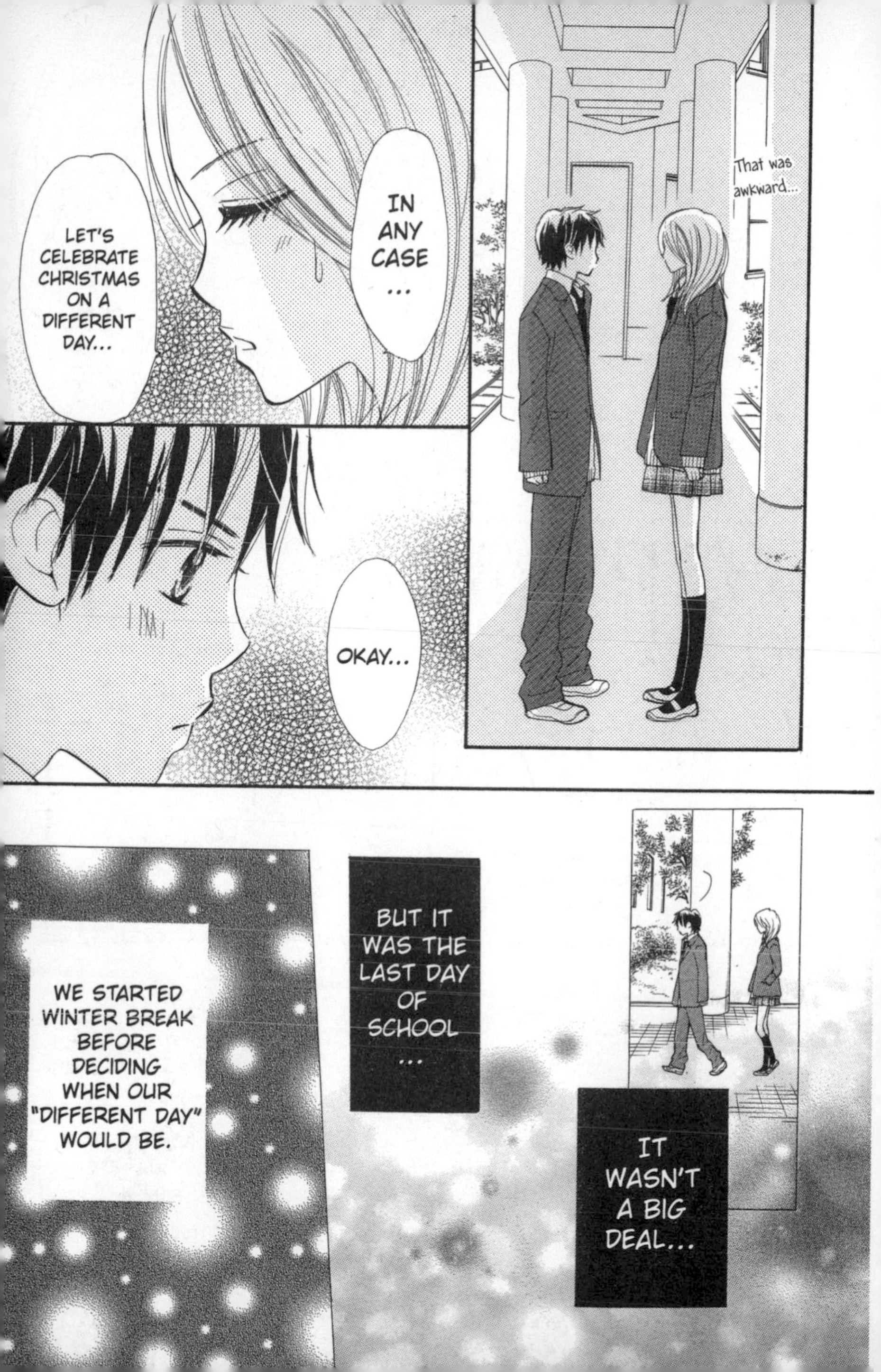

That was awkward...
IN ANY CASE...
LET'S CELEBRATE CHRISTMAS ON A DIFFERENT DAY...
OKAY...
BUT IT WAS THE LAST DAY OF SCHOOL...
IT WASN'T A BIG DEAL...
WE STARTED WINTER BREAK BEFORE DECIDING WHEN OUR "DIFFERENT DAY" WOULD BE.

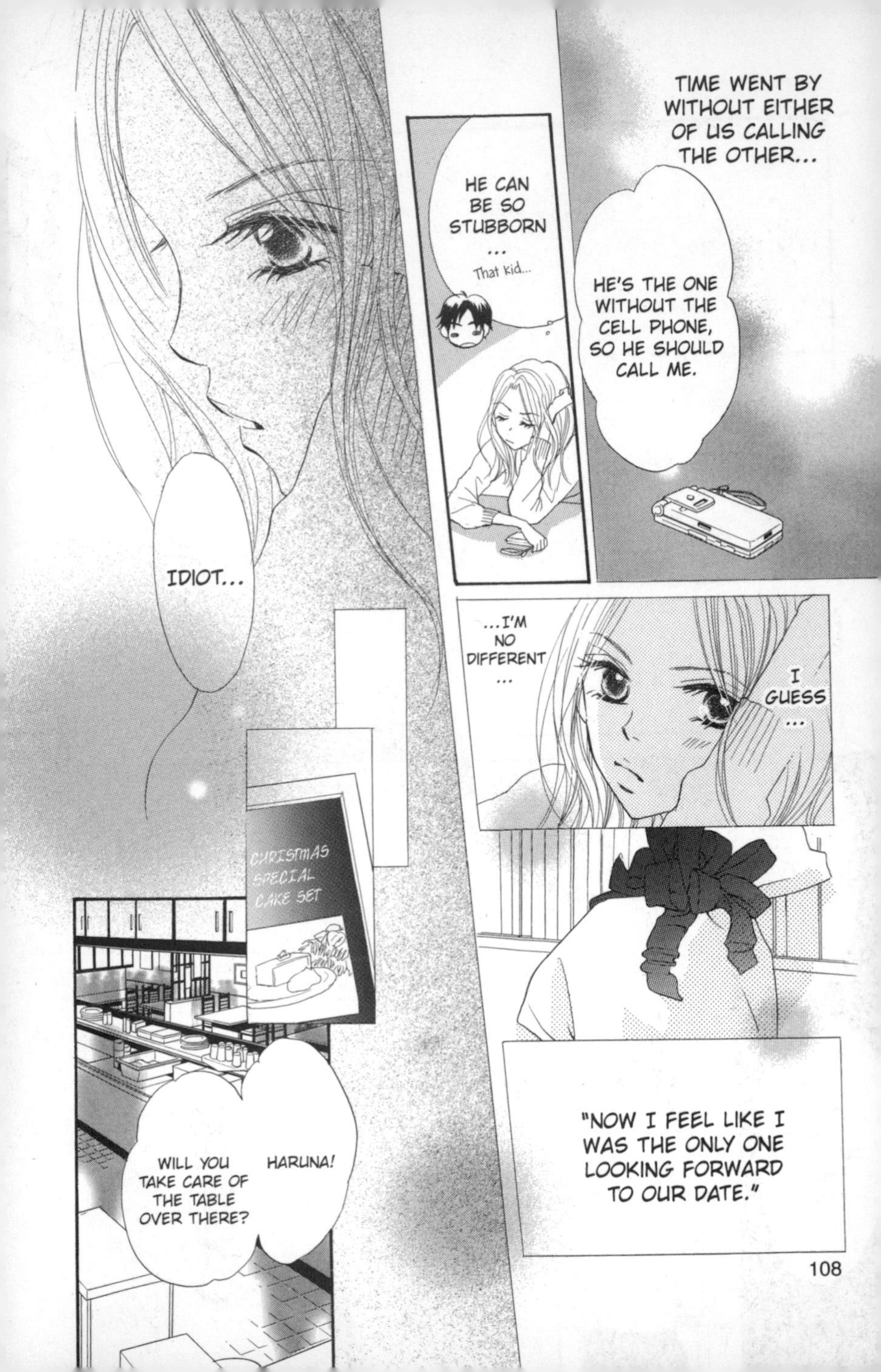
TIME WENT BY WITHOUT EITHER OF US CALLING THE OTHER...
HE'S THE ONE WITHOUT THE CELL PHONE, SO HE SHOULD CALL ME.
HE CAN BE SO STUBBORN ...
That kid...
IDIOT...
...I'M NO DIFFERENT ...
I GUESS ...
"NOW I FEEL LIKE I WAS THE ONLY ONE LOOKING FORWARD TO OUR DATE."
CHRISTMAS SPECIAL CAKE SET
HARUNA!
WILL YOU TAKE CARE OF THE TABLE OVER THERE?

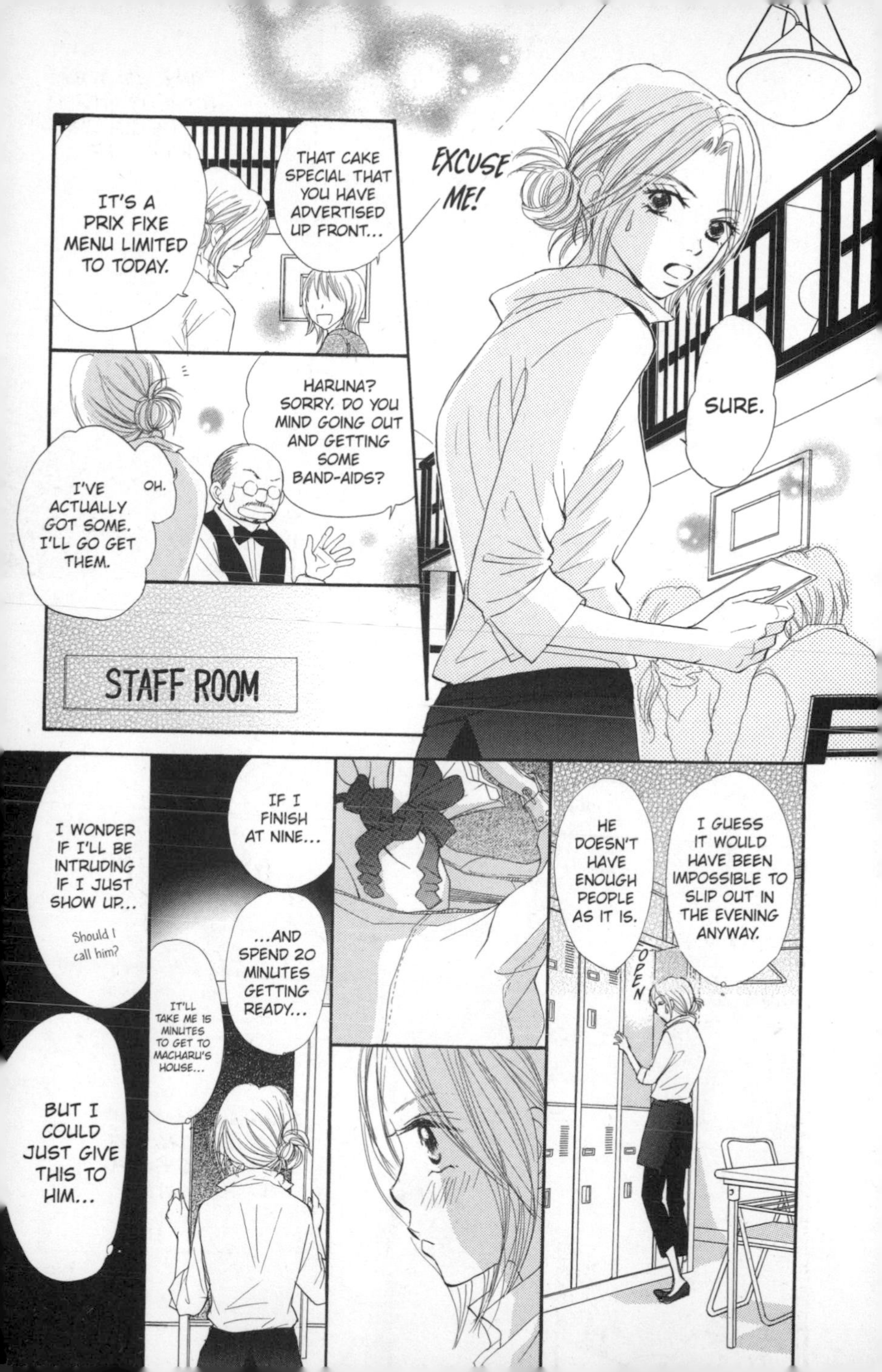
EXCUSE ME!
SURE.
THAT CAKE SPECIAL THAT YOU HAVE ADVERTISED UP FRONT...
IT'S A PRIX FIXE MENU LIMITED TO TODAY.
HARUNA? SORRY. DO YOU MIND GOING OUT AND GETTING SOME BAND-AIDS?
OH.
I'VE ACTUALLY GOT SOME. I'LL GO GET THEM.
STAFF ROOM
I GUESS IT WOULD HAVE BEEN IMPOSSIBLE TO SLIP OUT IN THE EVENING ANYWAY.
HE DOESN'T HAVE ENOUGH PEOPLE AS IT IS.
OPEN
IF I FINISH AT NINE...
...AND SPEND 20 MINUTES GETTING READY...
IT'LL TAKE ME 15 MINUTES TO GET TO MACHARU'S HOUSE...
I WONDER IF I'LL BE INTRUDING IF I JUST SHOW UP...
Should I call him?
BUT I COULD JUST GIVE THIS TO HIM...

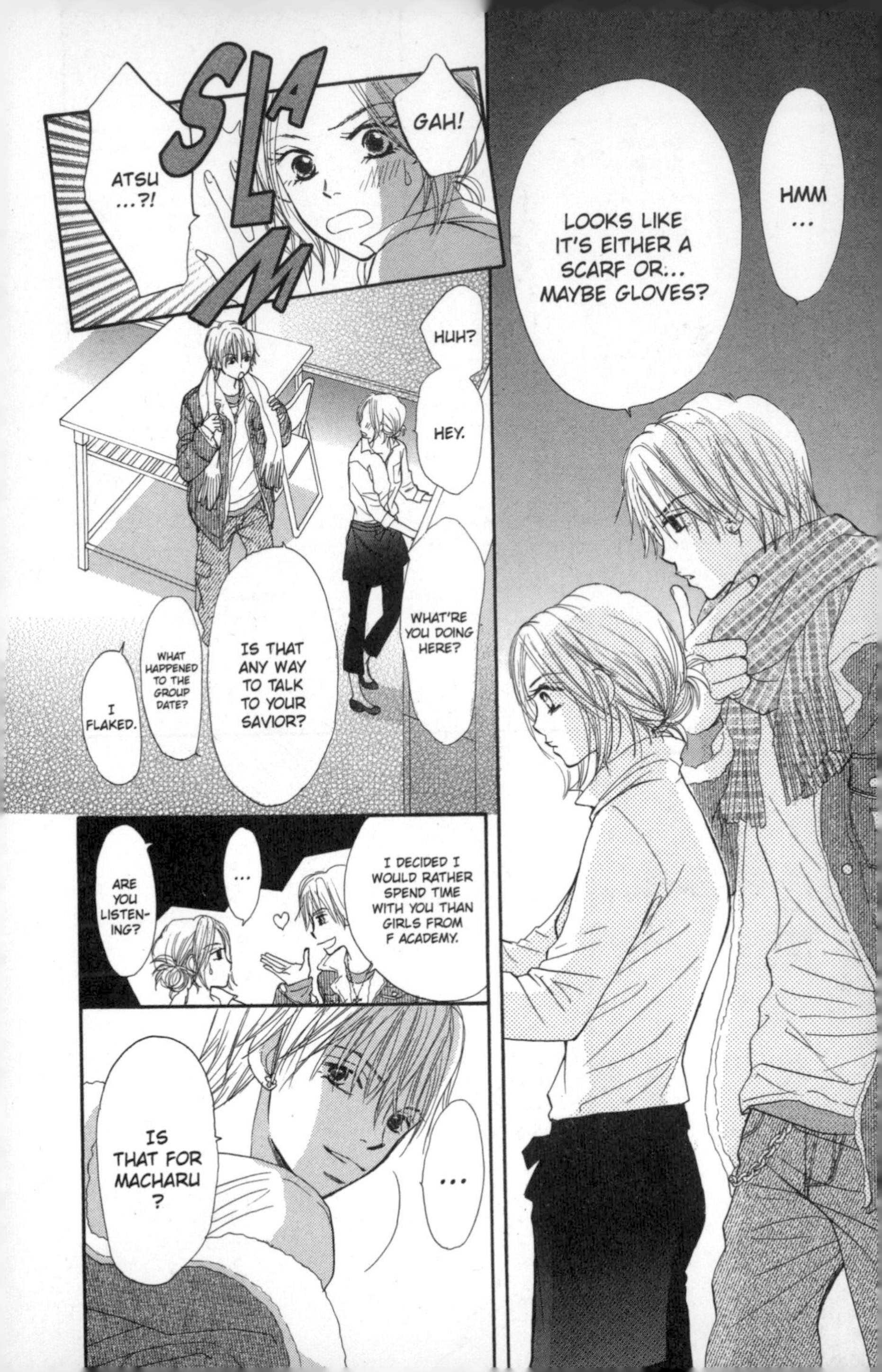
HMM ...
LOOKS LIKE IT'S EITHER A SCARF OR... MAYBE GLOVES?
GAH!
SLAM
ATSU ...?!
HUH?
HEY.
WHAT'RE YOU DOING HERE?
IS THAT ANY WAY TO TALK TO YOUR SAVIOR?
WHAT HAPPENED TO THE GROUP DATE?
I FLAKED.
I DECIDED I WOULD RATHER SPEND TIME WITH YOU THAN GIRLS FROM F ACADEMY.
...
ARE YOU LISTENING?
...
IS THAT FOR MACHARU ?

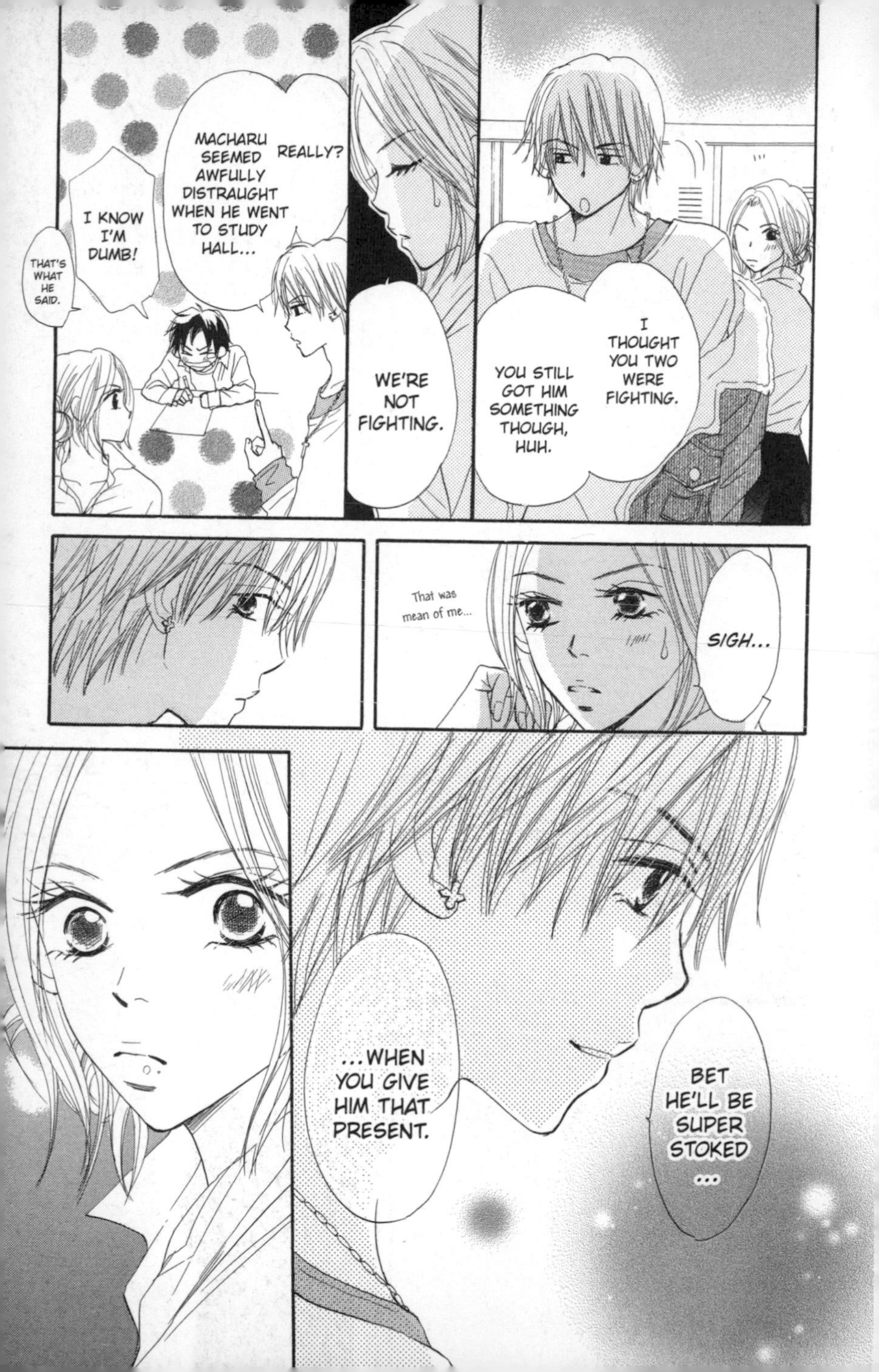
I THOUGHT YOU TWO WERE FIGHTING.
YOU STILL GOT HIM SOMETHING THOUGH, HUH.
WE'RE NOT FIGHTING.
MACHARU SEEMED AWFULLY DISTRAUGHT WHEN HE WENT TO STUDY HALL...
REALLY?
I KNOW I'M DUMB!
THAT'S WHAT HE SAID.
SIGH...
That was mean of me...
BET HE'LL BE SUPER STOKED...
...WHEN YOU GIVE HIM THAT PRESENT.

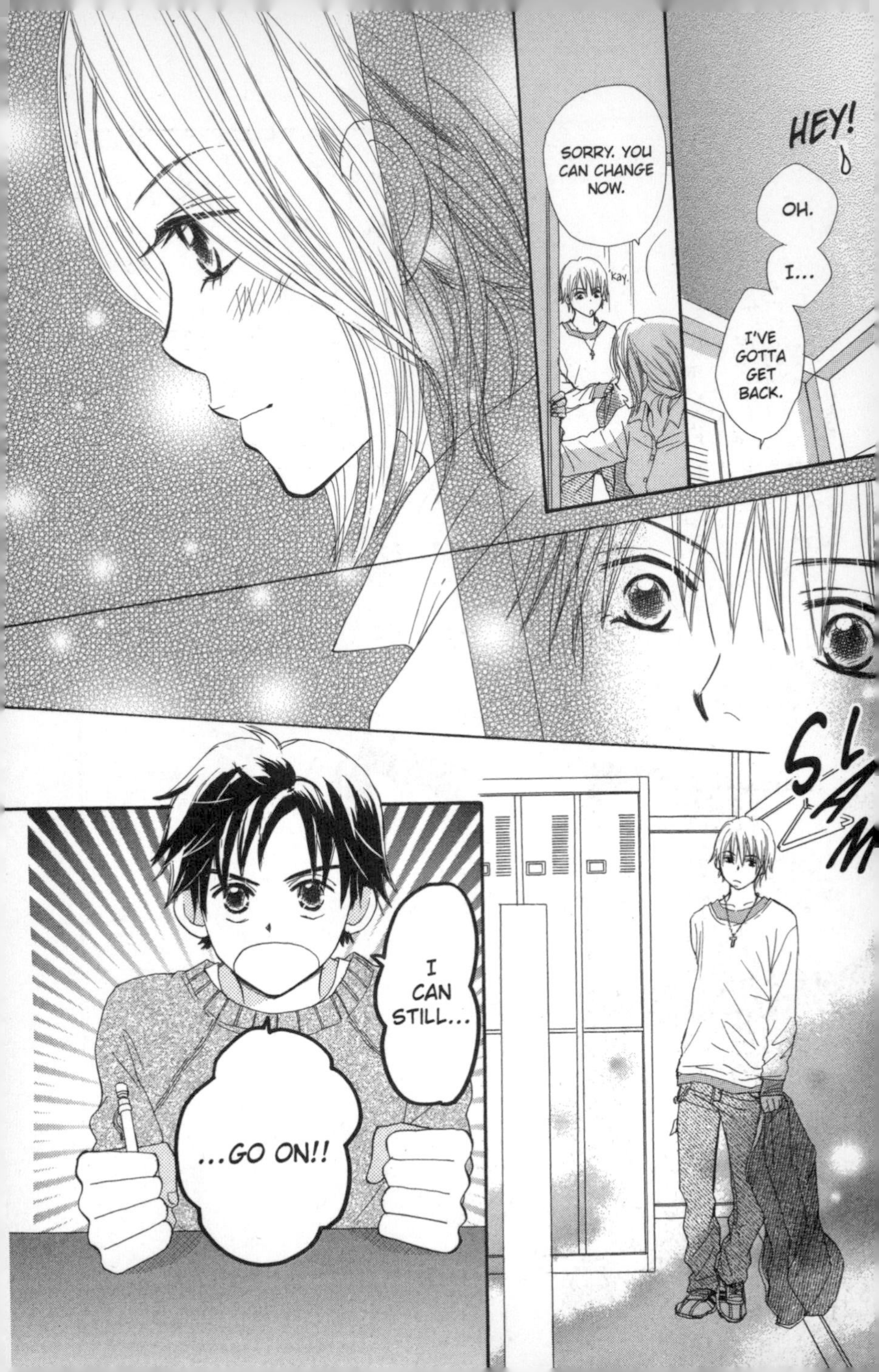
HEY!
OH.
I...
I'VE GOTTA GET BACK.
SORRY. YOU CAN CHANGE NOW.
'kay.
SLAM
I CAN STILL...
...GO ON!!

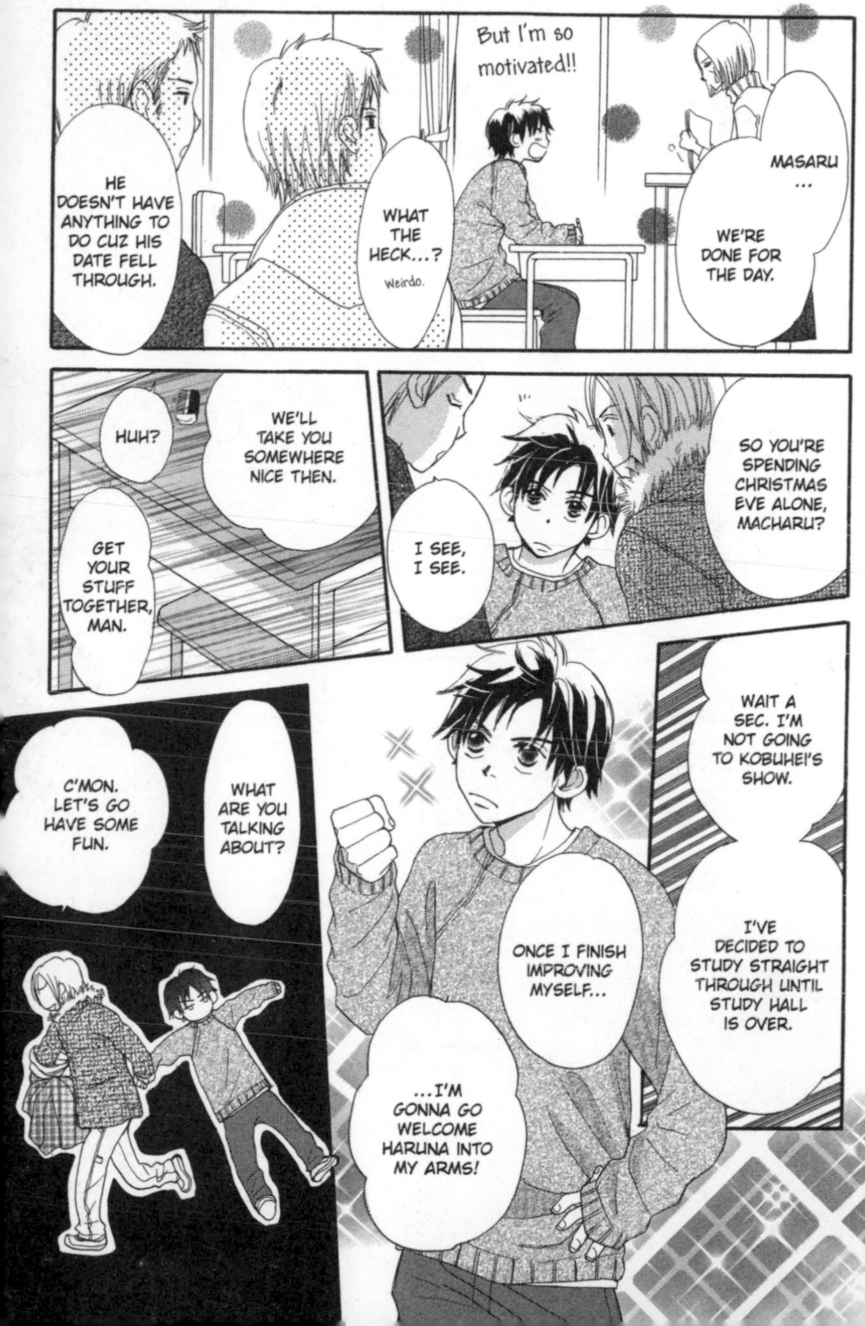
MASARU ...
WE'RE DONE FOR THE DAY.
But I'm so motivated!!
WHAT THE HECK...?
Weirdo.
HE DOESN'T HAVE ANYTHING TO DO CUZ HIS DATE FELL THROUGH.
SO YOU'RE SPENDING CHRISTMAS EVE ALONE, MACHARU?
I SEE, I SEE.
WE'LL TAKE YOU SOMEWHERE NICE THEN.
HUH?
GET YOUR STUFF TOGETHER, MAN.
WAIT A SEC. I'M NOT GOING TO KOBUHEI'S SHOW.
I'VE DECIDED TO STUDY STRAIGHT THROUGH UNTIL STUDY HALL IS OVER.
ONCE I FINISH IMPROVING MYSELF...
...I'M GONNA GO WELCOME HARUNA INTO MY ARMS!
WHAT ARE YOU TALKING ABOUT?
C'MON. LET'S GO HAVE SOME FUN.

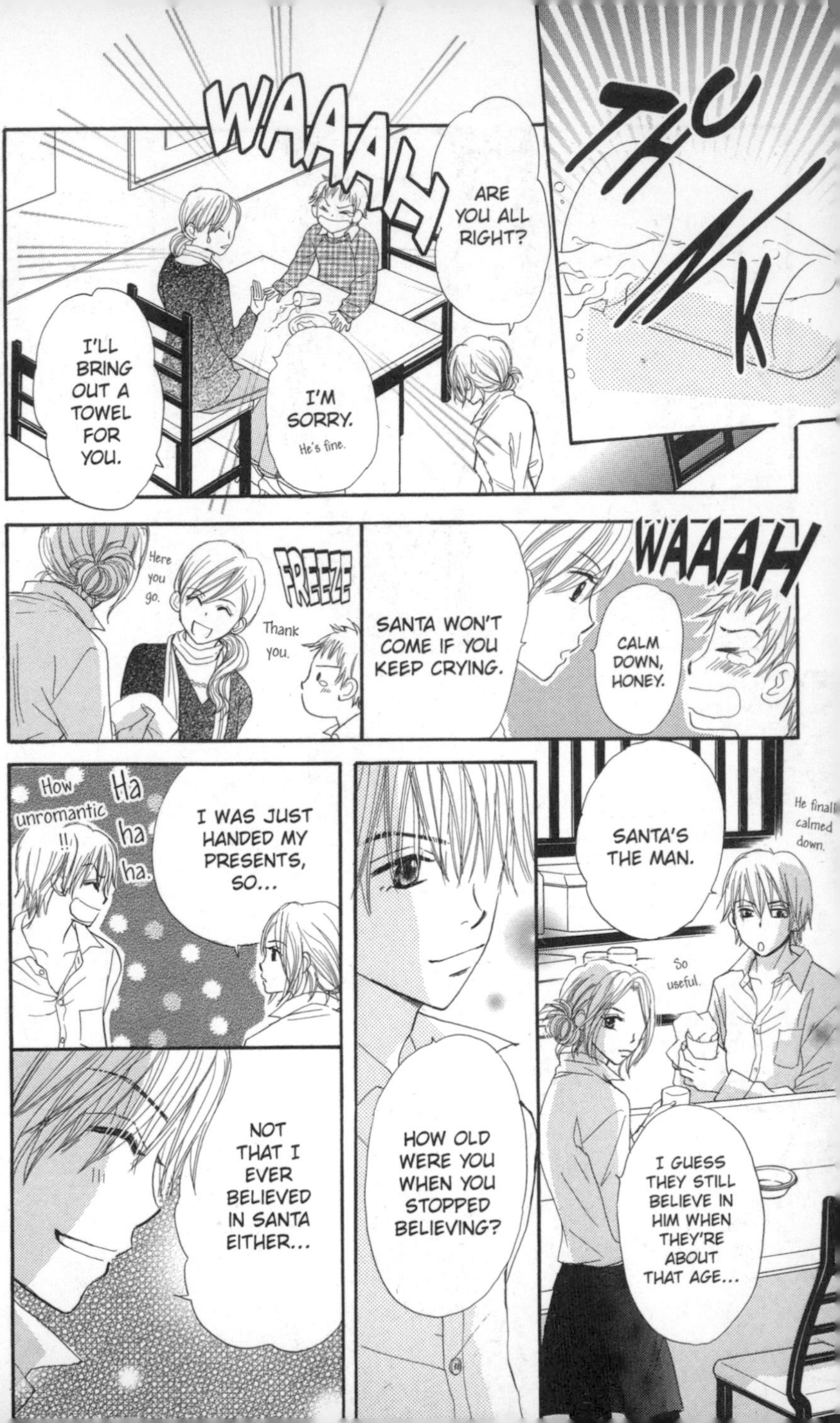
THUNK
WAAAH
ARE YOU ALL RIGHT?
I'M SORRY.
He's fine.
I'LL BRING OUT A TOWEL FOR YOU.
WAAAH
CALM DOWN, HONEY.
SANTA WON'T COME IF YOU KEEP CRYING.
FREEZE
Thank you.
Here you go.
He finall calmed down.
SANTA'S THE MAN.
So useful.
I GUESS THEY STILL BELIEVE IN HIM WHEN THEY'RE ABOUT THAT AGE...
HOW OLD WERE YOU WHEN YOU STOPPED BELIEVING?
I WAS JUST HANDED MY PRESENTS, SO...
Ha ha ha.
How unromantic !!
NOT THAT I EVER BELIEVED IN SANTA EITHER...

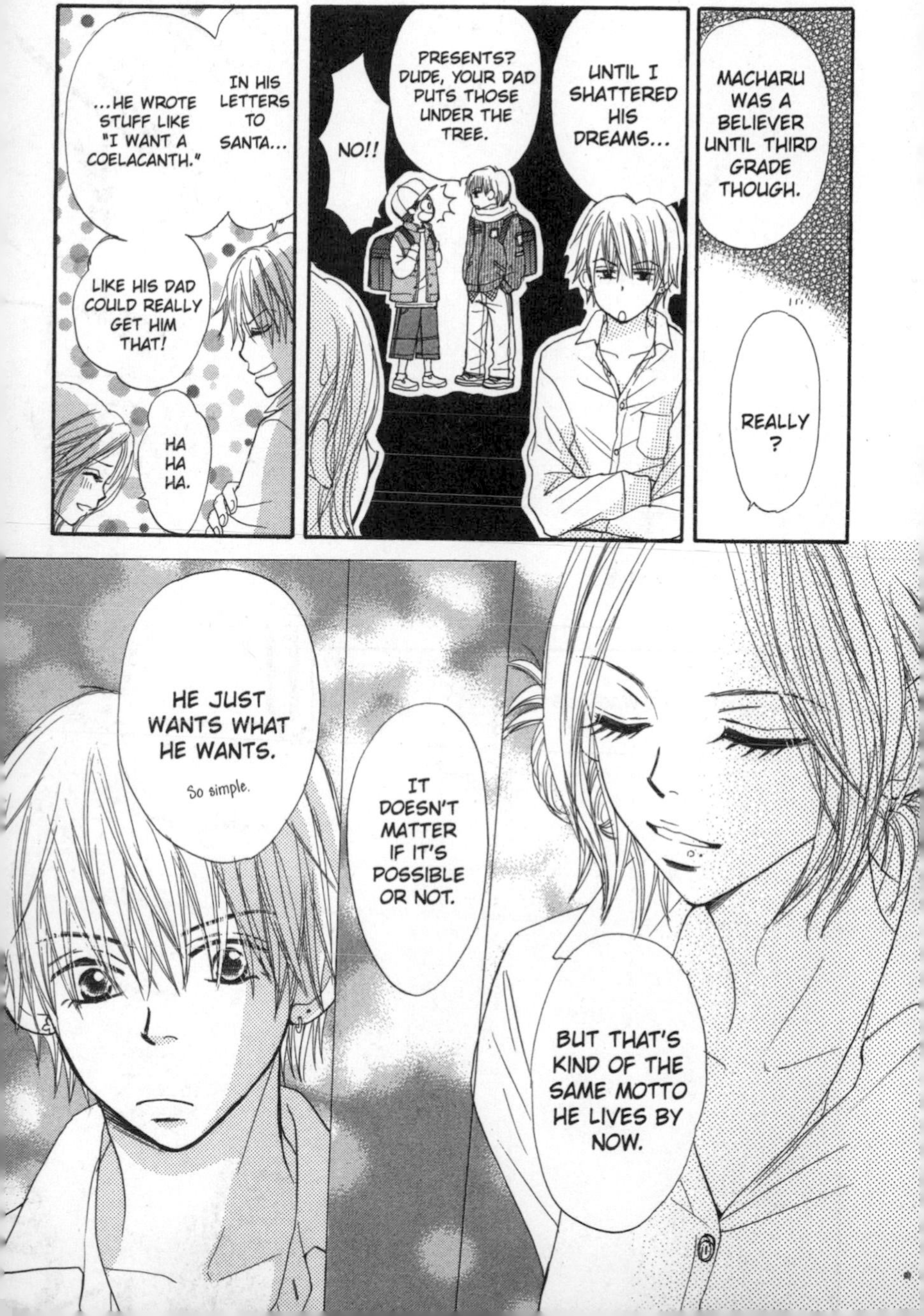
MACHARU WAS A BELIEVER UNTIL THIRD GRADE THOUGH.
REALLY?
UNTIL I SHATTERED HIS DREAMS...
PRESENTS? DUDE, YOUR DAD PUTS THOSE UNDER THE TREE.
NO!!
IN HIS LETTERS TO SANTA...
...HE WROTE STUFF LIKE "I WANT A COELACANTH."
LIKE HIS DAD COULD REALLY GET HIM THAT!
HA HA HA.
HE JUST WANTS WHAT HE WANTS.
So simple.
IT DOESN'T MATTER IF IT'S POSSIBLE OR NOT.
BUT THAT'S KIND OF THE SAME MOTTO HE LIVES BY NOW.

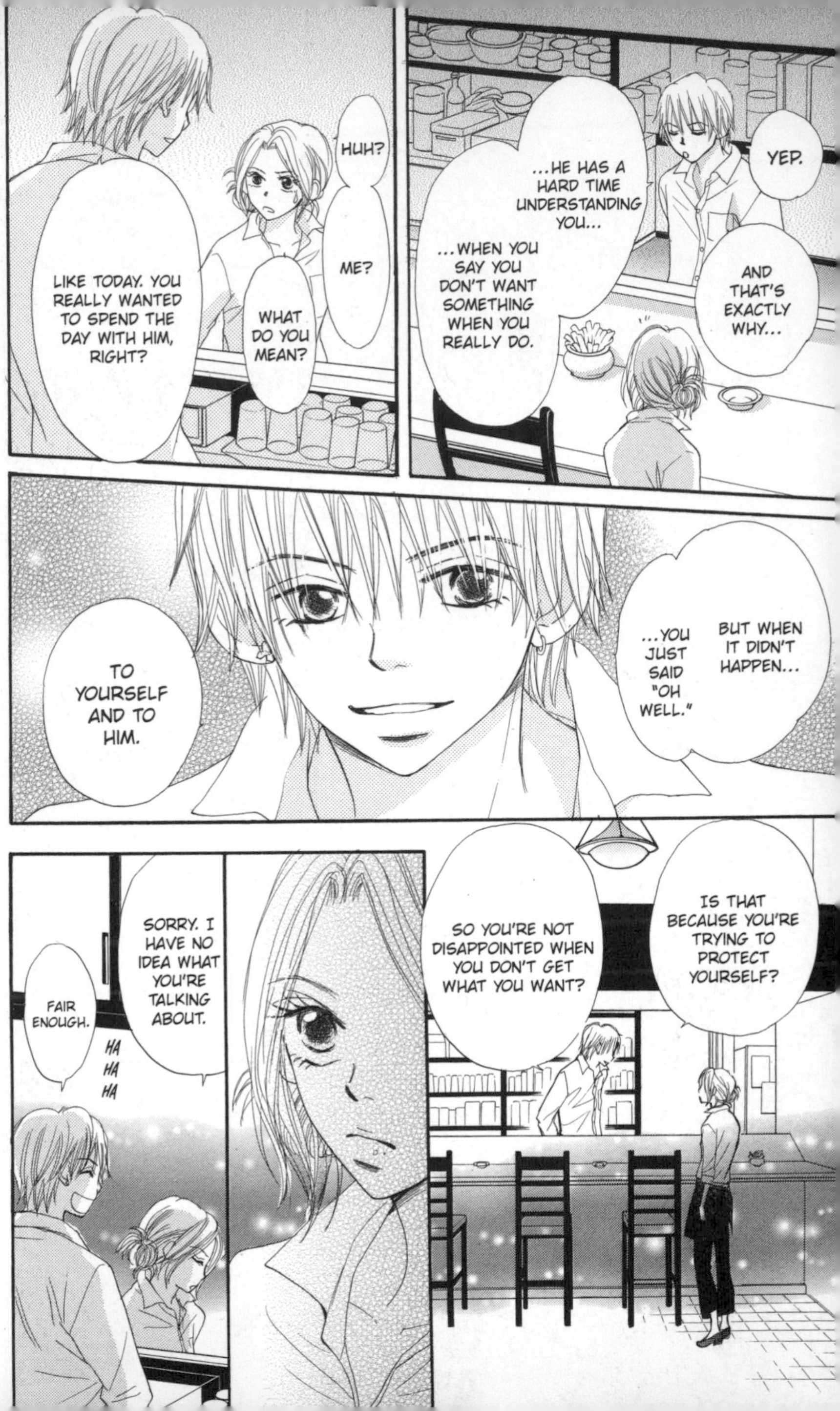
YEP.
AND THAT'S EXACTLY WHY...
...HE HAS A HARD TIME UNDERSTANDING YOU...
...WHEN YOU SAY YOU DON'T WANT SOMETHING WHEN YOU REALLY DO.
HUH?
ME?
WHAT DO YOU MEAN?
LIKE TODAY. YOU REALLY WANTED TO SPEND THE DAY WITH HIM, RIGHT?
BUT WHEN IT DIDN'T HAPPEN...
...YOU JUST SAID "OH WELL."
TO YOURSELF AND TO HIM.
IS THAT BECAUSE YOU'RE TRYING TO PROTECT YOURSELF?
SO YOU'RE NOT DISAPPOINTED WHEN YOU DON'T GET WHAT YOU WANT?
SORRY. I HAVE NO IDEA WHAT YOU'RE TALKING ABOUT.
HA HA HA
FAIR ENOUGH.

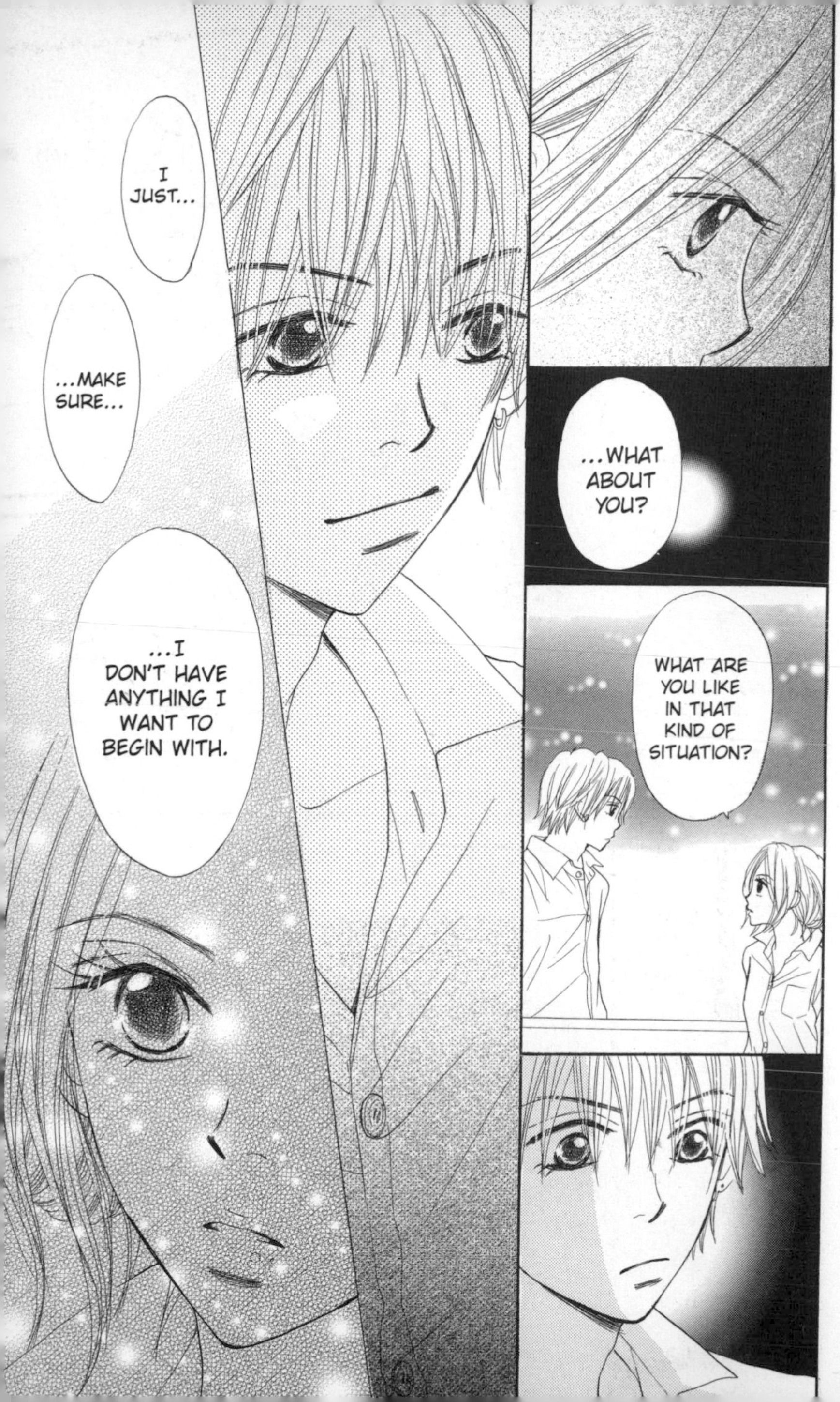
...WHAT ABOUT YOU?
WHAT ARE YOU LIKE IN THAT KIND OF SITUATION?
I JUST...
...MAKE SURE...
...I DON'T HAVE ANYTHING I WANT TO BEGIN WITH.

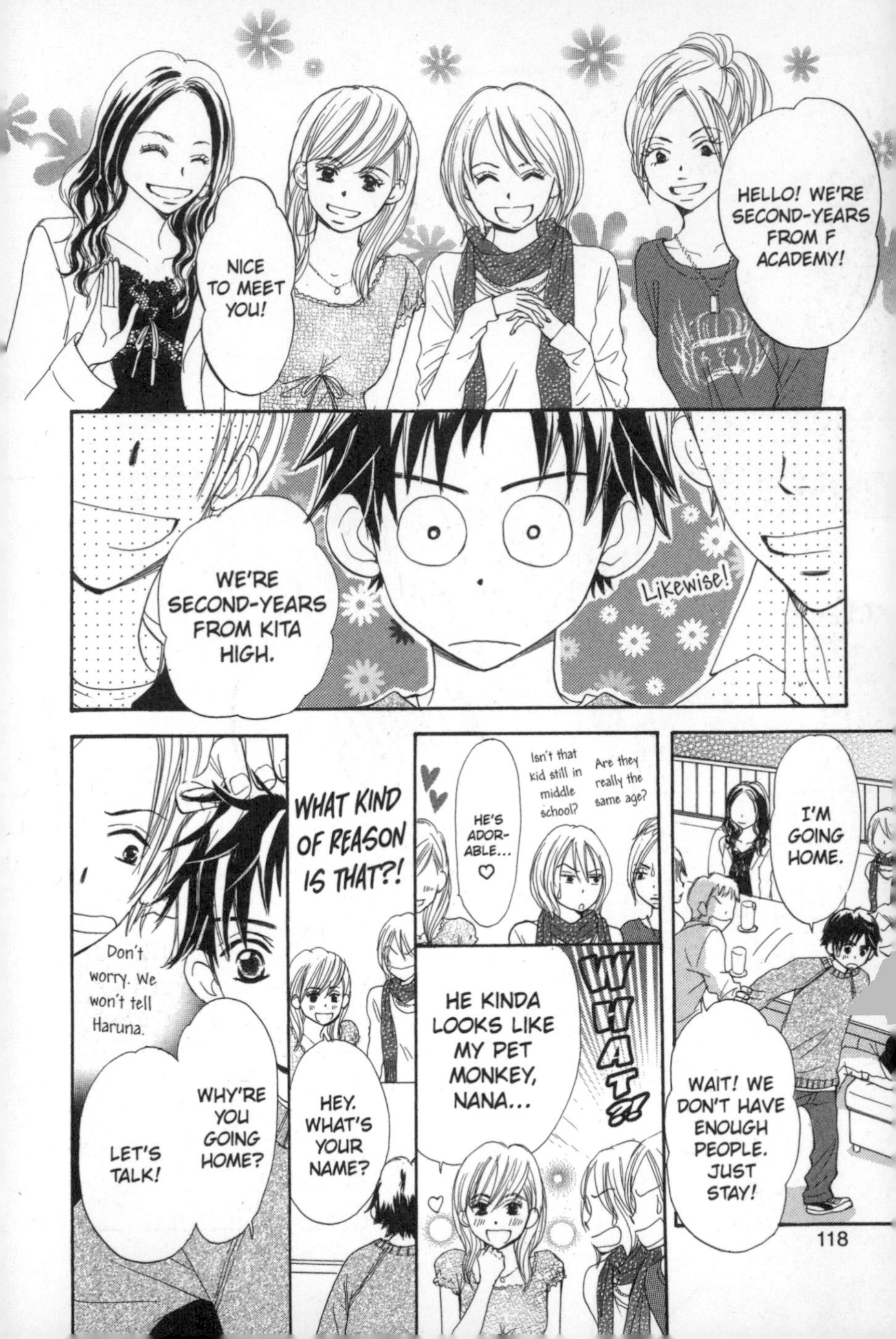
HELLO! WE'RE SECOND-YEARS FROM F ACADEMY!
NICE TO MEET YOU!
Likewise!
WE'RE SECOND-YEARS FROM KITA HIGH.
I'M GOING HOME.
WAIT! WE DON'T HAVE ENOUGH PEOPLE. JUST STAY!
Are they really the same age?
Isn't that kid still in middle school?
HE'S ADORABLE... ♡
WHAT?!
HE KINDA LOOKS LIKE MY PET MONKEY, NANA...
WHAT KIND OF REASON IS THAT?!
HEY. WHAT'S YOUR NAME?
Don't worry. We won't tell Haruna.
WHY'RE YOU GOING HOME?
LET'S TALK!

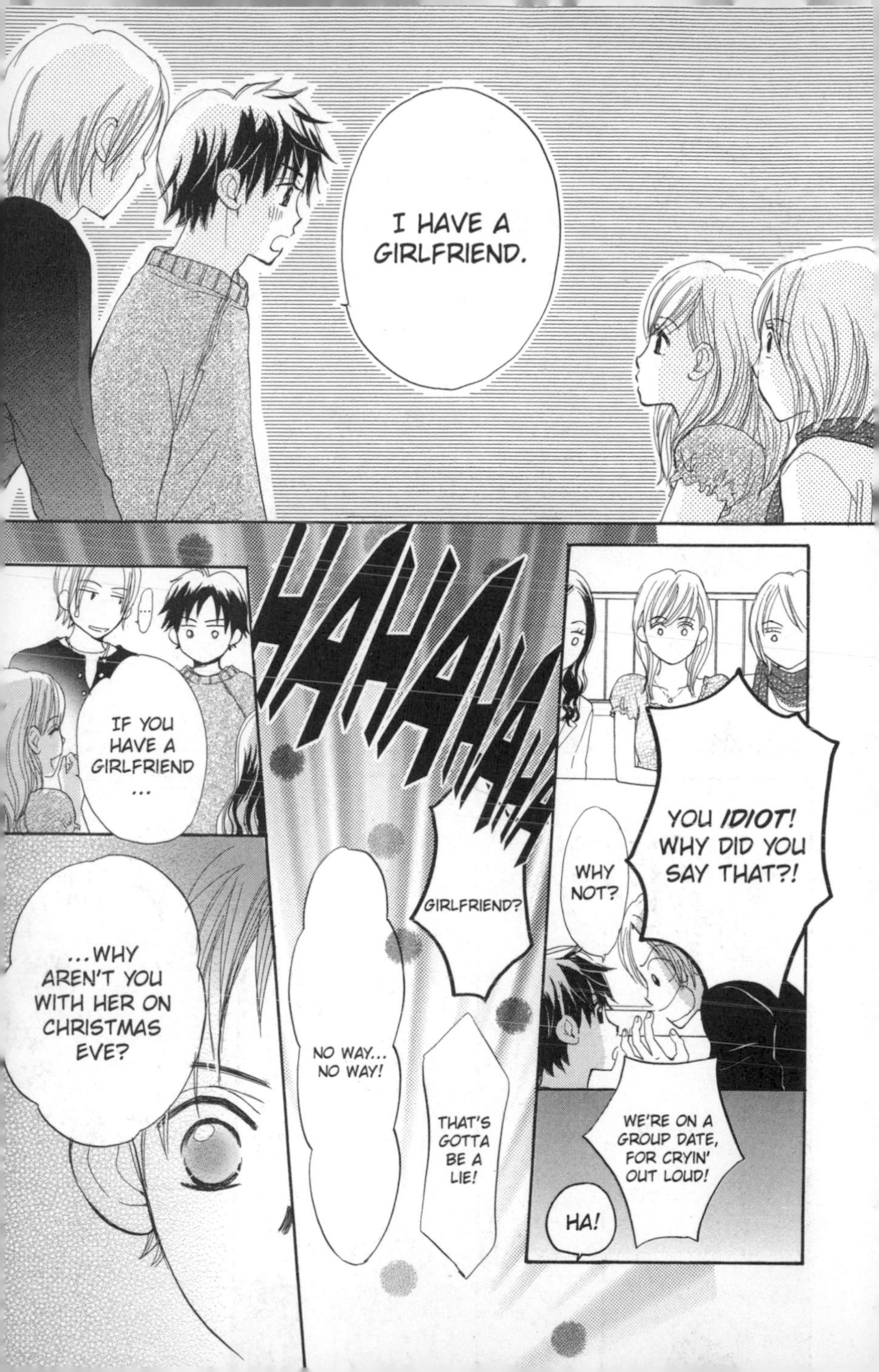
I HAVE A GIRLFRIEND.
YOU IDIOT! WHY DID YOU SAY THAT?!
WHY NOT?
WE'RE ON A GROUP DATE, FOR CRYIN' OUT LOUD!
HA!
HAHAHAHA
GIRLFRIEND?
THAT'S GOTTA BE A LIE!
NO WAY... NO WAY!
...
IF YOU HAVE A GIRLFRIEND ...
...WHY AREN'T YOU WITH HER ON CHRISTMAS EVE?

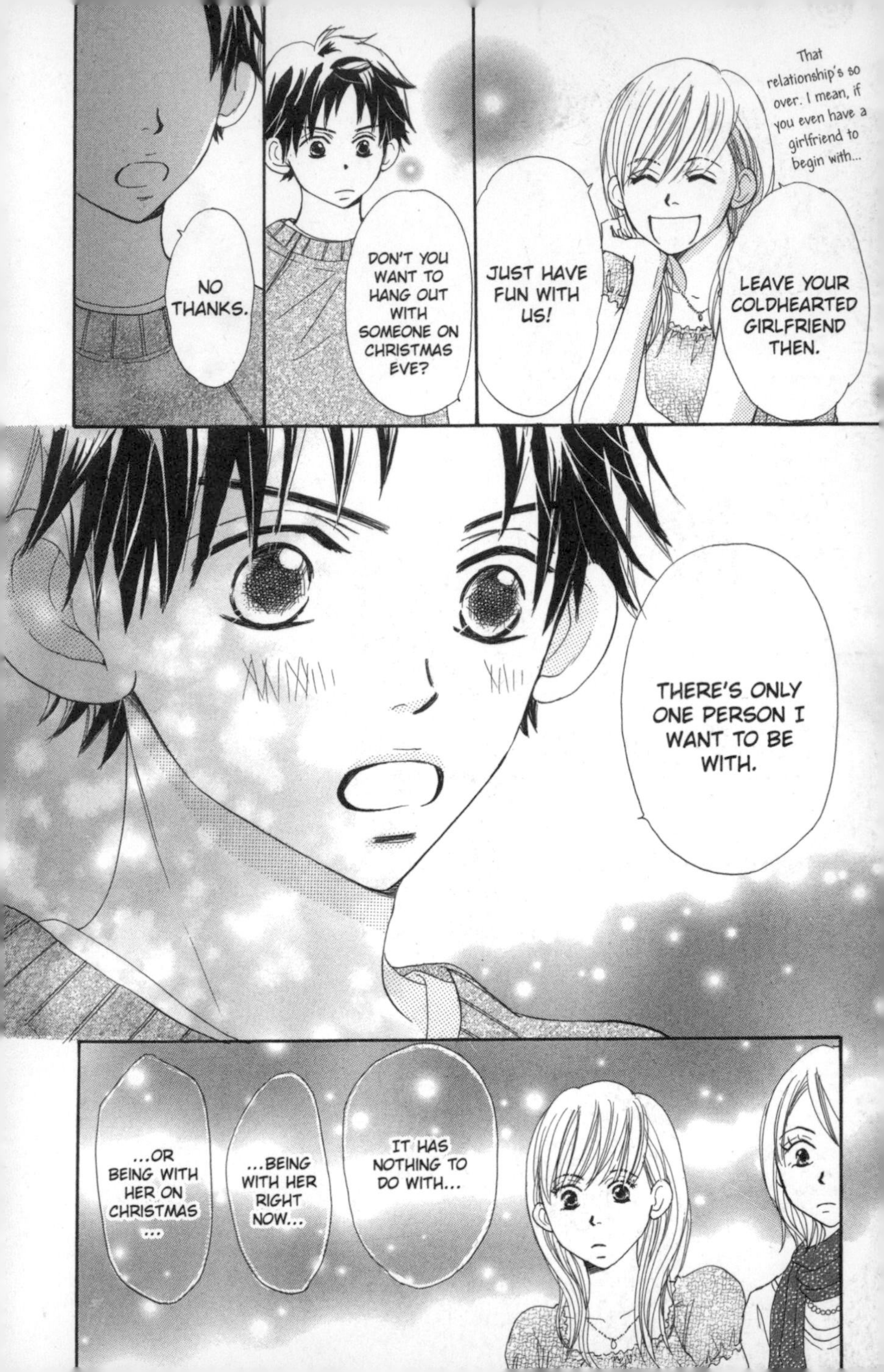
That relationship's so over. I mean, if you even have a girlfriend to begin with...
LEAVE YOUR COLDHEARTED GIRLFRIEND THEN.
JUST HAVE FUN WITH US!
DON'T YOU WANT TO HANG OUT WITH SOMEONE ON CHRISTMAS EVE?
NO THANKS.
THERE'S ONLY ONE PERSON I WANT TO BE WITH.
IT HAS NOTHING TO DO WITH...
...BEING WITH HER RIGHT NOW...
...OR BEING WITH HER ON CHRISTMAS ...

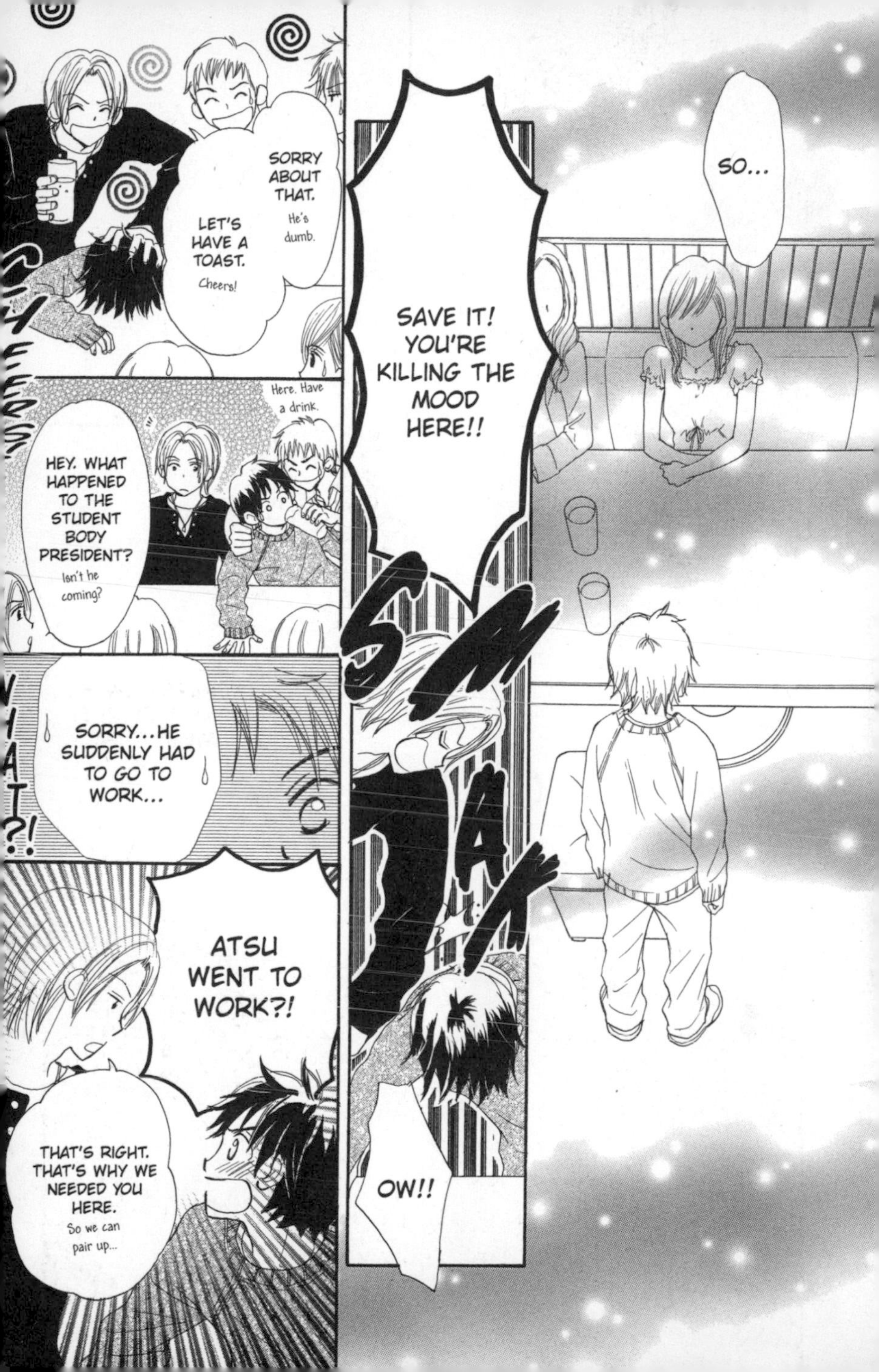
SO...
SAVE IT! YOU'RE KILLING THE MOOD HERE!!
SMACK
OW!!
SORRY ABOUT THAT.
He's dumb.
LET'S HAVE A TOAST.
Cheers!
CHEERS
Here. Have a drink.
HEY. WHAT HAPPENED TO THE STUDENT BODY PRESIDENT?
Isn't he coming?
SORRY...HE SUDDENLY HAD TO GO TO WORK...
WHAT?!
ATSU WENT TO WORK?!
THAT'S RIGHT. THAT'S WHY WE NEEDED YOU HERE.
So we can pair up...

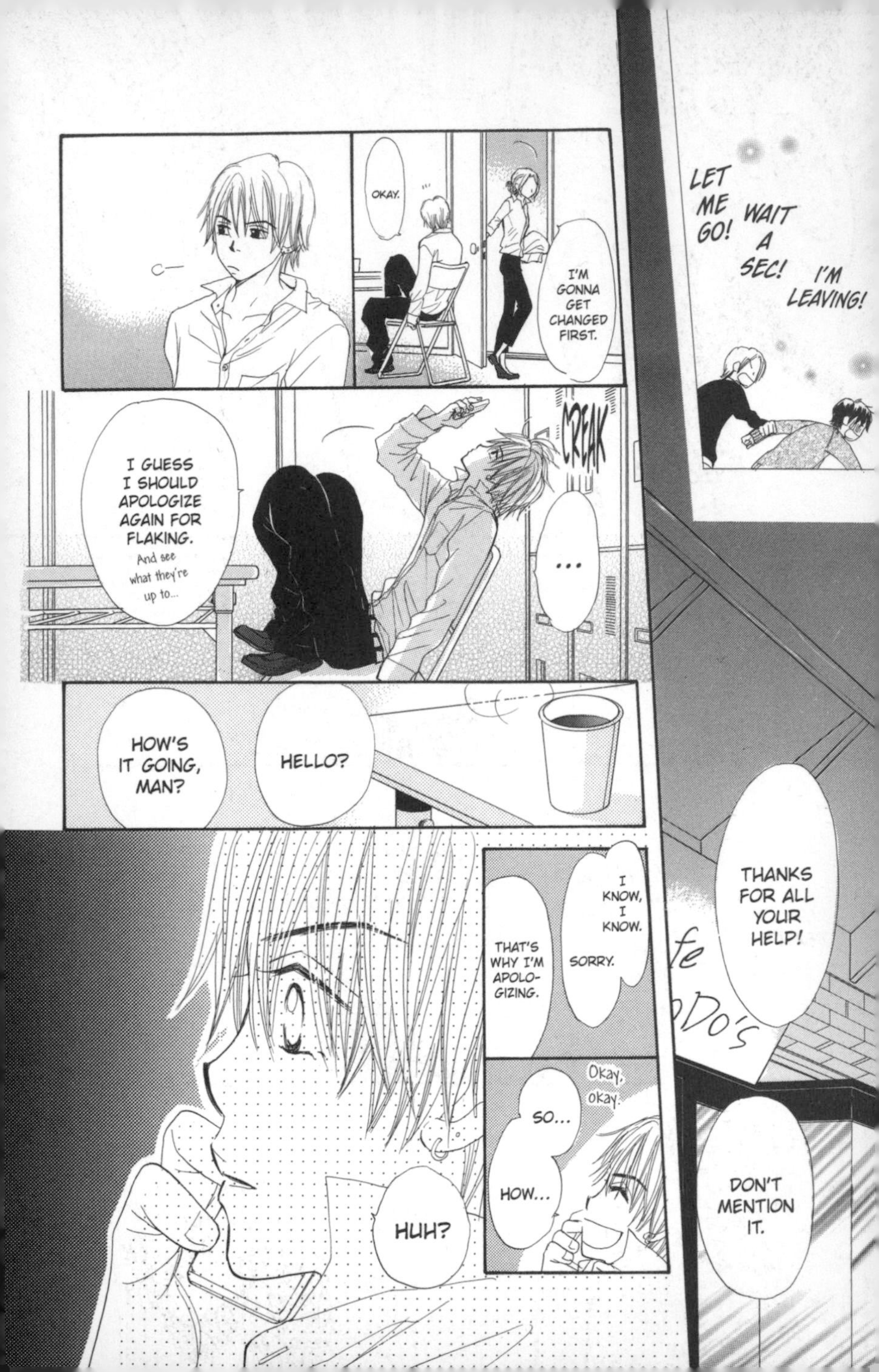
LET ME GO!
WAIT A SEC!
I'M LEAVING!
THANKS FOR ALL YOUR HELP!
DON'T MENTION IT.
I'M GONNA GET CHANGED FIRST.
...
OKAY.
CREAK
...
I GUESS I SHOULD APOLOGIZE AGAIN FOR FLAKING.
And see what they're up to...
HELLO?
HOW'S IT GOING, MAN?
I KNOW, I KNOW.
SORRY.
THAT'S WHY I'M APOLOGIZING.
Okay, okay.
SO...
HOW...
HUH?

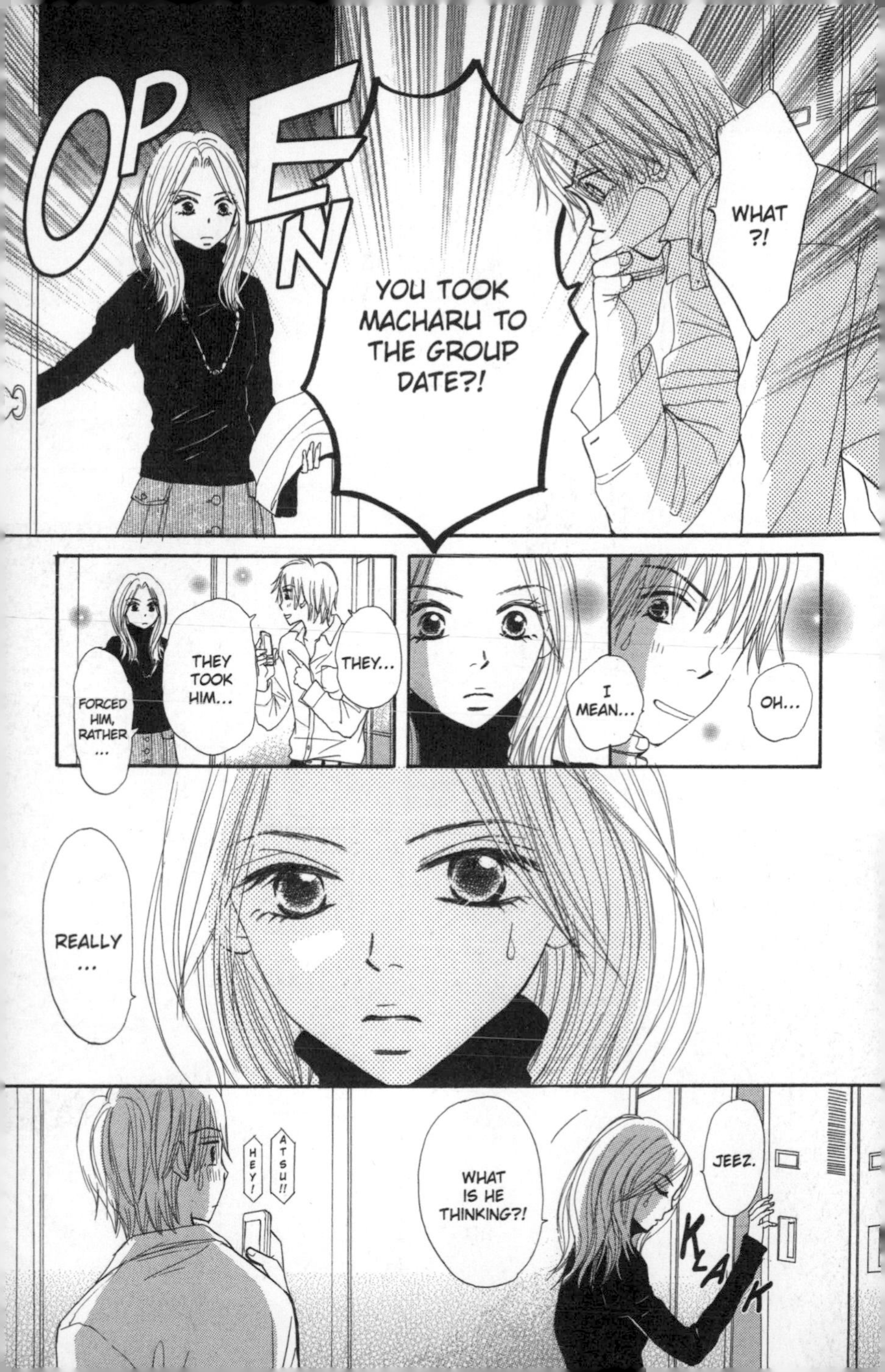
WHAT ?!
YOU TOOK MACHARU TO THE GROUP DATE?!
OPEN
OH...
I MEAN...
THEY...
THEY TOOK HIM...
FORCED HIM, RATHER ...
REALLY ...
JEEZ.
KLAK
WHAT IS HE THINKING?!
ATSU!!
HEY!

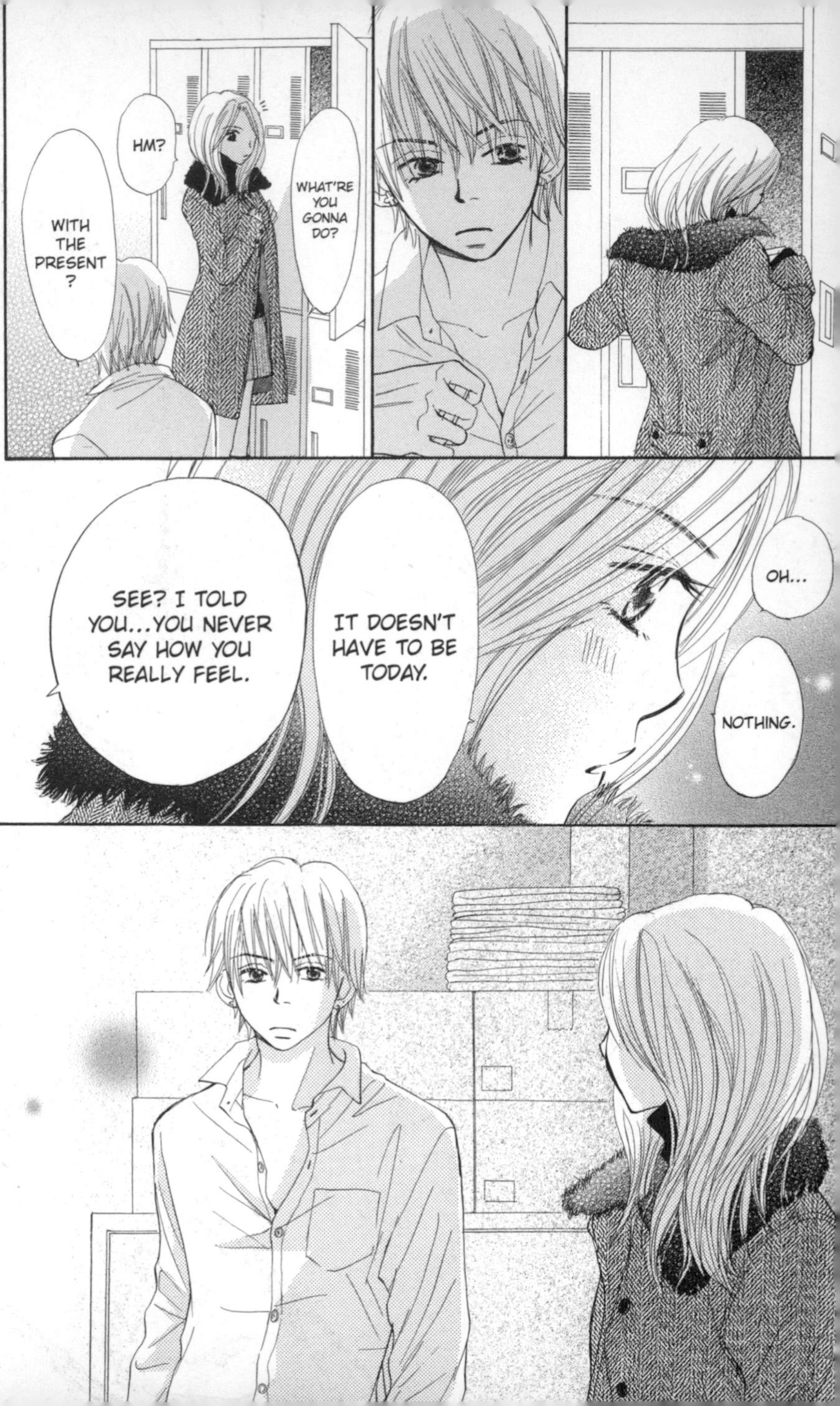
WHAT'RE YOU GONNA DO?
HM?
WITH THE PRESENT?
OH...
NOTHING.
IT DOESN'T HAVE TO BE TODAY.
SEE? I TOLD YOU...YOU NEVER SAY HOW YOU REALLY FEEL.

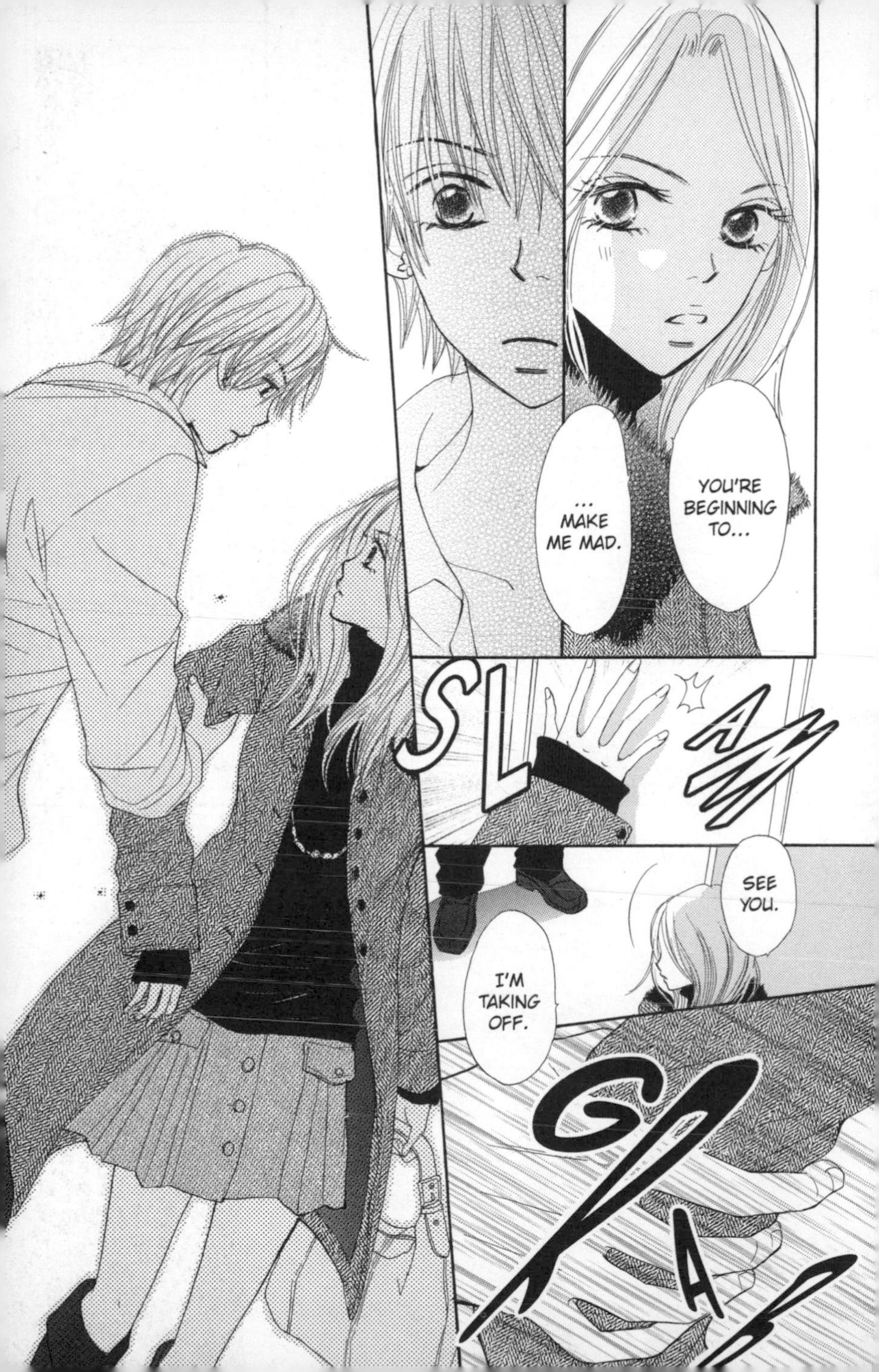
YOU'RE BEGINNING TO...
... MAKE ME MAD.
SLAM
SEE YOU.
I'M TAKING OFF.
GRAB

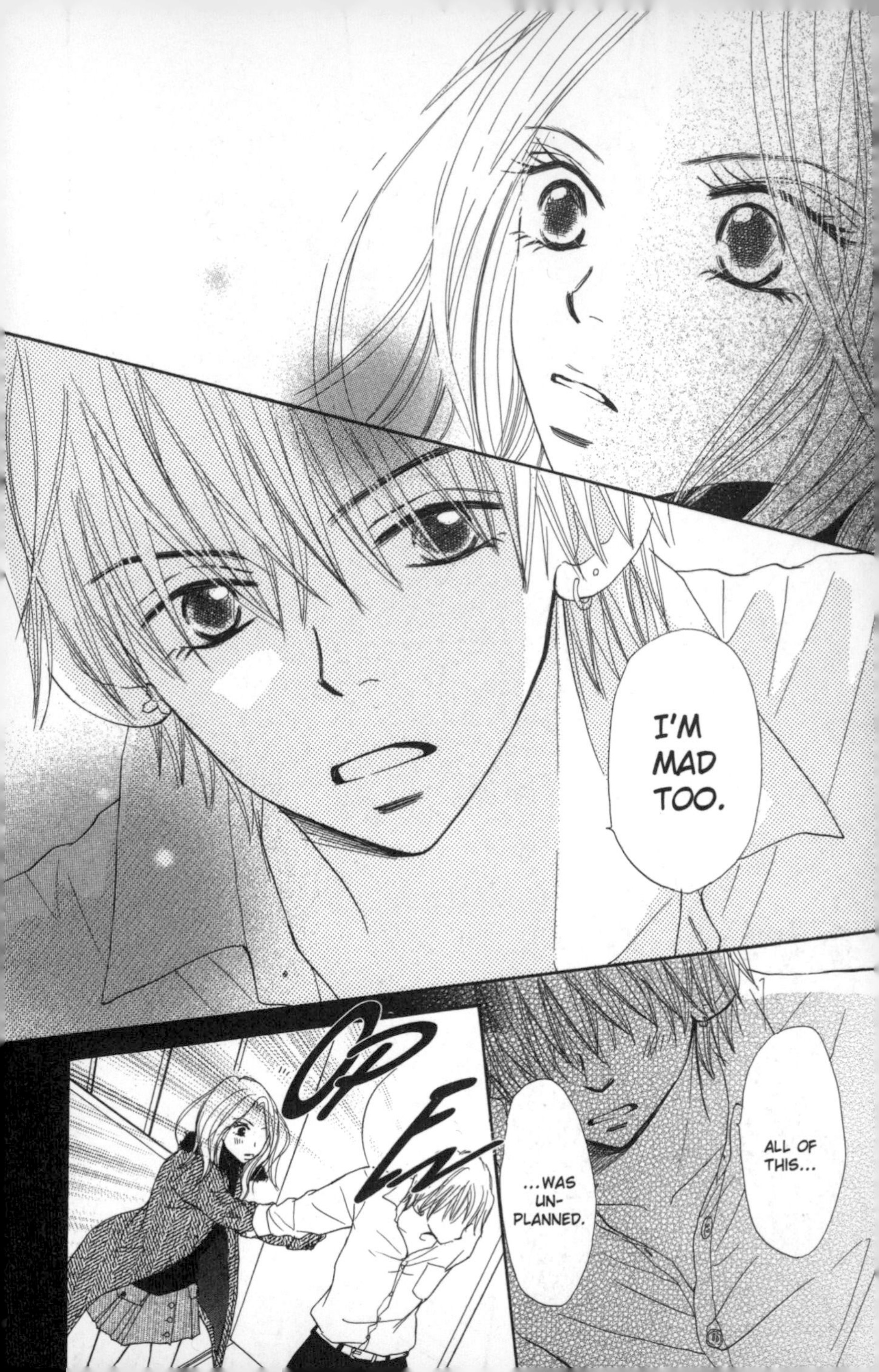
I'M MAD TOO.
ALL OF THIS...
...WAS UN-PLANNED.

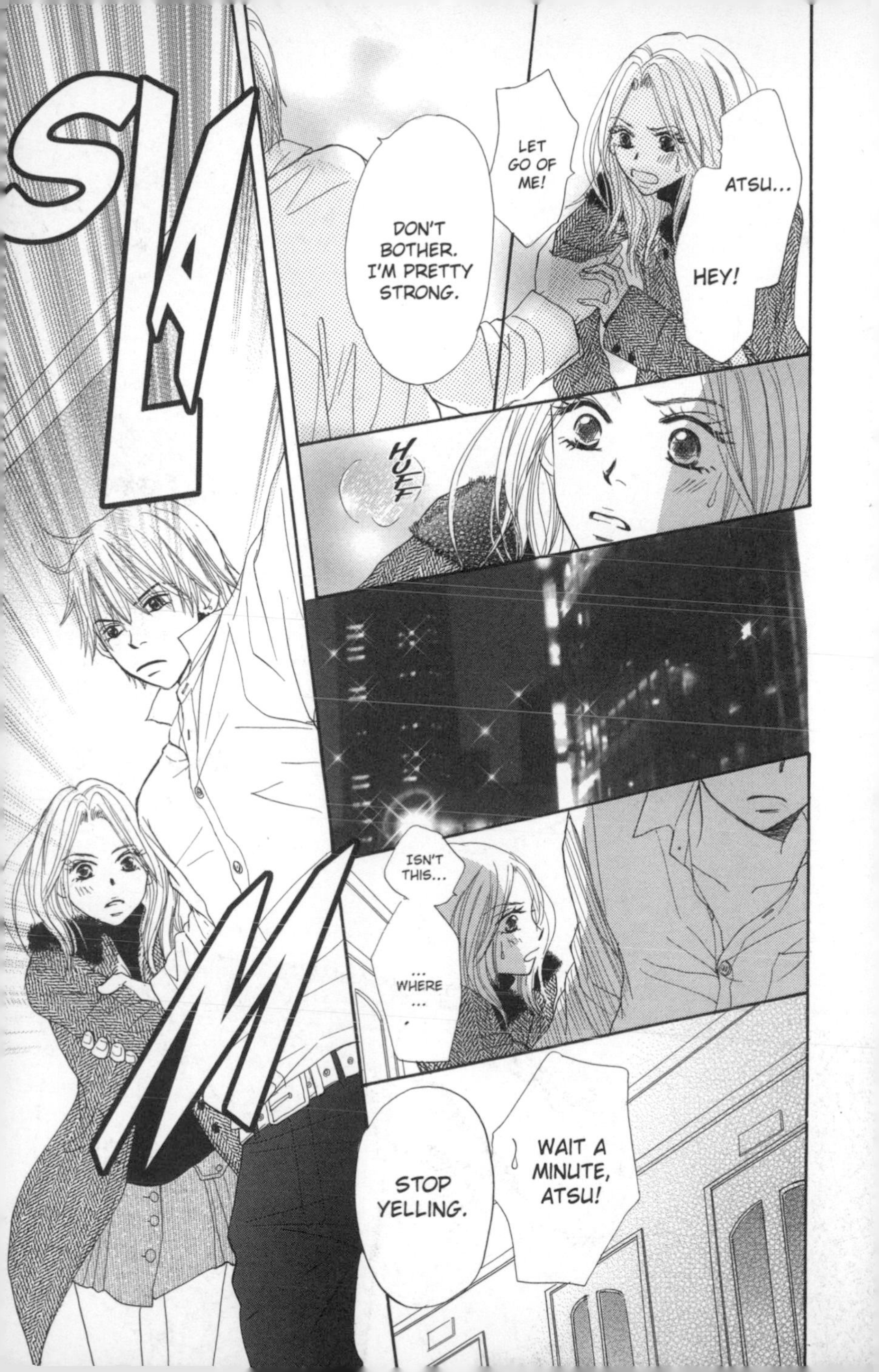
ATSU...
HEY!
LET GO OF ME!
DON'T BOTHER. I'M PRETTY STRONG.
HUFF
ISN'T THIS...
...WHERE...
WAIT A MINUTE, ATSU!
STOP YELLING.
SLAM

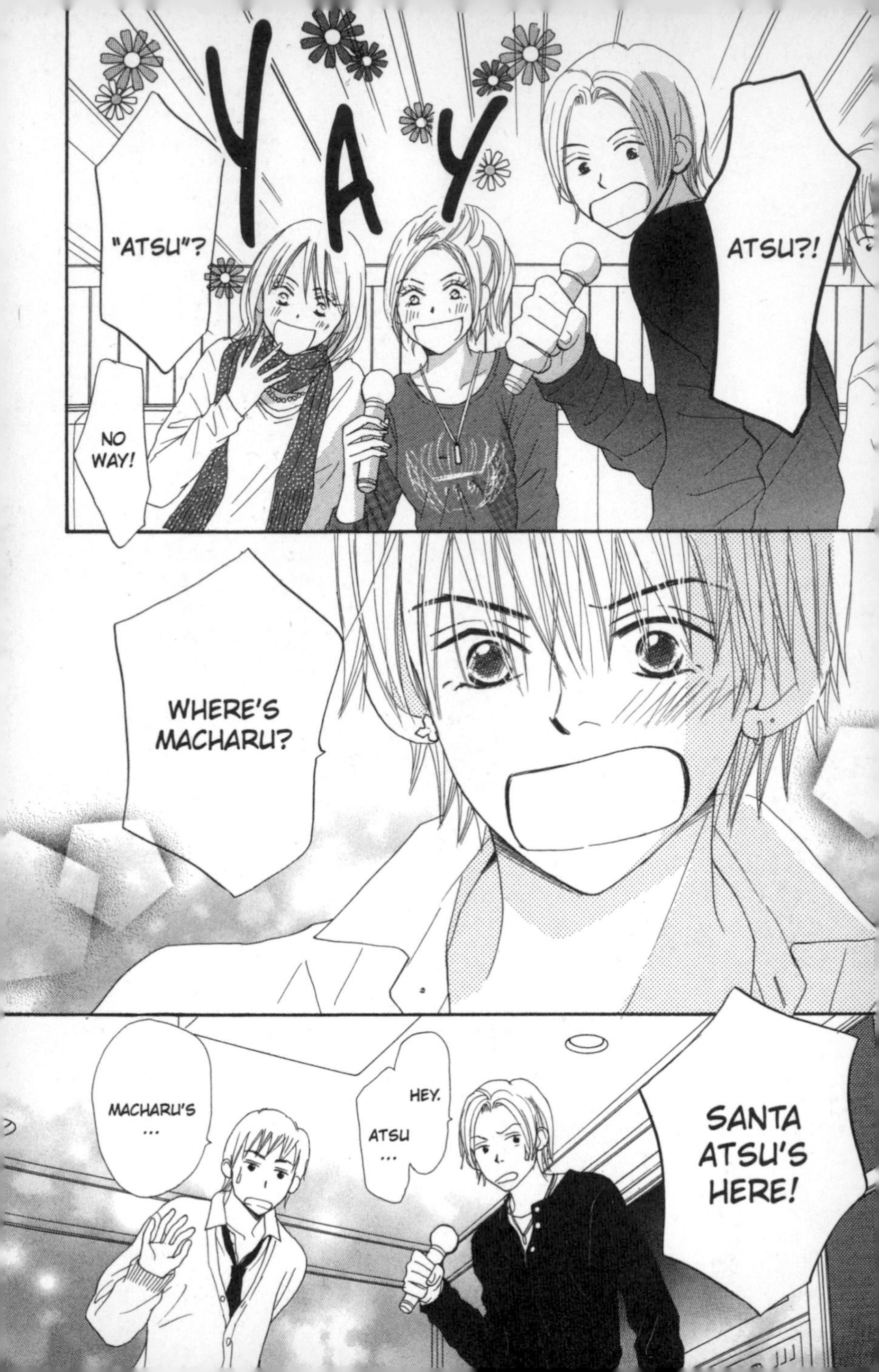
ATSU?!
YAY
"ATSU"?
NO WAY!
WHERE'S MACHARU?
SANTA ATSU'S HERE!
HEY. ATSU ...
MACHARU'S ...

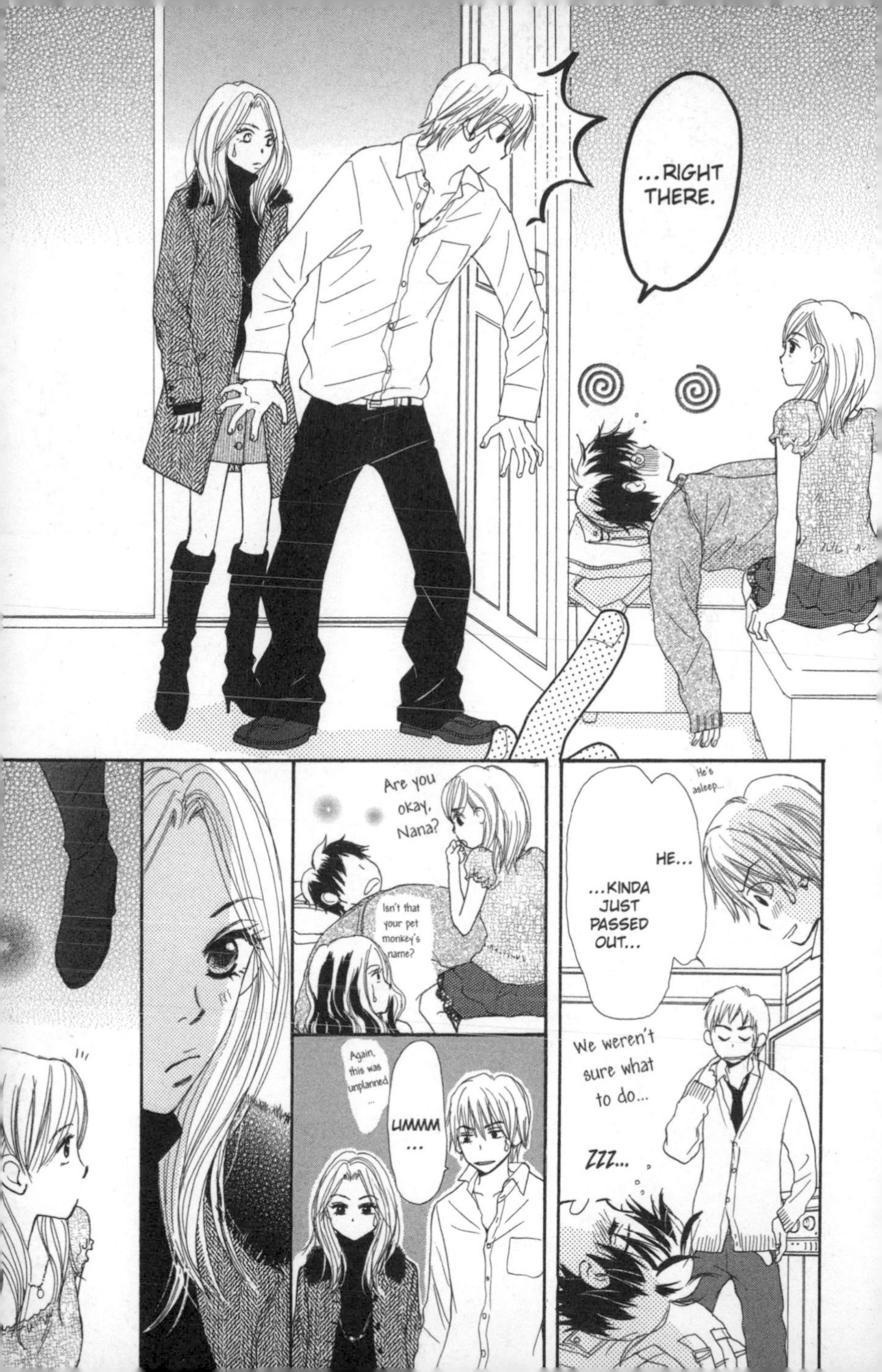
...RIGHT THERE.
He's asleep...
HE... ...KINDA JUST PASSED OUT...
We weren't sure what to do...
ZZZ...
Are you okay, Nana?
Isn't that your pet monkey's name?
Again, this was unplanned...
UMMM...

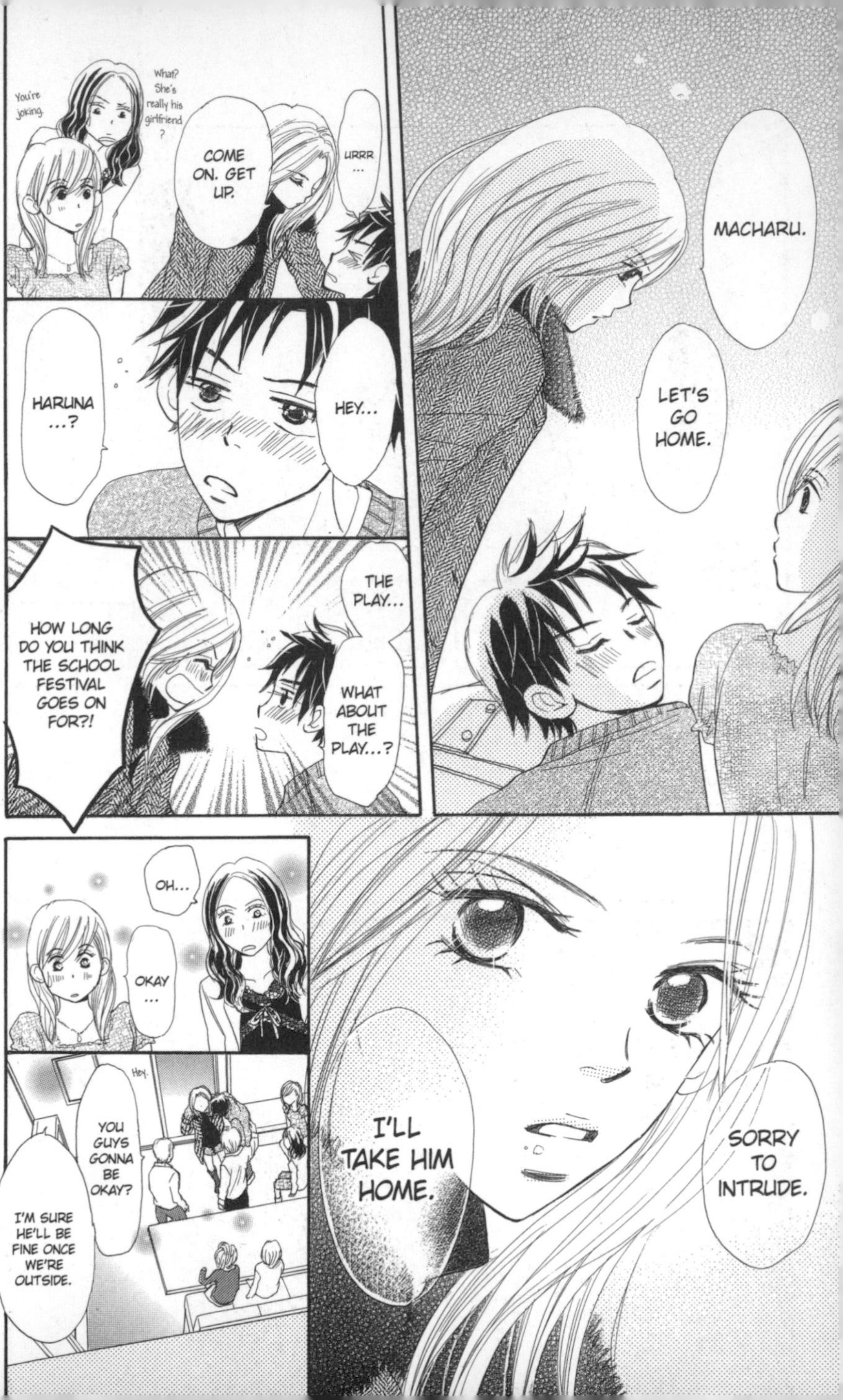
MACHARU.
LET'S GO HOME.
URRR...
COME ON. GET UP.
What? She's really his girlfriend?
You're joking.
HEY...
HARUNA...?
THE PLAY...
WHAT ABOUT THE PLAY...?
HOW LONG DO YOU THINK THE SCHOOL FESTIVAL GOES ON FOR?!
SORRY TO INTRUDE.
I'LL TAKE HIM HOME.
OH...
OKAY...
Hey.
YOU GUYS GONNA BE OKAY?
I'M SURE HE'LL BE FINE ONCE WE'RE OUTSIDE.

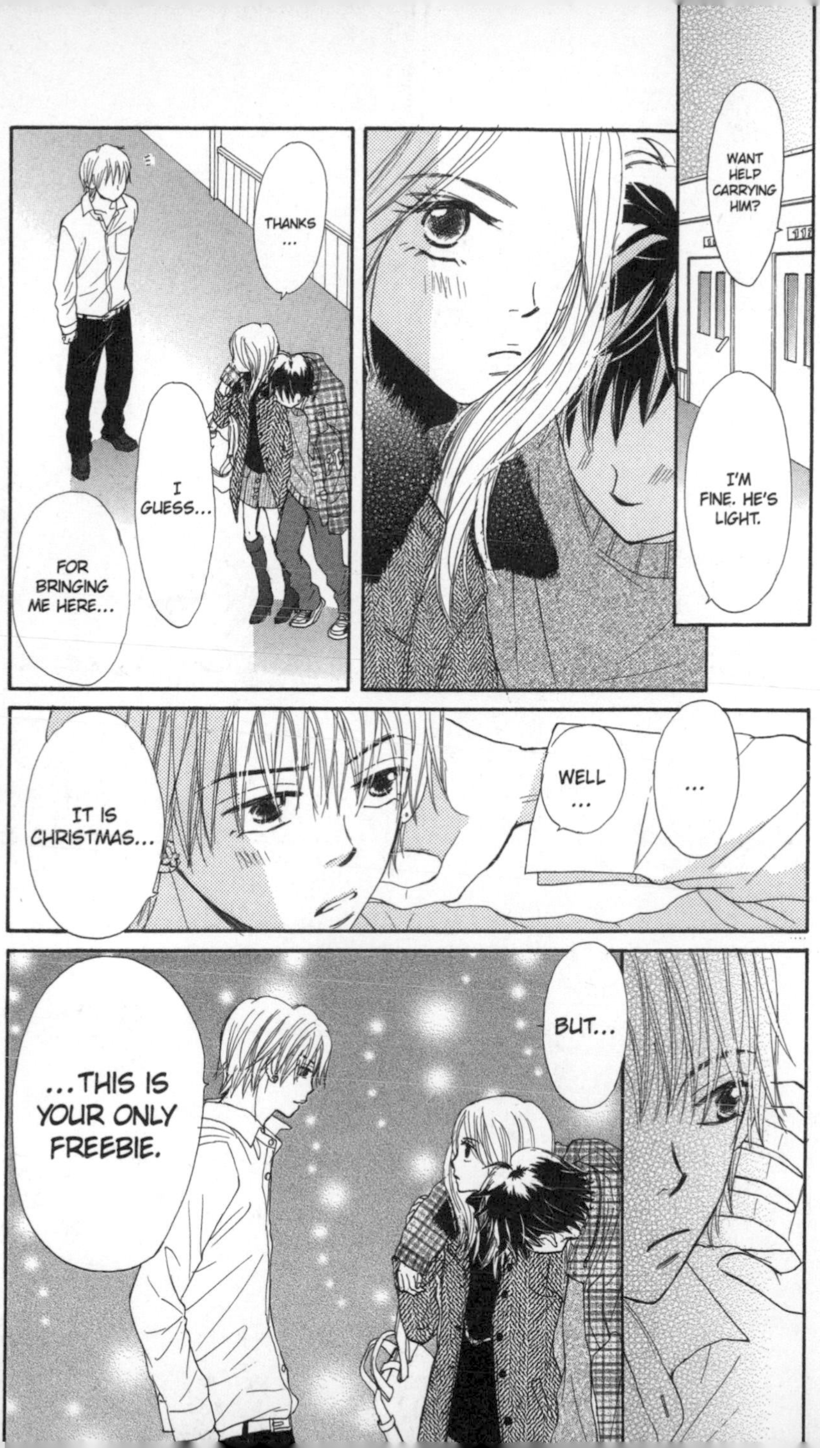
WANT HELP CARRYING HIM?
I'M FINE. HE'S LIGHT.
THANKS ...
I GUESS...
FOR BRINGING ME HERE...
...
WELL ...
IT IS CHRISTMAS...
BUT...
...THIS IS YOUR ONLY FREEBIE.

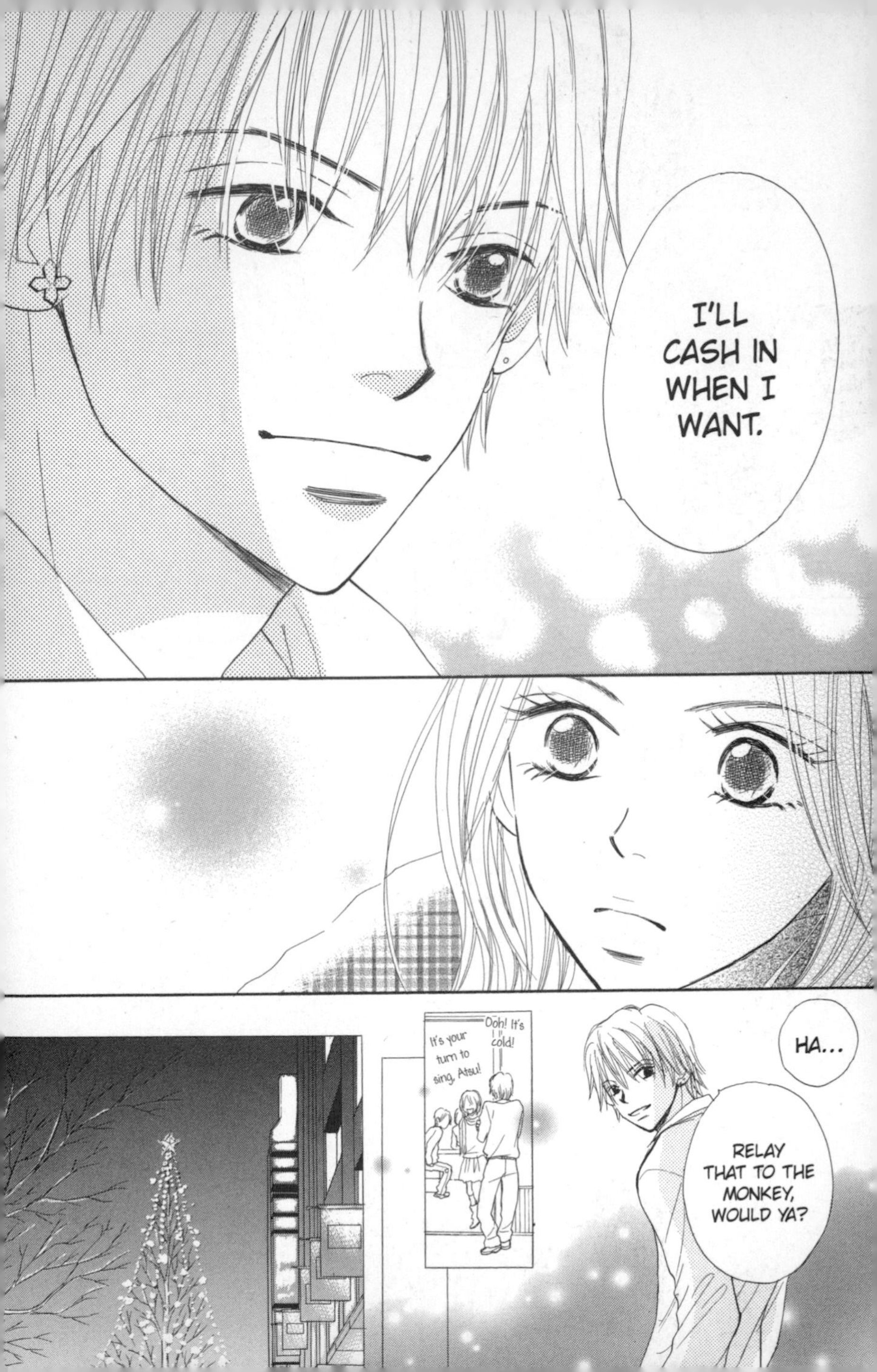
I'LL CASH IN WHEN I WANT.
HA...
RELAY THAT TO THE MONKEY, WOULD YA?
Ooh! It's cold!
It's your turn to sing, Atsu!

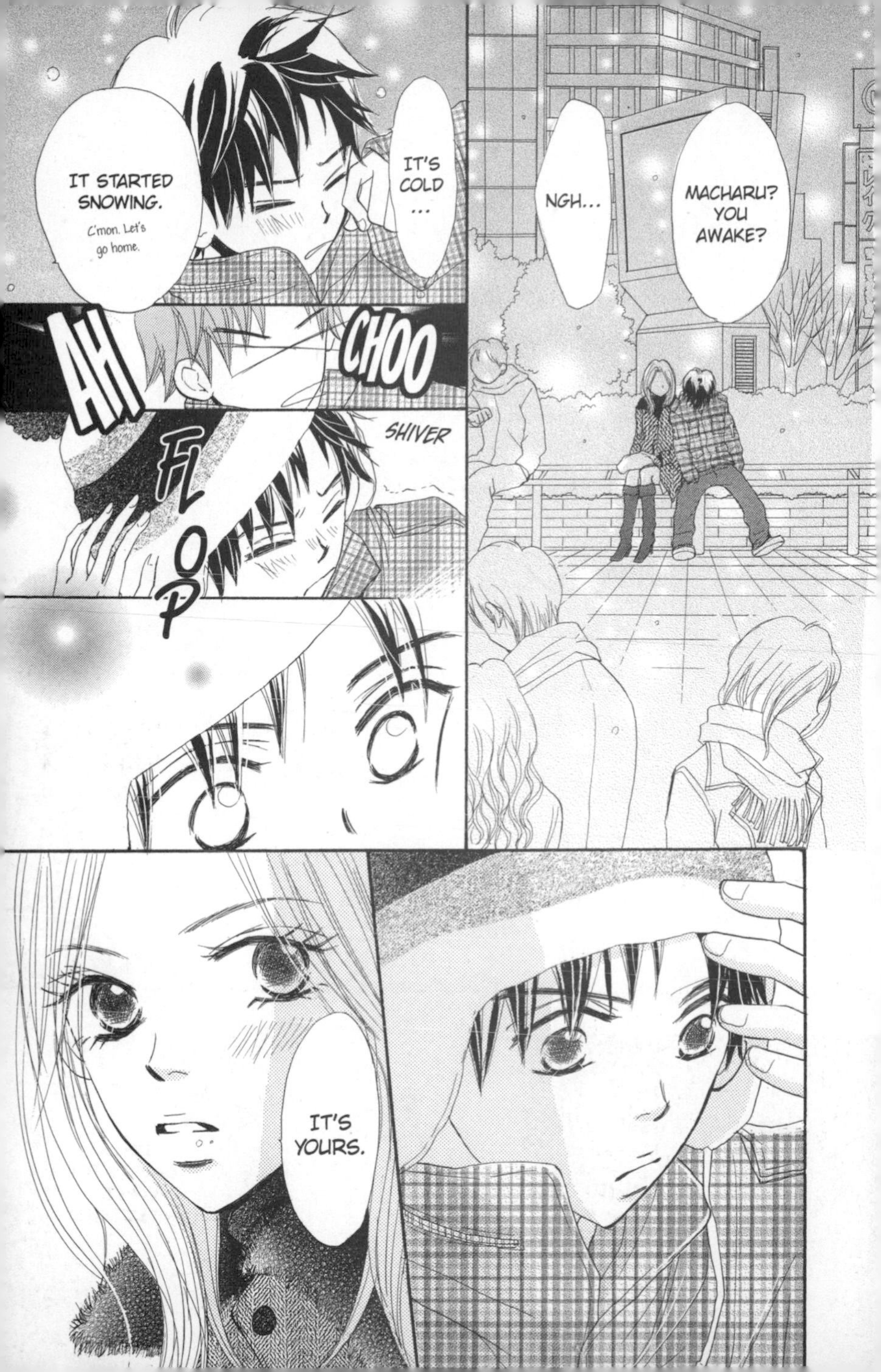
MACHARU? YOU AWAKE?
NGH...
IT'S COLD...
IT STARTED SNOWING.
C'mon. Let's go home.
AH
CHOO
SHIVER
FLOP
IT'S YOURS.

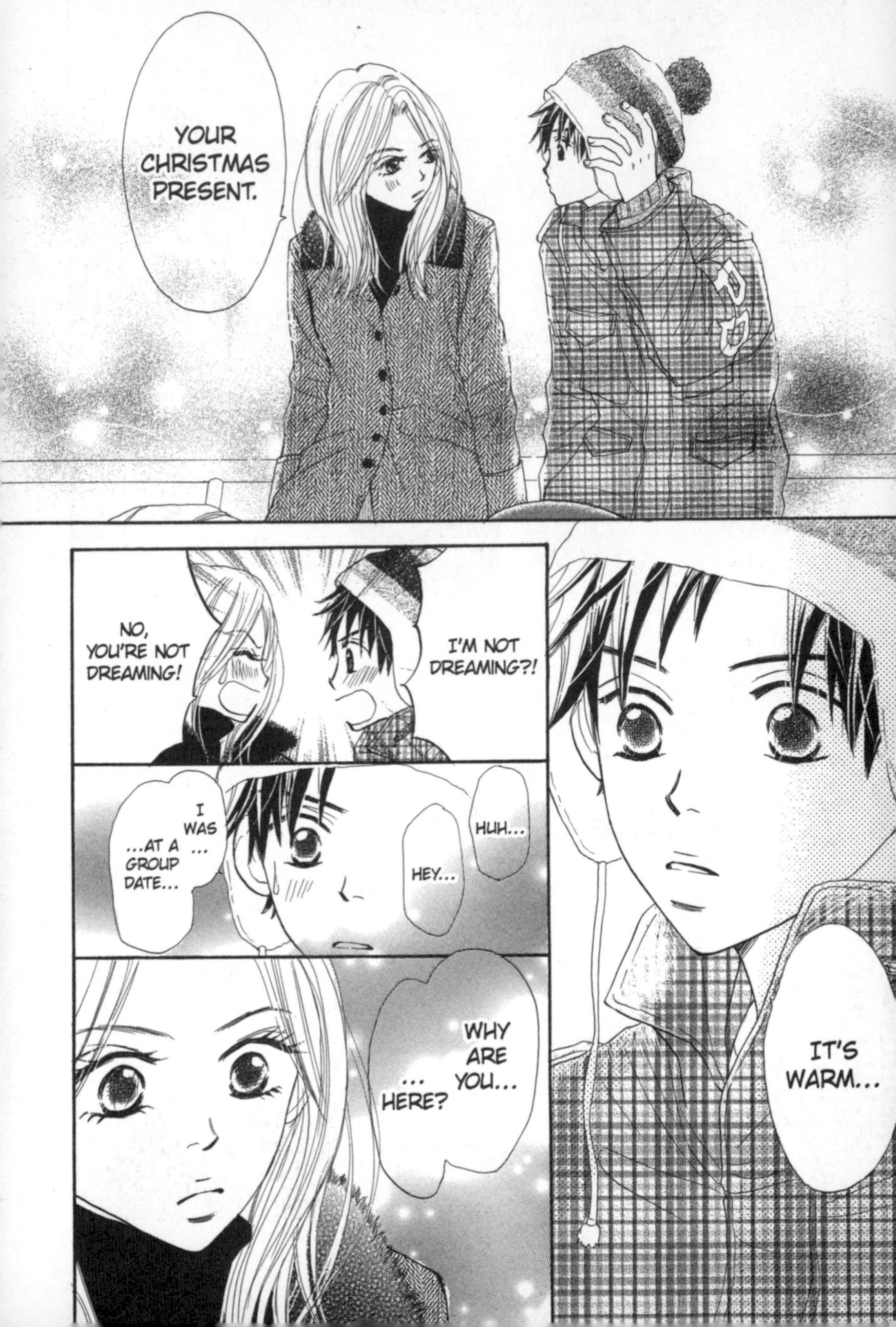
YOUR CHRISTMAS PRESENT.
IT'S WARM...
I'M NOT DREAMING?!
NO, YOU'RE NOT DREAMING!
HUH...
HEY...
I WAS...
...AT A GROUP DATE...
WHY ARE YOU...
...HERE?

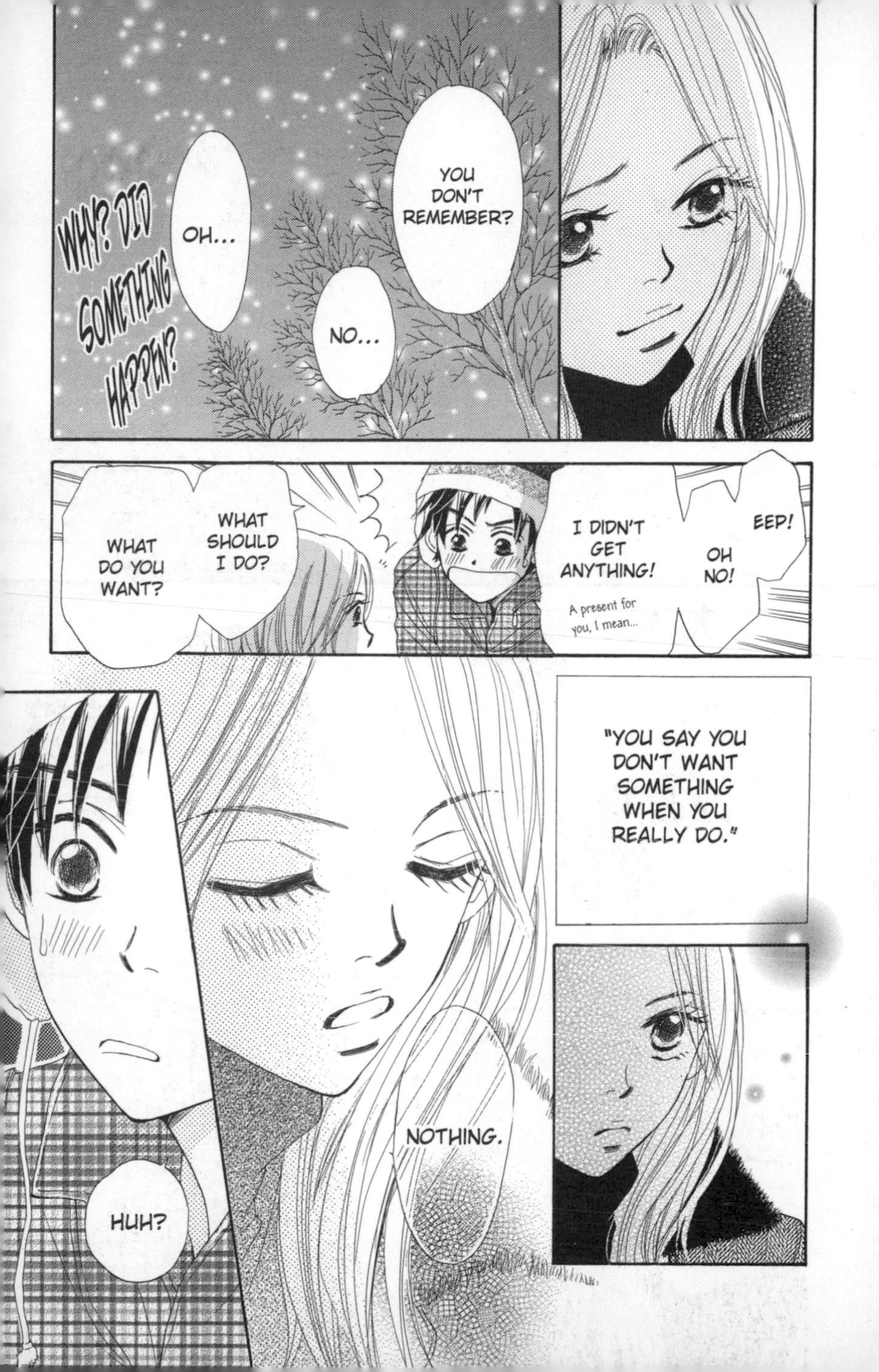
YOU DON'T REMEMBER?
NO...
OH...
WHY? DID SOMETHING HAPPEN?
EEP!
OH NO!
I DIDN'T GET ANYTHING!
A present for you, I mean...
WHAT SHOULD I DO?
WHAT DO YOU WANT?
"YOU SAY YOU DON'T WANT SOMETHING WHEN YOU REALLY DO."
NOTHING.
HUH?

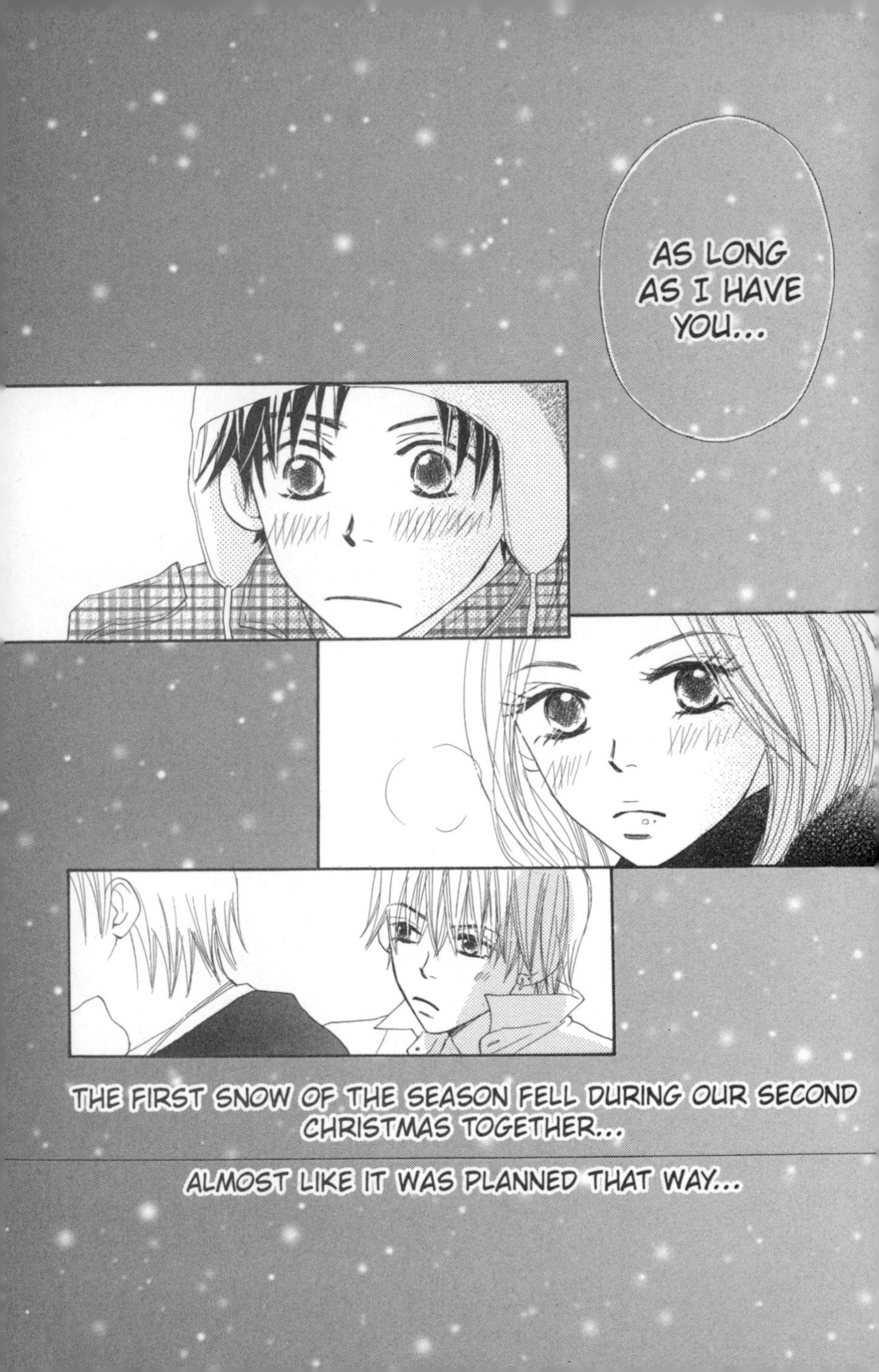
AS LONG AS I HAVE YOU...
THE FIRST SNOW OF THE SEASON FELL DURING OUR SECOND CHRISTMAS TOGETHER...
ALMOST LIKE IT WAS PLANNED THAT WAY...

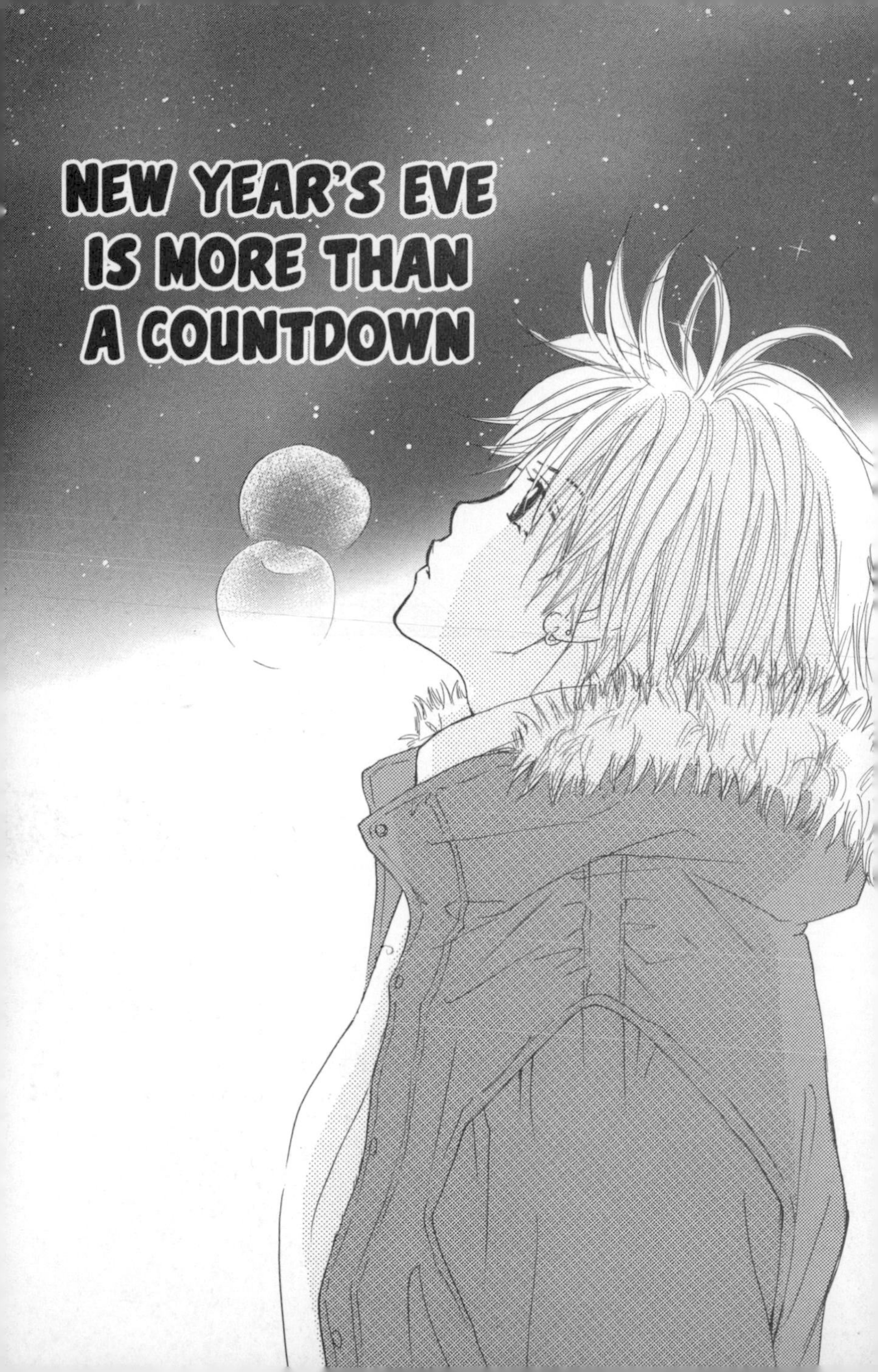
NEW YEAR'S EVE IS MORE THAN A COUNTDOWN

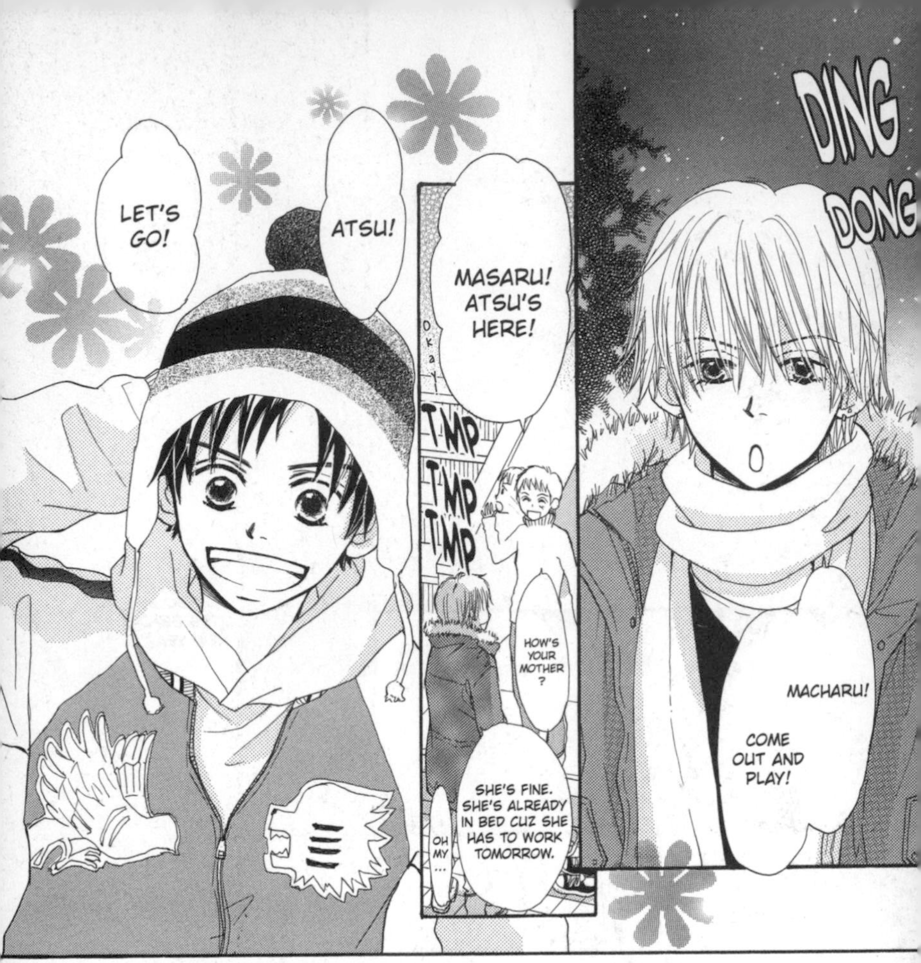
DING DONG
MACHARU!
COME OUT AND PLAY!
MASARU! ATSU'S HERE!
Okay
TMP TMP TMP
HOW'S YOUR MOTHER?
SHE'S FINE. SHE'S ALREADY IN BED CUZ SHE HAS TO WORK TOMORROW.
OH MY...
ATSU!
LET'S GO!

Monkey High!

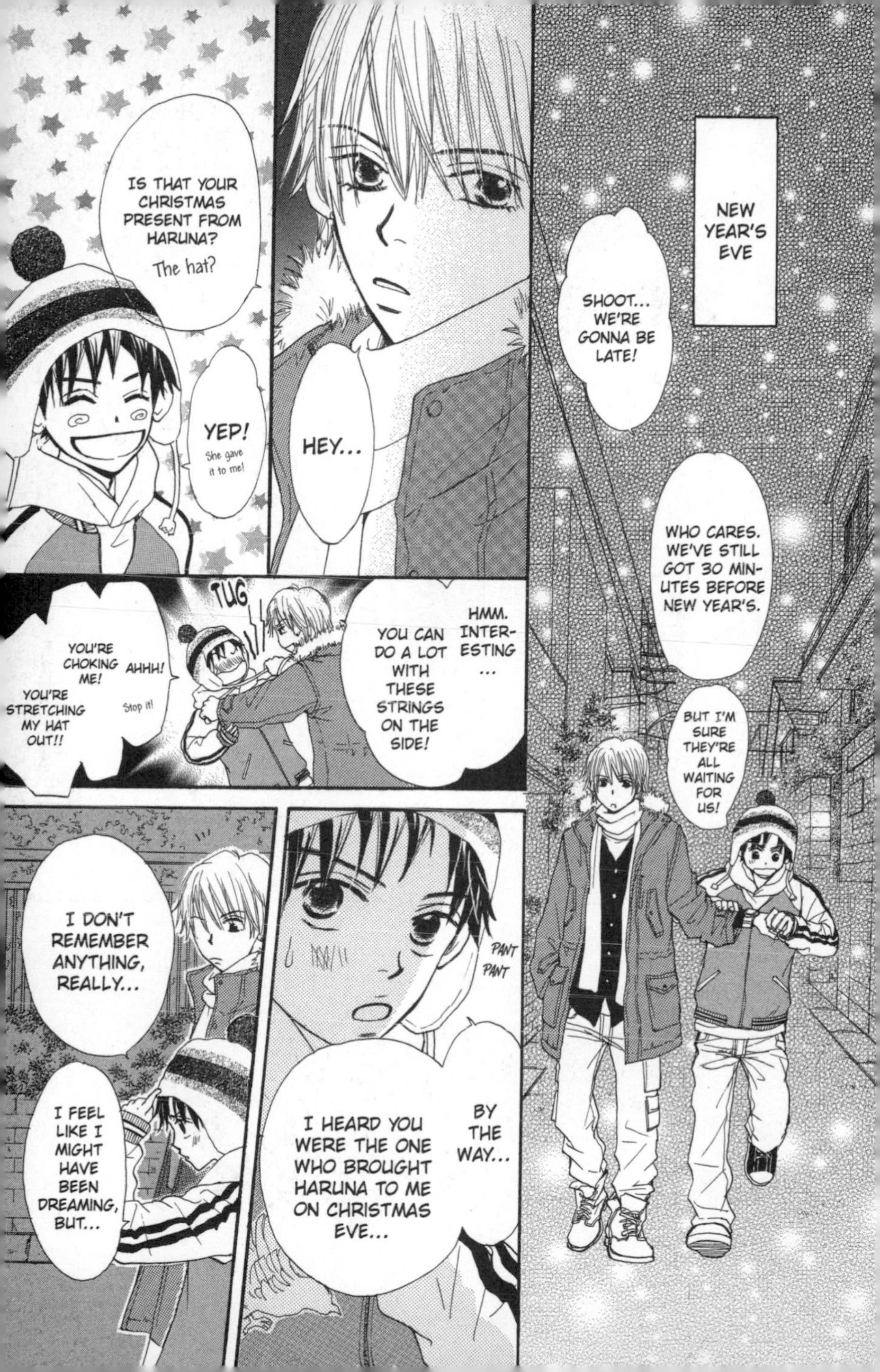
NEW YEAR'S EVE
SHOOT... WE'RE GONNA BE LATE!
WHO CARES. WE'VE STILL GOT 30 MIN-UTES BEFORE NEW YEAR'S.
BUT I'M SURE THEY'RE ALL WAITING FOR US!
HEY...
IS THAT YOUR CHRISTMAS PRESENT FROM HARUNA? The hat?
YEP! She gave it to me!
HMM. INTER-ESTING...
YOU CAN DO A LOT WITH THESE STRINGS ON THE SIDE!
TUG
AHHH!
YOU'RE CHOKING ME! YOU'RE STRETCHING MY HAT OUT!!
Stop it!
BY THE WAY...
I HEARD YOU WERE THE ONE WHO BROUGHT HARUNA TO ME ON CHRISTMAS EVE...
PANT PANT
I DON'T REMEMBER ANYTHING, REALLY...
I FEEL LIKE I MIGHT HAVE BEEN DREAMING, BUT...

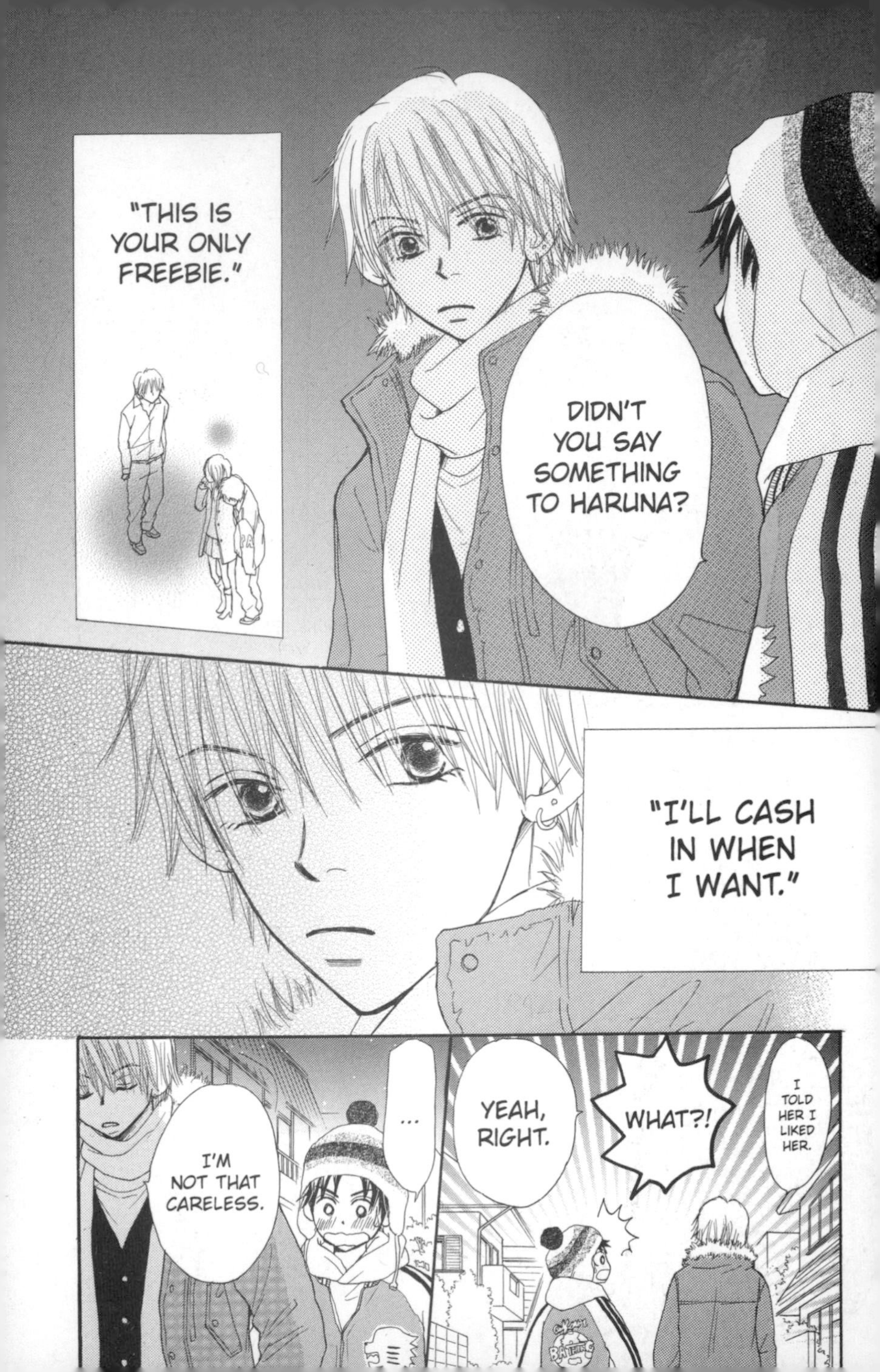
DIDN'T YOU SAY SOMETHING TO HARUNA?
"THIS IS YOUR ONLY FREEBIE."
"I'LL CASH IN WHEN I WANT."
I TOLD HER I LIKED HER.
WHAT?!
YEAH, RIGHT.
...
I'M NOT THAT CARELESS.

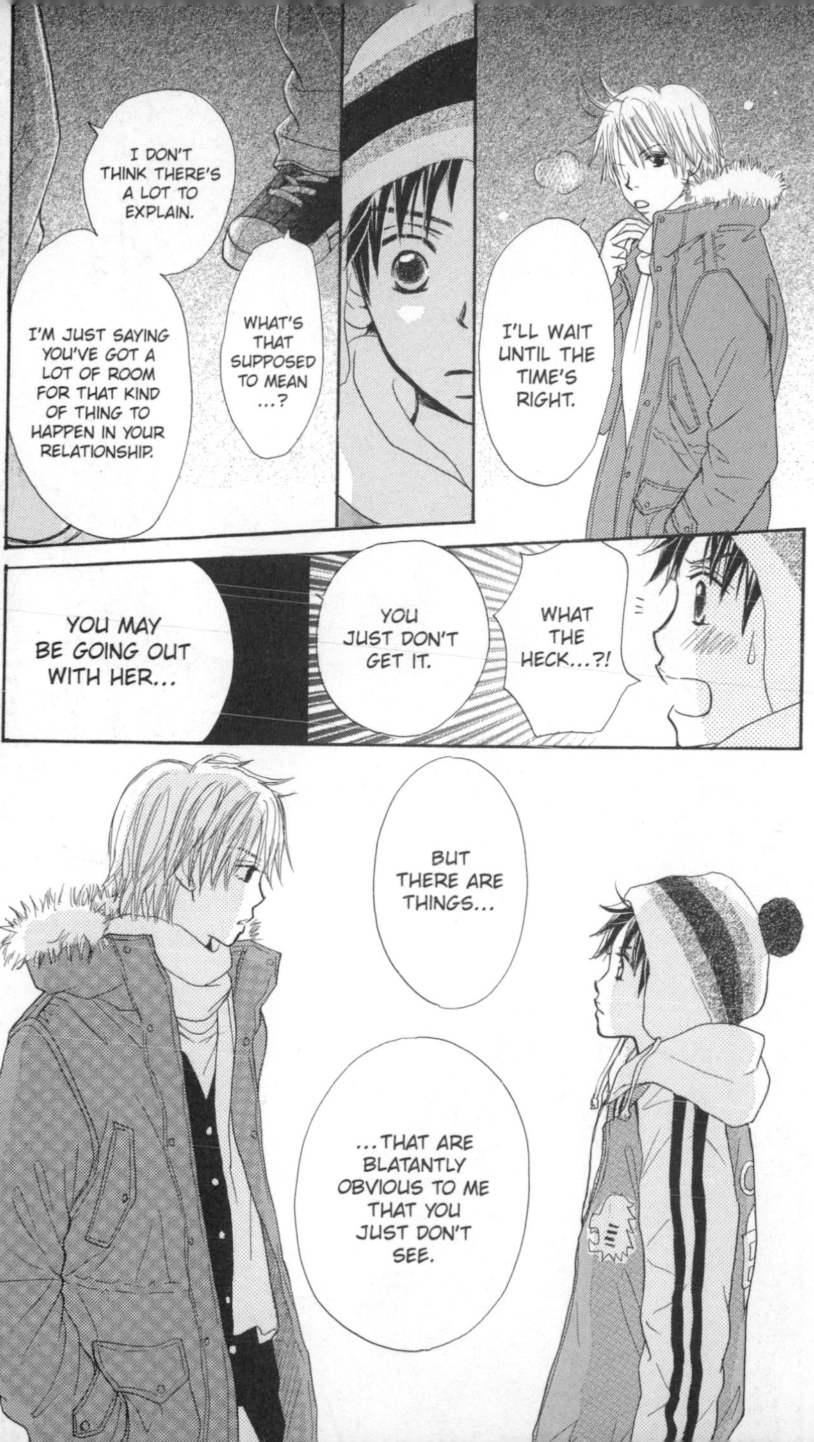
I'LL WAIT UNTIL THE TIME'S RIGHT.
WHAT'S THAT SUPPOSED TO MEAN ...?
I DON'T THINK THERE'S A LOT TO EXPLAIN.
I'M JUST SAYING YOU'VE GOT A LOT OF ROOM FOR THAT KIND OF THING TO HAPPEN IN YOUR RELATIONSHIP.
WHAT THE HECK...?!
YOU JUST DON'T GET IT.
YOU MAY BE GOING OUT WITH HER...
BUT THERE ARE THINGS...
...THAT ARE BLATANTLY OBVIOUS TO ME THAT YOU JUST DON'T SEE.

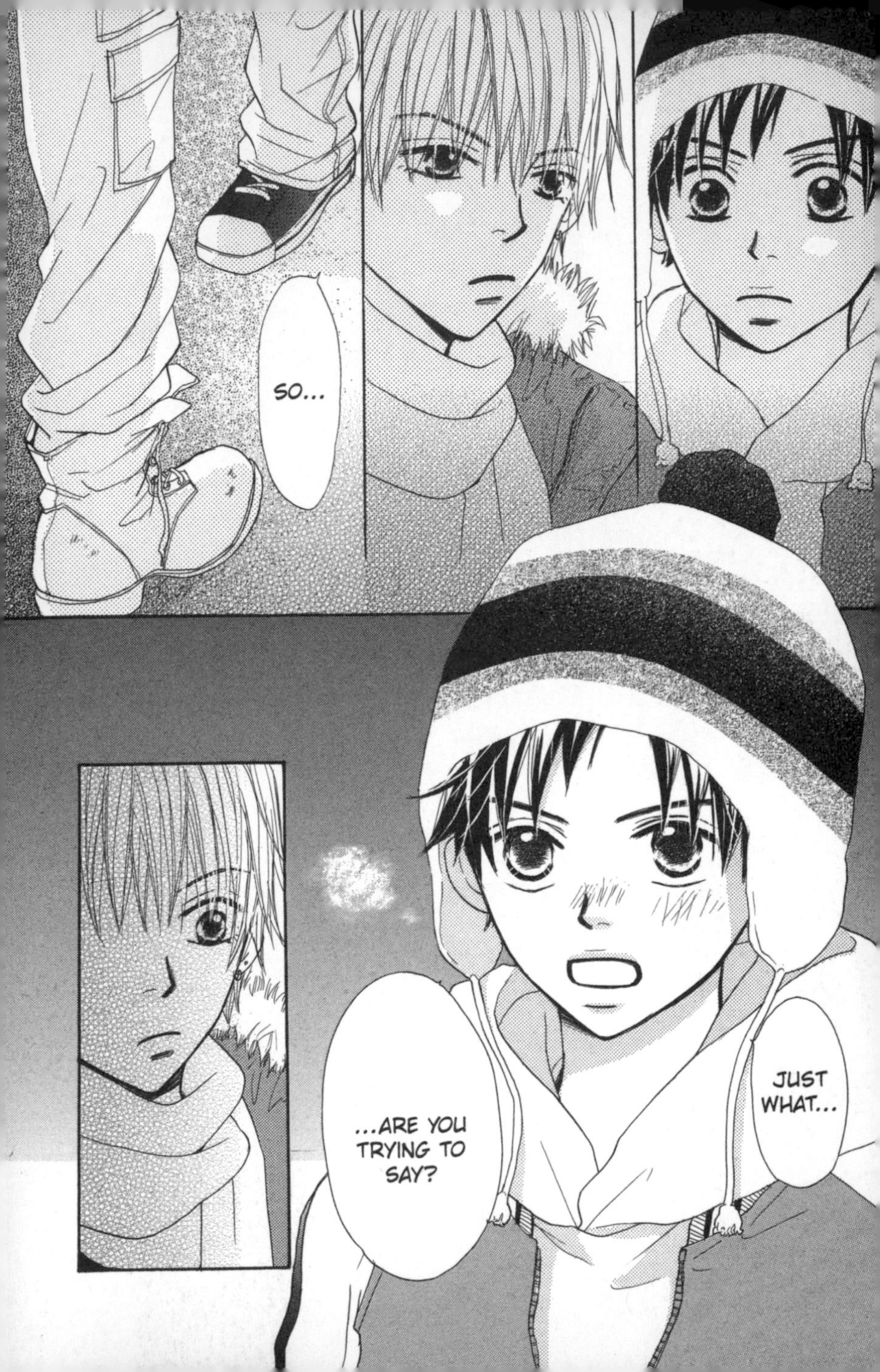
SO...
JUST WHAT...
...ARE YOU TRYING TO SAY?

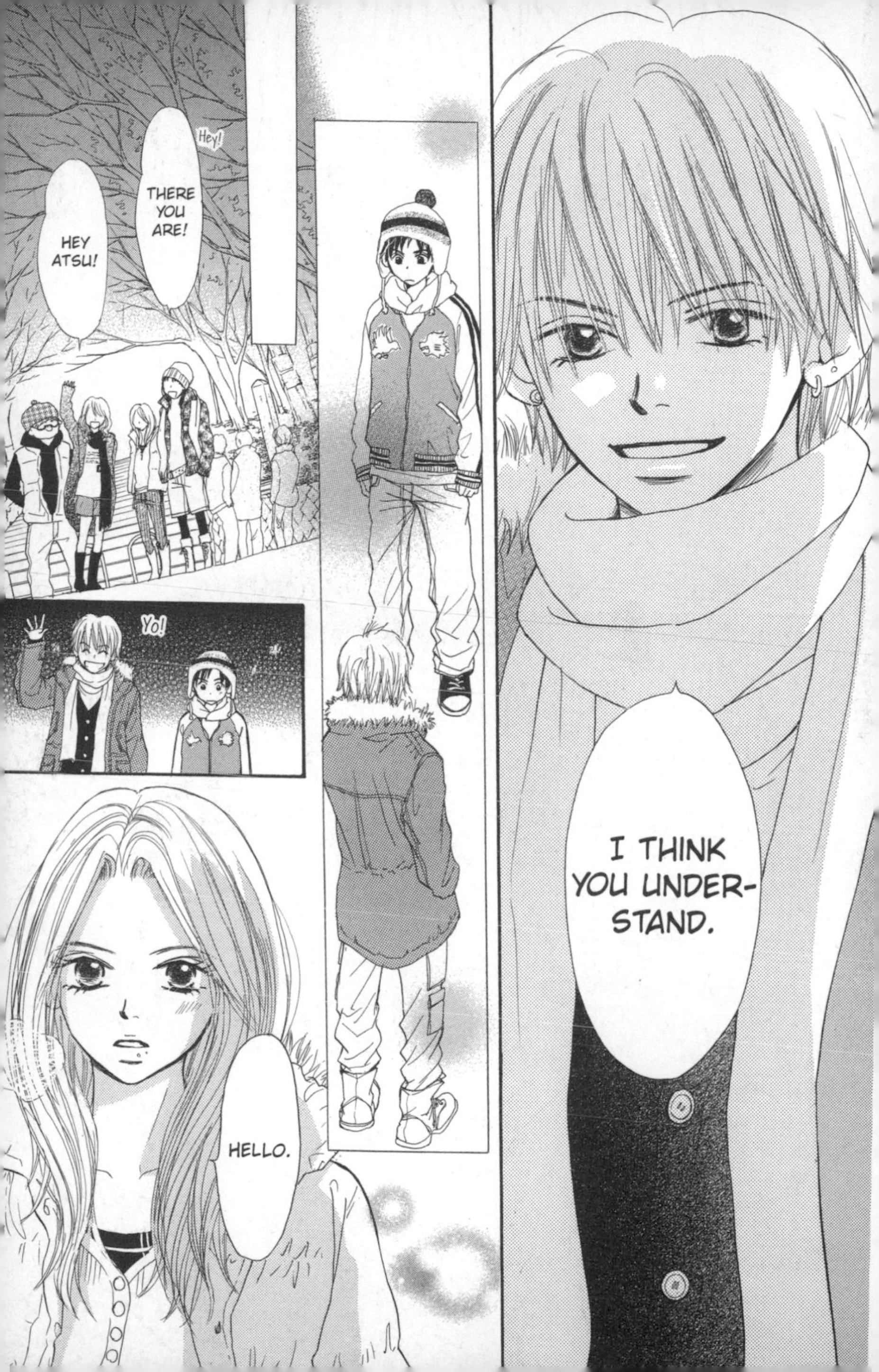
I THINK YOU UNDER-STAND.
Hey!
THERE YOU ARE!
HEY ATSU!
Yo!
HELLO.

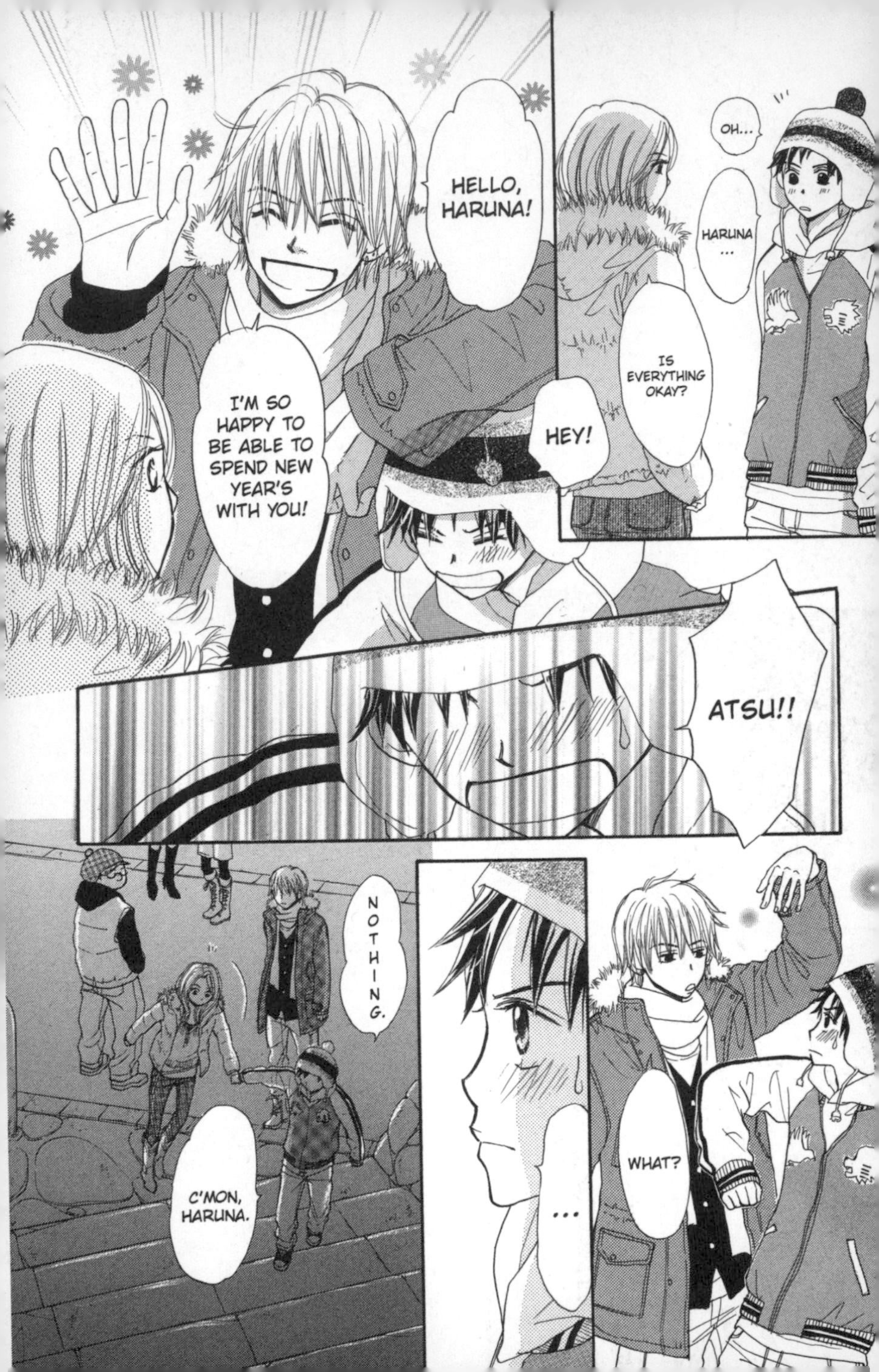
OH...
HARUNA ...
IS EVERYTHING OKAY?
HELLO, HARUNA!
I'M SO HAPPY TO BE ABLE TO SPEND NEW YEAR'S WITH YOU!
HEY!
ATSU!!
WHAT?
...
NOTHING.
C'MON, HARUNA.

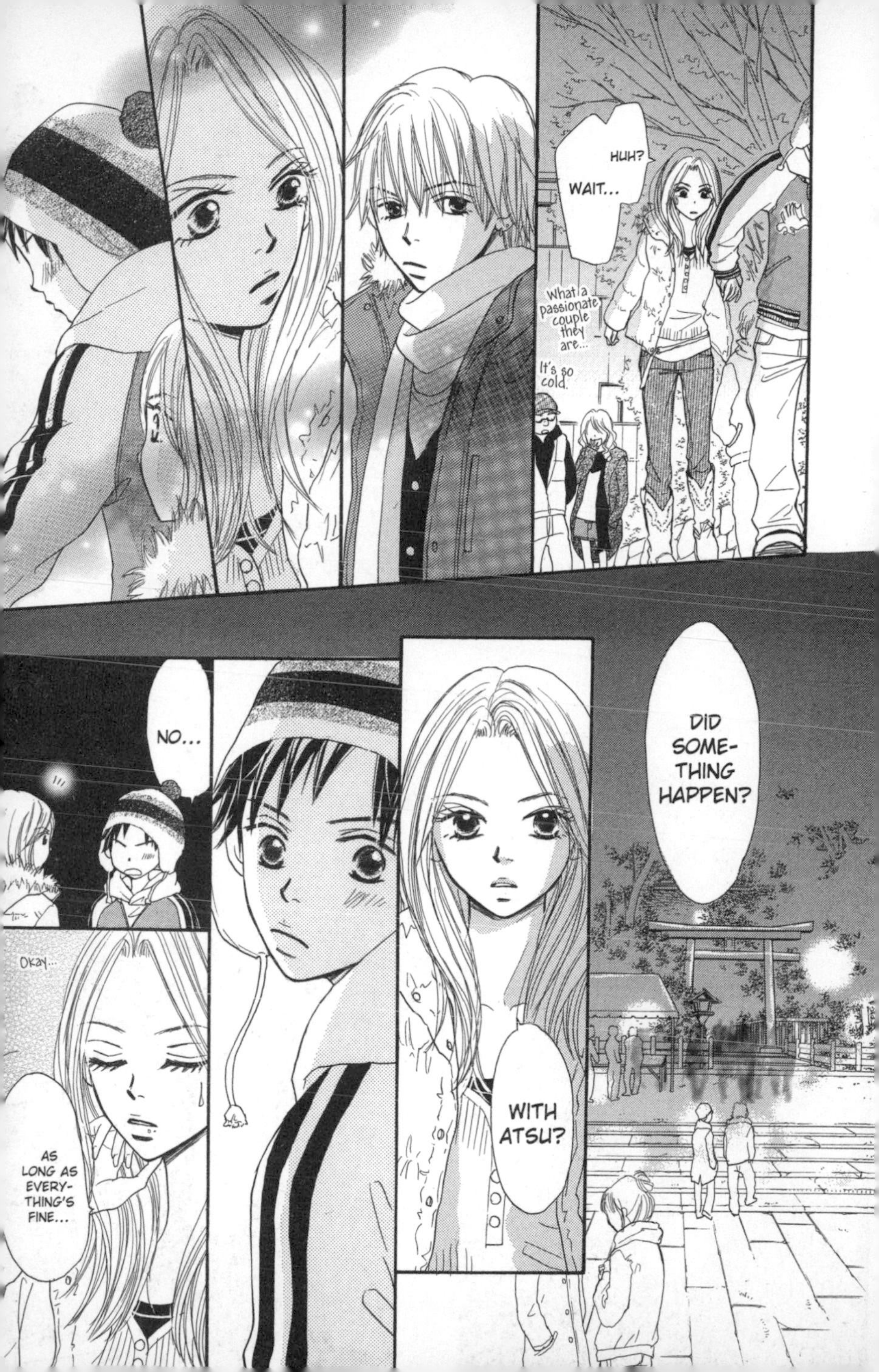
HUH?
WAIT...
What a passionate couple they are...
It's so cold.
DID SOME-THING HAPPEN?
WITH ATSU?
NO...
Okay...
AS LONG AS EVERY-THING'S FINE...

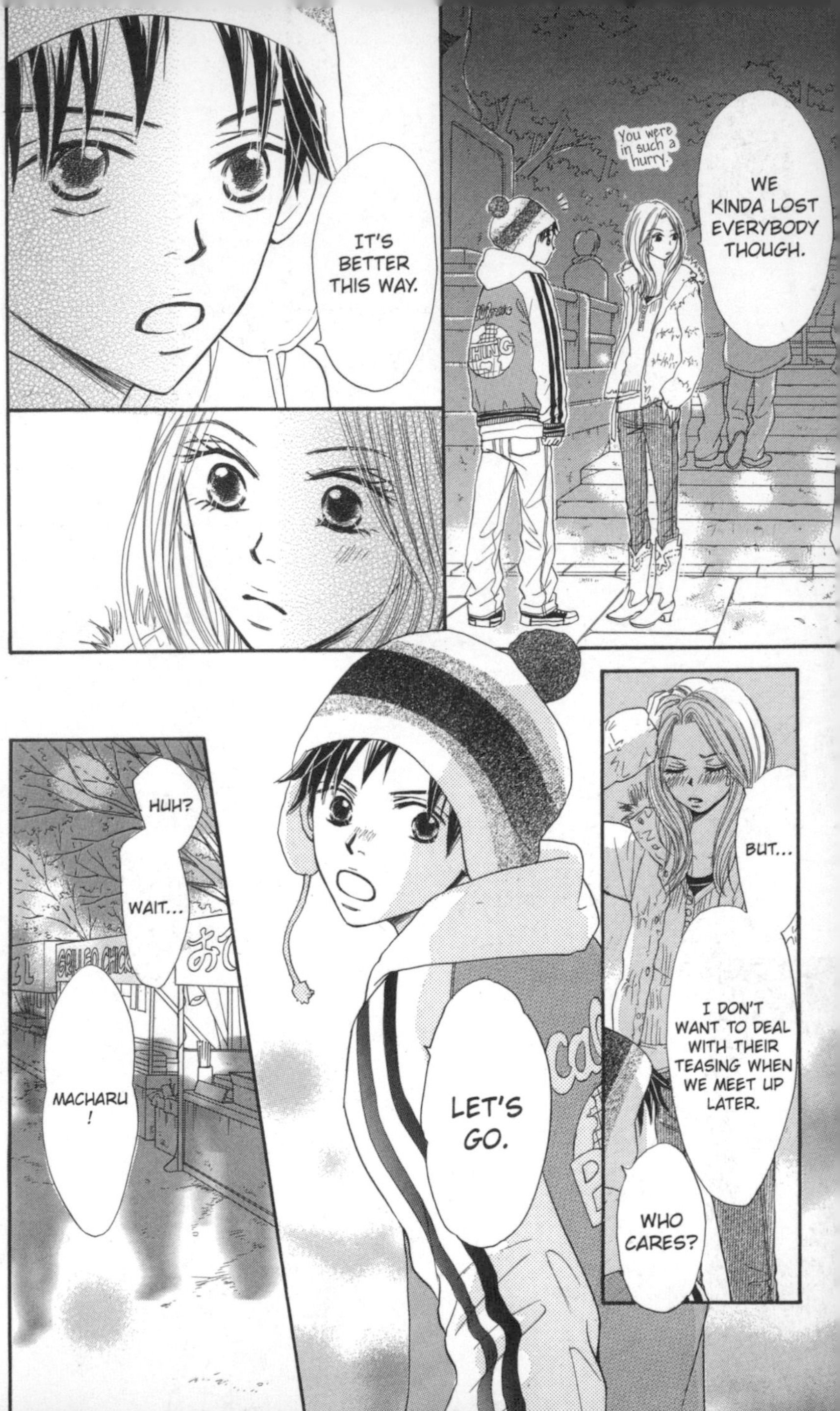
WE KINDA LOST EVERYBODY THOUGH.
You were in such a hurry.
IT'S BETTER THIS WAY.
BUT...
I DON'T WANT TO DEAL WITH THEIR TEASING WHEN WE MEET UP LATER.
WHO CARES?
LET'S GO.
HUH?
WAIT...
MACHARU!

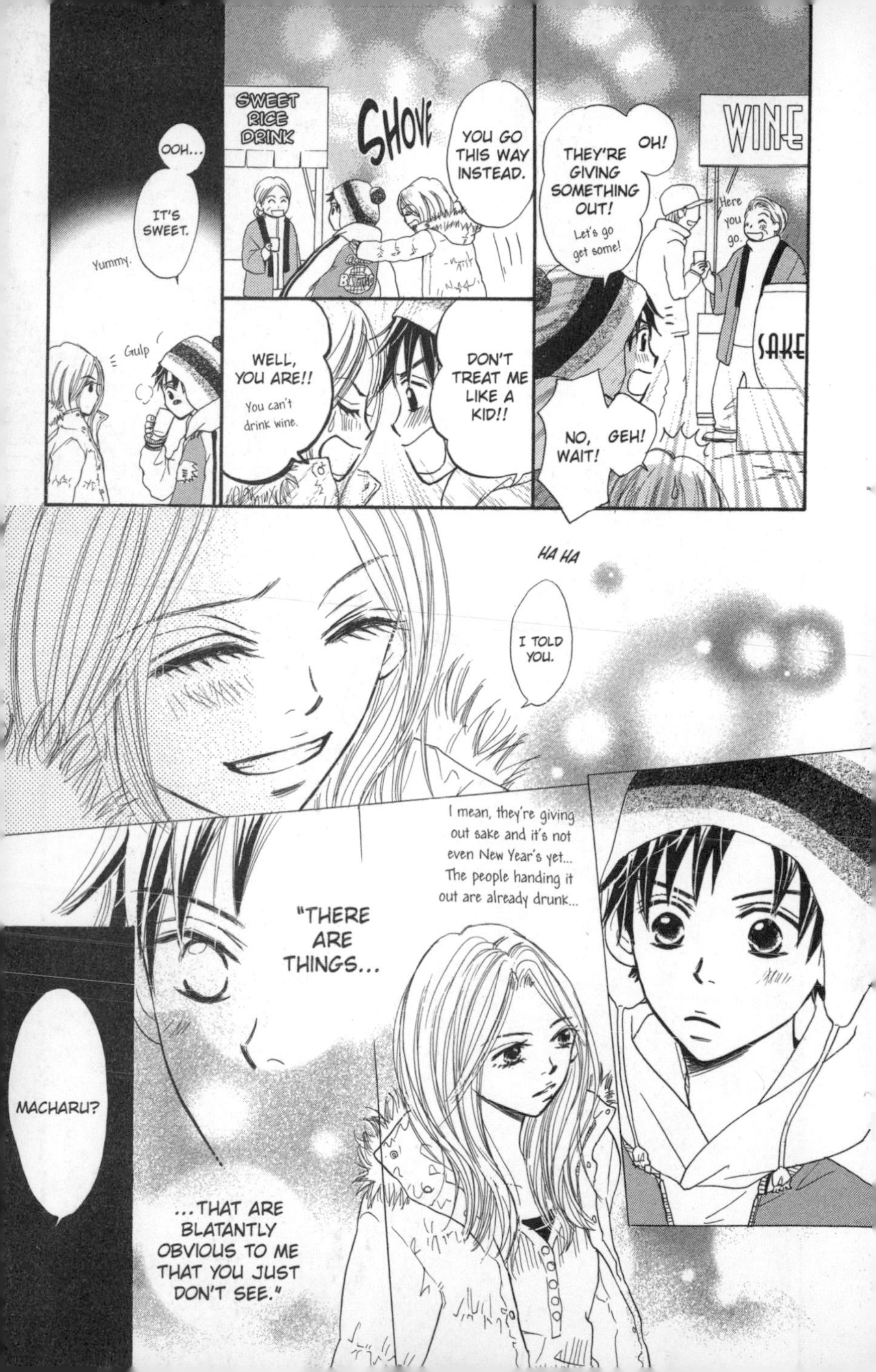
WINE
OH!
THEY'RE GIVING SOMETHING OUT!
Let's go get some!
Here you go.
SAKE
GEH!
NO, WAIT!
YOU GO THIS WAY INSTEAD.
SHOVE
SWEET RICE DRINK
DON'T TREAT ME LIKE A KID!!
WELL, YOU ARE!!
You can't drink wine.
OOH...
IT'S SWEET.
Yummy.
Gulp
HA HA
I TOLD YOU.
I mean, they're giving out sake and it's not even New Year's yet... The people handing it out are already drunk...
"THERE ARE THINGS...
...THAT ARE BLATANTLY OBVIOUS TO ME THAT YOU JUST DON'T SEE."
MACHARU?

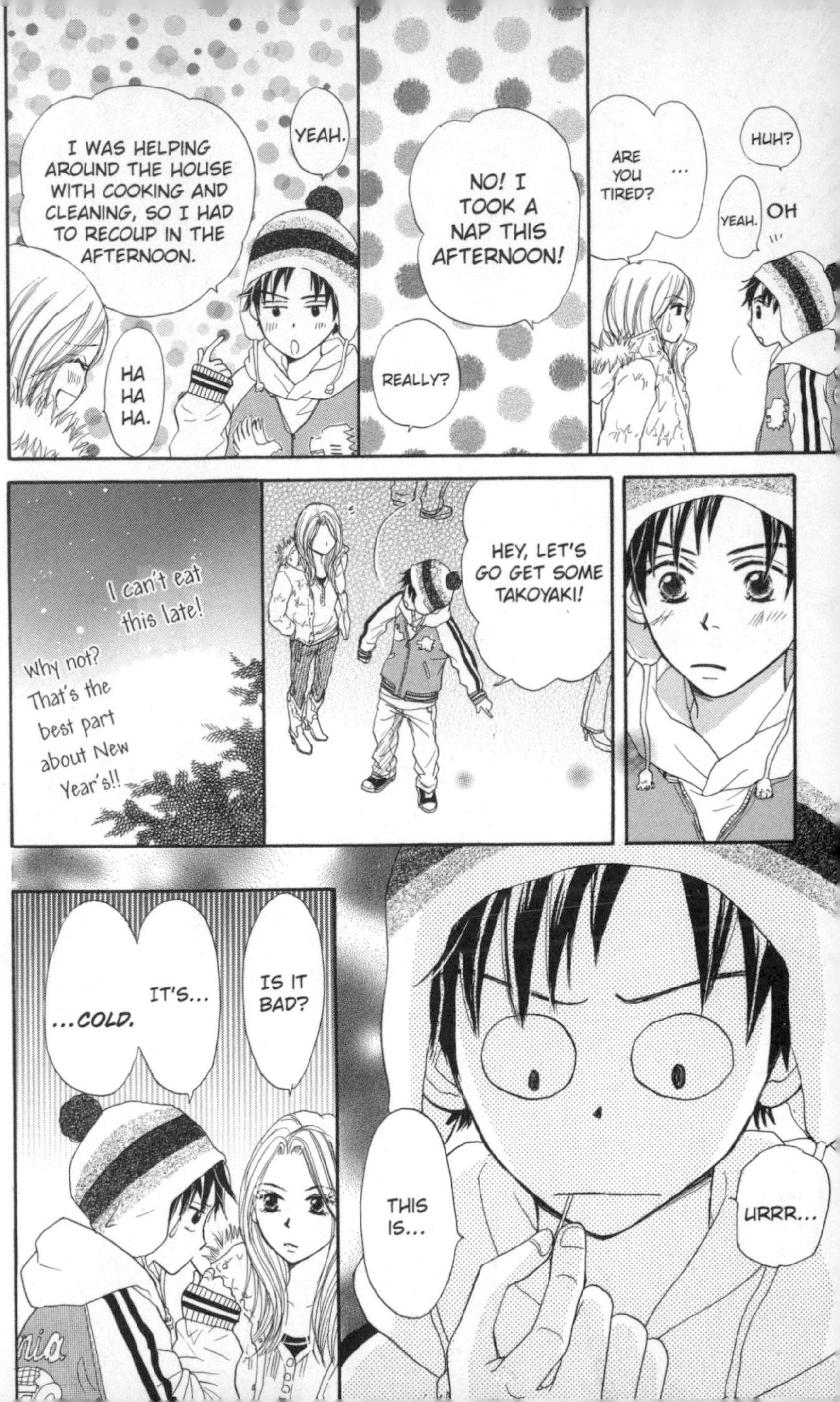
HUH?
ARE YOU TIRED? ...
OH
YEAH.
NO! I TOOK A NAP THIS AFTERNOON!
REALLY?
YEAH.
I WAS HELPING AROUND THE HOUSE WITH COOKING AND CLEANING, SO I HAD TO RECOUP IN THE AFTERNOON.
HA HA HA.
HEY, LET'S GO GET SOME TAKOYAKI!
I can't eat this late!
Why not? That's the best part about New Year's!!
URRR...
THIS IS...
IS IT BAD?
IT'S...
...COLD.

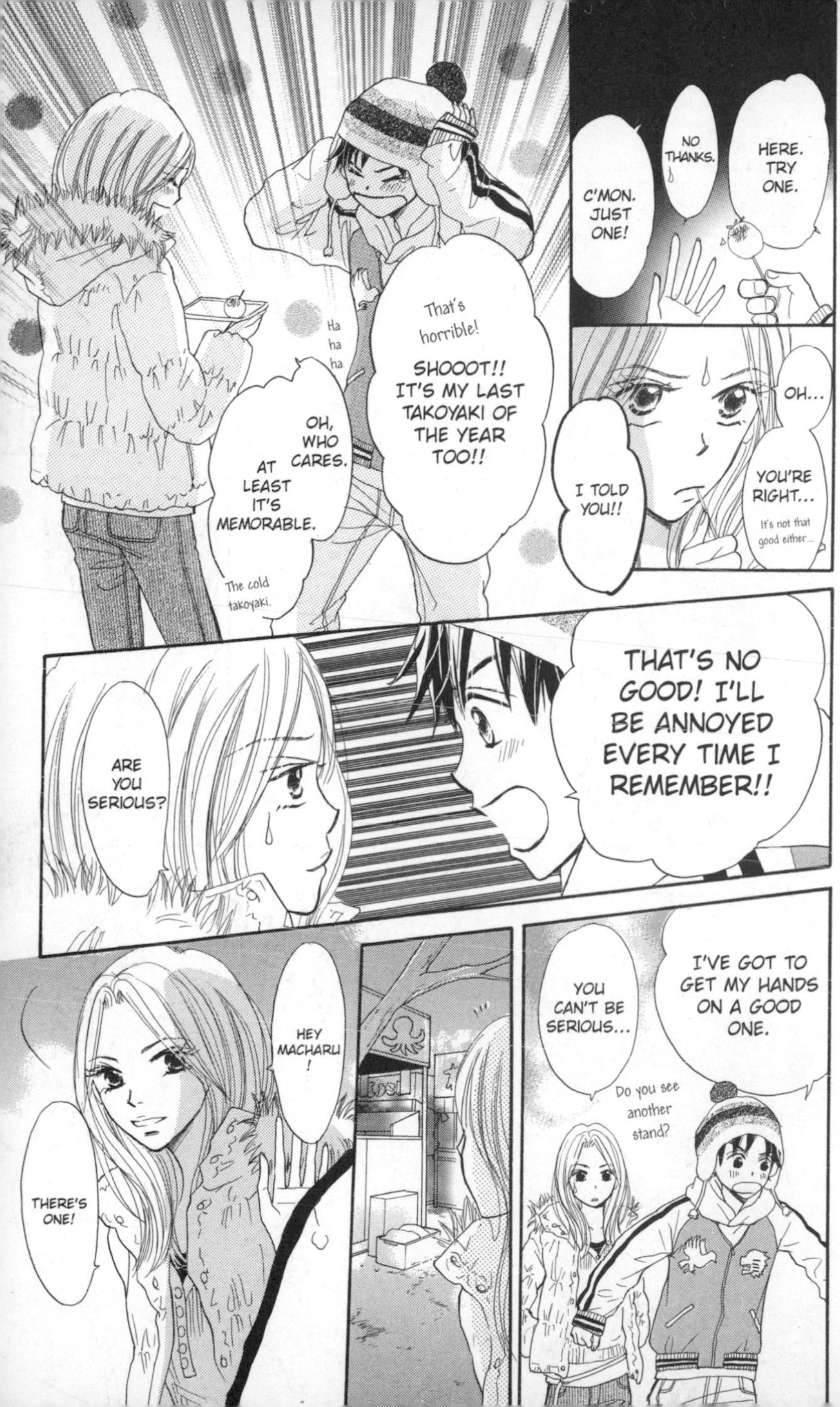
HERE. TRY ONE.
NO THANKS.
C'MON. JUST ONE!
OH...
YOU'RE RIGHT...
It's not that good either...
I TOLD YOU!!
That's horrible!
SHOOOT!! IT'S MY LAST TAKOYAKI OF THE YEAR TOO!!
Ha ha ha
OH, WHO CARES. AT LEAST IT'S MEMORABLE.
The cold takoyaki.
THAT'S NO GOOD! I'LL BE ANNOYED EVERY TIME I REMEMBER!!
ARE YOU SERIOUS?
I'VE GOT TO GET MY HANDS ON A GOOD ONE.
YOU CAN'T BE SERIOUS...
Do you see another stand?
HEY MACHARU!
THERE'S ONE!

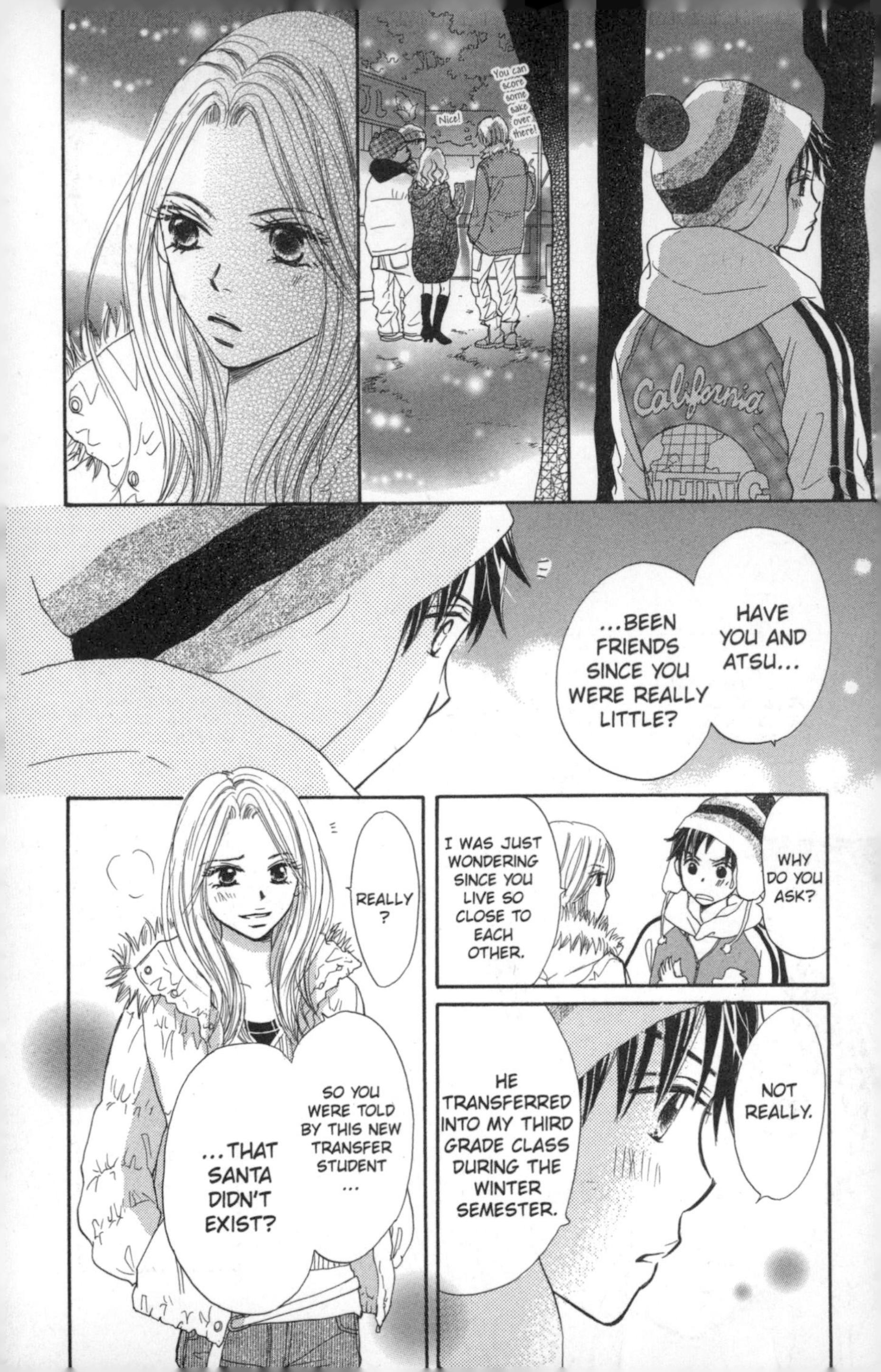
You can score some sake over there!
Nice!
HAVE YOU AND ATSU...
...BEEN FRIENDS SINCE YOU WERE REALLY LITTLE?
WHY DO YOU ASK?
I WAS JUST WONDERING SINCE YOU LIVE SO CLOSE TO EACH OTHER.
NOT REALLY.
HE TRANSFERRED INTO MY THIRD GRADE CLASS DURING THE WINTER SEMESTER.
REALLY?
SO YOU WERE TOLD BY THIS NEW TRANSFER STUDENT...
...THAT SANTA DIDN'T EXIST?

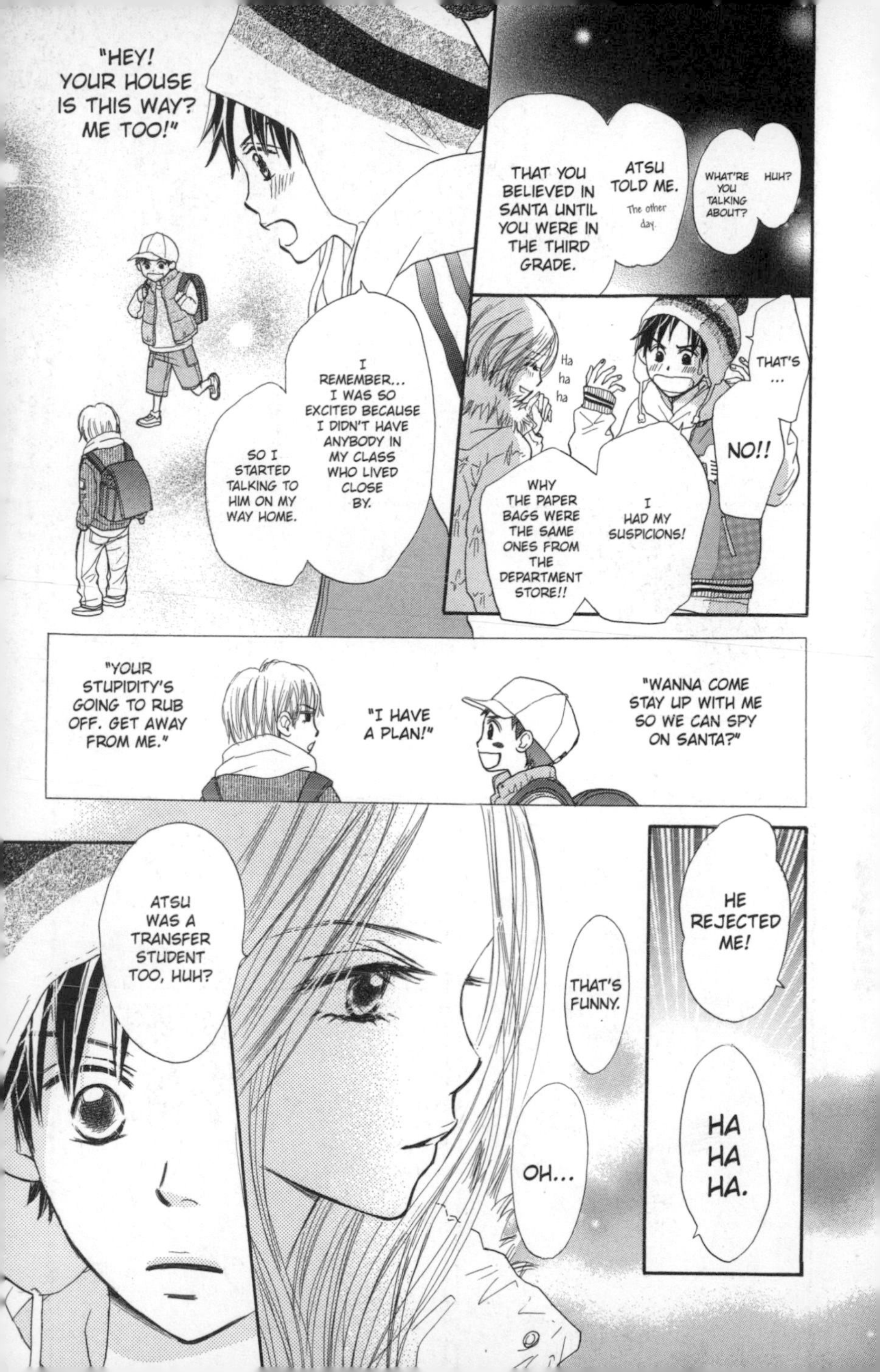
HUH?
WHAT'RE YOU TALKING ABOUT?
ATSU TOLD ME.
The other day.
THAT YOU BELIEVED IN SANTA UNTIL YOU WERE IN THE THIRD GRADE.
THAT'S...
NO!!
I HAD MY SUSPICIONS!
WHY THE PAPER BAGS WERE THE SAME ONES FROM THE DEPARTMENT STORE!!
Ha ha ha
"HEY! YOUR HOUSE IS THIS WAY? ME TOO!"
I REMEMBER... I WAS SO EXCITED BECAUSE I DIDN'T HAVE ANYBODY IN MY CLASS WHO LIVED CLOSE BY.
SO I STARTED TALKING TO HIM ON MY WAY HOME.
"WANNA COME STAY UP WITH ME SO WE CAN SPY ON SANTA?"
"I HAVE A PLAN!"
"YOUR STUPIDITY'S GOING TO RUB OFF. GET AWAY FROM ME."
HE REJECTED ME!
HA HA HA.
THAT'S FUNNY.
OH...
ATSU WAS A TRANSFER STUDENT TOO, HUH?

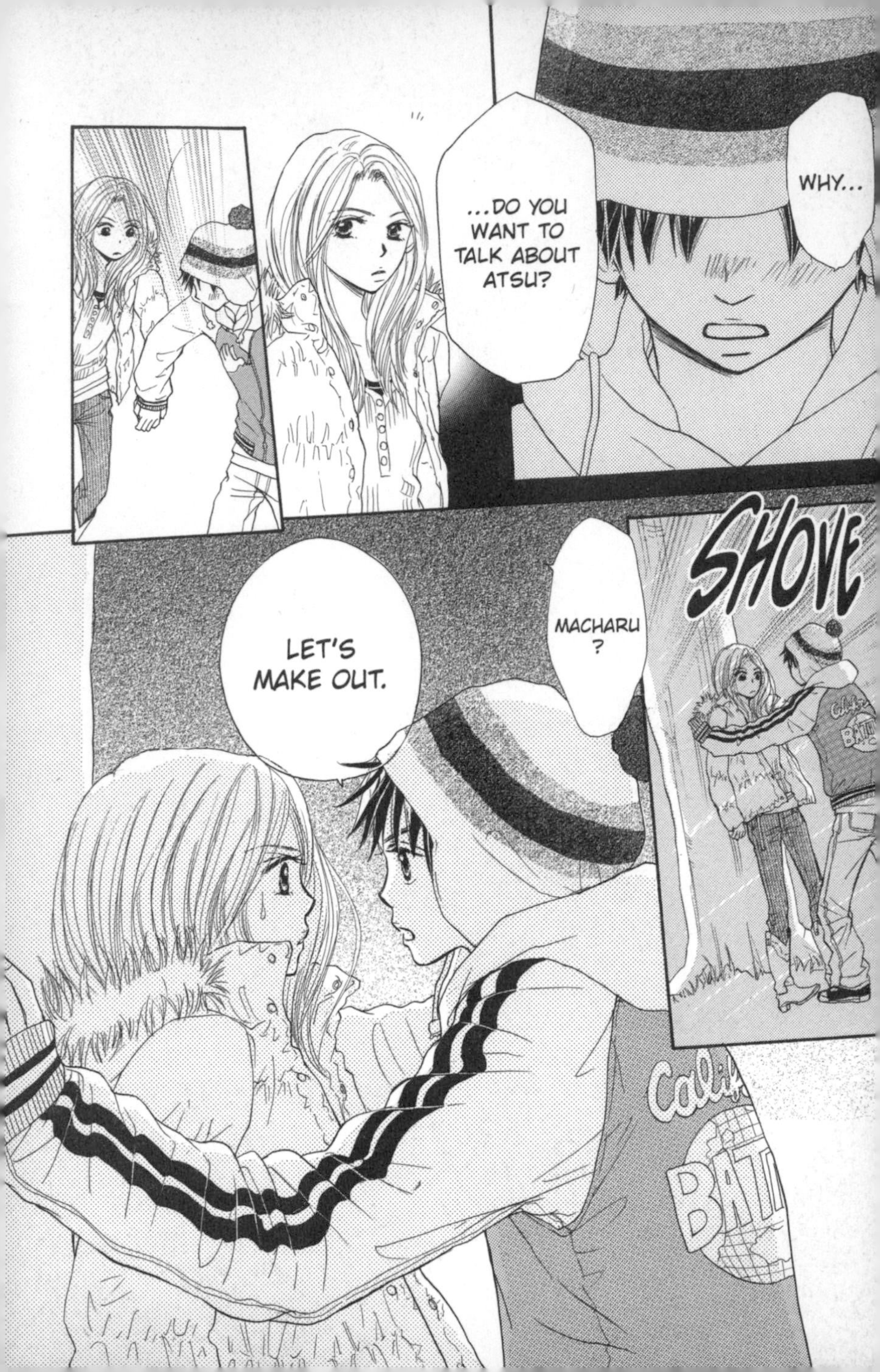
WHY...
...DO YOU WANT TO TALK ABOUT ATSU?
SHOVE
MACHARU?
LET'S MAKE OUT.

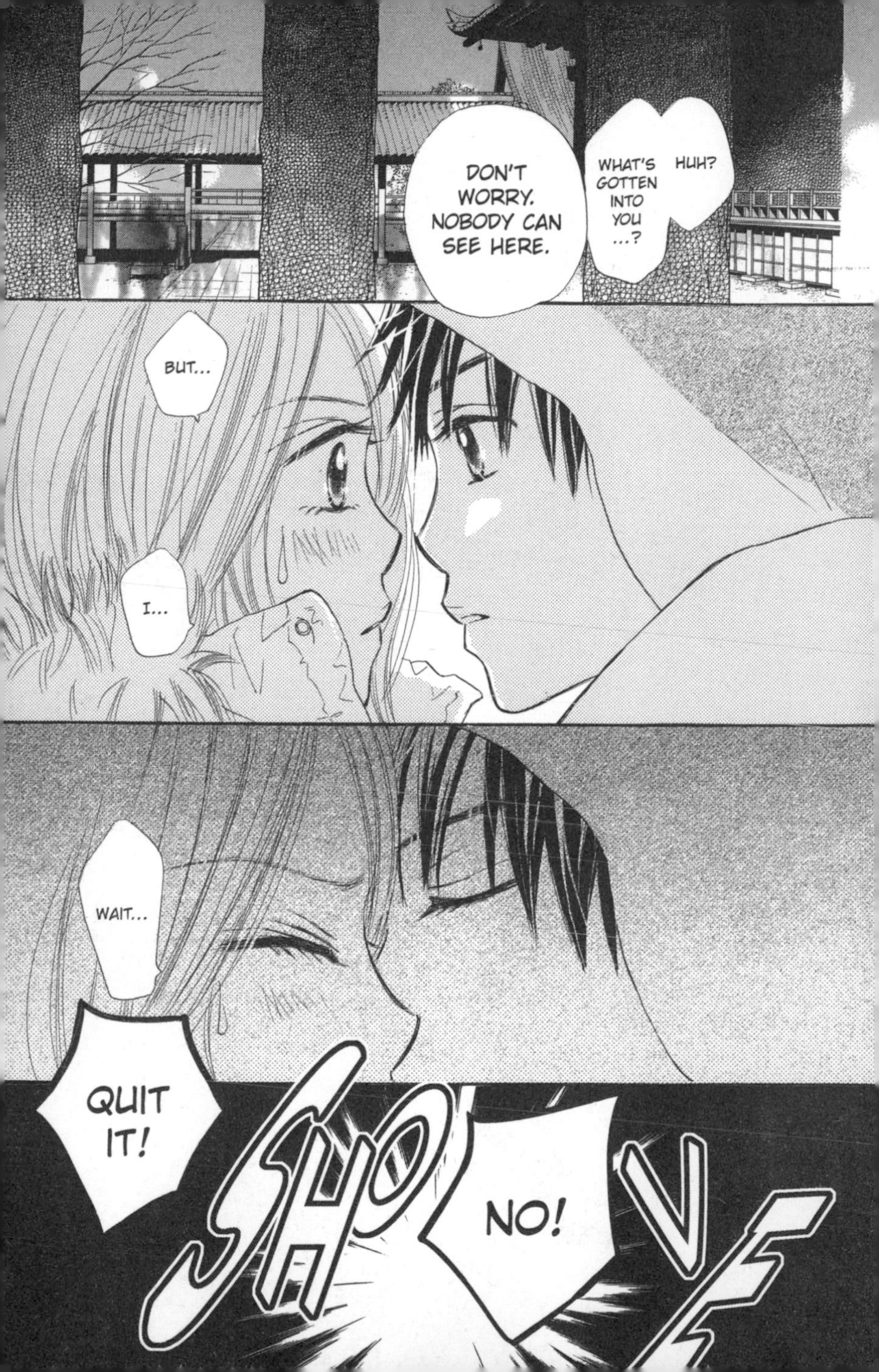
HUH?
WHAT'S GOTTEN INTO YOU ...?
DON'T WORRY. NOBODY CAN SEE HERE.
BUT...
I...
WAIT...
QUIT IT!
NO!
SHOVE

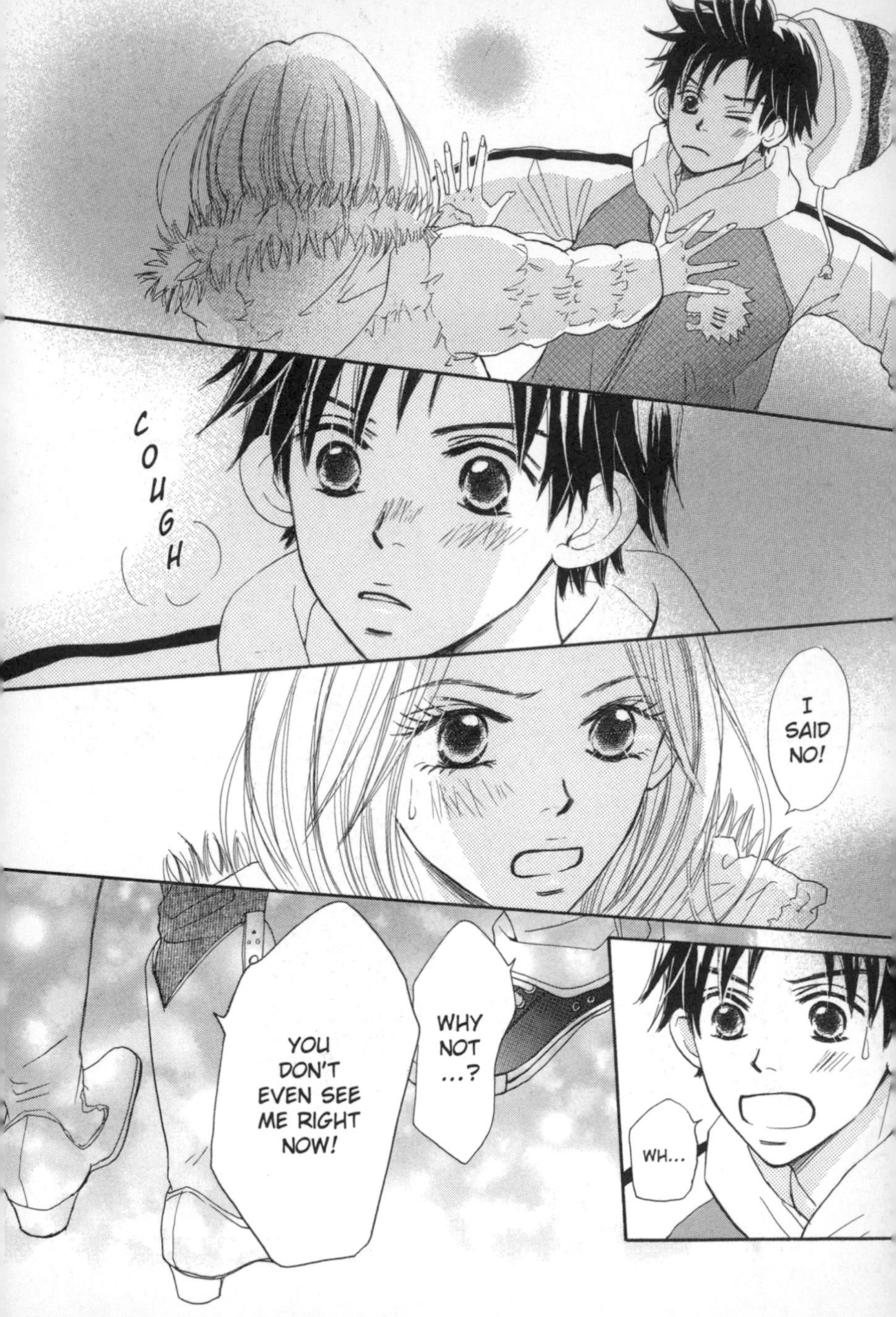
COUGH
I SAID NO!
WH...
WHY NOT ...?
YOU DON'T EVEN SEE ME RIGHT NOW!

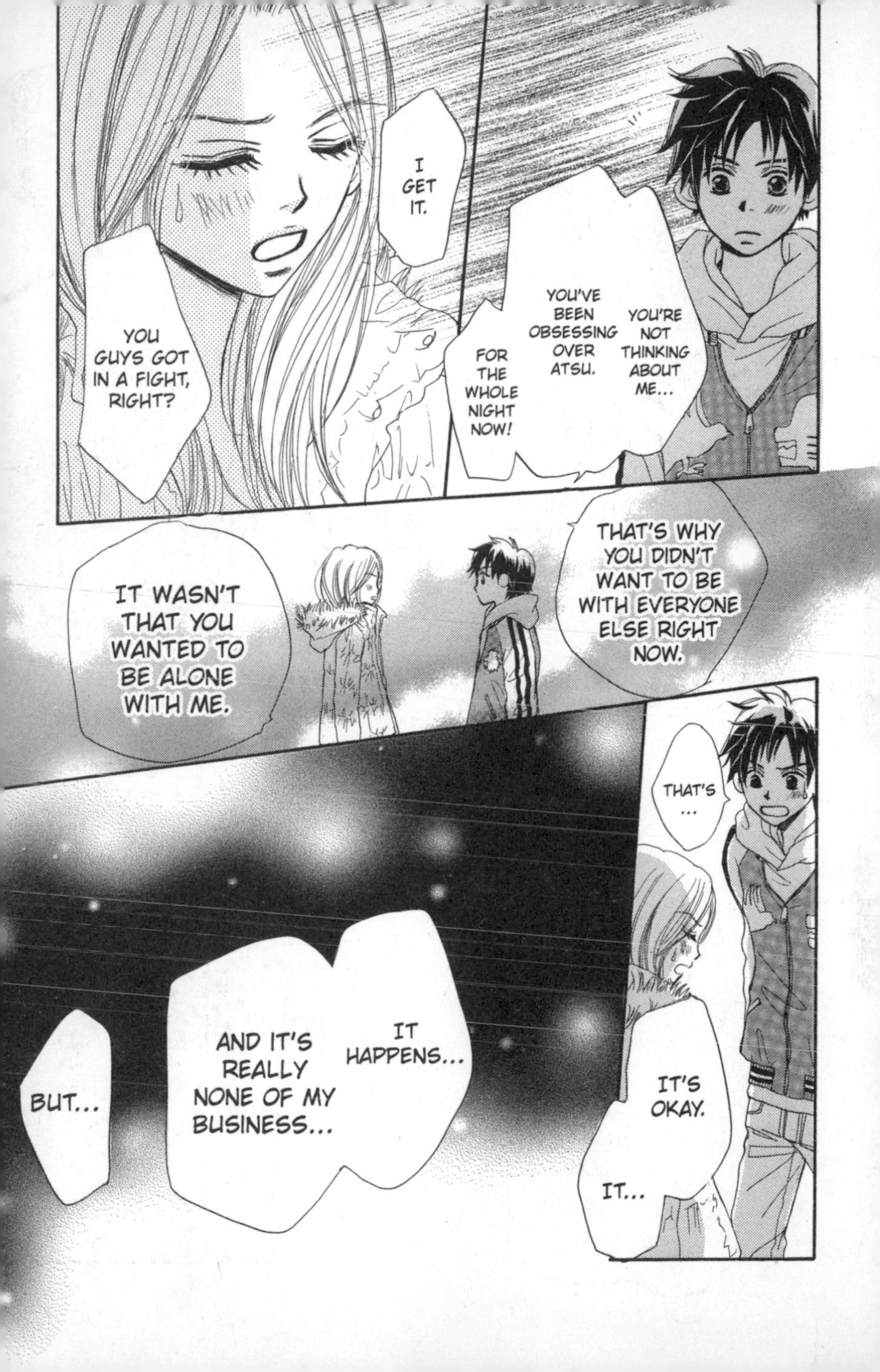
YOU'RE NOT THINKING ABOUT ME...
YOU'VE BEEN OBSESSING OVER ATSU.
FOR THE WHOLE NIGHT NOW!
I GET IT.
YOU GUYS GOT IN A FIGHT, RIGHT?
THAT'S WHY YOU DIDN'T WANT TO BE WITH EVERYONE ELSE RIGHT NOW.
IT WASN'T THAT YOU WANTED TO BE ALONE WITH ME.
THAT'S...
IT'S OKAY.
IT...
IT HAPPENS...
AND IT'S REALLY NONE OF MY BUSINESS...
BUT...

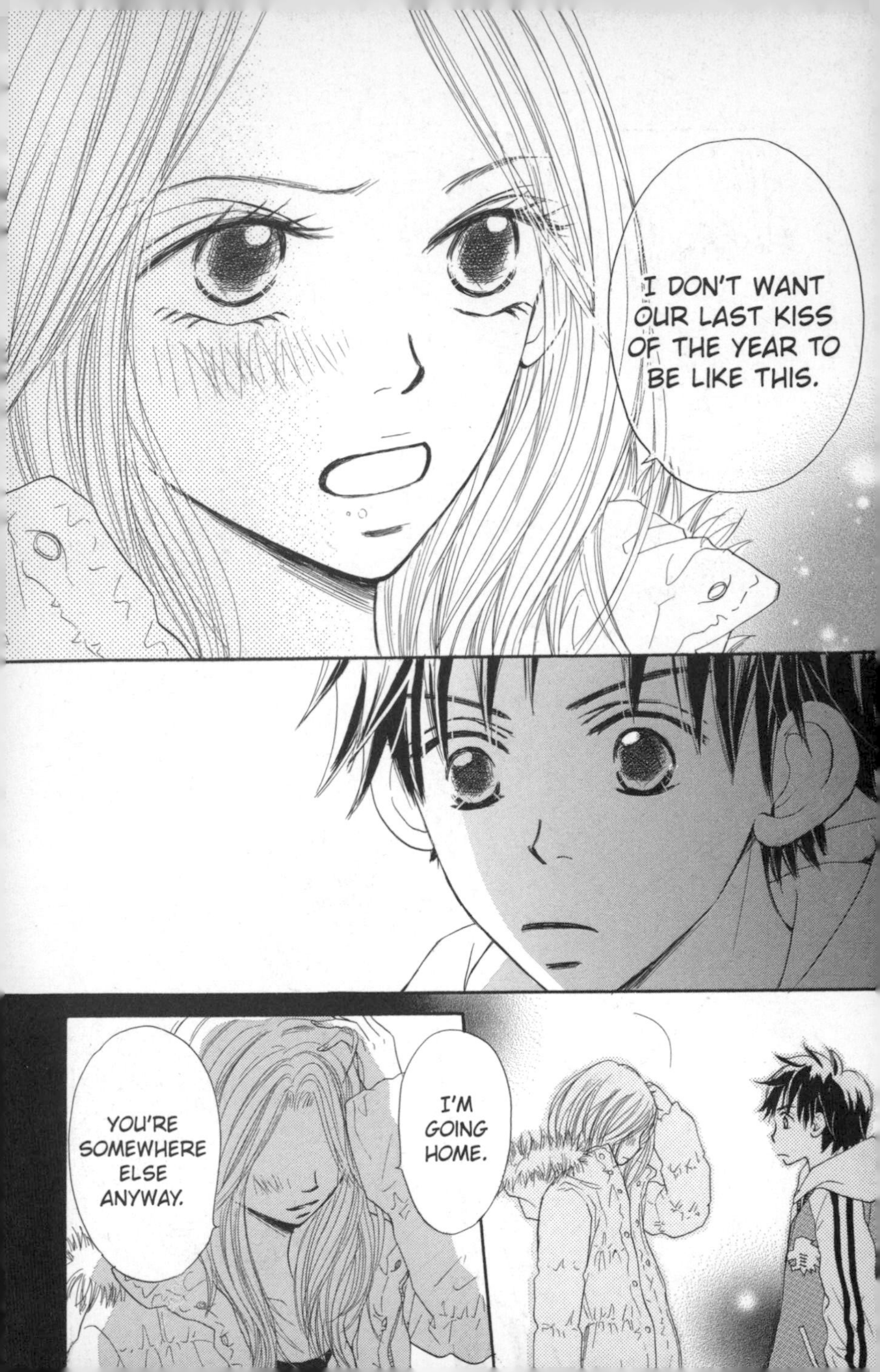
I DON'T WANT OUR LAST KISS OF THE YEAR TO BE LIKE THIS.
I'M GOING HOME.
YOU'RE SOMEWHERE ELSE ANYWAY.

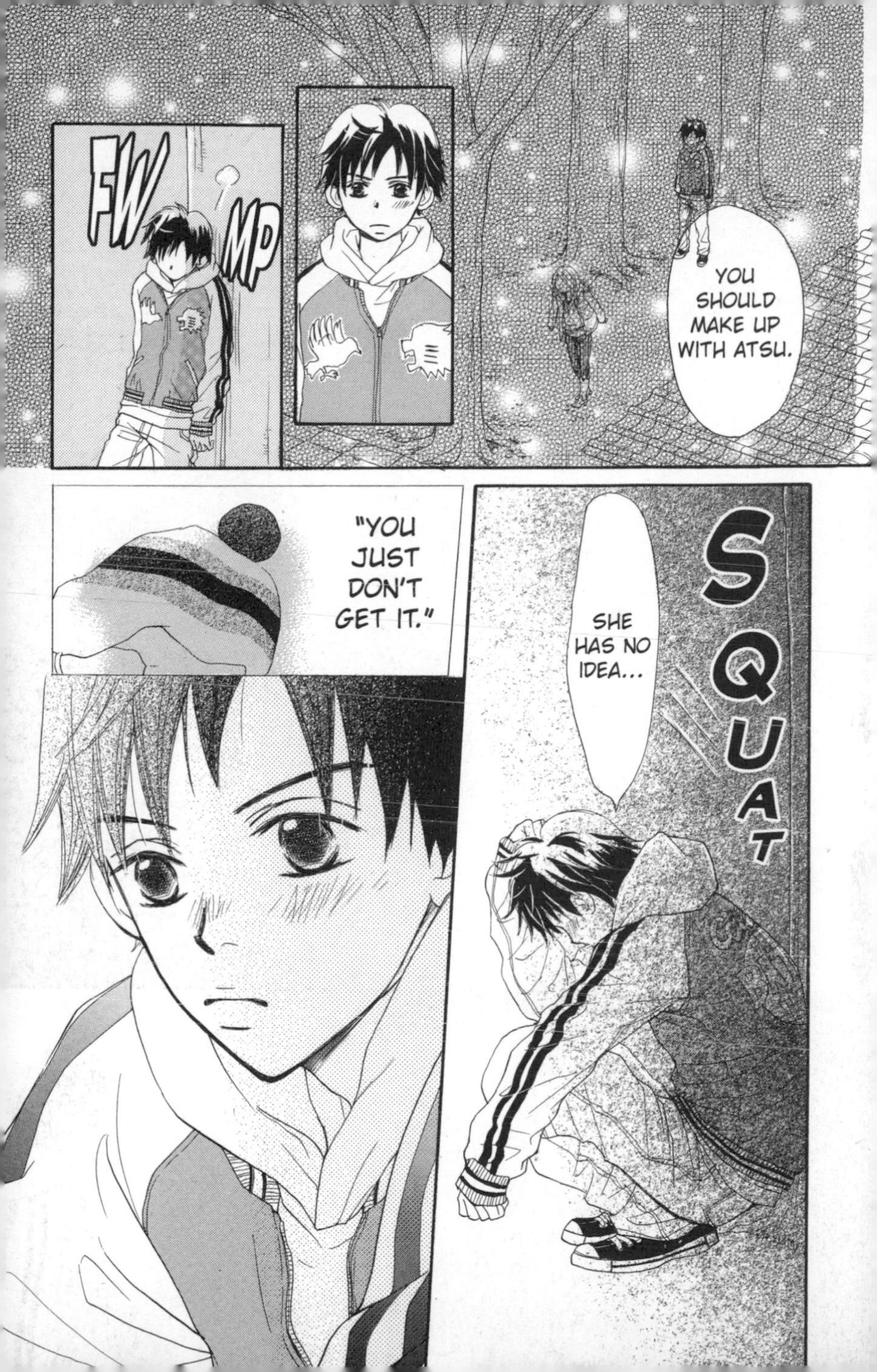
YOU SHOULD MAKE UP WITH ATSU.
FWMP
SQUAT
SHE HAS NO IDEA...
"YOU JUST DON'T GET IT."

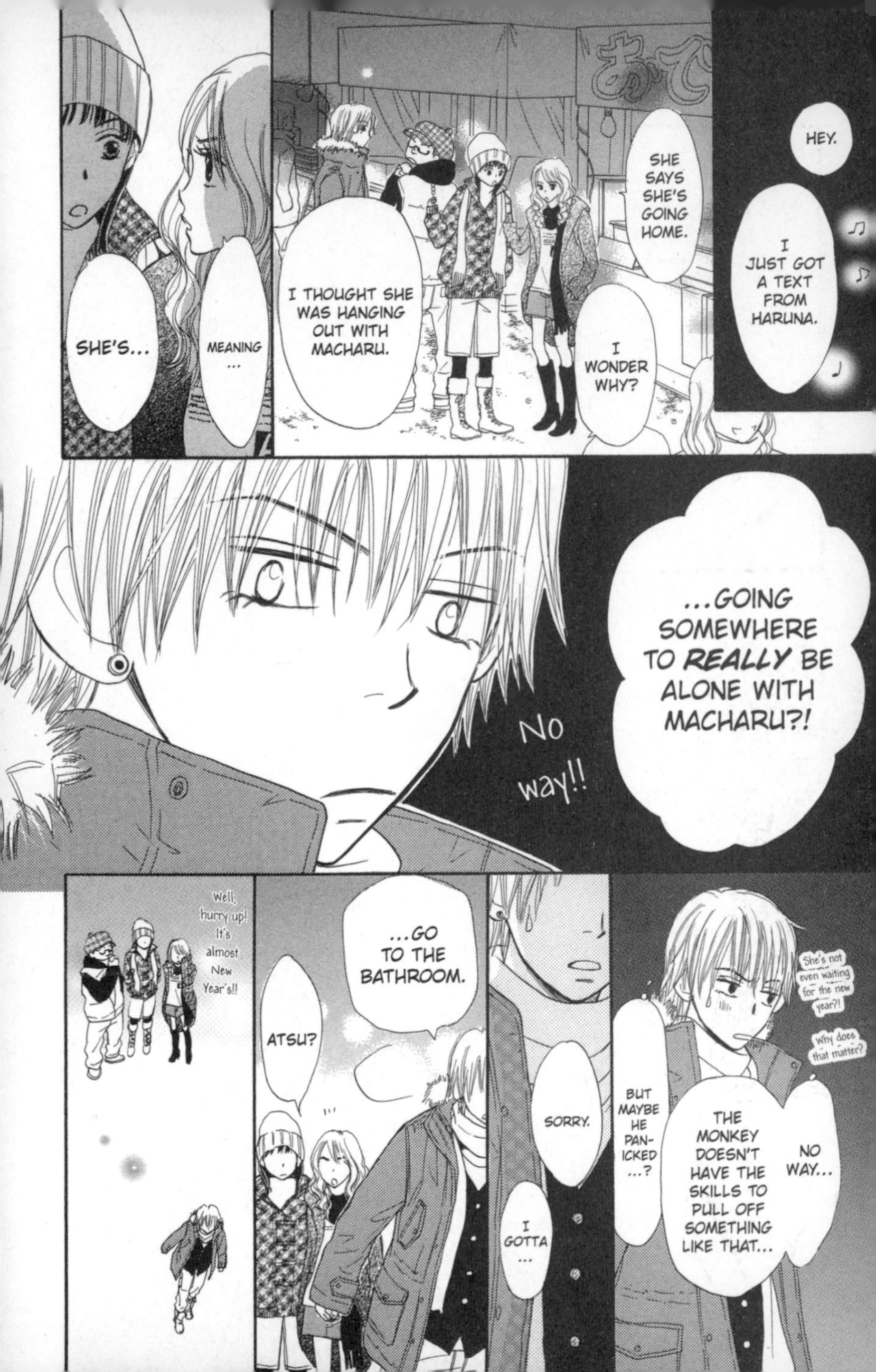
HEY.
I JUST GOT A TEXT FROM HARUNA.
SHE SAYS SHE'S GOING HOME.
I WONDER WHY?
I THOUGHT SHE WAS HANGING OUT WITH MACHARU.
MEANING ...
SHE'S...
...GOING SOMEWHERE TO REALLY BE ALONE WITH MACHARU?!
No way!!
She's not even waiting for the new year?!
Why does that matter?
NO WAY...
THE MONKEY DOESN'T HAVE THE SKILLS TO PULL OFF SOMETHING LIKE THAT...
BUT MAYBE HE PAN-ICKED ...?
SORRY.
I GOTTA ...
...GO TO THE BATHROOM.
ATSU?
Well, hurry up! It's almost New Year's!!

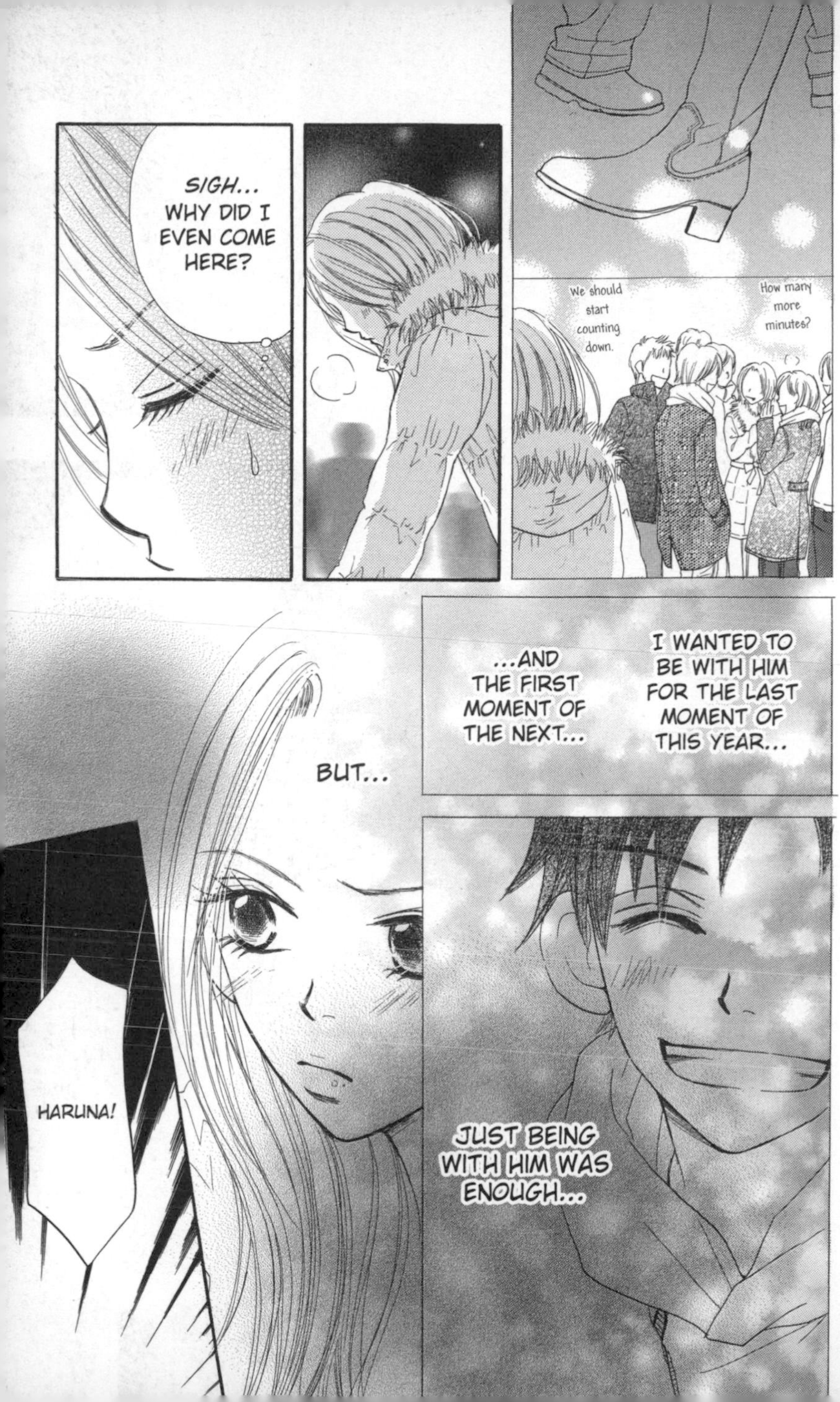
How many more minutes?
We should start counting down.
SIGH... WHY DID I EVEN COME HERE?
I WANTED TO BE WITH HIM FOR THE LAST MOMENT OF THIS YEAR...
...AND THE FIRST MOMENT OF THE NEXT...
BUT...
JUST BEING WITH HIM WAS ENOUGH...
HARUNA!

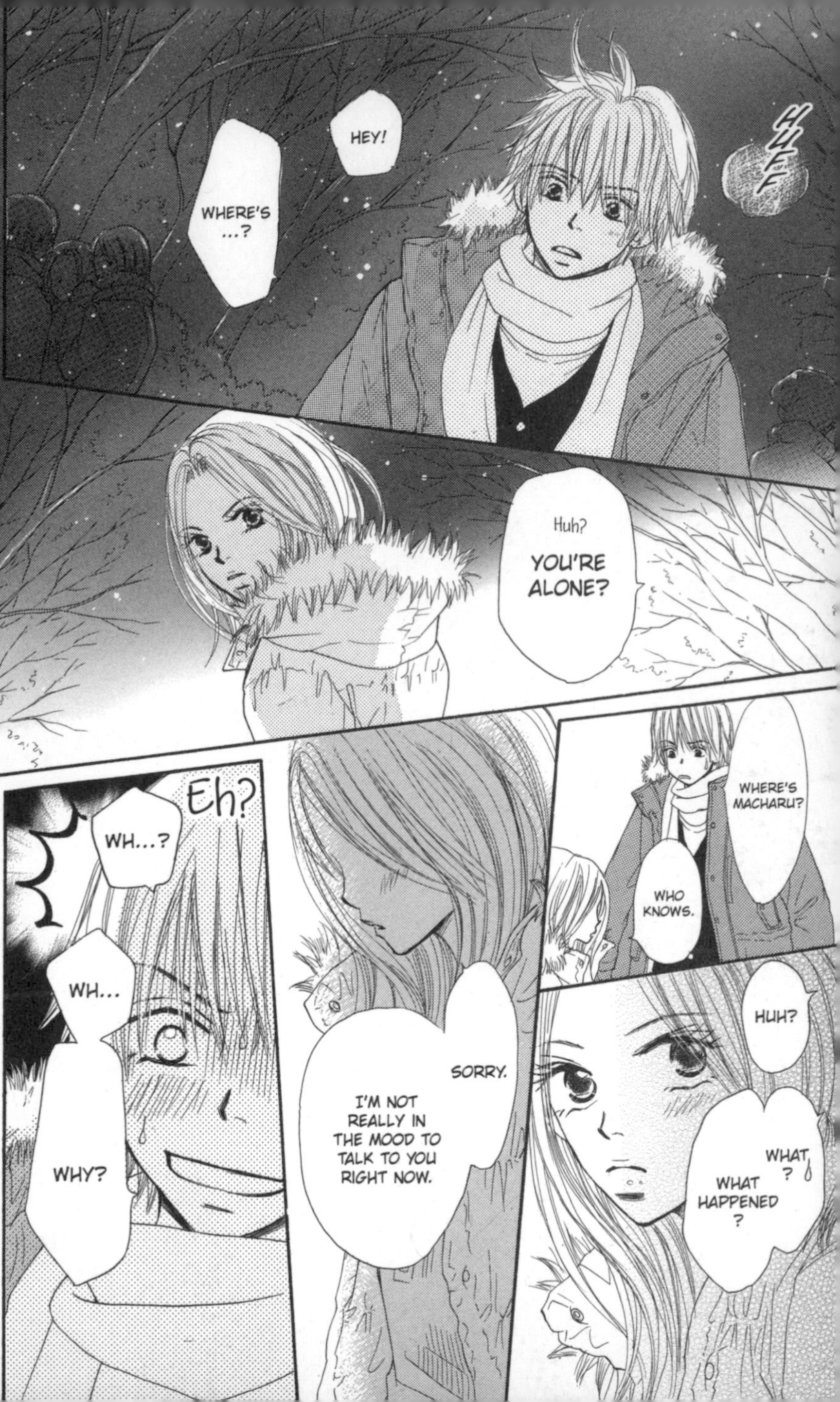
HUFF
HEY!
WHERE'S ...?
Huh?
YOU'RE ALONE?
WHERE'S MACHARU?
WHO KNOWS.
HUH?
WHAT?
WHAT HAPPENED?
SORRY.
I'M NOT REALLY IN THE MOOD TO TALK TO YOU RIGHT NOW.
Eh?
WH...?
WH...
WHY?

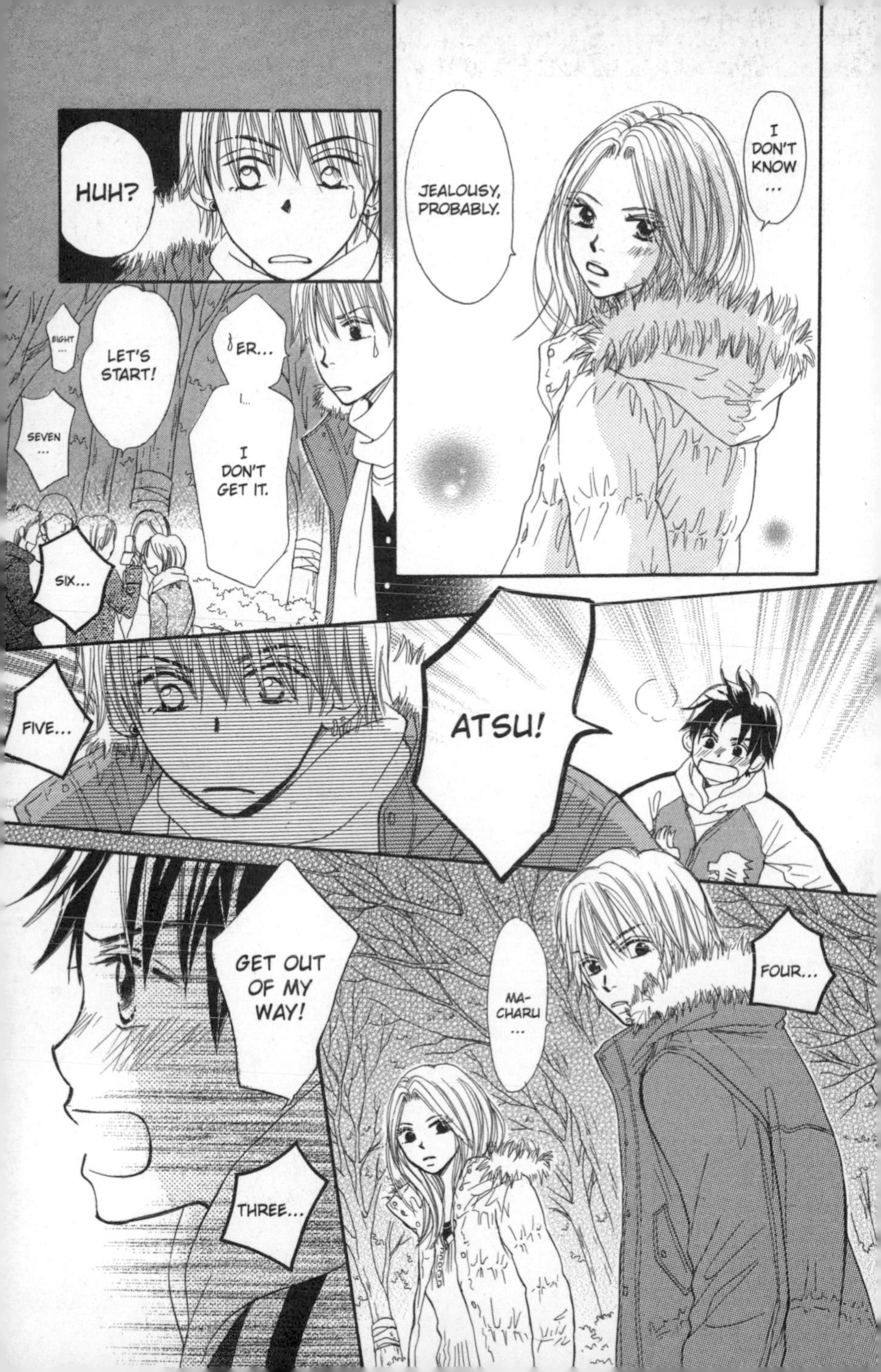
I DON'T KNOW...
JEALOUSY, PROBABLY.
HUH?
ER...
I...
I DON'T GET IT.
LET'S START!
EIGHT...
SEVEN...
SIX...
ATSU!
FIVE...
FOUR...
MA-CHARU...
GET OUT OF MY WAY!
THREE...

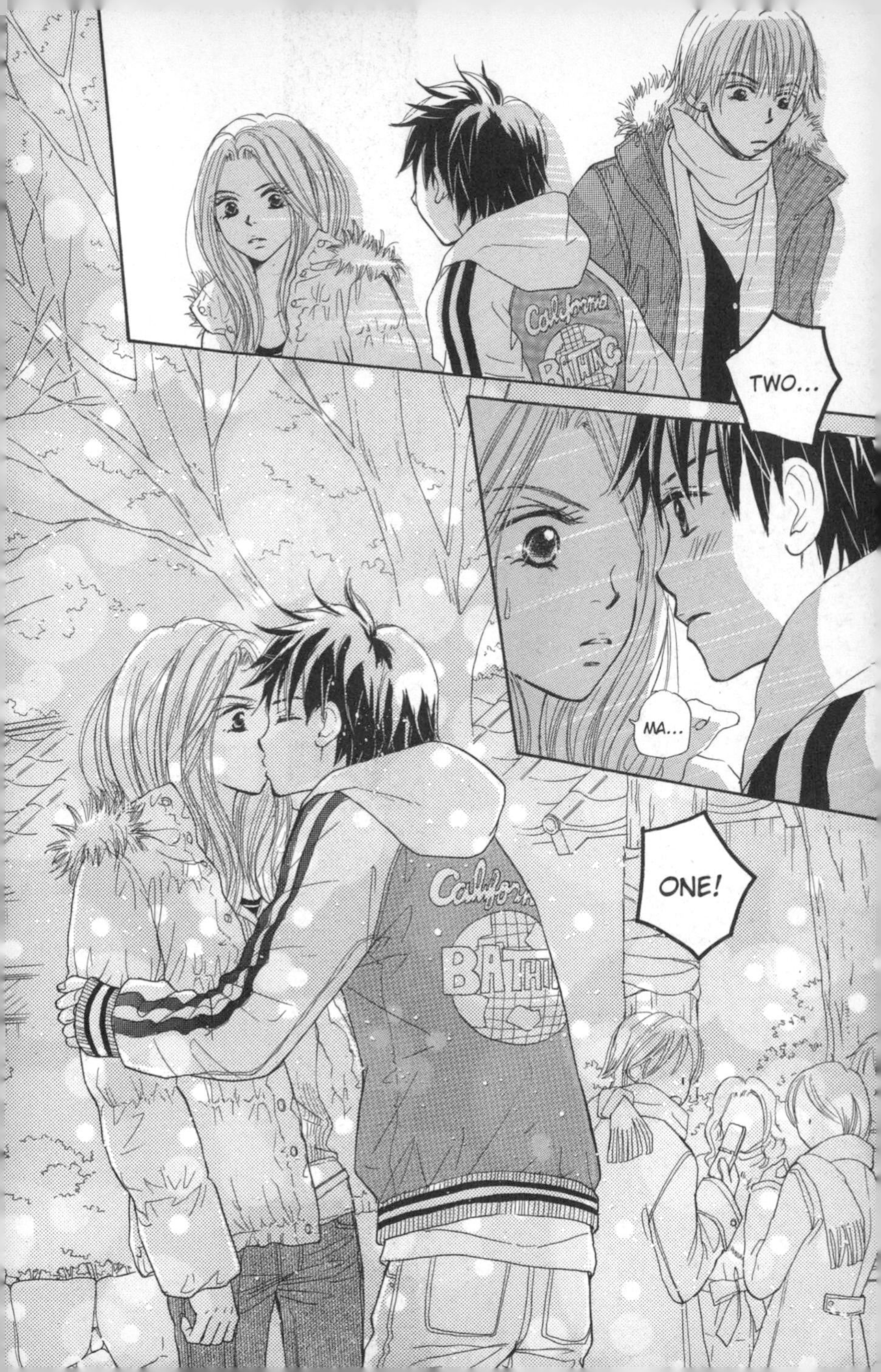
TWO...
MA...
ONE!

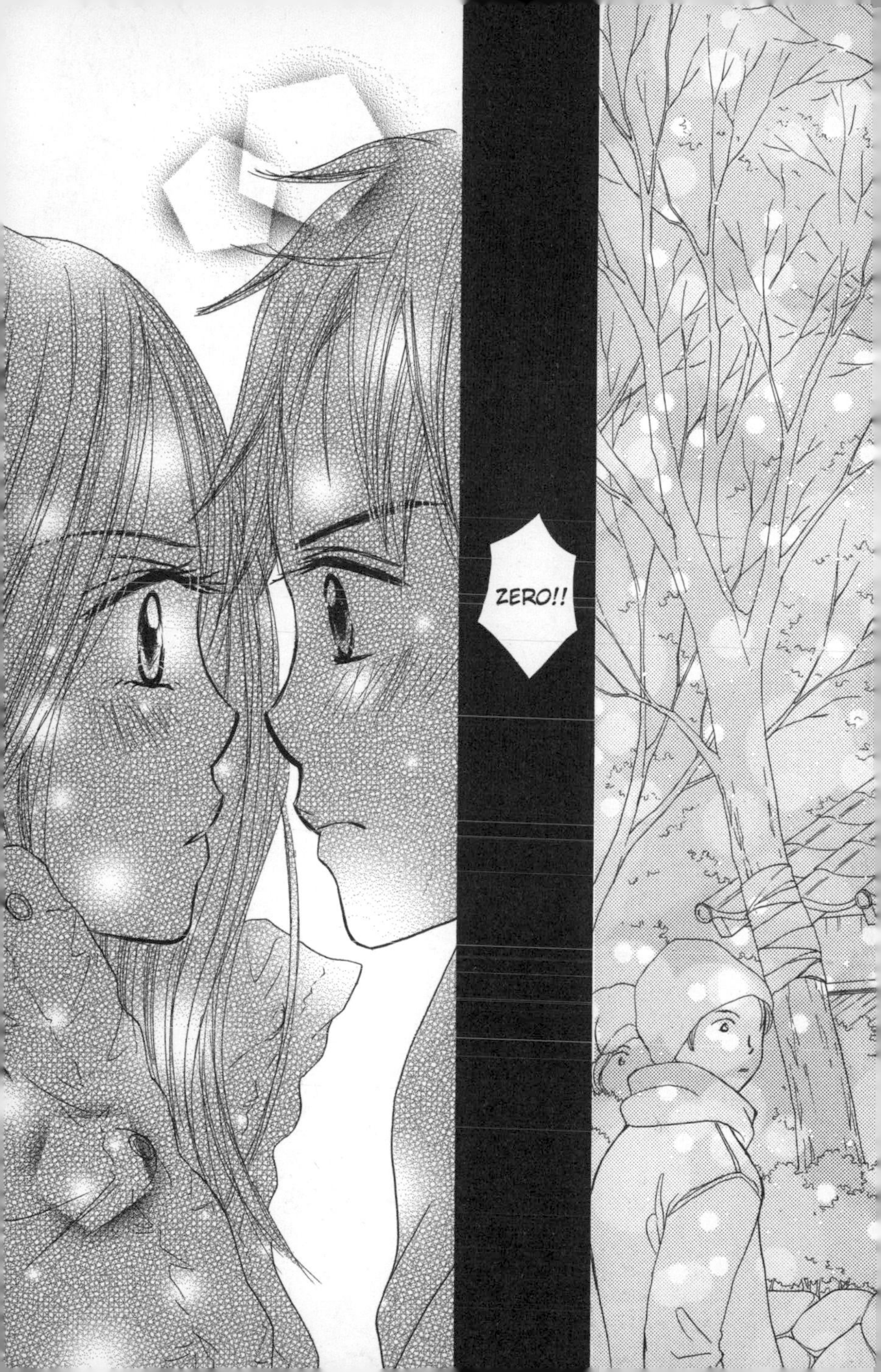
ZERO!!

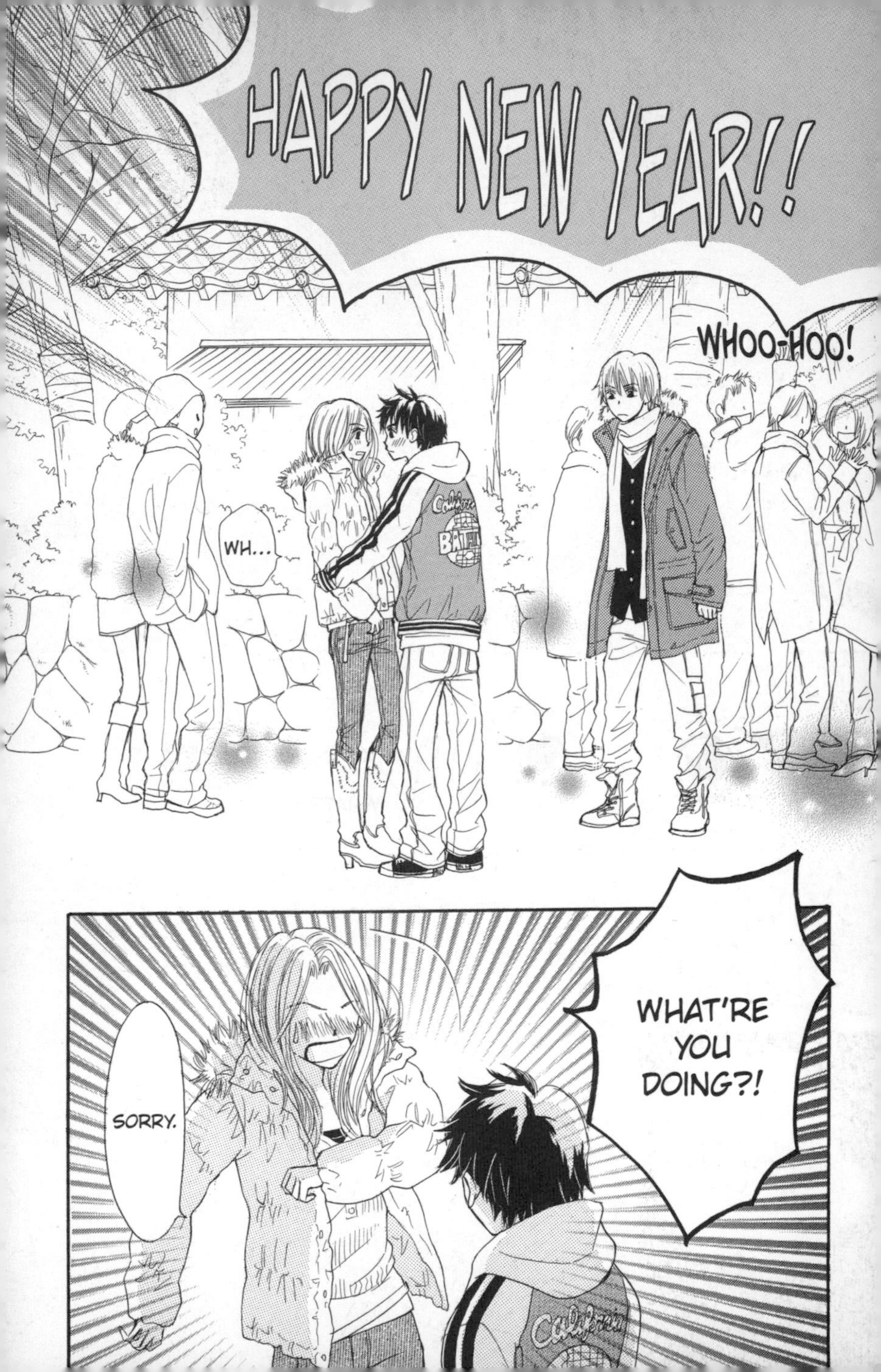
HAPPY NEW YEAR!!
WHOO-HOO!
WH...
WHAT'RE YOU DOING?!
SORRY.

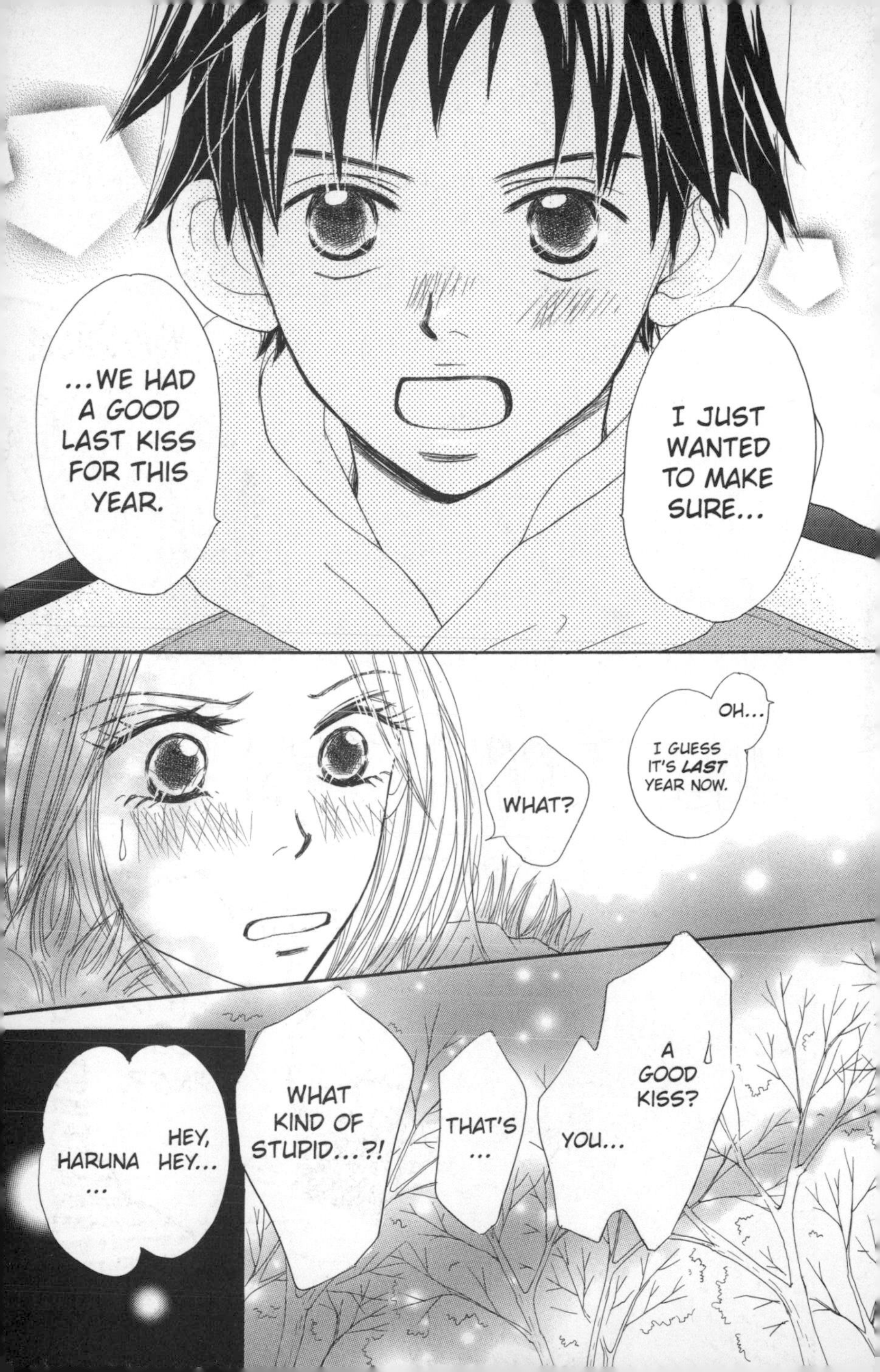
I JUST WANTED TO MAKE SURE...
...WE HAD A GOOD LAST KISS FOR THIS YEAR.
OH...
I GUESS IT'S *LAST* YEAR NOW.
WHAT?
A GOOD KISS?
YOU...
THAT'S ...
WHAT KIND OF STUPID...?!
HEY, HEY...
HARUNA ...

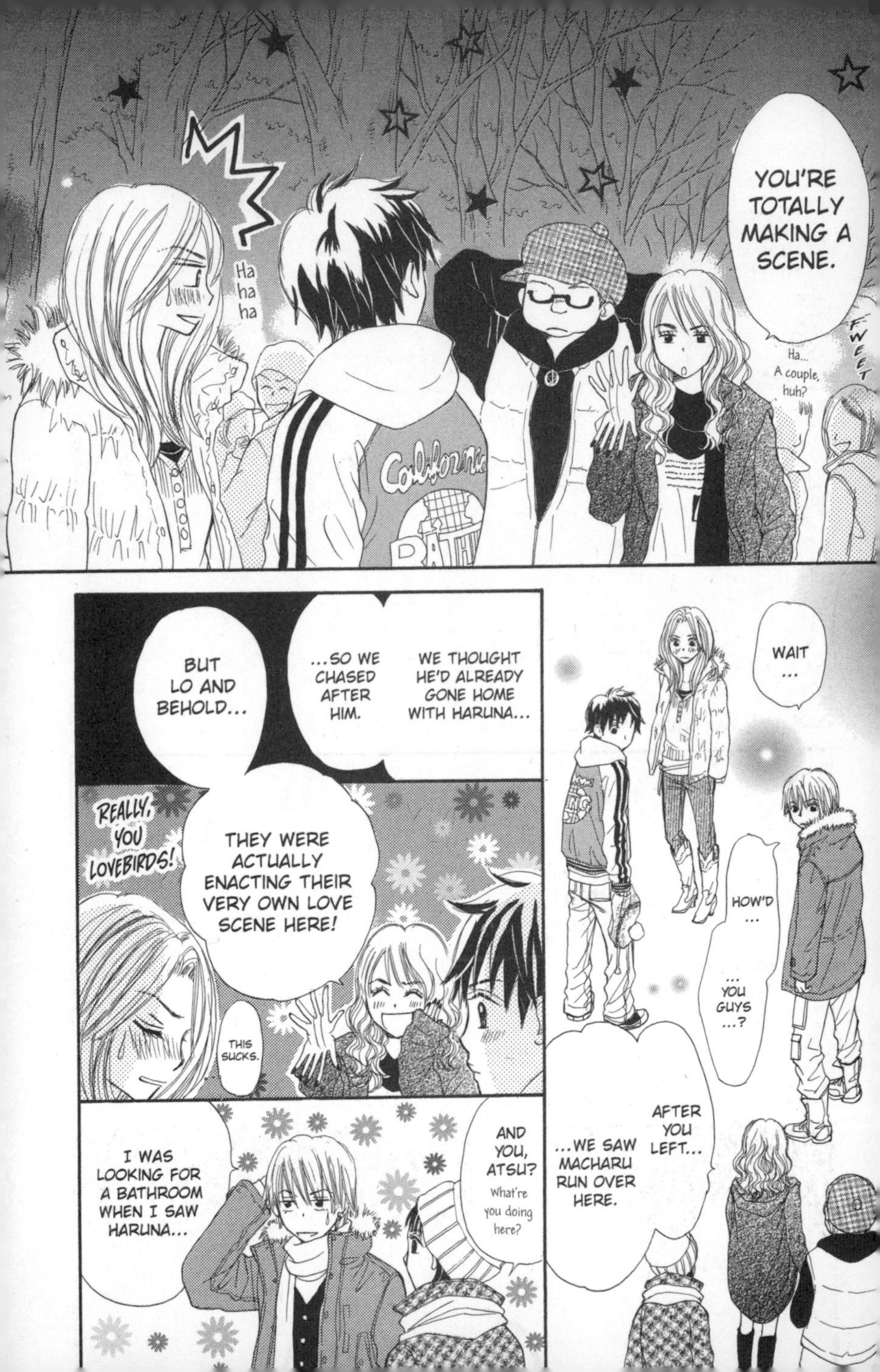
YOU'RE TOTALLY MAKING A SCENE.
F-WEET
Ha... A couple, huh?
Ha ha ha
WAIT ...
HOW'D ...
... YOU GUYS ...?
AFTER YOU LEFT...
...WE SAW MACHARU RUN OVER HERE.
WE THOUGHT HE'D ALREADY GONE HOME WITH HARUNA...
...SO WE CHASED AFTER HIM.
BUT LO AND BEHOLD...
THEY WERE ACTUALLY ENACTING THEIR VERY OWN LOVE SCENE HERE!
REALLY, YOU LOVEBIRDS!
THIS SUCKS.
AND YOU, ATSU?
What're you doing here?
I WAS LOOKING FOR A BATHROOM WHEN I SAW HARUNA...

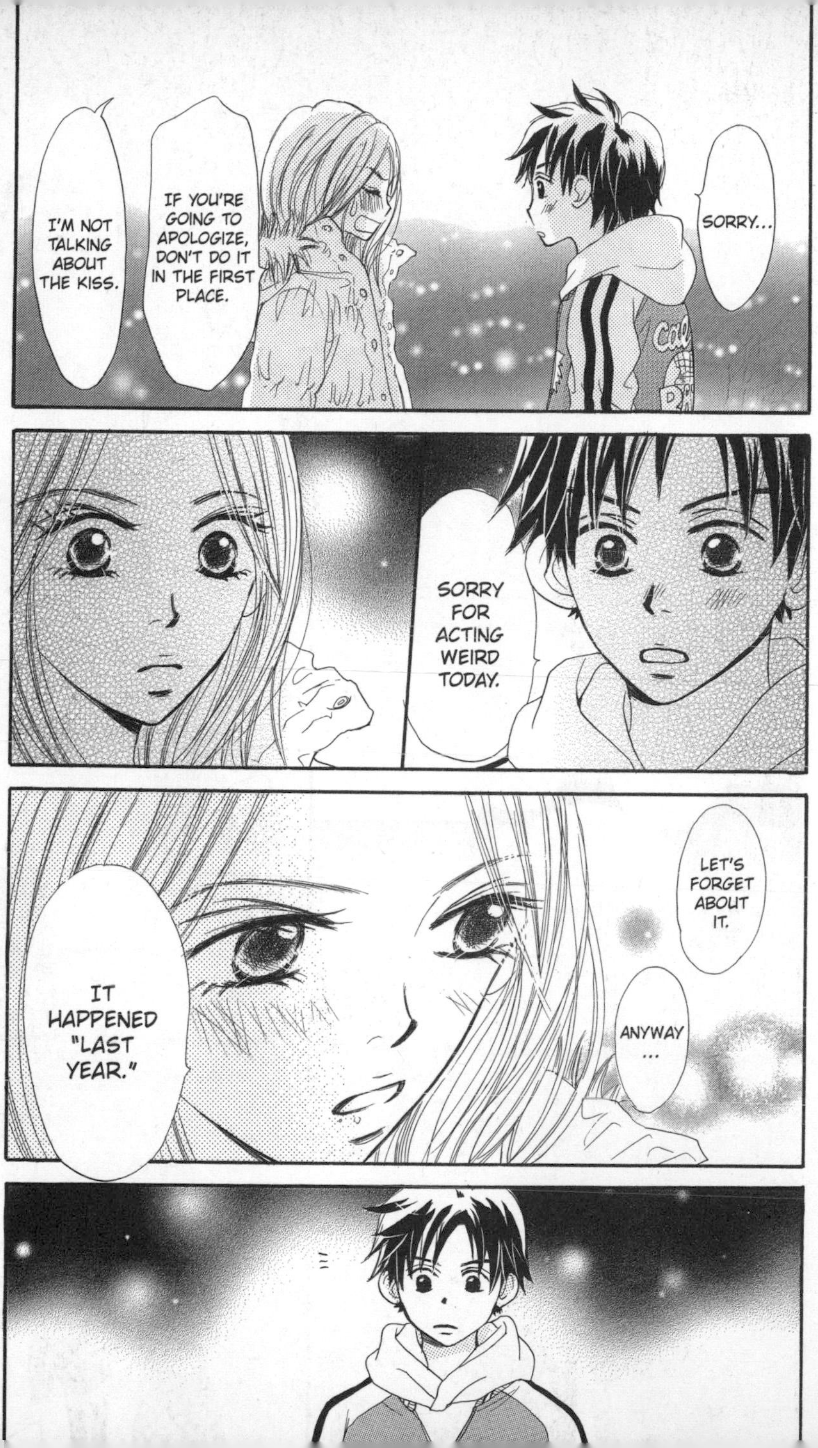
SORRY...
IF YOU'RE GOING TO APOLOGIZE, DON'T DO IT IN THE FIRST PLACE.
I'M NOT TALKING ABOUT THE KISS.
SORRY FOR ACTING WEIRD TODAY.
LET'S FORGET ABOUT IT.
ANYWAY...
IT HAPPENED "LAST YEAR."

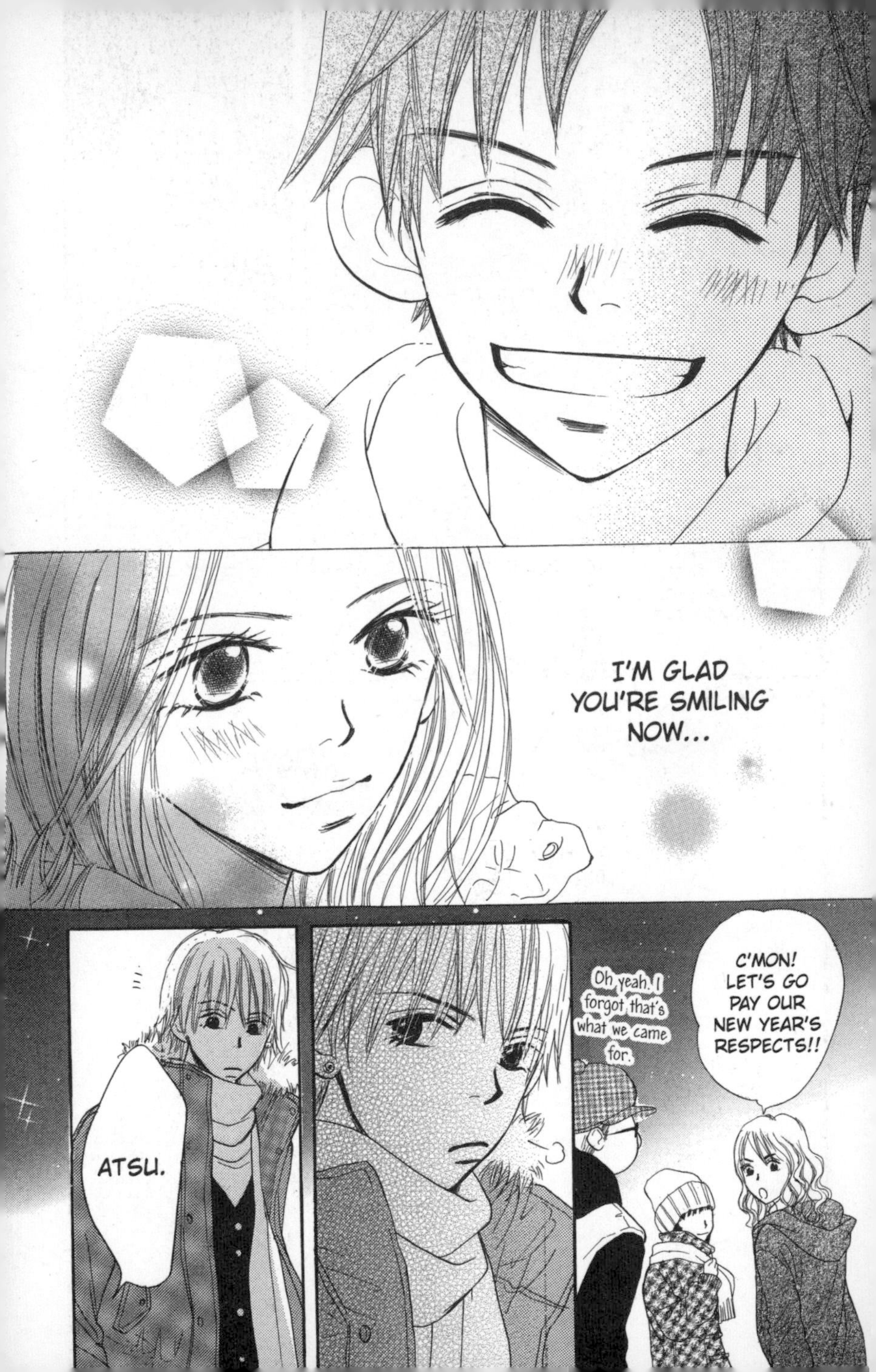
I'M GLAD YOU'RE SMILING NOW...
C'MON! LET'S GO PAY OUR NEW YEAR'S RESPECTS!!
Oh yeah. I forgot that's what we came for.
ATSU.

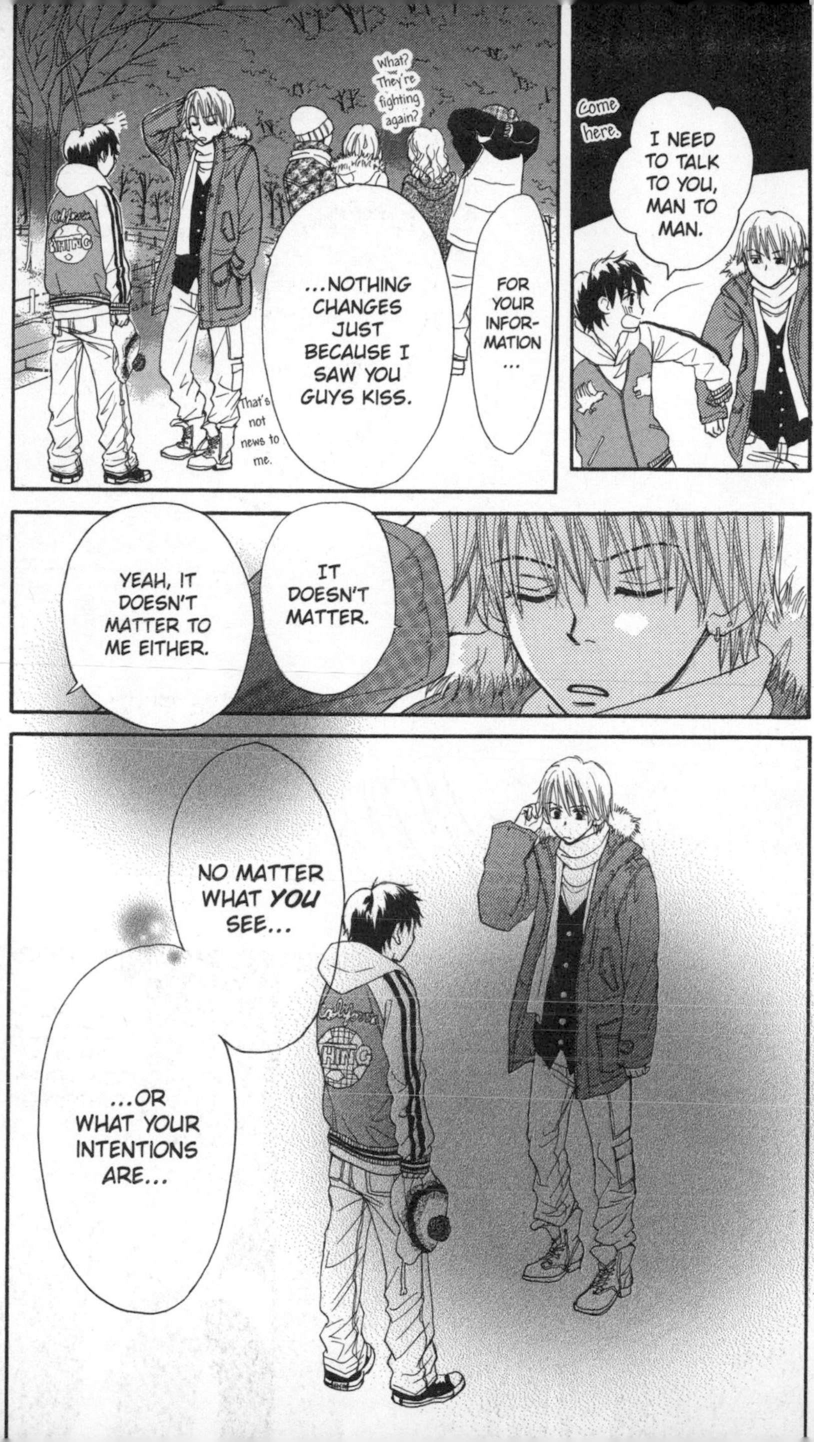
Come here.
I NEED TO TALK TO YOU, MAN TO MAN.
What? They're fighting again?
FOR YOUR INFORMATION...
...NOTHING CHANGES JUST BECAUSE I SAW YOU GUYS KISS.
That's not news to me.
IT DOESN'T MATTER.
YEAH, IT DOESN'T MATTER TO ME EITHER.
NO MATTER WHAT *YOU* SEE...
...OR WHAT YOUR INTENTIONS ARE...

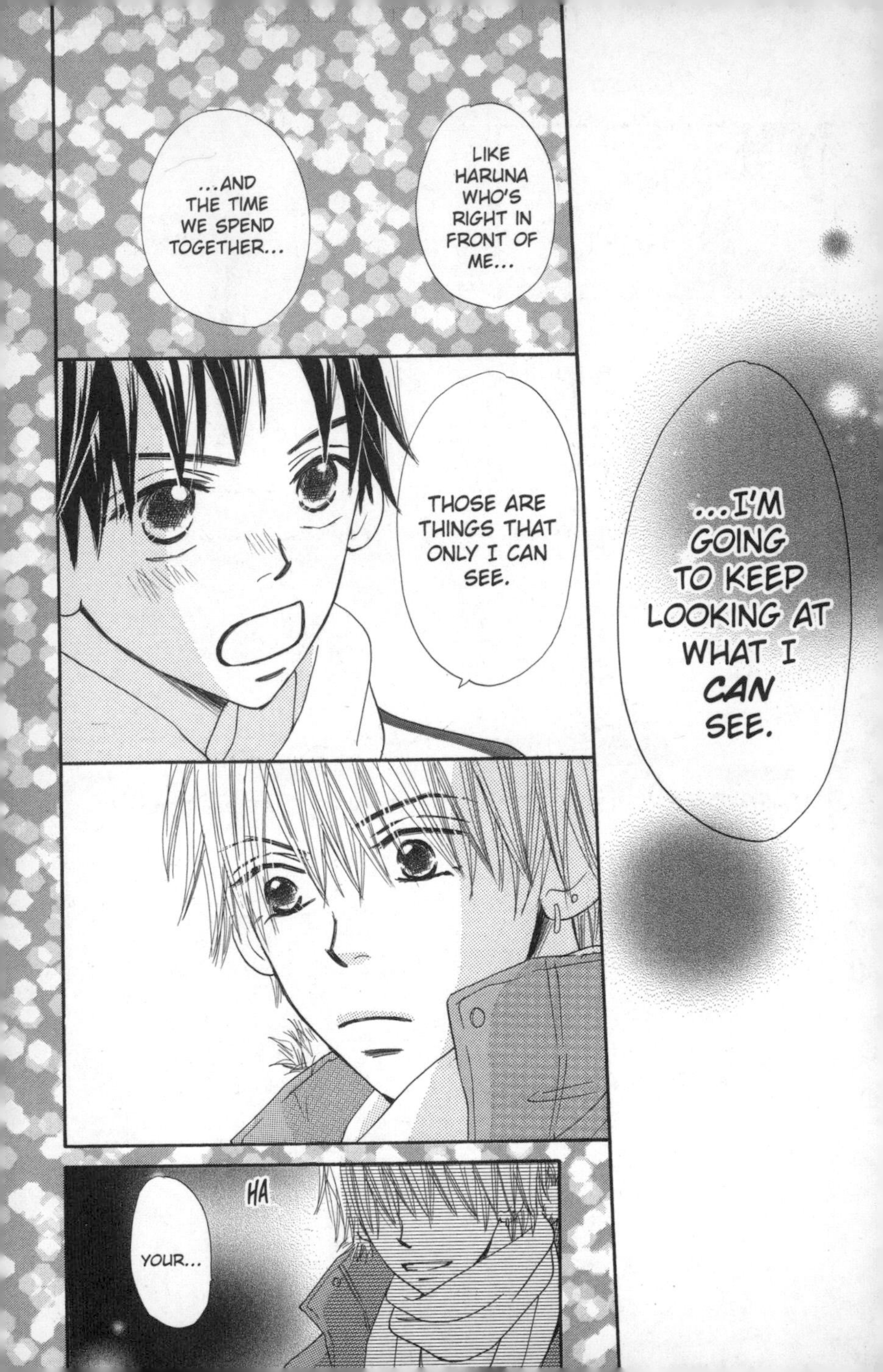
LIKE HARUNA WHO'S RIGHT IN FRONT OF ME...
...AND THE TIME WE SPEND TOGETHER...
THOSE ARE THINGS THAT ONLY I CAN SEE.
...I'M GOING TO KEEP LOOKING AT WHAT I CAN SEE.
HA
YOUR...

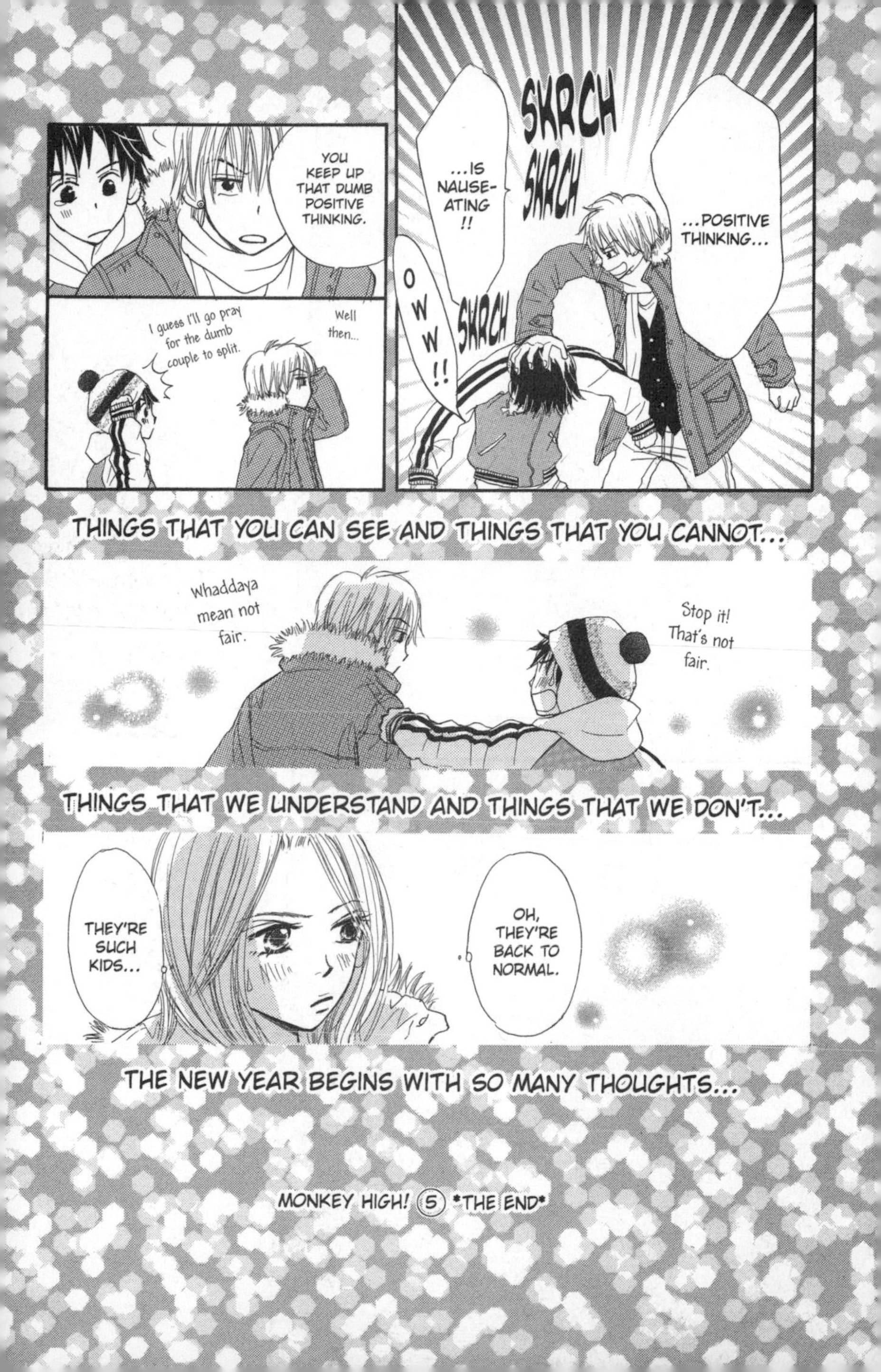

...POSITIVE THINKING...
SKRCH
SKRCH
...IS NAUSE-ATING!!
SKRCH
OWW!!
YOU KEEP UP THAT DUMB POSITIVE THINKING.
Well then...
I guess I'll go pray for the dumb couple to split.
THINGS THAT YOU CAN SEE AND THINGS THAT YOU CANNOT...
Stop it! That's not fair.
Whaddaya mean not fair.
THINGS THAT WE UNDERSTAND AND THINGS THAT WE DON'T...
OH, THEY'RE BACK TO NORMAL.
THEY'RE SUCH KIDS...
THE NEW YEAR BEGINS WITH SO MANY THOUGHTS...
MONKEY HIGH! 5 *THE END*

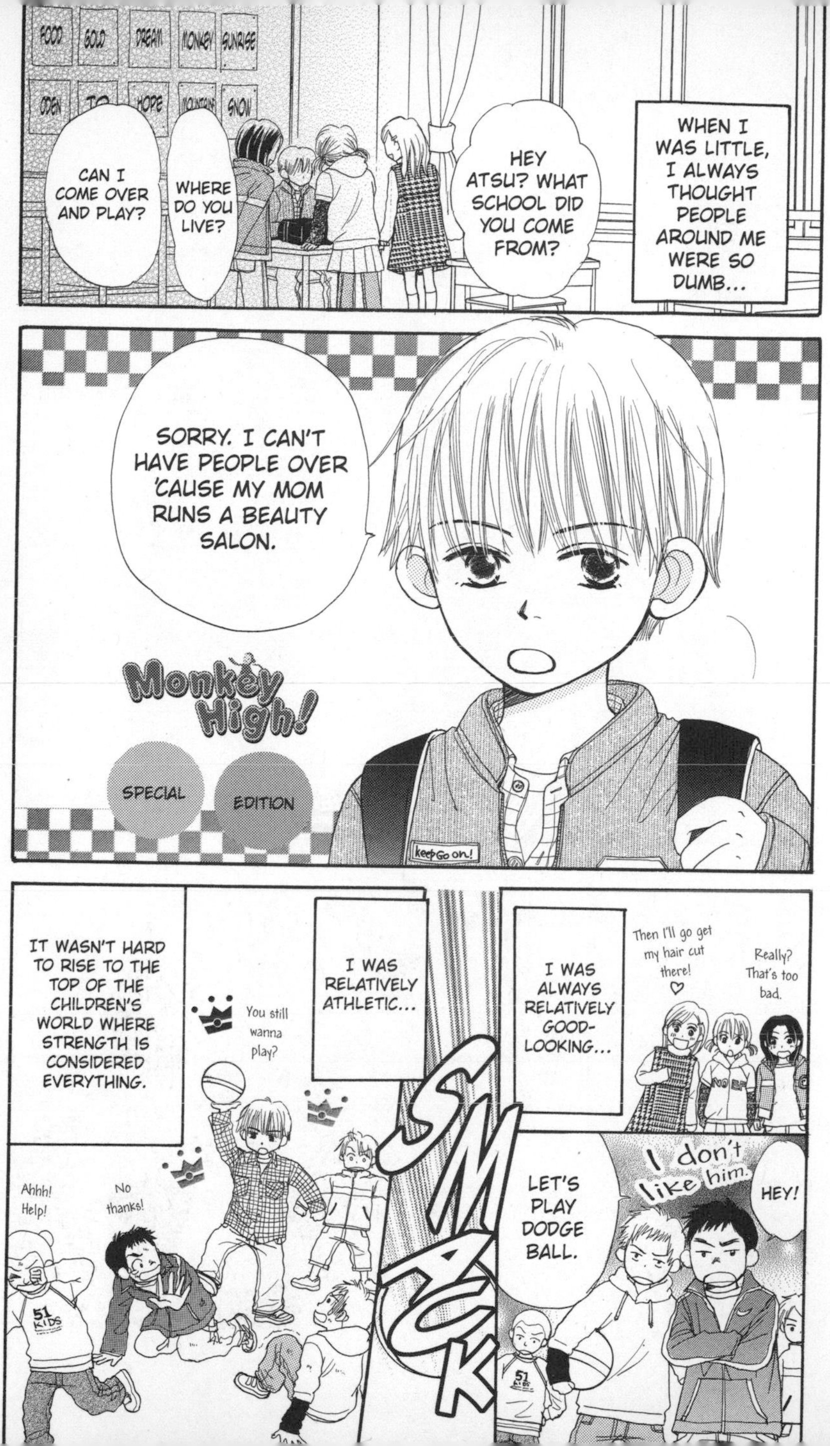
WHEN I WAS LITTLE, I ALWAYS THOUGHT PEOPLE AROUND ME WERE SO DUMB...
HEY ATSU? WHAT SCHOOL DID YOU COME FROM?
WHERE DO YOU LIVE?
CAN I COME OVER AND PLAY?
SORRY. I CAN'T HAVE PEOPLE OVER 'CAUSE MY MOM RUNS A BEAUTY SALON.
Monkey High!
SPECIAL EDITION
keep Go on!
I WAS ALWAYS RELATIVELY GOOD-LOOKING...
Really? That's too bad.
Then I'll go get my hair cut there! ♡
HEY!
I don't like him.
LET'S PLAY DODGE BALL.
SMACK
I WAS RELATIVELY ATHLETIC...
IT WASN'T HARD TO RISE TO THE TOP OF THE CHILDREN'S WORLD WHERE STRENGTH IS CONSIDERED EVERYTHING.
You still wanna play?
No thanks!
Ahhh! Help!

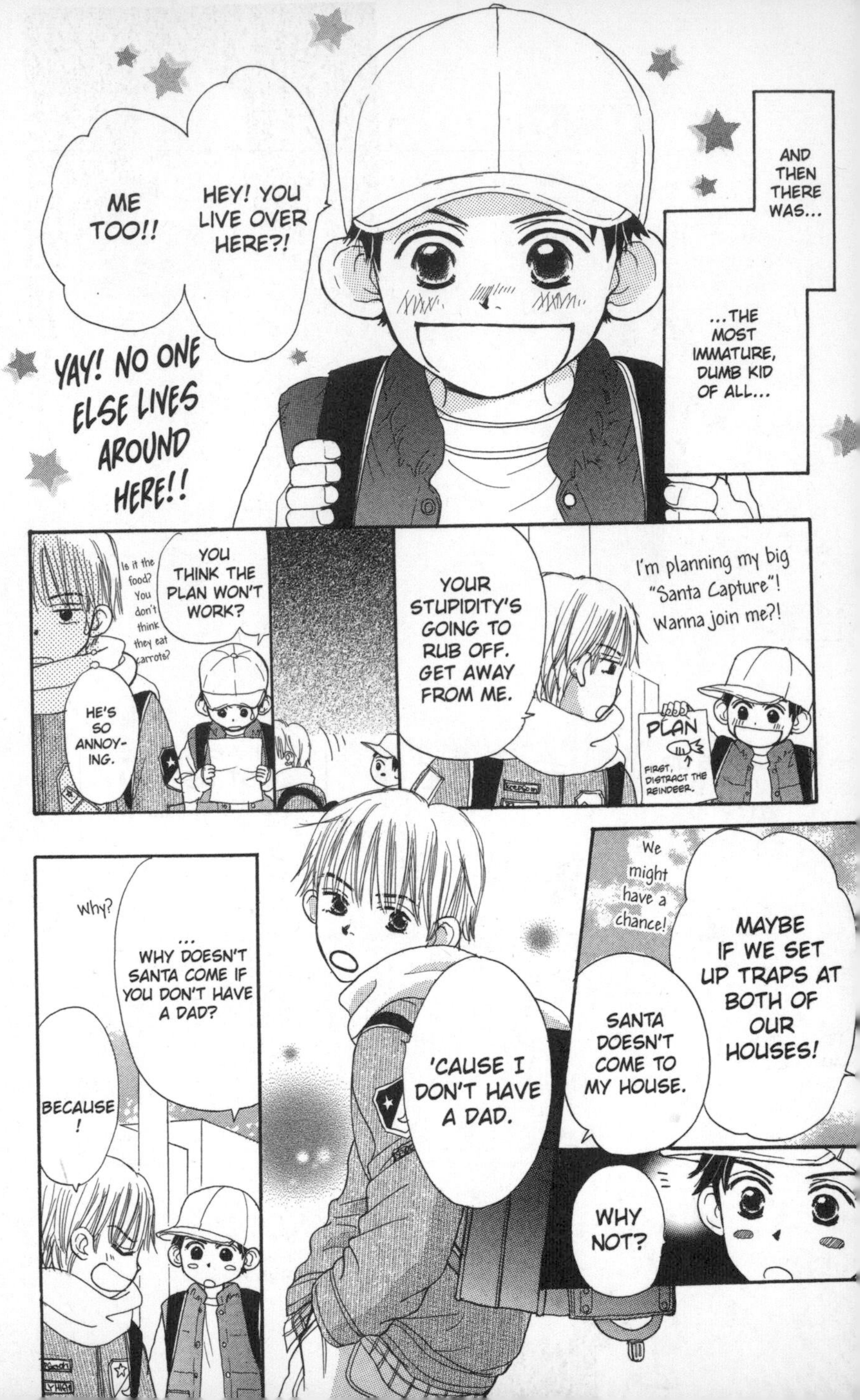
AND THEN THERE WAS...
...THE MOST IMMATURE, DUMB KID OF ALL...
HEY! YOU LIVE OVER HERE?!
ME TOO!!
YAY! NO ONE ELSE LIVES AROUND HERE!!
I'm planning my big "Santa Capture"! Wanna join me?!
PLAN
FIRST, DISTRACT THE REINDEER.
YOUR STUPIDITY'S GOING TO RUB OFF. GET AWAY FROM ME.
YOU THINK THE PLAN WON'T WORK?
Is it the food? You don't think they eat carrots?
HE'S SO ANNOYING.
MAYBE IF WE SET UP TRAPS AT BOTH OF OUR HOUSES!
We might have a chance!
SANTA DOESN'T COME TO MY HOUSE.
WHY NOT?
'CAUSE I DON'T HAVE A DAD.
Why?
...WHY DOESN'T SANTA COME IF YOU DON'T HAVE A DAD?
BECAUSE!

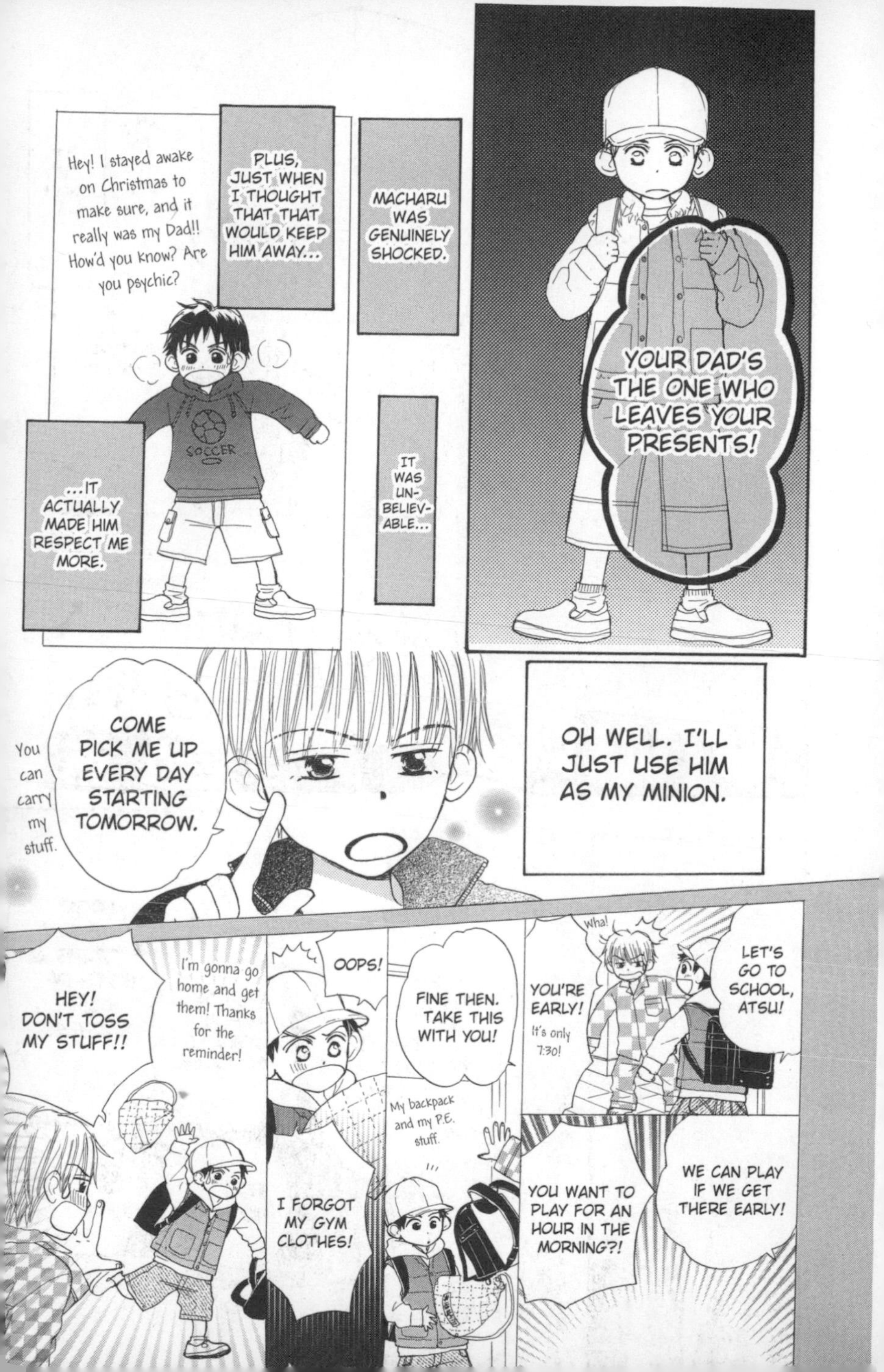
YOUR DAD'S THE ONE WHO LEAVES YOUR PRESENTS!
MACHARU WAS GENUINELY SHOCKED.
IT WAS UN-BELIEV-ABLE...
PLUS, JUST WHEN I THOUGHT THAT THAT WOULD KEEP HIM AWAY...
Hey! I stayed awake on Christmas to make sure, and it really was my Dad!! How'd you know? Are you psychic?
...IT ACTUALLY MADE HIM RESPECT ME MORE.
OH WELL. I'LL JUST USE HIM AS MY MINION.
COME PICK ME UP EVERY DAY STARTING TOMORROW.
You can carry my stuff.
LET'S GO TO SCHOOL, ATSU!
Wha!
YOU'RE EARLY!
It's only 7:30!
WE CAN PLAY IF WE GET THERE EARLY!
YOU WANT TO PLAY FOR AN HOUR IN THE MORNING?!
FINE THEN. TAKE THIS WITH YOU!
My backpack and my P.E. stuff.
OOPS!
I FORGOT MY GYM CLOTHES!
I'm gonna go home and get them! Thanks for the reminder!
HEY! DON'T TOSS MY STUFF!!

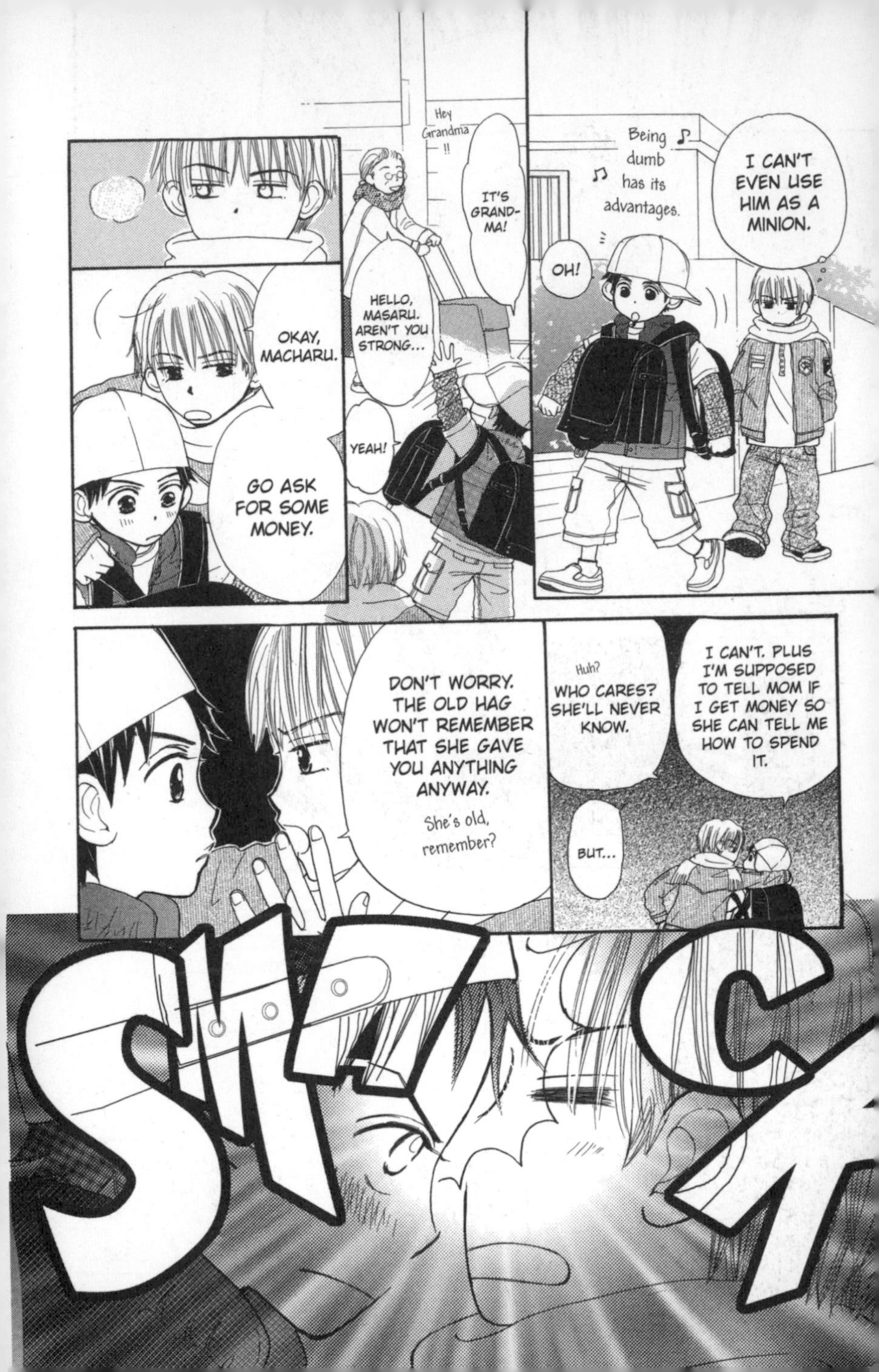
I CAN'T EVEN USE HIM AS A MINION.
Being dumb has its advantages.
OH!
Hey Grandma !!
IT'S GRANDMA!
HELLO, MASARU. AREN'T YOU STRONG...
YEAH!
OKAY, MACHARU.
GO ASK FOR SOME MONEY.
I CAN'T. PLUS I'M SUPPOSED TO TELL MOM IF I GET MONEY SO SHE CAN TELL ME HOW TO SPEND IT.
Huh?
WHO CARES? SHE'LL NEVER KNOW.
BUT...
DON'T WORRY. THE OLD HAG WON'T REMEMBER THAT SHE GAVE YOU ANYTHING ANYWAY.
She's old, remember?
SMACK

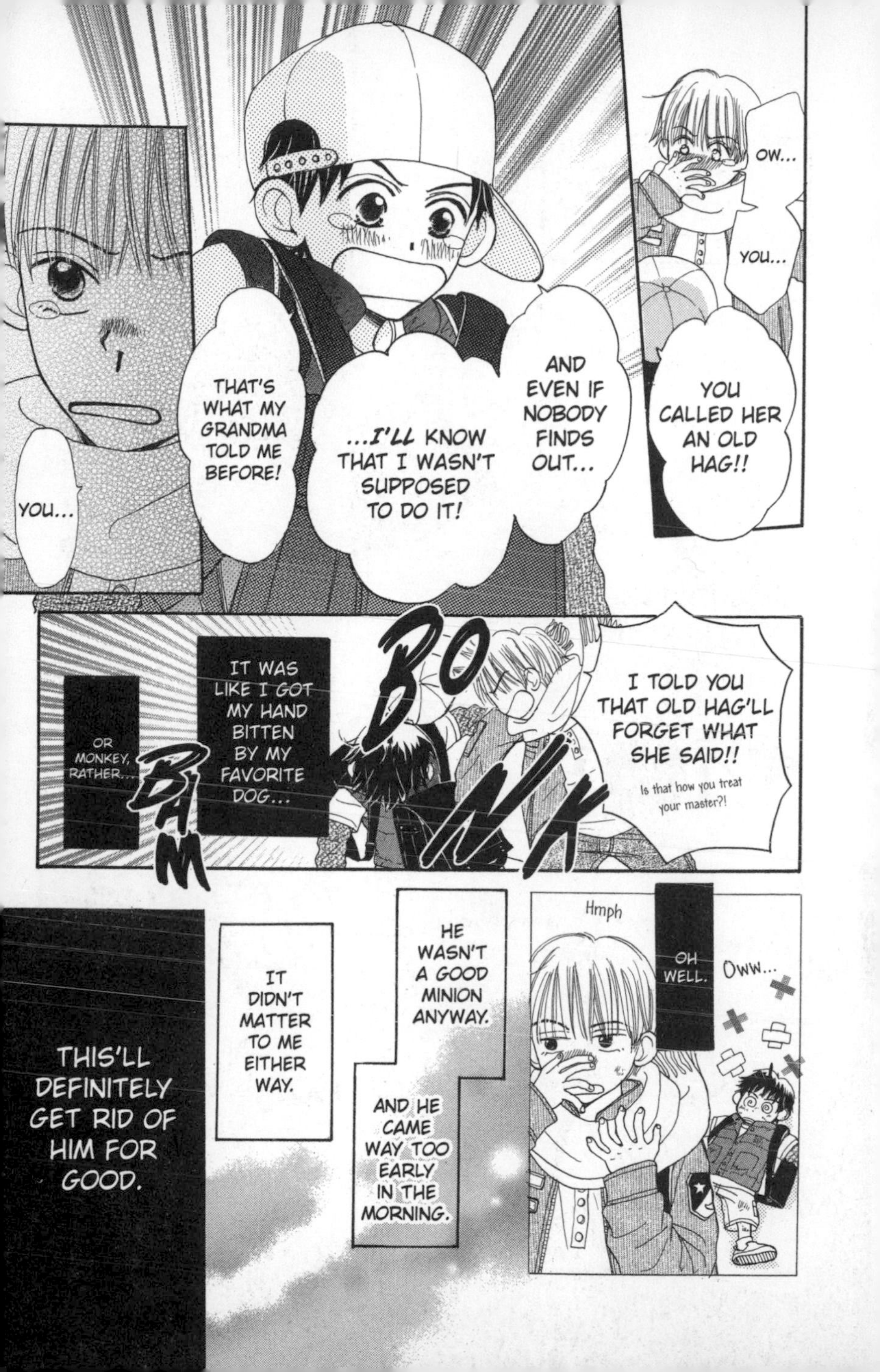
OW...
YOU...
YOU CALLED HER AN OLD HAG!!
AND EVEN IF NOBODY FINDS OUT...
...I'LL KNOW THAT I WASN'T SUPPOSED TO DO IT!
THAT'S WHAT MY GRANDMA TOLD ME BEFORE!
YOU...
I TOLD YOU THAT OLD HAG'LL FORGET WHAT SHE SAID!!
Is that how you treat your master?!
BONK
IT WAS LIKE I GOT MY HAND BITTEN BY MY FAVORITE DOG...
OR MONKEY, RATHER...
BAM
Hmph
OH WELL.
Oww...
HE WASN'T A GOOD MINION ANYWAY.
AND HE CAME WAY TOO EARLY IN THE MORNING.
IT DIDN'T MATTER TO ME EITHER WAY.
THIS'LL DEFINITELY GET RID OF HIM FOR GOOD.

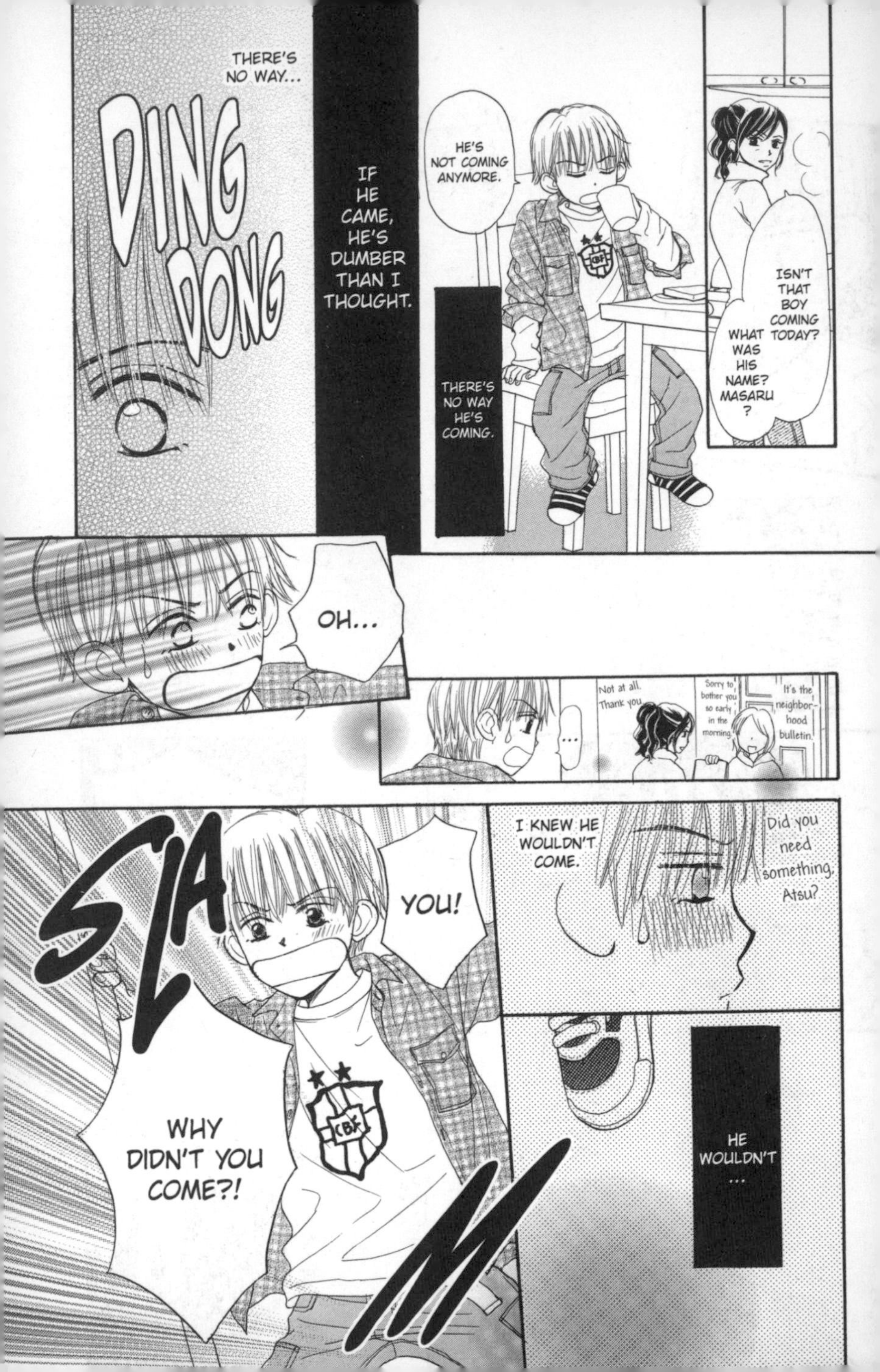
ISN'T THAT BOY COMING TODAY?
WHAT WAS HIS NAME? MASARU?
HE'S NOT COMING ANYMORE.
THERE'S NO WAY HE'S COMING.
IF HE CAME, HE'S DUMBER THAN I THOUGHT.
THERE'S NO WAY...
DING DONG
OH...
It's the neighborhood bulletin.
Sorry to bother you so early in the morning.
Not at all. Thank you.
...
Did you need something, Atsu?
I KNEW HE WOULDN'T COME.
HE WOULDN'T...
SLAM
YOU!
WHY DIDN'T YOU COME?!

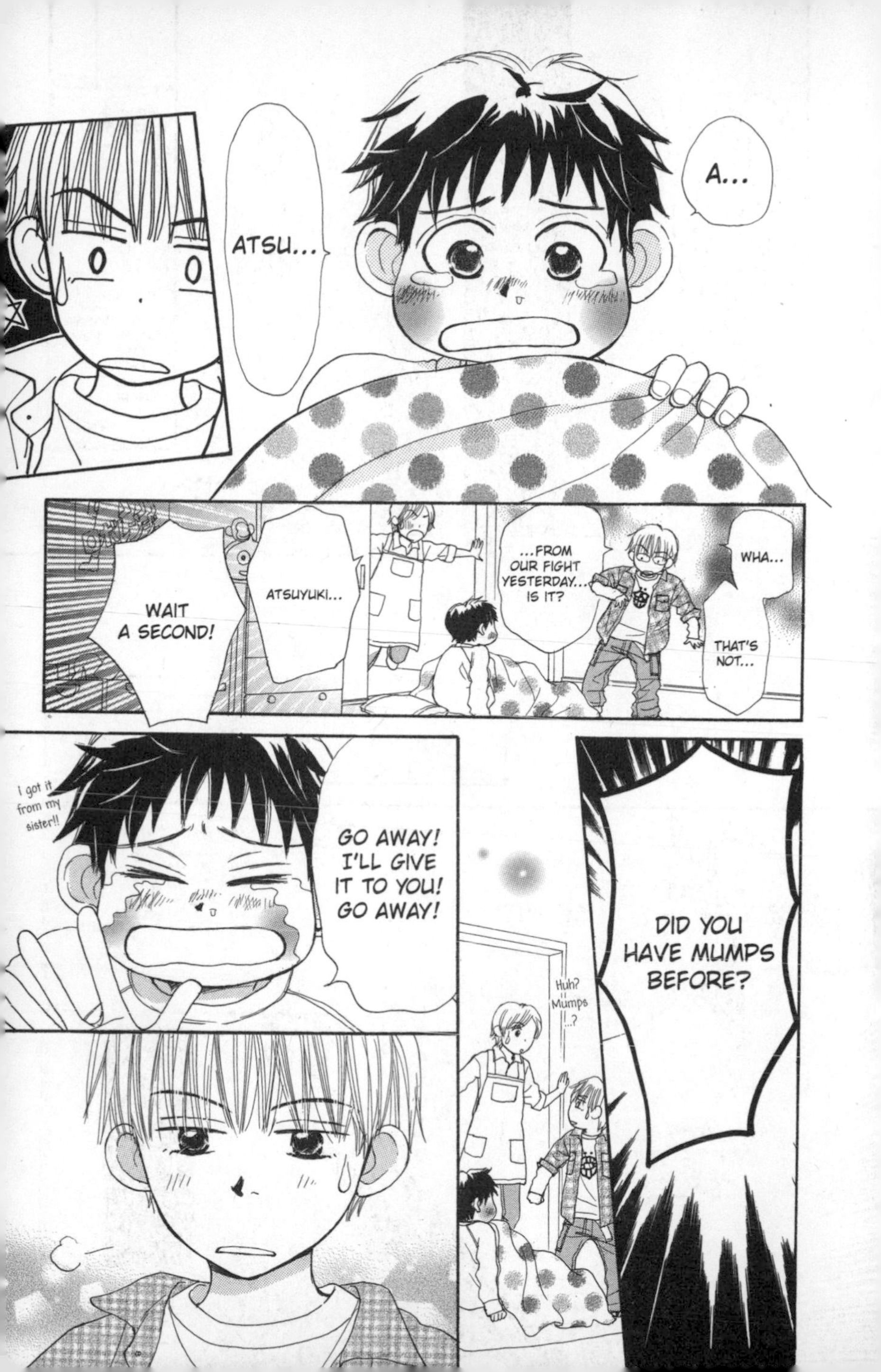
A...
ATSU...
WHA...
THAT'S NOT...
...FROM OUR FIGHT YESTERDAY... IS IT?
ATSUYUKI...
WAIT A SECOND!
DID YOU HAVE MUMPS BEFORE?
Huh? Mumps ...?
GO AWAY! I'LL GIVE IT TO YOU! GO AWAY!
I got it from my sister!!

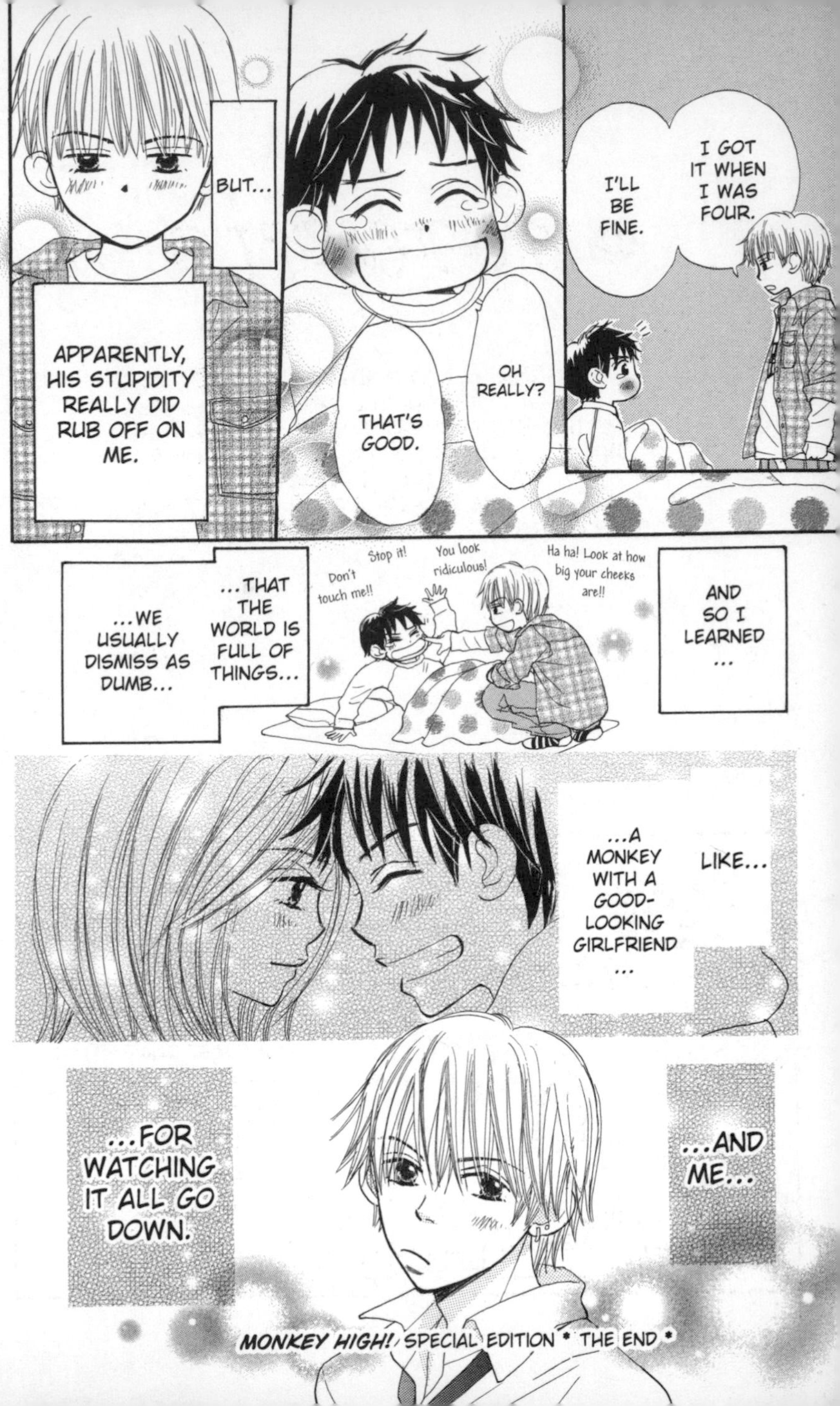
I GOT IT WHEN I WAS FOUR.
I'LL BE FINE.
OH REALLY?
THAT'S GOOD.
BUT...
APPARENTLY, HIS STUPIDITY REALLY DID RUB OFF ON ME.
AND SO I LEARNED...
Ha ha! Look at how big your cheeks are!!
You look ridiculous!
Stop it!
Don't touch me!!
...THAT THE WORLD IS FULL OF THINGS...
...WE USUALLY DISMISS AS DUMB...
LIKE...
...A MONKEY WITH A GOOD-LOOKING GIRLFRIEND...
...AND ME...
...FOR WATCHING IT ALL GO DOWN.
MONKEY HIGH! SPECIAL EDITION * THE END *

POSTSCRIPT

THANK YOU SO MUCH FOR READING!
I'M SHOUKO AKIRA.
VOLUME 5! I CAN'T BELIEVE IT! THANK YOU SO MUCH! IT'S NOT A DREAM, IS IT?! VOLUME 5...
I STILL CAN'T BELIEVE IT...
WELL, I'D LIKE TO KEEP UP THE TRADITION OF COMMENTING ON EACH OF THE STORIES...

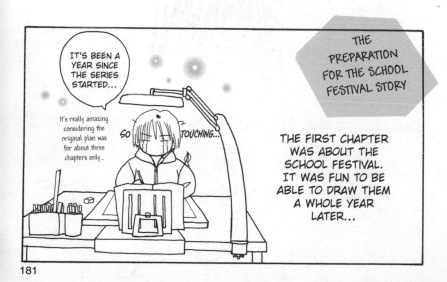

THE PREPARATION FOR THE SCHOOL FESTIVAL STORY
THE FIRST CHAPTER WAS ABOUT THE SCHOOL FESTIVAL. IT WAS FUN TO BE ABLE TO DRAW THEM A WHOLE YEAR LATER...
IT'S BEEN A YEAR SINCE THE SERIES STARTED...
SO TOUCHING...
It's really amazing considering the original plan was for about three chapters only...

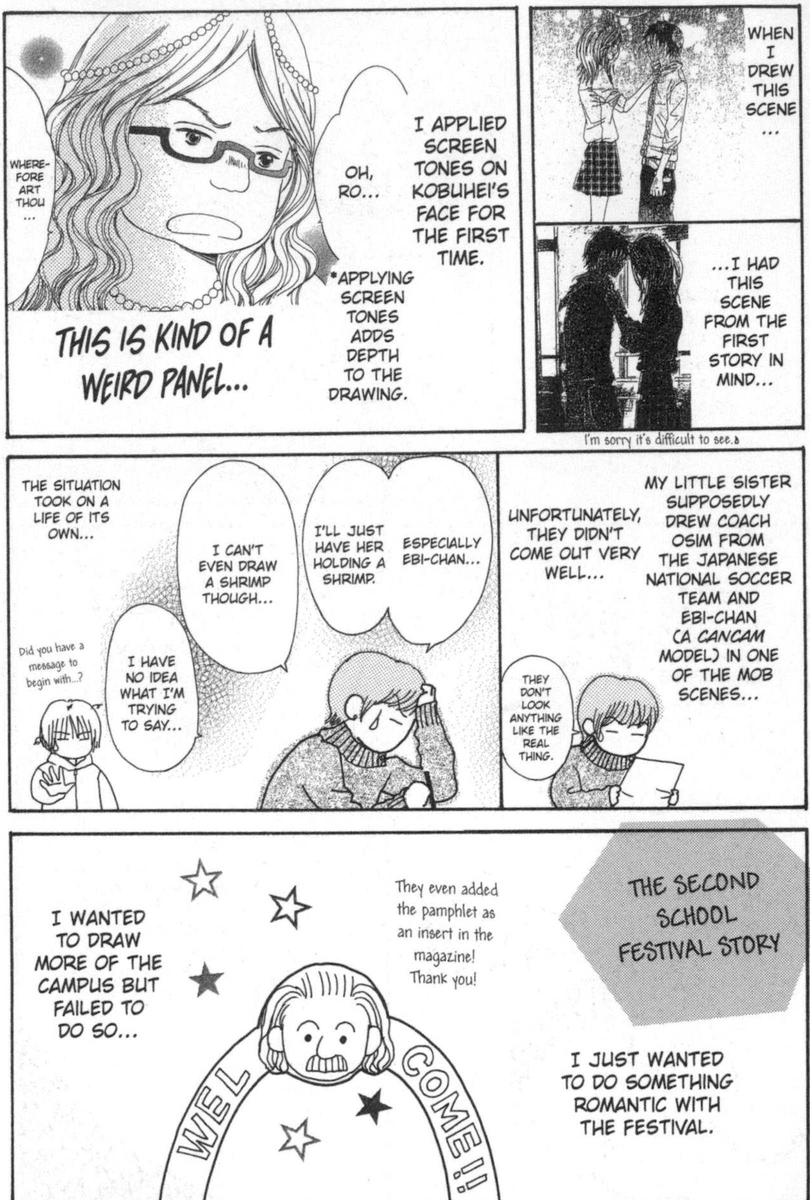
WHEN I DREW THIS SCENE...
...I HAD THIS SCENE FROM THE FIRST STORY IN MIND...
I'm sorry it's difficult to see.
I APPLIED SCREEN TONES ON KOBUHEI'S FACE FOR THE FIRST TIME.
OH, RO...
*APPLYING SCREEN TONES ADDS DEPTH TO THE DRAWING.
WHERE-FORE ART THOU...
THIS IS KIND OF A WEIRD PANEL...
MY LITTLE SISTER SUPPOSEDLY DREW COACH OSIM FROM THE JAPANESE NATIONAL SOCCER TEAM AND EBI-CHAN (A *CANCAM* MODEL) IN ONE OF THE MOB SCENES...
UNFORTUNATELY, THEY DIDN'T COME OUT VERY WELL...
THEY DON'T LOOK ANYTHING LIKE THE REAL THING.
ESPECIALLY EBI-CHAN...
I'LL JUST HAVE HER HOLDING A SHRIMP.
I CAN'T EVEN DRAW A SHRIMP THOUGH...
THE SITUATION TOOK ON A LIFE OF ITS OWN...
I HAVE NO IDEA WHAT I'M TRYING TO SAY...
Did you have a message to begin with...?
THE SECOND SCHOOL FESTIVAL STORY
I JUST WANTED TO DO SOMETHING ROMANTIC WITH THE FESTIVAL.
They even added the pamphlet as an insert in the magazine! Thank you!
I WANTED TO DRAW MORE OF THE CAMPUS BUT FAILED TO DO SO...
WEL COME!!

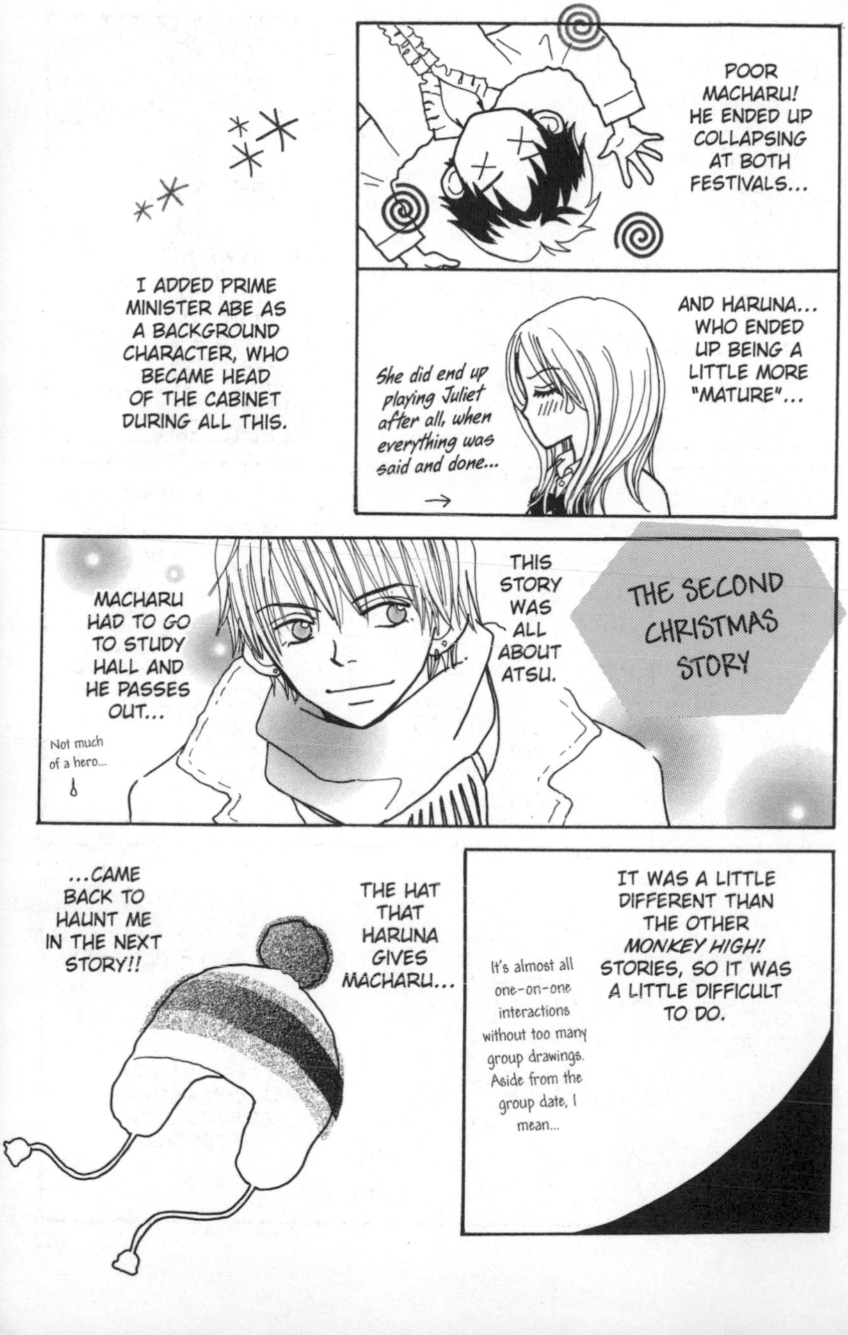
POOR MACHARU! HE ENDED UP COLLAPSING AT BOTH FESTIVALS...
AND HARUNA... WHO ENDED UP BEING A LITTLE MORE "MATURE"...
She did end up playing Juliet after all, when everything was said and done...
I ADDED PRIME MINISTER ABE AS A BACKGROUND CHARACTER, WHO BECAME HEAD OF THE CABINET DURING ALL THIS.
THE SECOND CHRISTMAS STORY
THIS STORY WAS ALL ABOUT ATSU.
MACHARU HAD TO GO TO STUDY HALL AND HE PASSES OUT...
Not much of a hero...
IT WAS A LITTLE DIFFERENT THAN THE OTHER *MONKEY HIGH!* STORIES, SO IT WAS A LITTLE DIFFICULT TO DO.
It's almost all one-on-one interactions without too many group drawings. Aside from the group date, I mean...
THE HAT THAT HARUNA GIVES MACHARU...
...CAME BACK TO HAUNT ME IN THE NEXT STORY!!

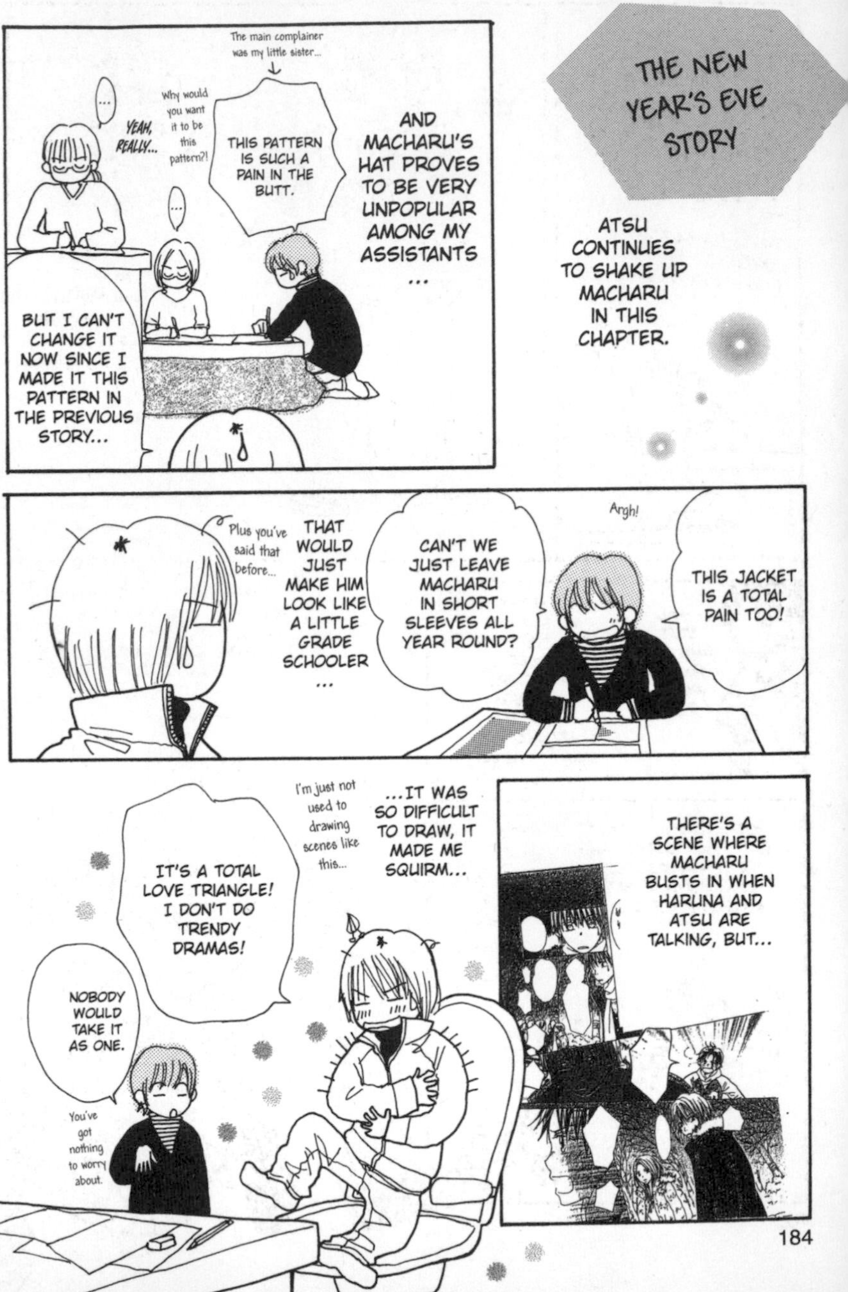
THE NEW YEAR'S EVE STORY
ATSU CONTINUES TO SHAKE UP MACHARU IN THIS CHAPTER.
The main complainer was my little sister...
AND MACHARU'S HAT PROVES TO BE VERY UNPOPULAR AMONG MY ASSISTANTS...
THIS PATTERN IS SUCH A PAIN IN THE BUTT.
Why would you want it to be this pattern?!
YEAH, REALLY...
...
...
BUT I CAN'T CHANGE IT NOW SINCE I MADE IT THIS PATTERN IN THE PREVIOUS STORY...
Argh!
THIS JACKET IS A TOTAL PAIN TOO!
CAN'T WE JUST LEAVE MACHARU IN SHORT SLEEVES ALL YEAR ROUND?
THAT WOULD JUST MAKE HIM LOOK LIKE A LITTLE GRADE SCHOOLER...
Plus you've said that before...
THERE'S A SCENE WHERE MACHARU BUSTS IN WHEN HARUNA AND ATSU ARE TALKING, BUT...
...IT WAS SO DIFFICULT TO DRAW, IT MADE ME SQUIRM...
I'm just not used to drawing scenes like this...
IT'S A TOTAL LOVE TRIANGLE! I DON'T DO TRENDY DRAMAS!
NOBODY WOULD TAKE IT AS ONE.
You've got nothing to worry about.

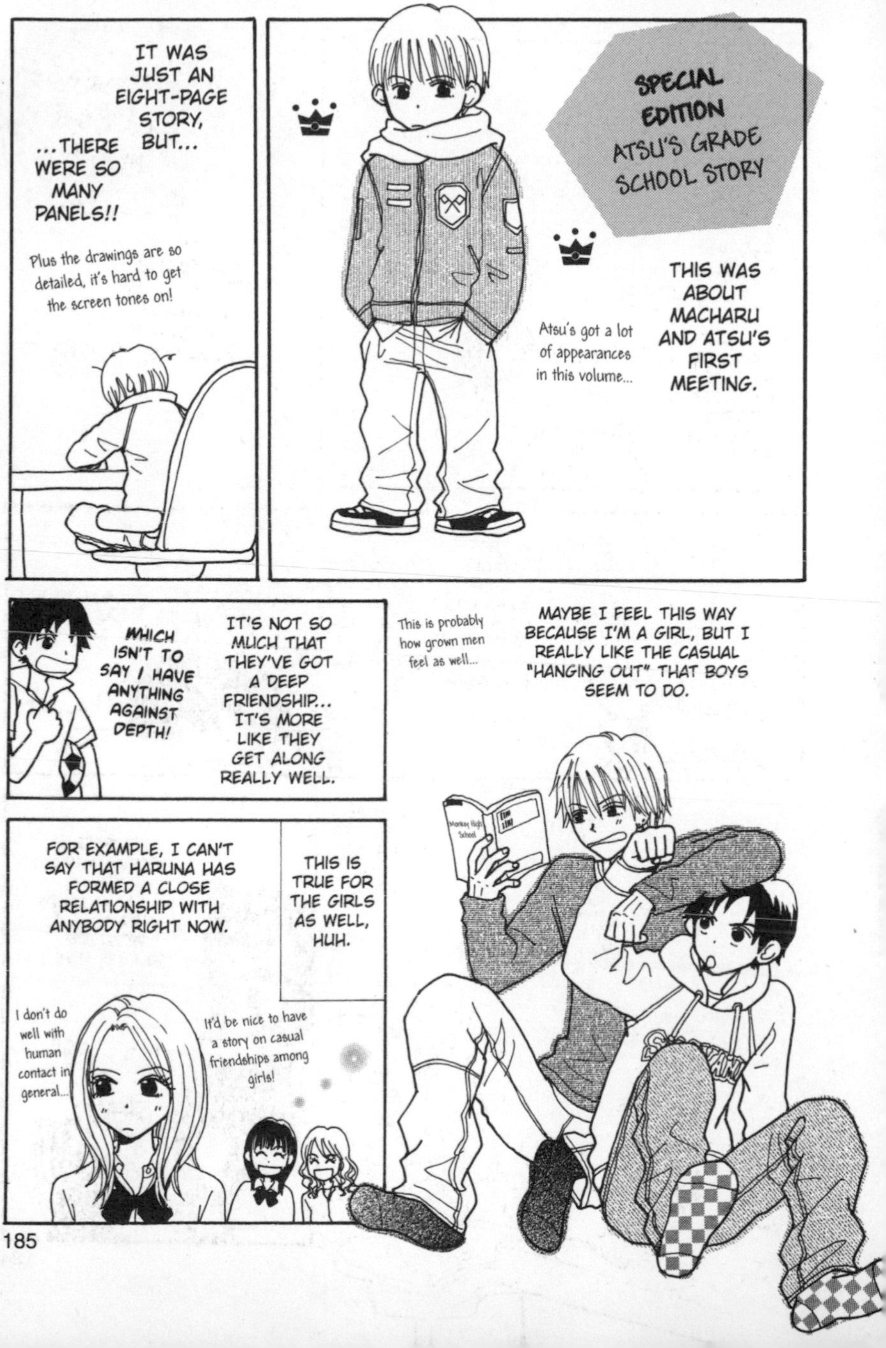
SPECIAL EDITION
ATSU'S GRADE SCHOOL STORY
THIS WAS ABOUT MACHARU AND ATSU'S FIRST MEETING.
Atsu's got a lot of appearances in this volume...
IT WAS JUST AN EIGHT-PAGE STORY, BUT...
...THERE WERE SO MANY PANELS!!
Plus the drawings are so detailed, it's hard to get the screen tones on!
MAYBE I FEEL THIS WAY BECAUSE I'M A GIRL, BUT I REALLY LIKE THE CASUAL "HANGING OUT" THAT BOYS SEEM TO DO.
This is probably how grown men feel as well...
IT'S NOT SO MUCH THAT THEY'VE GOT A DEEP FRIENDSHIP... IT'S MORE LIKE THEY GET ALONG REALLY WELL.
WHICH ISN'T TO SAY I HAVE ANYTHING AGAINST DEPTH!
Monkey High School
THIS IS TRUE FOR THE GIRLS AS WELL, HUH.
FOR EXAMPLE, I CAN'T SAY THAT HARUNA HAS FORMED A CLOSE RELATIONSHIP WITH ANYBODY RIGHT NOW.
It'd be nice to have a story on casual friendships among girls!
I don't do well with human contact in general...

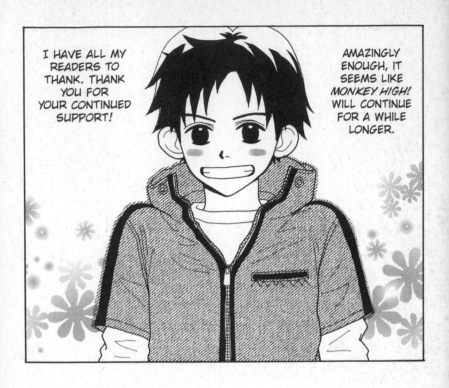

AMAZINGLY ENOUGH, IT SEEMS LIKE *MONKEY HIGH!* WILL CONTINUE FOR A WHILE LONGER.
I HAVE ALL MY READERS TO THANK. THANK YOU FOR YOUR CONTINUED SUPPORT!

I'D LIKE TO THANK EVERYBODY WHO HELPS ME: MY EDITOR, MY COORDINATOR, MY DESIGNER, MY FAMILY, FRIENDS AND ALL MY READERS. ANYBODY AND EVERYBODY WHO ARE INVOLVED IN MY MANGA PROCESS... THANK YOU SO VERY MUCH!

IT HASN'T BEEN THE EASIEST OF JOURNEYS TO GET HERE, BUT I WILL CONTINUE TO POUR MY HEART AND SOUL INTO DRAWING, SO I ASK FOR YOUR CONTINUED SUPPORT. THANK YOU.

February 2007
Shouko Akira

Slightly confused by all the monkeying around?
Here are some notes to help you out!

Page 4: **Masaru**
Even though everyone refers to him by his nickname, Macharu's real name is "Masaru," which means "superior" in Japanese. Interestingly enough, *saru* by itself means "monkey."

Page 6, panel 1: *Sumanai*
A play in Japan that was based on *Monty Python and the Holy Grail*.

Page 54: *Betsucomi*
A monthly Japanese *shojo manga* (girls' comics) magazine published by Shogakukan.

Page 54: **Kitakou**
The syllables "ki," "ta," "ko," and "u" spell out *Kitakou*, which translates to "Kita High."

Page 148, panel 5: **Takoyaki**
Takoyaki are dough balls with pieces of octopus in them. They are made using a hotplate and are often sold at Japanese festivals. *Tako* means "octopus" in Japanese.

Page 182, panel 4: **Ebi-chan**
Nickname for Yuri Ebihara, a model and actress who got her start in *CanCam*. *Ebi* means "shrimp" in Japanese.

Page 182, panel 4: *CanCam*
A Japanese fashion magazine published by Shogakukan that's aimed at women in their early twenties.

I can't believe this is volume 5! Thank you so much. Check out the number of bananas on the spine [of the original Japanese version] as well as the number of fingers the monkey holds up on the front cover.

—Shouko Akira

Wow!

Already volume 5?!

Shouko Akira was born on September 10th and grew up in Kyoto. She currently lives in Tokyo and loves soccer, cycling, and Yoshimoto Shin Kigeki (a comedy stage show based out of Osaka). Most of her works revolve around school life and love, including *Times Two*, a collection of five romantic short stories.

MONKEY HIGH!
VOL. 5
The Shojo Beat Manga Edition

STORY AND ART BY
SHOUKO AKIRA

Translation & Adaptation/Mai Ihara
Touch-up Art & Lettering/John Hunt
Design/Hidemi Dunn
Editor/Amy Yu

Editor in Chief, Books/Alvin Lu
Editor in Chief, Magazines/Marc Weidenbaum
VP, Publishing Licensing/Rika Inouye
VP, Sales & Product Marketing/Gonzalo Ferreyra
VP, Creative/Linda Espinosa
Publisher/Hyoe Narita

SARUYAMA! 5 by Shouko AKIRA © 2007 Shouko AKIRA
All rights reserved.
Original Japanese edition published in 2007 by Shogakukan Inc., Tokyo.

The stories, characters and incidents mentioned in this publication
are entirely fictional.

Printed in Canada

Published by VIZ Media, LLC
P.O. Box 77010
San Francisco, CA 94107

Shojo Beat Manga Edition
10 9 8 7 6 5 4 3 2 1
First printing, March 2009

www.viz.com

store.viz.com

PARENTAL ADVISORY
MONKEY HIGH! is rated T for Teen
and is recommended for ages 13 and up.
This volume contains suggestive themes.
ratings.viz.com